PENGUIN BOOKS

THE AUTHENTIC GOSPEL OF JESUS

Geza Vermes was born in Hungary in 1924. He studied in Budapest and Louvain, where he read Oriental history and languages and in 1953 obtained a doctorate in theology with a dissertation on the Dead Sea Scrolls. From 1957 to 1991 he taught at the Universities of Newcastle and Oxford. His pioneering work on the Dead Sea Scrolls and the historical figure of Jesus led to his appointment as the first Professor of Jewish Studies at Oxford, where he is now Professor Emeritus. Since 1991 he has been director of the Forum for Qumran Research at the Oxford Centre for Hebrew and Jewish Studies. Professor Vermes is a Fellow of the British Academy and of the European Academy of Arts, Sciences and Humanities, the holder of an Oxford D.Litt. and of honorary doctorates from several British universities. Professor Vermes's books include *The Complete Dead Sea Scrolls in English* (1997) and *The Changing Faces of Jesus* (2000), both published by Penguin.

GEZA VERMES

The Authentic Gospel of Jesus

PENGUIN BOOKS

For Margaret and Ian
with love

PENGUIN BOOKS

Published by the Penguin Group
Penguin Books Ltd, 80 Strand, London WC2R 0RL, England
Penguin Group (USA) Inc., 375 Hudson Street, New York, New York 10014, USA
Penguin Books Australia Ltd, 250 Camberwell Road, Camberwell, Victoria 3124, Australia
Penguin Books Canada Ltd, 10 Alcorn Avenue, Toronto, Ontario, Canada M4V 3B2
Penguin Books India (P) Ltd, 11 Community Centre, Panchsheel Park, New Delhi – 110 017, India
Penguin Group (NZ), Cnr Airborne and Rosedale Roads, Albany, Auckland 1310, New Zealand
Penguin Books (South Africa) (Pty) Ltd, 24 Sturdee Avenue, Rosebank 2196, South Africa

Penguin Books Ltd, Registered Offices: 80 Strand, London WC2R 0RL, England

www.penguin.com

Published by Allen Lane 2003
Published in Penguin Books 2004
6

Typeset by Rowland Phototypesetting Ltd, Bury St Edmunds, Suffolk
Printed in England by Clays Ltd, St Ives plc

Contents

Prologue: A fifth book on Jesus?

The historical Jesus, a religious genius who lived, taught and died in Jewish Palestine in the first century of the time reckoning named after him, has been at the centre of my scholarly preoccupation since the late 1960s. Acting as a sympathetic historian and discarding denominational biases, both the deification of Jesus by Christians and his traditional Jewish caricature as an apostate, a magician and an enemy of the people of Israel, I have simply tried to put the record straight and to reconstruct a genuine likeness of Yeshua, son of Joseph of the Galilean townlet of Nazareth.

The original project developed into a trilogy. In 1973 appeared *Jesus the Jew*, a work which purported to discover and sketch the true personality of Jesus within the setting of his authentic historical milieu. It was followed in 1983 by a first essay to piece together the original doctrinal, religious and ethical message of the Gospel in *Jesus and the World of Judaism*, a volume which also contained two methodological essays to justify my special way of proceeding. Yet another ten years had passed before I was ready to present in 1993 the final part of the trilogy under the self-explanatory title *The Religion of Jesus the Jew*. Being historically inspired, the series was based exclusively on the least theologically motivated sources of the life and teaching of Jesus, the Synoptic Gospels of Mark, Matthew and Luke. Then in the late 1990s I undertook a fresh re-examination of the material; it saw the light of day in the spring of 2000 under the title *The Changing Faces of Jesus*. Here I adopted a two-pronged approach, simultaneously historical and literary, to the various representations of Jesus, seeking to identify his diverse portrayals in the whole of the New Testament. I started with the latest and doctrinally most advanced Gospel of John, and progressed in a descending order of theological sophistication through the epistles of St Paul and the other letter-writers to the Acts of the Apostles, to the Synoptic Gospels and finally to the Jesus image concealed beneath Luke, Matthew and Mark. The structure of the book reminds one of an archaeological excavation performed on literary sources. The dig starts with the top layer, the most recent of them all, and descends as it were to the pre-Gospel Jesus who is identified with the help of a historico-literary analysis of the Synoptic material merged with the ideas and realities of the Jewish world in which Jesus lived.

After four books on Jesus why did I decide to write a fifth one? The idea arose from a prompting by Stefan McGrath, my friendly editor at Penguin, who suggested shortly after the publication of *The Changing Faces of Jesus* that I should devise a companion volume to it. Reflecting on the matter, it struck me that I had never tried my hand at a critical interpretation of the Gospel text itself. Perhaps this is how I should have started the Jesus project years ago, I said to myself, but maybe it is better late than never. Thus was conceived *The Authentic Gospel of Jesus*, known for a while at Penguin Books as 'Untitled on Christ'. This new book was to collect, thematically classify, and succinctly comment on every word attributed to Jesus in the Gospels of Matthew, Mark and Luke. Thus the reader would be enabled to discover between the covers of a single book all the material which is usually treated in three separate volumes of Gospel commentary.

In the present venture my first goal is to expound all the sayings which Jesus supposedly uttered, but the ultimate purpose of the book is the rediscovery of the genuine religious message preached and practised by him. The doctrinal and moral statements are divided into nine chapters corresponding to nine literary categories: (1) narratives and commands; (2) controversy stories; (3) words of wisdom; (4) parables; (5) biblical quotations; (6) prayers; (7) son of Man sayings; (8) sayings about the Kingdom of God; and (9) eschatological rules of behaviour.

The succinct commentary attached to the quotations attempts to distinguish the diverse levels of superimposed meanings with a view to establishing, if possible, their primary setting and significance in the life of Jesus. In the tenth and final chapter I endeavour first to formulate, and then in the Appendix to apply, the principles which allow the determination of the parameters of authenticity, or in plain language to distinguish the genuine or probably genuine sayings of Jesus from those which are unlikely to be authentic. As a result an approximation of his real teaching emerges, distinguished from the successive revised and enlarged editions produced by the evangelists, the early church and two millennia of Christianity.

Finally, on the basis of the maxims judged most likely to be genuine, I will attempt to outline the personality of the real Jesus and the quintessence of his authentic eschatological gospel.[1] A parting forward glance will seek to assess the relationship between the historical Jesus and Christianity from the point of view of a detached twenty-first-century observer . . . confidently assuming that such an uncommon animal as a *detached* observer actually exists.

My especial gratitude is due to my wife, the first critical reader of these pages. She is a biochemist, not a biblical scholar, yet she has greatly helped to improve the clarity and logic of the presentation of the book by applying to it the trained mind of an experimental scientist. We often argued, but she got the better of me most of the time.

Some years ago, on commissioning an article on the Scrolls, the editor of *The New York Review of Books* warned me: 'Remember that three quarters of my readers are chemists. Bear them in mind when you write.' What splendid advice!

Oxford, G.V.
May 2002

1. The terms 'eschatology' and 'eschatological' will regularly appear in the forthcoming pages. They signify what Jesus and his contemporaries thought to be the final period of the present era and all matters relating to it.

A Note on the Sources

To facilitate the task of those readers for whom this is the first attempt at a critical reading of the sayings of Jesus, I will provide a brief summary of essential information concerning the sources on which the present study is based.

Chief among these are the official or canonical Gospels,[1] especially Matthew, Mark and Luke, and to a smaller extent the Gospel of John, also called the Fourth Gospel. Quite exceptionally I will refer to the non-canonical Gospel of Thomas, a collection of maxims ascribed to Jesus.

Before describing the individual Gospels a few general remarks seem to be appropriate. The four Gospels are conceived as accounts conveying the life story and the message of Jesus. In their final version, that is to say in the form in which they have reached us, the aim of these Gospels was to transmit, not the report of a chronicler, but the doctrinal message of the early church. Their purpose was primarily didactic, not historical.

Like all ancient sources, they must be subjected to a critical analysis if we are to grasp the reality and authentic significance of the events and the teaching contained in them. Ideally this analysis should be applied to the original language of the teaching of Jesus, who spoke Aramaic. Aramaic was the Semitic tongue used by most of his compatriots, which is closely related to Hebrew, the language of the Jewish Bible (the Old Testament). However, our four Gospels have survived in Greek, and scholars unanimously maintain that they were directly

1. In the following pages, the word 'gospel' in lower case designates the message of Jesus, the 'good news'. When it refers to one of the books of the New Testament such as Gospel of Mark, it is written with a capital G.

composed in Greek; they are not translations from a Semitic original. It is true that we learn from the second-century bishop Papias, quoted by the church historian Eusebius in the fourth century, that the evangelist Matthew was acquainted with a collection of Aramaic sayings of Jesus. But apart from this second-hand reference to them no trace of these Aramaic sayings is extant. Did Papias allude to a Semitic draft of our first Gospel? Surely not, since the canonical Matthew, with its stories, genealogies, polemics and parables, can hardly be described as an anthology of logia or maxims. Did the Jewish branch of primitive Christianity, the so-called Ebionites, produce an Aramaic Gospel? It is possible, but such a Gospel, written by Judaeo-Christians who were soon castigated as heretics by the non-Jewish majority of the church for not believing in the divinity of Jesus, would have made no mark on our existing four documents.

This means that none of the canonical Gospels can reach back directly to Jesus. Since during the first centuries of Christianity the vast majority of the members of the church were Greek-speaking, non-Jewish inhabitants of the Roman empire, they needed the teaching of Jesus in Greek. As a result, with the exception of a few quotations in the Greek Gospels themselves, such as *Abba*, 'Father' (Mark 14:36) or *Talitha cum*, 'Little girl, get up' (Mark 5:41), the Aramaic originals of the sayings of Jesus have all been allowed to fade from the memory. In short, at a very early stage, say by the end of the first century AD, an Aramaic Gospel would have been completely useless for the Gentile Christians of Antioch, Alexandria, Ephesus, Corinth or Rome for whom Matthew, Mark and Luke (himself a Gentile) had to cater.

The canonical Gospels fall into two groups: Matthew, Mark and Luke on the one hand, and John on the other. The first three are known as the *Synoptic* Gospels, because they reflect the same general point of view, follow the same story line, use nearly the same words, and can be set out in three parallel columns in a Gospel *synopsis*.[2] They are considered to be the earliest Gospels. Mainstream scholarly opinion holds the Gospel of Mark to be the oldest. It is addressed to a non-Jewish audience shortly after the fall of Jerusalem in AD 70. The same Papias,

2. Cf. *Gospel Parallels: A Synopsis of the First Three Gospels*, ed. Burton H. Throckmorton Jr. (Nashville, Tenn., 1979).

already quoted, asserts that Mark was the interpreter of Peter, whom he accompanied to Rome. The Gospels of Matthew and Luke are slightly more recent than Mark; they may be placed between AD 80 and 100. The same Papias of the second century labels Matthew as an evangelist, and Luke is first mentioned as the author of a Gospel in a list of the books of the New Testament in a fragment called the Muratorian canon, around AD 180. Mark and Matthew were most probably Jews, but Luke the physician, an associate of Paul, was a Greek. We have no solid evidence to prove that any of the Synoptic evangelists was a close associate of Jesus, but we can safely assume that all three belonged to the apostolic age (the second half of the first century AD).

The similarities and differences between the Synoptic Gospels gave rise to many debates on the so-called synoptic problem. The classic solution, the 'two-source theory', maintains that Mark is an independent composition and that Matthew and Luke rely on Mark into which they insert the contents of another hypothetical compilation consisting mainly of sayings. This hypothetical compilation is designated as *Q*, derived from the German word for 'source', *Quelle*. Matthew and Luke include further material peculiar to each of them. They are abbreviated as *M* for Matthew's special material and *L* for Luke's. The consensus of scholarly opinion considers the Synoptic Gospels as the version of the teaching of Jesus which has undergone the least amount of doctrinal manipulation. Mark, Matthew and Luke are therefore the most important sources in our inquiry.

The identity of the fourth evangelist is uncertain. He is held by Christian tradition to be identical with the apostle John, son of Zebedee, but this claim is not backed by any solid historical evidence. This Gospel has little in common with Mark, Matthew and Luke and the doctrinal development contained in it points to a period after the Synoptics in the beginning of the second century AD (roughly AD 100–110). The bulk of the long, rambling and repetitious speeches of Jesus included in John reflect the ideas of an author steeped in Hellenistic philosophical and mystical speculation, who reshaped the portrait of Jesus two to three generations after his death. This writer can scarcely be identical with the apostle John who is described in the Acts of the Apostles as an 'uneducated, common man' (Acts 4:13). The violent antisemitism of the fourth evangelist makes it even questionable that he was a Jew.[3] In consequence, apart from the small number of sayings which echo the Synoptics, the words of Jesus peculiar to the Fourth Gospel will not be taken into account in our investigation.

The apocryphal Gospel of Thomas purports to record secret sayings of Jesus. Written in Greek perhaps in the middle of the second century AD and preserved for posterity in a third- or fourth-century Egyptian Coptic translation,[4] it will only occasionally be discussed. A good many of the direct parallels to the Synoptic Gospels contained in it have been reworked and they are often tainted with heretical ('Gnostic') ideas.[5]

The first attestation of a list of the Gospels and the other books of the New Testament is contained in the Muratorian canon. Its original Greek text dates to around AD 180. The canonical status of the four Gospels has thereafter never been questioned, but that of other New Testament texts, especially the Book of Revelation, continued to be debated until the fourth century.

The text of the New Testament has been preserved in Greek manuscripts from which the ancient and modern translations have been made.[6] The oldest papyrus fragments of the New Testament date to *c.* AD 125–150, and the most ancient codices (the Sinaiticus and the Vaticanus) to the fourth century. I will occasionally take into account textual variants attested in the Gospel manuscripts. As far as the *agrapha*, or sayings of Jesus found in the writings of later church fathers but unrecorded anywhere in the four Gospels, are concerned, I deem them too unreliable to be considered in a quest for the authentic teaching of Jesus.[7]

3. For a more detailed discussion see my *The Changing Faces of Jesus*, 6–21.
4. See *Q Thomas Reader*, ed. John S. Kloppenborg, Marvin W. Meyer, *et al.* (Sonoma, Calif., 1990).
5. For the sake of completeness, I should like to draw attention to two sayings attributed to Jesus which are preserved in the New Testament outside the Gospels. In Acts 20:35 Paul cites Jesus as declaring: 'It is more blessed to give than to receive.' No identical formula can be found in any of the Gospels, but insistence on extreme generosity is a characteristic trait of the teaching of Jesus. Again, according to Paul 'the Lord commanded that those who proclaim the gospel should get their living by the gospel' (1 Cor. 9:14), which is a maxim similar to Luke 10:7, 'For the labourer deserves his wages'.
6. See Bruce M. Metzger, *The Text of the New Testament*, 3rd edn. (New York, 1992).
7. Joachim Jeremias, *Unknown Sayings of Jesus*, 2nd edn. (London, 1964).

In order to understand the Gospel evidence within its historical framework, the accounts of the evangelists must be compared with the many parallels preserved in Jewish writings of the intertestamental age (*c.* 200 BC – AD 200) and in rabbinic literature. Although the latter was recorded in script roughly between AD 200 and 500, it none the less comprises many religious traditions which stem from, or even antedate, the age of the Gospels. These writings have survived in Hebrew and Aramaic and thus bring us near to the ideas of Jesus, and to their expression in words and images. Without their study, it is often impossible to catch the nuances or even the basic meaning of the sayings, parables and Bible interpretation handed down by the evangelists in the name of Jesus.

The main branches of intertestamental literature are the Apocrypha, the Pseudepigrapha, the Dead Sea Scrolls and the writings of the Jewish philosopher Philo of Alexandria and the historian Flavius Josephus, both active in the first century AD.

The *Apocrypha* (literally 'hidden' writings) begin with 1 and 2 Esdras and finish with 1 and 2 Maccabees. They are included in the Greek translation of the Old Testament, known as the Septuagint.[8] The Jews of the Hellenistic diaspora venerated them as holy books, and so did the early Hellenistic church. Roman Catholics continue to regard them as Holy Scripture. However, the Palestinian Jews excluded them from their canon at the end of the first century AD, and so, under Jewish influence, did Protestants in the sixteenth century. The Apocrypha date to the first and second centuries BC. With the exception of the Wisdom of Solomon and 2 Maccabees, which were composed in Greek, all the writings of the Apocrypha were originally written in Hebrew or Aramaic and subsequently translated into Greek. We now possess fragments of the Book of Tobit in Aramaic and Hebrew, and substantial sections of Ecclesiasticus or Wisdom of Jesus son of Sira in Hebrew, thanks to the Dead Sea Scrolls and to the Cairo Geniza. The Geniza, a medieval depository of discarded Jewish manuscripts attached to a synagogue in old Cairo, was discovered at the end of the nineteenth century and the bulk of its contents is now in the University Library of Cambridge.

8. See Bruce M. Metzger, *An Introduction to the Apocrypha* (New York, 1977).

Pseudepigrapha (literally 'falsely entitled' writings) is the umbrella term applied to a collection of Jewish non-canonical religious books which have been preserved in various ancient translations (Greek, Latin, Syriac, Ethiopian, etc.) in Christian churches.[9] Several of these works, first and foremost the Book of Jubilees, an enlarged version of the biblical book of Genesis, and the apocalyptic work known as the First Book of Enoch, are now in part available in their original Hebrew (Jubilees) and Aramaic (Enoch), thanks to the Qumran finds. The Dead Sea Scrolls have also revealed a number of previously unknown documents belonging to this class of literature. These Pseudepigrapha came into being during a period of over four centuries (*c.* 250 BC – AD 200), and some of them exercised considerable influence both on Jewish and on Christian circles. For instance, in the New Testament the Letter of Jude, verse 14, cites the Book of Enoch as an authoritative sacred writing.

The *Dead Sea Scrolls* designate over eight hundred original manuscripts discovered between 1947 and 1956 in eleven caves in the neighbourhood of Qumran, not far from Jericho and close to the Dead Sea. A quarter of them represent the Hebrew Scripture and the rest are biblical translations into Greek and Aramaic as well as religious writings of various kinds. Many of them disclose for the first time the rules, hymns, Bible exegesis, etc. of a Jewish sect which occupied the area of Qumran from the end of the second century BC until the destruction of the settlement by the Romans in AD 68. Most of these manuscripts, dating from the late third century BC to the middle of the first century AD, existed during the lifetime of Jesus. They reveal many similarities with the New Testament and thus contribute substantially to our understanding of Jesus and his teaching.[10]

Two important Jewish writers of the first century AD shed considerable light on the world of the Gospels and of St Paul. The Egyptian Philo of Alexandria (*c.* 20 BC – AD 50) is an invaluable witness to the philosophy, law, ethics and theology of Hellenistic Judaism in the age of Jesus. Philo also acted as one of the ambassadors of the Alexandrian Jews who were sent to Rome to plead the cause of their co-religionists

9. See *The Old Testament Pseudepigrapha* I–II, ed. James H. Charlesworth (London, 1983).

10. See Geza Vermes, *The Complete Dead Sea Scrolls in English* (London, 1998).

with the emperor Gaius Caligula. Philo never mentions Jesus or the Christian church. The large corpus of his writings is available in a bilingual Greek–English edition.[11] Flavius Josephus, a Jewish priest from Jerusalem whose Hebrew name was Joseph son of Mattatyahu (AD 37 – *c.* 100), is our most precious source of Jewish history, religion and culture of the intertestamental age and of the first century AD in particular. His two major works, *The Jewish War* and *Jewish Antiquities*, as well as his *Life* and his apologia for the Jews entitled *Against Apion*, contain a priceless mine of information for the interpreter of the sayings of Jesus.[12] The *Jewish Antiquities* includes passages on John the Baptist, Jesus and his brother James.

Rabbinic literature, the final group of texts, which may be used for comparison in the study of the sayings of Jesus, consists of two sections: legal and interpretative.

The legal section includes the *Mishnah* (teaching) and the *Tosefta* (supplement), i.e. legal rulings not directly associated with the Bible, which are credited to Palestinian rabbis called *Tannaim* or Mishnah teachers of the first and second century AD. The Talmud (doctrine) is a further development of the laws of the Mishnah by rabbis of the Land of Israel in the third and fourth century AD and by rabbis of Babylonia in the third to the fifth century. The former collection is known as the Palestinian or Jerusalem Talmud and the latter as the Babylonian Talmud.

The most important Bible commentaries are the *Tannaitic Midrashim* (plural of Midrash, works of Scripture exegesis) on the Law of Moses ascribed to the Tannaim of the first two centuries AD; the *Midrash Rabbah*, or Large Midrash, on the Torah and the five Rolls (Ruth, Ecclesiastes, Song of Songs, Lamentations and Esther) produced by rabbis of various eras; and the *Targumim* (plural of Targum, translation) covering a variety of popular Aramaic versions of the Hebrew Bible classified as the Targum of Onkelos on the Torah, various recensions of the Palestinian Targum on the Torah, the Targum of Jonathan on the Prophets, etc.

11. See *Philo* I–X, ed. F. H. Colson and G. H. Whitaker, Loeb Classical Library (London and Cambridge, Mass., 1962).

12. See *Josephus* I–IX, ed. H. St J. Thackeray *et al.*, Loeb Classical Library (London and Cambridge, Mass., 1926–65).

As a final point of clarification, I would like to note that some New Testament scholars mistakenly argue that the time gap between the Gospels (dating from *c.* AD 70 to 110) and the rabbinic writings (dating to between AD 200 and 500) rules out the use of these writings as comparative material in the study of the sayings of Jesus. In other words, they adopt the simplistic view that the date of a tradition transmitted in a work is the same as the date of the redaction of that work. In consequence, they overlook the fact that in the Mishnah, Midrash, Talmud and Targum the rabbis endeavoured to safeguard and transmit to posterity a large quantity of old teachings many of which can be traced to the age of Jesus and even to pre-Christian times. Indeed, when a saying of Jesus coincides with that of a later rabbi, it is more likely that they both reflect a common Jewish traditional teaching dating back at least to the first century AD than that the rabbi actually borrowed from Jesus. The profound rabbinic dislike for Christianity makes it well-nigh unthinkable for Jews of the Talmudic period to accept and acknowledge as doctrinally sound any doctrine presumed to have originated with Jesus.[13]

A classified register of authentic and inauthentic sayings may be found on pages 419–36. In addition, an index of Gospel citations will make it easy for the reader to find the pages in this book where a particular word of Jesus is discussed.

13. A dictum of Rabbi Abbahu of Caesarea, a third-century contemporary of Origen, is almost certainly alluding to Jesus: 'If a man says to you, "I am God", he lies. "I am the son of Man" [a human being], at the end he will be sorry [since like every human being, he will die]. "I will go up to heaven", he has said this, but will not fulfil it' (yTaan 65b). The second quotation from Jesus appears in the Babylonian Talmud (bAbodah zara 16b–17a) attributed to first–second century AD rabbis or Tannaim. The famous R. Eliezer ben Hyrcanus remembers that a Jewish Christian, called Jacob of Kfar Sekhaniah, interpreted, 'You shall not bring the hire of a harlot . . . into the house of . . . your God' (Deut. 23:18), in the sense that such money was fit only for the construction of a latrine for the high priest. When Eliezer confessed that he could not understand this exposition, Jacob presented him with an exegesis attributed to Jesus, who apparently linked Micah 1:7, 'From the hire of a harlot she gathered them, and to the hire of a harlot they shall return', to Deuteronomy 23:18 to arrive at the explanation: 'From the place of filth they have come, and to the place of filth they will return.' Eliezer was impressed by Jesus' interpretative skill and on this account he was charged with heresy and excommunicated by other rabbis.

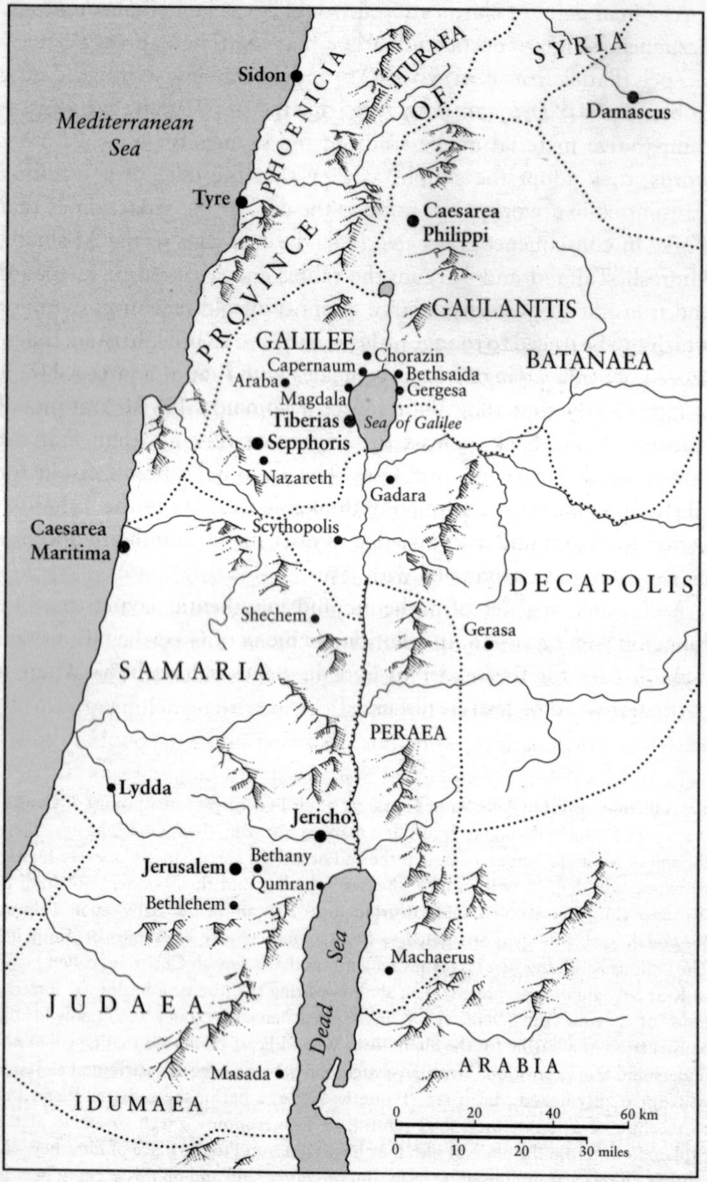

Palestine in the age of Jesus

I

Narratives and Commands

Narratives and commands occur in those Gospel passages which quote direct speech by Jesus when reporting episodes in his life. These words placed on his lips are built into the account to lend liveliness and colour to the story. Scholarly interpreters in general reject the authenticity of such sayings and assign them to the evangelists. The bulk of the material comes from Mark and the triple tradition (Mark, Matthew and Luke), that is to say those sources which supply the main 'biographical' narrative of the Gospels. The majority of the passages relate to healing or exorcism, which in addition to teaching constitute the main features of the public activity of Jesus. The special traditions contained in Matthew and Luke complete the evidence. The negative characteristic of these texts is that they include no preaching or instruction. Nevertheless, the commands occurring in the accounts of exorcism are significant. They reveal what kind of a person Jesus was and the nature of the religious attitude he expected from his followers. These narrative portions have yet another important contribution to make. They allow a better perception of Jesus against his background by throwing light on the peculiarities of the society in which he lived. Thus the teacher and his audience appear in the temporal and spatial framework of the real world.

Each individual quotation of words ascribed to Jesus will be given in its context before being subjected to analysis. As a rule, the Revised Standard Version (RSV) will be used. Only Mark, the oldest Gospel, is reproduced when Matthew and Luke do not depart from it in any meaningful fashion. When they do, the variant readings appear in square brackets.

I. MARK WITH MATTHEW AND/OR LUKE

1. Call of the first disciples (Mark 1:16–18; Matt. 4:18–20)

And passing along the Sea of Galilee he saw [two brothers (Matt.)] Simon [who is called Peter (Matt.)] and Andrew the brother of Simon casting a net into the sea; for they were fishermen. And Jesus said to them, *Follow me and I will make you fishers of men.* And immediately they left their nets and followed him.

Mark and Matthew offer a vivid description of the call of two Galilean fishermen, Simon(-Peter) and Andrew, to join Jesus. Fishing is chosen as the symbol of Jesus' mission, and Simon and Andrew are ordered to spiritualize their profession: instead of fish, they will have to 'catch' humans. Later, in the course of an unexpectedly successful fishing trip on the lake, Jesus repeats that symbolic fishing will be Peter's future vocation (Luke 5:10; cf. no. 34 below).

The phrase 'fishers of men' was not created by Jesus or by the writers of the Gospels. The imagery is biblical. It appears in Jeremiah 16:16 where the wicked Jews are delivered by God to 'many fishers', and those who escape them will fall prey to 'many hunters'. A similar metaphor is used by the prophet Habakkuk. In his vision God transforms men into fish and allows their enemies to drag them out with nets (1:14–15; cf. also Amos 4:2). Closer to Jesus' time, the poet responsible for one of the Qumran Thanksgiving Hymns echoes Jeremiah. He sees the children of iniquity either caught in the net of fishermen or captured by hunters (1QH 13 [formerly 5]: 8).

Nevertheless, when we compare the New Testament usage with the terminology of the prophets and of the Dead Sea writings, we are struck by one notable difference. In the biblical and Scroll imagery both the fishermen and the hunters are hostile figures sent by God to punish the guilty. By contrast, the 'fishers of men' spoken of by Jesus are emissaries dispatched to rescue men. The metaphor is neither simple nor straightforward. How can being caught in a net be beneficial to a fish? The image could be a church creation at a time when the reality of fishing was no longer part of the everyday experience of urban Christians in Syria, Asia Minor or Greece, living far away from the Sea of Galilee. For them, 'fishers of men' simply meant saviours. Nevertheless, it is more likely that we are facing here a new twist added to the imagery by Jesus. The parable of the net (Matt. 13:47–50; see chapter 4, no. 20) applies the metaphor to the situation of the final age. There the fishermen's job is to separate the good fish from the bad in preparation for the Last Judgement. They, like the harvesters in the parables of the sower, are the chosen agents of the coming Kingdom of God. A fresh slant given to a common idiom is typical of the metaphorical language of Jesus.

2. The first exorcism of Jesus (Mark 1:23–25; Luke 4:33–35)

And immediately there was in their synagogue a man with an unclean spirit; and he cried out [with a loud voice, Ah! (Luke)] 'What have you to do with us, Jesus of Nazareth? Have you come to destroy us? I know who you are, the Holy One of God.' But Jesus rebuked him, saying, *Be silent and come out of him!*

In the account of an exorcism which is located in the synagogue of Capernaum, the evangelists quote the conversation between the demoniac and Jesus: 'What have you to do with us?' the demons scream. Jesus silences[1] and expels them (Mark 1:25; Luke 4:35). Similar orders are addressed to evil spirits in Mark 5:8: 'Come out of the man, you unclean spirit!', and in Matthew 8:32, 'Go!' These are standard formulae used by Jewish exorcists, and the Greek terms correspond to the Hebrew *tse* (from the verb *yatsa*), and the Aramaic *poq* (from the verb *npaq*), signifying 'depart', 'go', or 'come out'.

References to exorcism occur in the Dead Sea Scrolls too, but the Qumran writers employ only generic expressions such as 'rebuking', 'frightening' or 'terrifying' evil spirits (1QapGen 20:29; 4Q510,4; 511, fr. 8). Flavius Josephus provides the full description of an exorcism performed by a Jew called Eleazar, and witnessed by the future emperor Vespasian, but does not cite the formula itself (*Jewish*

1. For the same command employed in calming the storm, cf. Mark 4:39.

Antiquities 8:46–47.). The Babylonian Talmud, in contrast, contains the words which two renowned Tannaitic rabbis of the early second century AD, Simeon ben Yohai and Eleazar ben Yose, are said to have pronounced when expelling a named demon from the daughter of a Roman emperor: 'Ben Temalion, *come out*! Ben Temalion, *come out*!' (bMeilah 17b). The evangelists testify to Jesus using the normal Jewish exorcistic terminology of his age. 'Come out' may be Jesus' own words.

3. Jesus departs from Capernaum (Mark 1:35–38; Luke 4:42–43)

And in the morning, a great while before day, he rose and went out to a lonely place, and there he prayed. And Simon and those who were with him pursued him, and they found him and said to him, 'Everyone is searching for you.' And he said to them, *Let us go on to the next towns that I may preach there also; for that is why I came out.*

I must preach the good news of the kingdom of God to the other cities also; for I was sent for this purpose (Luke).

The evangelists report that after an extended healing session in Capernaum Jesus sought to escape to the wilderness. His deeds and his words show that he liked to pray in solitary places (see Matt. 6:6; cf. chapter 6, no. 7). The saying helps along the narrative which next describes how Jesus preached and expelled demons all over Galilee (Mark 1:39; Matt. 4:23; Luke 4:44). In Mark Jesus himself decides to set out on his mission ('I came out'), whereas the more theologically minded Luke attributes his departure to the will of God: 'I was sent for this purpose' with a view to announcing 'the good news of the kingdom'.

4. Healing a leper (Mark 1:40–44; Matt. 8:2–4; Luke 5:12–14)

And a leper beseeching him and kneeling said to him, '[Lord (Matt., Luke)] If you will, you can make me clean.' Moved with pity, he stretched out his hand and touched him, and said to him, *I will; be clean*. And immediately the leprosy left him and he was made clean. And he sternly charged him and sent him away at once, and said to him: *See that you say nothing to anyone; but go, show yourself to the priest, and offer for your cleansing what Moses commanded for a proof to the people.*

The healing imperative 'Be clean!' (Mark 1:41; Matt. 8:3; Luke 5:13) employed in connection with the curing of lepers resembles the formula of exorcism already encountered. This is the only Gospel episode containing the form of command associated with the removal of leprosy. The same verb 'to cleanse' may be read in the parallel story of Luke 17:17, and curing lepers is listed among the principal signs of the messianic age in Matthew 11:5 and Luke 7:22 (see chapter 5, no. 25).

The story-teller attributes to Jesus the command that the former leper should keep quiet about his recovery, an injunction which according to Mark the latter disobeyed (1:45).[2] The man was further ordered to obtain from a priest a certificate of cure in conformity with the Law (Lev. 13:49; 14:2). The attribution to Jesus of an emphatic injunction to observe a ritual precept is highly significant (cf. also Luke 17:14). The proclamation by the former leper about his miraculous cure is given in Mark 1:45 as the source of the growing reputation of Jesus. The order of secrecy concerning the charismatic powers of Jesus is a standard feature in the Synoptic Gospels (cf. Mark 5:43; 7:36; Matt. 9:30; Luke 8:56; see nos. 8, 10, 15, 29 below and p. 36).

2. Note, however, that Luke ascribes the dissemination of the news to other witnesses of the miracle (Luke 5:15).

5. The call of Levi (Mark 2:14; Matt. 9:9; Luke 5:27)

And as he passed on, he saw Levi the son of Alphaeus [a man called Matthew (Matt.)] sitting at the tax office, and he said to him, *Follow me.*

In describing the invitation to the tax-collector Levi son of Alphaeus, or Matthew, to join the company of Jesus, the narrator quotes a direct command: 'Follow me!' (Mark 2:14; Matt. 9:9; Luke 5:27). This is a standard formula which figures also in connection with the call of Simon and Andrew (Mark 1:17; Matt. 4:19 (cf. no. 1 above)), an anonymous disciple (Matt. 8:22; Luke 9:59), a rich man (Mark 10:21; Matt. 19:21; Luke 18:22), Philip (John 1:43) and Peter (John 21:19, 22). It simply means 'Accompany me' and not 'Imitate my example'.

6. Healing a man with a withered hand (Mark 3:1–3, 5; Matt. 12:9–10; Luke 6:6–8, 10)

Again he [Jesus] entered the synagogue, and a man was there who had a withered hand. And they watched him, to see whether he would heal him on the sabbath, so that they might accuse him. And he said to the man who had the withered hand, *Come here . . . Stretch out your hand.* And he stretched out and his hand was restored.

In the process of healing a man with a withered hand on the Sabbath, Jesus issues two brief instructions. The sick man is ordered to approach him (Mark 3:3; Luke 6:8), and later to stretch out his hand (Mark 3:5; Matt. 12:13; Luke 6:10). The meaning of both sayings is obvious. For the subsequent controversy about breaking the Law see chapter 2, no. 4.

7. Stilling the storm (Mark 4:36–40; Matt. 8:23–26; Luke 8:22–25)

And leaving the crowd, they took him with them in the boat, just as he was . . . And a great storm of wind arose, and the waves beat into the boat, so that the boat was already filling. But he was in the stern, asleep on the cushion; and they woke him and said to him, 'Teacher, do you not care if we perish?' And he awoke and rebuked the wind, and said to the sea, *Peace! Be still!* And the wind ceased, and there was a great calm. He said to them, *Why are you afraid? Have you no faith?*

The calming of the waves is effected by a brief double command of Jesus: 'Peace!' – 'Be still!' (Mark 4:39). 'Be still' is also used in exorcisms (cf. Mark 1:25 in no. 2 above). The story echoes the nature miracles of Jewish folklore. Thus in the Bible, too, Elijah declares that the restoration of rain after a period of drought will be effected by his word (1 Kings 17:1). Similarly in rabbinic literature the bringing and arresting of rain are attributed to the miracle-working prayers of Honi and Hanina ben Dosa.

The account illustrates one of the chief doctrines of Jesus. For him, lack of faith or pusillanimity was the greatest obstacle to religious well-being and the main barrier in front of a divinely inspired action (Matt. 6:30; Luke 12:28; Matt. 14:31; 16:8). The obverse of this statement is that faith as small as the proverbial mustard seed can enable a man to perform miracles (Matt. 17:20; Luke 17:6). Successful cures are often credited by the healer to the belief of the patient (Mark 5:34; Matt. 9:22; Luke 8:48; Mark 7:29; Matt. 15:28; Mark 10:52; Luke 18:42; 7:50; 17:19; Matt. 8:10; Luke 7:9; see nos. 9, 19, 28 below and chapter 8, no. 6).

8. The Gerasene demoniac (Mark 5:1–19; Matt. 8:28–34; Luke 8:26–39)

They came to the other side of the sea, to the country of the Gerasenes . . . There met him out of the tombs a man with an unclean spirit . . . And when he saw Jesus from afar, he ran and worshipped him; and crying out with a loud voice, he said, 'What have you to do with me, Jesus, Son of the Most High God? I adjure you by God, do not torment me.' For he had said to him, *Come out of the man, you unclean spirit!* And Jesus asked him, *What is your name?* He replied, 'My name is Legion; for we are many.' . . . The man who had been possessed with demons begged him that he might be with him. But he refused, and said to him, *Go home to your friends and tell them how much the Lord has done for you, and how he has had mercy on you.*

A standard formula of exorcism, 'Come out . . . you unclean spirit!' (Mark 5:8), is used by Jesus in the land of the Gerasenes (or Gergesenes) to cast out demons (see Mark 1:25 in no. 2 above). Readers may find it surprising that Jesus inquires the name of the evil spirit. The purpose of the question, no doubt attributable to the evangelists, was to obtain as much information as possible about the demon because according to popular wisdom such knowledge was helpful to exorcists. (For the story of Simeon ben Yohai and Ben Temalion, see no. 2 above.)

At the end of the account, the liberated man wished to follow Jesus (Mark 5:18; Luke 8:38), but instead he was sent away with the injunction to announce the cure to all and sundry in the neighbourhood. As a result the fame of Jesus spread in the Transjordanian Greek cities of the Decapolis (Mark 5:20). It should be noted that in contrast to Jesus' custom not to allow his charismatic achievements to be publicized, here he recommends the proclamation of the good news. The reason for this exception is that the rule of secrecy applied only in a Jewish setting (cf. Mark 1:44; 5:43; 7:36; see no. 4 above). The different behaviour prescribed for the pagan Gerasenes (Gergesenes) is probably due to the editor attributing to Jesus the later Gentile church's missionary attitude towards non-Jews outside Palestine.

9. Healing a woman (Mark 5:25–34; Matt. 9:20–22; Luke 8:43–48)

And there was a woman who had had a flow of blood for twelve years, and who had suffered much under many physicians ... She had heard the reports about Jesus, and came up behind him in the crowd and touched his garment. For she said, 'If I touch even his garments, I shall be made well.' And immediately the haemorrhage ceased ... And Jesus, perceiving in himself that power had gone forth from him, ... said, *Who touched my garments?* ... The woman ... fell down before him and told him the whole truth. And he said to her, *Daughter,*[3] *your faith has made you well; go in peace, and be healed of your disease.*

In this story of healing the evangelists present us with the surprising statement that in the midst of a bustling crowd Jesus sought to identify the person who had touched him. Apparently he noticed that some healing power had passed from him into someone through bodily contact. Indeed, we are told that the woman, who had suffered from haemorrhage for twelve years, was convinced that even the fringe of Jesus' garment could heal her (Matt. 9:20; Luke 8:44; cf. Mark 6:56; Matt. 14:36).

Fringes or tassels (*tsitsiyyot* in Hebrew and *kraspeda* in Greek) play a special role in miracle stories. For instance, children grasped those on the tunic of the charismatic grandson of Honi the Circle-Drawer when they begged him to bring rain (bTaan 23a). As the lower edge of the outer garment was not easily reachable, the keenness to touch it suggests that people attributed to these fringes some kind of imaginary power. According to a legend preserved in a Tannaitic midrash, the tassels worn by a young Jew in obedience to a biblical precept (Num. 15:37–39) miraculously enabled him to resist the charms of a beautiful high-class Gentile prostitute,[4] and were instrumental in converting her to the Jewish religion.

Here as in most similar stories, the miracle is attributed to the faith

3. Teachers and healers addressed their followers as 'son' or 'daughter'. See Mark 2:5; Matt. 9:2 in chapter 2, no. 1; see also CD 2:14 in the Dead Sea Scrolls.

4. Sifre on Numbers 15:37–41, ed. H. S. Horovitz, para. 115, pp. 128–9.

of the sick person, Jesus simply declaring the *fait accompli*: 'Your faith has made you well'. Nevertheless in the mind of the patient and of the onlookers the healing was the work of Jesus. Likewise in the Talmudic story of charismatic rain-making, despite his modest denials the rabbis were convinced that the rain was brought by Abba Hilkiah, grandson of Honi the Circle-Drawer (bTaan 23ab).

10. Raising the daughter of Jairus (Mark 5:22–24, 35–43; Matt. 9:18–19, 23–26; Luke 8:41–42, 49–56)

Then came one of the rulers of the synagogue, Jairus by name, . . . and besought him, saying, 'My little daughter is at the point of death. Come and lay your hands on her, so that she may . . . live'. And he went with him . . . While he was still speaking, there came from the ruler's house some who said, 'Your daughter is dead. Why trouble the Teacher any further?' But . . . Jesus said . . . , *Do not fear, only believe*. And he allowed no one to follow him except Peter and James and John . . . When they came to the house . . . he saw . . . people weeping and wailing loudly . . . He said to them, *Why do you make a tumult and weep? The child is not dead, but sleeping*. And they laughed at him. But he put them all outside, and took the child's father and mother and those who were with him, and went in . . . Taking her by the hand he said to her, *Talitha cum(i)*, which means, 'Little girl, I say to you, arise.' And immediately the girl got up and walked (she was twelve years of age) . . . And he strictly charged them that no one should know this (Mark, Luke).

Behold, a ruler came in and knelt before him, saying, 'My daughter has just died; but come and lay your hand on her, and she will live.' And Jesus followed him with his disciples . . . And when Jesus came to the ruler's house, and saw the flute players, and the crowd making a tumult, he said, *Depart; for the girl is not dead but sleeping*. . . . But . . . he went in and took her by the hand, and the girl arose. And the report of this went through the whole district (Matt.).

Jairus, the president of the synagogue in an unidentified Galilean village, was exhorted by Jesus not to despair when the news of the death of his daughter was brought to him. (For faith as the precondition of miracles, see no. 7 above.)

The account of the raising of the girl is detailed in Mark, abridged in Matthew, and confused in Luke. In Mark Jesus, accompanied to the house by his three favourite apostles, Peter, James and John, was met there by a crowd of wailers. He told them that the girl was only asleep.[5] The villagers found Jesus' comment ridiculous, but were promptly dismissed, so that the subsequent events were witnessed only by Jesus, his three favourite companions and the parents of the girl. However, according to Matthew's account the actual raising of the girl by Jesus took place without other spectators.

The child, we are told, was resurrected by a formula quoted in Mark in colloquial Aramaic: *Talitha cum*,[6] 'Little girl, I say to you, arise!' Literally it is a familiar reference to a girl child and means, 'Kid [i.e. little goat], get up!' The masculine form (*talya* instead of *talitha*) was used for boys. Matthew altogether omits the command, and Luke abbreviates it to 'Child, arise!' (Luke 8:54); for his Greek-speaking non-Jewish readers Aramaic would have been double Dutch.

Mark and Matthew simply note that the 'dead' girl rose from her bed. Luke, however, specifies that 'her spirit returned', thus specifying that this was a case of the resurrection of the dead and not the awakening of a person from a comatose sleep. According to Mark the girl 'immediately . . . walked', and all the astounded witnesses were ordered by Jesus to keep the story to themselves. In Luke only the parents were expressly bound to secrecy; Peter, James and John, the other witnesses, needed no such reminder. Matthew (9:26) omits the command and states instead that the news spread like wildfire throughout the whole district.

5. Note that in the Acts of the Apostles 20:9–12 Paul, before raising Eutychus, also declared that the young man was not dead but sleeping, although he had fallen from a third-storey window.

6. This is the best-attested form of the verb in New Testament manuscripts. It represents sloppy dialect, using the masculine form of the imperative (*cum*, properly transliterated as *qum*) linked to a feminine subject (*talitha*). Other manuscripts testify to an attempt to ensure grammatical correctness, using *cumi* (*qumi*), the feminine form of the imperative.

11. Feeding five thousand (Mark 6:31–43; Matt. 14:13–20; Luke 9:10–17)

And he said to them, *Come away by yourselves to a lonely place, and rest a while*. For many were coming and going, and they had no leisure even to eat . . . As he went ashore, he saw a great throng, and he had compassion on them . . . and he began to teach them many things. And when it grew late, his disciples . . . said, 'This is a lonely place . . . send them away to go into the country and villages . . . and buy themselves something to eat.' But he answered to them, *You give them something to eat*. And they said to him, 'Shall we go and buy two hundred denarii worth of bread . . . ?' And he said to them, *How many loaves have you? Go and see* . . . They said, 'Five, and two fish.' Then he commanded them all to sit down . . . by hundreds and by fifties. And taking the five loaves and two fish he . . . blessed [them] . . . And gave them to the disciples to set before the people . . . And they all ate and were satisfied.

The account of the miraculous feeding is given in context. Jesus' order to his disciples, 'Come away . . . and rest a while', serves as the connecting link between the preceding account of the return of the apostles from their first missionary journey and the present story of the miraculous feeding of five thousand Galileans. The number of the attendance seems to be exaggerated, as is often the case in Jewish story-telling from the Bible to Josephus. In any case, how could a speaker be heard and understood in the countryside by a multitude of five thousand? Being a good narrator, Mark records the fascinating detail that because of the milling crowd the disciples of Jesus were so busy that they could not find time to eat. So Master and apostles tried to escape on a boat, but the excited people outran them and awaited their arrival at the next landing place on the lake shore.

A long teaching session followed in the remote countryside, lasting until the late afternoon, by which time the audience was starving. The apostles suggested that the people should be dispatched to fend for themselves, but Jesus instructed them to provide for the audience.

They first intended to go and buy bread for two hundred denarii,[7] but Jesus told them to use their own rations: five loaves and two fish.

The multitude was then seated in groups of hundreds and fifties (Mark). Matthew does not specify the numbers and Luke speaks of groups of 'about fifty each'. These units recall the traditional biblical division of the people into thousands, hundreds, fifties and tens (Exod. 18:21), confirmed by the Dead Sea Scrolls (1QS 2:21; CD 13:1–2). Luke's '*about* fifty', attested by the majority of ancient manuscripts, may once again indicate his unfamiliarity with Jewish customs, unless it mechanically copies the phrase '*about* five thousand' which immediately precedes it.

The evangelists advance an unexpected detail to anticipate the suggestion that the 'miracle' was purely psychological, namely that a tiny amount of food made the crowd feel satisfied. The apostles, if I may be allowed a light-hearted remark, seem to play the role of agents of a 'Keep the Galilean countryside clean!' campaign. They go round and collect the debris left after the picnic, filling twelve baskets. This detail is meant to answer in advance doubters who might have questioned the reality of the miracle: even the leftovers exceeded the original quantity of bread and fish.

The story is modelled on the Old Testament precedent of the prophet Elisha feeding a hundred men with twenty loaves of barley bread: 'And they ate, and had some left' (2 Kings 4:42–44). The surplus is an essential element in the tale.

12. Walking on the water (Mark 6:45–51; Matt. 14:22–27, 32)

Immediately he made his disciples get into the boat and go before him to the other side to Bethsaida . . . And . . . he went up on the mountain to pray. And when evening came, the boat was out on the sea and he was alone on the land. And he saw that they were making headway painfully, for the wind was against them. And about the fourth watch of the night he came to them, walking

7. A denarius was the daily wage of a labourer.

on the sea . . . But when they saw him walking on the sea they thought it was a ghost . . . But immediately he spoke to them and said, *Take heart, it is I; have no fear*. And he got into the boat with them and the wind ceased.

This is a folk legend – the exhausted disciples imagined they saw a ghost walking on the water – in which the emphasis is laid on Jesus' customary exhortation to faith, without which no miraculous escape from danger is possible (see also nos. 7 and 9 above).

13. Healing a deaf-mute (Mark 7:32–36)

And they brought to him a man who was deaf and had an impediment in his speech; and they besought him to lay his hand upon him. And taking him aside from the multitude privately, he put his fingers into his ears, and he spat and touched his tongue; and looking up to heaven, he sighed, and said to him, *Ephphatha*, that is, 'Be opened'. And his ears were opened, his tongue was released, and he spoke plainly. And he charged them to tell no one; but the more he charged them the more zealously they proclaimed it.

Mark alone recounts the healing of a deaf-mute near the Sea of Galilee. This time the event is not placed on a Sabbath, and the healing entails therapeutic acts. Jesus puts his fingers into the man's ears and touches his tongue with his saliva, then utters the command quoted in the original Aramaic: '*Ephphatha*' ('Be opened'). In a description of the messianic future (Isa. 35:5) the same verb is used to allude to the miraculous opening of the ears of the deaf in the eschatological age.

The spittle of Jesus also served for the healing of the eyes of a blind man (Mark 8:23). In John 9:6, too, Jesus spat on the ground and treated the eyes of another blind man with the mud thus made. Belief in the curative and magical power of human saliva is attested in rabbinic literature.[8] Spitting in the context of a magical action was

8. Cf. L. Blau, *Altjüdisches Zauberwesen* (Strassburg, 1898), 162.

forbidden by the rabbis; 'Abba Shaul said in the name of R. Akiba: "He who whispers (an incantation) over a wound . . . and spits (on it) has no portion in the world to come"' (tSanhedrin 12:10). In the Roman world, Tacitus reports that the emperor Vespasian had restored vision to a blind man by means of *oris excremento*, his saliva (*Histories* iv.81). Jesus is portrayed as employing the popular, though by present-day standards rather unhygienic, healing methods of his time.

14. Feeding four thousand (Mark 8:1–9; Matt. 15:32–38; Mark 8:17–21; Matt. 16:8–10)

In those days, when again a great crowd had gathered, and they had nothing to eat, he called his disciples to him, and said to them, *I have compassion on the crowd, because they have been with me now three days, and have nothing to eat; and if I send them away hungry to their homes, they will faint on the way; and some of them have come a long way.* And the disciples answered him, 'How can one feed these men with bread here in the desert?' And he asked them, *How many loaves have you?* They said, 'Seven.' . . . And he commanded the crowd to sit down on the ground . . . And they ate, and were satisfied . . . And there were about four thousand people [besides women and children (Matt.)].

Why do you discuss the fact that you have no bread? Do you not yet perceive or understand? Are your hearts hardened? Having eyes, do you not see, and having ears do you not hear? And do you not remember? When I broke the five loaves for the five thousand, how many baskets full of broken pieces did you take up? . . . And the seven for the four thousand, how many baskets full of broken pieces did you take up? . . . Do you not yet understand? (Mark 8:17–21; Matt. 16:8–10).

Though the story is very similar to the miraculous feeding reported in no. 11 above, several important details have been changed. The crowd is smaller: 4,000 instead of 5,000.[9] On the other hand the quantity of bread has grown from five to seven loaves and the number of fish is vaguely described in Mark and Matthew as 'a few'. The area here designated 'a desert' (*erêmia*) is farther from civilization than the 'desert place' (*erêmos topos*) of the first account: there it seemed possible to purchase food in neighbouring villages, whereas here shops are too far away. In the present story, as in Mark 6:34 and Matthew 14:14, Jesus' action springs from compassion for his tired and hungry audience. His question about the loaves of bread figures in both Mark and Matthew, but all the words of Jesus could be ascribed to the narrator without altering the meaning or the impact of the story.

The details of both miraculous feedings – the number of people, the number of loaves, and that of the baskets filled with leftovers – are repeated in Mark 8:17–21 and Matthew 16:8–10 in connection with Jesus' advice to abstain from the leaven of the Pharisees. The lesson he draws from it is the usual one: the necessity of faith.

15. Healing a blind man in Bethsaida (Mark 8:22–26)

Some people brought to him a blind man, and begged him to touch him. And he took the blind man by the hand, and led him out of the village; and when he had spit on his eyes and laid his hands upon him, he asked him, *Do you see anything?* And he looked up and said, 'I see men, but they look like trees, walking.' Then again he laid his hands upon his eyes; and he looked intently and was restored, and saw everything clearly. And he sent him away to his home, saying, *Do not even enter the village.*

Like in the story of the deaf-mute (see no. 13 above), Jesus uses his saliva as a medicinal substance, but he also lays his hands on the blind man as an act of healing and blessing. The action takes place outside the inhabited area and without witnesses, and while instantaneous, the healing is not complete since the man's vision remains blurred and

9. In Matthew 15:38, as earlier in Matthew 14:21, only the male members of the audience are counted.

distorted. As a result, the laying-on of hands has to be repeated. The story is unique in so far as normally Jesus' intervention is presented as an instant and total success. The healing finally accomplished, Jesus, as usual (see nos. 4, 10, 13, 29), insists on the avoidance of publicity, and to ensure discretion he forbids the man to re-enter the village.

16. Confession of Peter (Mark 8:27–33; Matt. 16:13–16, 20–23; Luke 9:18–22)

And Jesus went on with his disciples, to the villages of Caesarea Philippi; and on the way he asked his disciples, *Who do men say that I am* [*that the son of Man is* (Matt.)]? And they told him, 'John the Baptist; and others say, Elijah; and others [Jeremiah or (Matt.)] one of the prophets.' And he asked them, *But who do you say that I am?* Peter answered him, 'You are the Christ' [the Son of the living God (Matt.), 'The Christ of God' (Luke)]. And he charged them to tell no one about him. And he began to teach them that the son of Man must suffer many things . . . and be killed, and after three days rise again . . . And Peter took him, and began to rebuke him. But . . . he rebuked Peter, and said, *Get behind me, Satan! For you are not on the side of God, but of men.*

Two questions introduce the significant declaration of Peter concerning the messianic identity of Jesus. The first is aimed at outsiders: 'Who do men say that I am? [that the son of Man is? (Matt.)]' (Mark 8:27; Matt. 16:13; Luke 9:18). The two phrases using either 'I' (Mark, Luke) or 'the son of Man' (Matt.) are identical in meaning, that is to say, 'the son of Man' = 'I' (see chapter 7). In fact some manuscripts of Matthew and several ancient versions combine both formulae so as to read: 'Who do men say that I, the son of Man, am?' Peter reports three (or four) opinions attributed to outsiders ('men'). For them Jesus is John the Baptist, or Elijah, (or Jeremiah (Matt.)), or one of the prophets.

This reply elicits from Jesus a further question concerning the apostles' view (Mark 8:29; Matt. 16:15; Luke 9:20). Peter's words are substantially the same in all three Gospels, namely that Jesus is the

Messiah, but there are slight terminological variations: 'You are the Christ' (Mark) – 'You are the Christ, the Son of the living God' (Matt.) – 'The Christ of God' (Luke). The composite title, 'the Christ, the Son of God', appears also in Matthew 26:63 and is slightly modified in Mark 14:61, 'the Christ, the Son of the Blessed'. 'Christ' and 'Son of God' are used as synonyms.

The Synoptists place the first announcement of Jesus' death and resurrection immediately after Peter's confession of his Messiahship. The words of Jesus infuriate Peter, whose comment in turn provokes a sharp rebuke: Jesus calls him 'Satan' (Mark 8:33; Matt. 16:23). Peter's reaction indicates that for him and his companions the 'Messiah – Son of God' could not be a failure, neither was he expected to die. Put differently, they shared the common Jewish concept of a triumphant Anointed of the Lord (for fuller details, see chapter 7). As for the prediction of resurrection following death, it is hard to imagine how an announcement of Jesus' triumph could have made Peter so indignant as to rebuke him. The resurrection part of the prediction is probably a later editorial supplement.

17. Healing of an epileptic boy (Mark 9:14–27; Matt. 17:14–18; Luke 9:38–43)

And when they came to the disciples, they saw a great crowd about them, and scribes arguing with them . . . And he asked them, *What are you discussing with them?* And one of the crowd answered him, 'Teacher, I brought my son to you, for he has a dumb spirit . . . and I asked your disciples to cast it out, and they were not able.' And he answered them, *O faithless* [*and perverse* (Matt., Luke)] *generation, how long am I to be with you? How long am I to bear with you? Bring him to me*. And they brought the boy to him; and when the spirit saw him, immediately it convulsed the boy, and he fell on the ground and rolled about, foaming at the mouth. And Jesus asked his father, *How long has he had this?* And he said, 'From childhood . . . but if you can do anything, have pity on us and help us.' And Jesus said to him, *If you can! All things are possible to him who believes*. Immediately the father of the child cried out and said, 'I believe; help my unbelief!' . . . Jesus . . . rebuked the unclean spirit, saying to it, *You dumb and deaf spirit, I command you, come out of him, and never enter him again.* And after crying out and convulsing him terribly, it came out, and the boy was like a corpse . . . But Jesus took him by the hand and lifted him up, and he arose.

The disciples of Jesus, after their failure to expel a demon from a dumb boy, were challenged by local scribes. Jesus apparently did not know what the debate was about, nor was he aware of the length of the boy's illness, and consequently had to inquire. Such questions are typical in the account of Mark, who had no scruples in admitting lack of knowledge on the part of Jesus (cf. Mark 9:33 in no. 18 below). By the time Matthew and Luke wrote their Gospels, an imperfection of this kind could no longer be attributed to the Son of God. In consequence, they omitted the questions.

When Jesus found out the cause of the argument, he angrily castigated the apostles' lack of faith (Mark 9:19; Matt. 17:17; Luke 9:41; cf. John 14:9; see also no. 8 above). The distraught father's prayer was not couched in the right terms either: 'if you can do anything'. Hence the disillusioned and tolerant sigh ascribed to Jesus: 'If you can!' (Mark 9:23).

The solemn form of exorcism pronounced by Jesus was intended to remedy the disciples' inability to cope with the possessed: 'You dumb and deaf spirit, I command you, come out of him, and never enter him again!' (see also nos. 2 and 8 above). It was generally thought that the exorcized demon could return to the same person.[10] Note that the exorcist Eleazar, described by Josephus, also adjured the demon never to revisit its former victim (*Antiquities* 8:46–7). This would imply, in modern parlance, awareness that the effect of an exorcism might be temporary, producing remission rather than cure.

10. Matt. 12:44–45; Luke 11:24–26; see chapter 3, no. 3, n. 1; chapter 4, no. 10.

18. Dispute about greatness (Mark 9:33–34; Matt. 18:1; Luke 9:46)

And they came to Capernaum; and when he was in the house he asked them, *What were you discussing on the way?* But they were silent; for . . . they had discussed with one another who was the greatest.

Mark again depicts Jesus as ignorant of the thoughts of his disciples (cf. no. 17 above). As before, the question is omitted in Matthew and Luke. In fact Luke (9:47) explicitly denies any lack of knowledge on Jesus' part: 'Jesus perceived the thought of their hearts.' This is a later attempt to rectify the tradition of Mark.

19. Healing a blind man (Mark 10:46–52; Matt. 20:29–34; Luke 18:35–43)

And as he was leaving Jericho . . . Bartimaeus, a blind beggar, . . . began to cry out and say, 'Jesus, Son of David, have mercy on me!' . . . And Jesus stopped and said, *Call him* . . . And throwing off his mantle, he sprang up and came to Jesus. And Jesus said to him, *What do you want me to do for you?* And the blind man said to him, 'Master, let me receive my sight.' And Jesus said to him, *Go your way; your faith has made you well.*

Having heard the plea for help of the blind Bartimaeus, Jesus told his followers to bring him near (Mark 10:49). One would have expected him to address the beggar directly, but the story-teller sought to enhance his stature and made him employ assistants to handle menial tasks. The cure is once more ascribed to faith (see also no. 7 above).

20. Entry into Jerusalem (Mark 11:1–3; Matt. 21:1–3; Luke 19:29–31)

And when they drew near to Jerusalem, to Bethphage and Bethany, at the Mount of Olives, he sent two of his disciples and said to them, *Go into the village opposite you, and immediately as you enter it you will find a colt tied, on which no one has ever sat* [*an ass tied, and a colt with her* (Matt.)]; *untie it* [*them* (Matt.)] *and bring it* [*them* (Matt.)] *to me. If anyone says to you, 'Why are you doing this?' say, 'The Lord has need of it* [*them* (Matt.)] and will send it [*them* (Matt.)] *back here immediately.'*

In the account of the preparation of Passover in Bethany Jesus gives detailed instructions to his disciples. Mark and Luke speak of a colt to be borrowed on which Jesus was to make his solemn entry into Jerusalem. Riding, rather than walking, into the holy city for Passover was nothing unusual, according to rabbinic tradition. The Palestinian Talmud records that before Passover ass-drivers did flourishing business in carrying pilgrims to Jerusalem (yBer 13d). In particular the rich preferred to ride on donkeys to the Temple mount and thus publicly demonstrate their higher social status (yPes 31b).

In order to associate the event with a messianic prophecy, Matthew re-wrote Mark, and introduced a she-ass as well as her colt. His story is laboured and artificial. The quotation 'Tell the daughter of Zion, Behold, your king is coming to you, humble, and mounted on *an ass*, and on *a colt, the foal of an ass*' (Matt. 21:5) does not come directly from the Hebrew Bible or from the Greek Septuagint, but results from a combination of Isaiah 62:11 with an otherwise unknown form of Zechariah 9:9. Matthew's understanding of the text is idiosyncratic. He deliberately overlooks that in the poetry of Zechariah 'a colt, the foal of an ass' is a mere literary parallelism. The prophet envisaged a single donkey and not a mother together with her young. Nevertheless the Greek Matthew (21:7) speaks of *two* animals: the garments were placed on '*them*', and in some curious way Jesus was sitting on them (two donkeys)![11] No native Semitic speaker would have made such a mistake.

21. The cursing of the fig tree (Mark 11:12–14; Matt. 21:18–19)

On the following day, when they came from Bethany, he was hungry. And seeing in the distance a fig tree in leaf, he went to see if he could find anything on it. When he came to it, he found nothing but leaves, for it was not the season for figs. And he said to it, *May no one ever eat from you again.* [And the fig tree withered at once (Matt.).]

This is a real curiosity. The hungry Jesus of Mark apparently behaved illogically and cursed a fig tree for being fruitless when it was not the season for figs. Matthew ignores this curious detail. He reports instead that Jesus' curse killed the tree at once. It is interesting to recall that according to Flavius Josephus fig trees produced fruit during ten of the twelve months in the year around the Sea of Galilee (*War* 3:518). One could speculate that Jesus forgot that Jerusalem had a harsher climate, and expected too much from a Judaean fig tree.

22. Prediction of the destruction of the Temple (Mark 13:1–2; Matt. 24:1–2; Luke 21:5–6)

And as he came out of the temple, one of his disciples said to him, '. . . Do you see these great buildings?' And Jesus said to him, *There will not be left here one stone upon another that will not be thrown down.*

The Eschatological Discourse (Mark 13; Matt. 24; Luke 21) is introduced by a question addressed to Jesus about the splendour of the

11. Some copyists were puzzled and replaced 'them' by 'it' so as to conform to the single colt of Mark and Luke.

Temple. The succinct announcement of the destruction of the sanctuary, given in direct speech by Jesus, triggers off a query about the exact moment of the catastrophe. The answer follows in the Discourse, which will be considered in chapter 8.

23. Preparation for Passover (Mark 14:12–15; Matt. 26:17–18; Luke 22:7–12)

And on the first day of unleavened bread, . . . his disciples said to him, 'Where will you have us go and prepare for you to eat the passover?' And he sent two of his disciples and said to them, *Go into the city, and a man carrying a jar of water will meet you; follow him, and wherever he enters, say to the householder, 'The Teacher says, Where is my guest room, where I am to eat the passover with my disciples?' And he will show you a large upper room furnished and ready; there prepare for us* (Mark, Luke).

Go into the city to a certain one, and say to him, 'The Teacher says, My time is at hand; I will keep the passover at your house with my disciples' (Matt.).

From Bethany, Jesus dispatched two of his disciples (Mark),[12] or all of them (Matt.), with full instructions about where to make arrangements for the Passover dinner. In Mark the directives have a mysterious, vaguely prophetic character. The apostles will come across someone who will lead them to the right address. Matthew dispenses with the cloak-and-dagger preface of Mark, and substitutes for it a terse and prosaic order issued by Jesus.

12. In Luke (22:8–9) Jesus takes the initiative and chooses Peter and John as emissaries (see no. 38 below) who then ask for instructions.

24. Jesus in Gethsemane (Mark 14:32–42; Matt. 26:36–46; Luke 22:40–46)

And they went to a place which was called Gethsemane; and he said to his disciples, *Sit here, while I pray*. And he took with him Peter and James and John . . . And said to them, *My soul is very sorrowful, even to death; remain here, and watch* . . . And he came and found them sleeping, and said to Peter, *Simon, are you asleep? Could you not watch one hour? Watch and pray that you may not enter into temptation; the spirit is indeed willing, but the flesh is weak* . . . And again he came and found them sleeping . . . And he came the third time, and said to them, *Are you still sleeping and taking your rest? It is enough; the hour has come; the Son of Man is betrayed into the hands of sinners. Rise, let us be going; see, my betrayer is at hand.*

After the Last Supper, Jesus invites his apostles to pray and be vigilant. Nevertheless he finds their leaders, Peter, James and John, asleep. As often happens, the close associates of Jesus are depicted in a bad light. For Peter's betrayal, see chapter 8, no. 31.

25. The arrest of Jesus (Mark 14:43–49; Matt. 26:47–56; Luke 22:47–53)

And . . . Judas came, . . . and with him a crowd with swords and clubs, from the chief priests and the scribes and the elders . . . And they laid hands on him and seized him . . . And Jesus said to them, *Have you come out as against a robber, with swords and clubs to capture me? Day after day I was with you in the temple teaching, and you did not seize me. But let the scriptures be fulfilled.*

But all this has taken place, that the scriptures of the prophets might be fulfilled (Matt.).

But this is your hour, and the power of darkness (Luke).

The armed group of law enforcers sent by the religious authorities (and guided by Judas) are confronted by Jesus. The question of why he was treated as a criminal, after having enjoyed freedom of speech in the Temple day after day, is directed to the authorities rather than to their emissaries. Mark and Matthew hint in vague terms that the event was the fulfilment of prophecy. Though no book, chapter or verse is quoted, the allusion may point to Isaiah 53:12 (cf. Luke 22:37; see chapter 5, no. 39). Without referring to the scriptures, Luke considers the happenings predestined: 'This is your hour, and the power of darkness.' The use of the argument from prophecy in connection with the passion and resurrection of Jesus was part of the apologetics of the primitive church and figures especially in exchanges with Jews who were familiar with the Bible.

26. Jesus and the High Priest (Mark 14:61–62; Matt. 26:63–64; Luke 22:67–70)

Again the high priest asked him, 'Are you the Christ, the Son of the Blessed?'

'I adjure you by the living God, tell us if you are the Christ, the Son of God' (Matt.).

And Jesus said, *I am* [*You have said so* (Matt.)]; *and you will see the Son of man seated at the right hand of Power, and coming with the clouds of heaven.*

'If you are the Christ, tell us.' But he said to them, *If I tell you, you will not believe; and if I ask you, you will not answer. But from now on the Son of man shall be seated at the right hand of the power of God.* And they all said, 'Are you the Son of God, then?' And he said to them, *You say that I am* (Luke).

The two sayings of Jesus which help along the narrative are the separate but similar answers to the questions, 'Are you the Christ?' (Mark, Matt., Luke) and again 'Are you the Son of God?' (Luke). The reply given by Jesus is equivocal in Matthew and in Luke. 'You have said so' and 'You say that I am' imply that Jesus would not have chosen to describe himself in these terms. On the first occasion in Luke, Jesus refuses to answer on account of his opponents' unwillingness to listen to him. The same attitude is implied in chapter 2, no. 10 (see also no. 27 below).

The plain affirmative reply in Mark – 'I am' – is the odd man out. It conflicts with the general line of reply ascribed to Jesus, which was 'You have said so' or 'You say that I am'. The phrase implies a negative answer according to rabbinic literature (see *The Changing Faces of Jesus*, 181–3). It should also be observed that in conformity with mainstream tradition some manuscripts of Mark's Gospel read 'You say that I am'. The main declaration about the Son of Man sitting next to God and coming with the clouds will be treated in chapter 5, no. 18, and in chapter 7, no. 20.

27. Jesus before Pilate (Mark 15:2; Matt. 27:11; Luke 23:3)

And Pilate asked him, 'Are you the King of the Jews?' And he answered him, *You have said so*.

To the Roman prefect's straight question concerning Jesus' royal aspirations, he gave his customary equivocal reply. The most likely meaning of 'You have said so' is that the words are Pilate's, but this is not how Jesus would identify himself.

II. MATTHEW AND LUKE (Q)

28. The centurion's servant (Matt. 8:5–13; Luke 7:1–10)

As he entered Capernaum, a centurion came forward to him, beseeching him and saying, 'Lord, my servant is lying paralysed at home, in terrible distress.' And he said to him, *I will come and heal him*. But the centurion answered him, 'Lord, I am not worthy to have you under my roof; but only say the word, and my servant will be healed.' . . . And to the centurion Jesus said, *Go; be it done for you as you have believed*. And the servant was healed at that very moment.

The two sentences directly attributed to Jesus figure at the beginning and the end of the conversation. In Capernaum a Roman centurion solicited Jesus' intervention on behalf of his paralysed servant (*pais*),[13] and he promptly volunteered his help. In the body of the story emphasis is laid on the unexpected faith of this Gentile (see chapter 8, no. 37), and in the concluding statement of Jesus the healing of the servant is presented as the sequel to the centurion's faith just as in the case of healing miracles among Jews (Matt. 8:13). The cure was performed from a distance. Healing *in absentia* without touching the patient is known also in rabbinic literature; it is attributed to Hanina ben Dosa, a younger contemporary of Jesus (yBer 9d; bBer 34b).

III. MATTHEW'S SPECIAL MATERIAL (*M*)

29. Healing two blind men (Matt. 9:27–31)

And as Jesus passed on from there, two blind men followed him, crying aloud, 'Have mercy on us, Son of David.' . . . Jesus said to them, *Do you believe that I am able to do this?* They said to him, 'Yes, Lord.' Then he touched their eyes, saying, *According to your faith be it done to you*. And their eyes were opened. And Jesus sternly charged them, *See that no one knows it*. But they went away and spread his fame through all that district.

The healing of two blind men is preceded in Matthew by the raising of the daughter of a nameless ruler (*archôn*)[14] in an unspecified Galilean locality. The story follows the normal pattern. Jesus first calls for an expression of belief in his healing power, then ascribes the miracle to the faith thus elicited, and finally orders the beneficiaries of the cure to keep it secret, which they disregard (see Mark 8:26; 10:51–52 in nos. 15 and 19 above).

13. The parallel account in Luke 7:2 speaks of a slave (*doulos*). John (4:46) in turn refers to the centurion's son (*huios*).

14. In Mark 5:22 he is named Jairus and is described as the president of a synagogue.

30. Peter's failure to walk on the water (Matt. 14:28–32)

And Peter answered him, 'Lord, if it is you, bid me come to you on the water.' He said, *Come* . . . When he saw the wind, he was afraid, and beginning to sink he cried out, 'Lord, save me.' Jesus immediately reached out his hand and caught him, saying to him, *O man of little faith, why did you doubt?* And when they got into the boat, the wind ceased.

In a Matthean supplement to the legend of Jesus' walking on the water (Mark 6:45–50; Matt. 14:22–27; cf. no. 12 above), Peter wishes to imitate his Master, but almost immediately sinks. The story serves to illustrate the necessity and power of faith and conversely the disastrous effect of pusillanimity.

31. Instruction by the risen Jesus to his disciples (Matt. 28:10)

Then Jesus said to them, *Do not be afraid; go and tell my brethren to go to Galilee, and there they will see me.*

The words put on the lips of Jesus by Matthew are part of the confused accounts of the 'post-resurrection' events. According to Mark 16:8, the women who went to complete the burial rites on Sunday at dawn ran away terrified from the empty tomb and 'said nothing to any one'. Luke 24:9, on the other hand, makes them report their experience to 'the eleven and to all the rest', but these did not believe the 'idle tale' of the women (Luke 24:11). However, two other disciples travelling to Emmaus met Jesus and immediately returned to Jerusalem to report the matter to the apostles, only to learn that by then Jesus had appeared to Simon Peter too (Luke 24:13–35). At that moment Jesus was seen by all of them. A session of final instruction followed, at the end of which Jesus took them to Bethany and on the same day he ascended to heaven (Luke 24:36–53).

Matthew gives a completely different version of the story. Mary Magdalene and the 'other' Mary left the empty tomb with a mixture of 'fear and great joy' (Matt. 28:8) and told the apostles what they had seen and heard. Yet in an inconsequential manner Matthew speaks of another encounter of the women with Jesus, who dispatches them to his 'brethren' with the message to meet him in Galilee. The directive is obeyed and the meeting with Jesus on a Galilean mountain constitutes the finale of the Gospel of Matthew. The story is a highly elaborate supplement which is absent from the other Gospels. It fills in the hole in Mark concerning the resurrection appearances of Jesus.

IV. LUKE'S SPECIAL MATERIAL (*L*)

32. The young Jesus in the Temple (Luke 2:48–49)

His mother said to him, 'Son, why have you treated us so? Behold, your father and I have been looking for you anxiously.' And he said to them, *How is it that you sought me? Did you not know that I must be in my Father's house?*

These are the only words ascribed to the twelve-year-old Jesus in the story of his first Passover pilgrimage to Jerusalem. It is generally accepted that the so-called Infancy Gospels belong to the genre of historically unreliable childhood tales, frequently attested in legends and folk literature. Wandering away from the family group, the youth spent his time listening to teachers in the Temple and astonishing them with his extraordinary cleverness. The anxious and no doubt angry Mary and Joseph discovered him after three days' search and gently took him to task. He answered them with the words quoted, displaying tolerant criticism. 'My Father's house' or literally 'what is my Father's' can designate either the Temple of Jerusalem, or more generally the affairs of God. The aim of the evangelist is to depict Jesus as a person who from the outset was totally devoted to the service of God. Bearing in mind the nature of the passage, the question of the authenticity of the spoken words hardly arises.

The precocious knowledge attributed to famous great men is part of folklore and legend; it can also be useful for self-aggrandizement. A suitable illustration may be found in the autobiography of Flavius Josephus. 'While still a mere boy,' he writes, 'about fourteen years old, I won universal applause for my love of letters; inasmuch that the chief priests and the leading men of the city used constantly to come to me for precise information about some particular in our ordinances' (*Life* 9).

33. Jesus in the synagogue of Nazareth (Luke 4:16–19, 21)

And he came to Nazareth . . . and he went to the synagogue . . . on the sabbath day. And he stood up to read; and there was given to him the book of the prophet Isaiah. He opened the book and found the place where it was written, 'The Spirit of the Lord is upon me . . .' . . . And he began to say to them, *Today this scripture has been fulfilled in your hearing.*

Luke alone describes a Sabbath service in the synagogue of Nazareth at which Jesus performed the role of reader of the prophetic section (*haftarah*) borrowed on that occasion from Isaiah. (For the discussion of the text itself, see chapter 5, no. 38.) Normally the reader had to recite the prescribed biblical text without jumping from one passage to another. Luke's quotation comes from the Greek Septuagint and not from the Hebrew Isaiah which would have been read in a Galilean synagogue. Even more strikingly, Jesus is said to have publicly asserted that the prophecy just recited has been realized in him. He nowhere else makes such a claim in connection with a specific quotation.

Moreover, contrary to the testimony of Mark and Matthew, according to whom neither his family nor the inhabitants of Nazareth held Jesus in high esteem, Luke suggests that the congregation of his home town reacted favourably to his words and congratulated themselves on having him as a fellow citizen (Luke 4:22). The phrase 'Is not this Joseph's son?' appears in Luke in a positive context as against the disparaging overtone of a similar question in Mark 6:3 and Matthew 13:55–56. Both these evangelists clearly attest that the people of

Nazareth were scandalized by Jesus.[15] In fact the clumsiness of Luke's story-telling culminates a few verses later (4:28–29) when after a religiously much less provocative statement of Jesus – 'No prophet is acceptable in his own country' (4:24) – the synagogue congregation of Nazareth suddenly turns into a lynch mob ready to murder Jesus.

34. Miraculous catch of fish (Luke 5:1, 3–6, 10)

He was standing by the lake of Gennesaret . . . Getting into one of the boats, which was Simon's, he asked him to put out a little from the land. And he sat down and taught the people from the boat. And when he had ceased speaking, he said to Simon, *Put out into the deep and let down your nets for a catch*. And Simon answered, 'Master, we toiled all night and took nothing! But at your word I will let down the nets.' And when they had done this, they enclosed a great shoal of fish . . . And Jesus said to Simon, *Do not be afraid; henceforth you will be catching men.*

Jesus is presented as directing the fishing operation; he tells the experts what to do. Peter, the head of a partnership with James and John, obeys Jesus even though this entails acting against his expert judgement, and is rewarded with a miraculous catch. Luke's account is the prelude to the announcement of the new profession of the apostles as symbolical 'catchers of men' and parallels the call of Peter and Andrew in Mark and Matthew (see no. 1 above).

15. Most New Testament scholars interpret the question about Jesus son of Joseph as a sign that after the first enthusiasm doubts began to creep into the minds of the people of Nazareth, marking three stages of an evolutionary process: (1) admiration; (2) doubt; (3) outrage. Yet it is hard to imagine how anyone reading Luke 4:22 on its own can conclude that a substantial change in attitude has been taking place between the beginning and the end of the same verse: 'And all spoke well of him, and wondered at the gracious words which proceeded from his mouth; and they said, "Is not this Joseph's son?"'

35. Raising the widow's son at Nain (Luke 7:11–15)

Soon afterward he went to a city called Nain . . . As he drew near to the gate of the city, behold, a man who had died was being carried out, the only son of his mother, and she was a widow . . . And when the Lord saw her, he had compassion on her and said to her, *Do not weep*. And he came and touched the bier, and the bearers stood still. And he said, *Young man, I say to you, arise*. And the dead man sat up, and began to speak. And he gave him to his mother.

Luke describes the entry of Jesus into the otherwise unknown Galilean village of Nain.[16] Having met there a funeral procession of the only son of a widow, he comforted the mother and ordered the dead man to get up. The formula 'Young man . . . arise' is similar to that employed by Jesus in connection with the raising of the daughter of Jairus, 'Little girl . . . arise' (see no. 10 above). Luke, with his usual lack of familiarity with Palestinian realities, remarks that the report about this miracle spread, not in Galilee as would be normal, but 'through the whole of Judaea and all the surrounding country' (Luke 7:17).

36. The cleansing of ten lepers (Luke 17:11–19)

On the way to Jerusalem he was passing along between Samaria and Galilee. And as he entered a village, he was met by ten lepers, who . . . lifted up their voices and said, 'Jesus, Master, have mercy on us.' . . . He said to them, *Go and show yourselves to the priests*. And . . . they were cleansed. Then one of them . . . turned back, praising God with a loud voice; and he fell on his face at Jesus' feet, giving him thanks. Now he was a Samaritan.

16. That Luke locates Nain in Galilee may be deduced from the dating of the episode 'soon afterward' or 'next day' following Jesus' visit to Capernaum (Luke 7:1, 11) The only Nain (variant reading Ain) known to Josephus is a place lying somewhere in southern Judaea, not far from the Idumaean border, which is too distant to be relevant here. Cf. *War* 4:511, 517.

Then Jesus said, *Were not ten cleansed? Where are the nine? Was no one found to return and give praise to God except this foreigner?* And he said to him, *Rise and go your way; your faith has made you well.*

This episode of ten lepers reported only by Luke repeats the theme of the healing of the one leper in no. 4 above. Here too Jesus stressed the duty to observe the ritual precepts, and associated the cure with the person's faith. The twist introduced by Luke consists in underlining that only the one Samaritan – and not the nine Jews – showed gratitude and returned to thank the healer. Luke is always keen on stressing that non-Jews, including Samaritans (see chapter 4, no. 28), are better than Jews. The account bears the mark of the theological ideology of the Gentile church, which chose Samaria as its first non-Jewish missionary territory (cf. Acts 8:4–25) despite Jesus' former prohibition on approaching Samaritans (Matt. 10:5; see chapter 8, no. 49).

37. Zacchaeus (Luke 19:1–6)

He entered Jericho . . . And there was a man named Zacchaeus; he was a chief tax collector, and rich. And he sought to see who Jesus was, but could not, on account of the crowd, because he was small of stature. So he . . . climbed up into a sycamore tree to see him . . . Jesus . . . looked up and said to him, *Zacchaeus, make haste and come down; for I must stay at your house today.* So he . . . came down, and received him joyfully.

Luke places a special narrative about the chief tax-collector of Jericho next to the account of the healing of Bartimaeus, the blind beggar from the same city (Mark 10:46–52; Matt. 20:29–34; Luke 18:35–43; cf. no. 19 above). The words cited are part of the narrative framework of the story, which serves as an illustration of Jesus' sympathy towards 'tax-collectors and sinners' (see chapter 7, no. 9, and chapter 8, no. 41).

38. Preparation for the Passover (Luke 22:8)

Jesus sent Peter and John, saying, *Go and prepare the passover for us, that we may eat it.*

In Luke's special formulation of the account, Jesus instructs Peter and John to make the necessary arrangements for the Passover meal. In Mark the disciples are not named, and in Matthew the command is addressed to all the close followers of Jesus. Cf. no. 23 above.

39. Journey to Emmaus (Luke 24:13–19)

That very day two of them [Jesus' disciples] were going to a village named Emmaus . . . While they were talking . . . Jesus himself drew near and went with them. But their eyes were kept from recognizing him. And he said to them, *What is this conversation which you are holding with each other as you walk?* . . . One of them . . . answered him, 'Are you the only visitor to Jerusalem who does not know the things that have happened there in these days?' And he said to them, *What things?*

The first resurrection appearance, recorded only by Luke, happens on the road to Emmaus where two dispirited disciples encounter a stranger – the unrecognized risen Jesus – who leads them on by inquiring about the subject of their conversation. This turns out to be the 'things' which constituted the talk of the town in Jerusalem. A further puzzled interjection by the stranger follows: 'What things?' The questions are part of the evangelist's lively descriptive narrative with no doctrinal or historical relevance.

40. Appearance of Jesus to his disciples in Jerusalem (Luke 24:36–43, 48–49)

Jesus himself stood among them [the disciples]. But they were startled . . . and supposed that they saw a spirit. And he said to them, *Why are you troubled, and why do questionings rise in your hearts?* . . . And while they still disbelieved for joy, and wondered, he said to them, *Have you anything here to eat?* They gave him a piece of broiled fish, and he . . . ate before them . . . *You are witnesses of these things. And behold, I send the promise of my Father upon you; but stay in the city, until you are clothed with power from on high.*

The scene is the gathering of the apostles after the arrival of the two disciples from Emmaus. The questions of Jesus were meant to reassure them as they were frightened by what they thought to be a ghost (cf. no. 12 above). His request for food was to prove that he was real flesh and blood, and not a disembodied spirit. The reference to the coming of the Holy Spirit, the instruction that the apostles should remain in Jerusalem and the concluding mention of the ascension of Jesus to heaven on Easter day itself (Luke 24:50–51) serve as connecting links between the end of Luke's Gospel and the opening chapter of the Acts of the Apostles.

REFLECTIONS

The words listed under the heading 'Narratives and Commands' contribute little to the study of the authentic teaching of Jesus, but they can help the reader to form a clearer image of the personality of Jesus as portrayed in the Synoptic Gospels. For notwithstanding the theological overtones of their narration, Mark, Matthew and Luke still supply a sketch of the career of a first-century rural Galilean prophet and holy man.

The first constant image we encounter in the Gospels is that of Jesus *qua* charismatic healer–exorcist – 'miracle-worker'. They show nothing theatrical in the actions of Jesus, who shunned the abracadabra of Jewish or pagan amulets and magical bowls and the various real or phoney medicines prescribed in them. He discarded even the less exotic characteristics of charismatic action attested in the respectable writings of the Apocrypha and the rest of ancient Jewish literature, including Josephus. Jesus did not make use of angelic wisdom as did Noah and Solomon according to post-biblical writings. Apart from his saliva, he employed no *materia medica*, no remedies such as the heart and liver of fish burnt by the young Tobit in order to keep the demon Asmodeus at a safe distance from his bride and himself (Tobit 8:2–3), or the gall of the same fish which he used to cure his father from blindness (Tobit 11:11–14). Jesus disdained the showy acting of Josephus' professional exorcist Eleazar, who filled a bowl with water for the expelled demon to knock over and thus allow the onlookers to witness its departure (Josephus, *Antiquities* 8:46–47). (Did he reckon that the exorcized man in his fit would spill the liquid?) Jesus did not even imitate the orthodox form of healing or expelling evil spirits in the name of God, but simply commanded the demon to quit, leprosy to disappear, the withered hand to stretch out, the deaf ear to open, the dead (or near dead?) to rise, and the storm to abate. The words ascribed to Jesus in the narrative context of healing and exorcism present him as a man of spiritual power filled with, and exuding, charismatic authority. This picture is similar to his description as a teacher who was unlike the ordinary scribes of his time on account of the masterfulness of his message: 'For he taught them as one who had authority' (Mark 1:22; Matt. 7:29; Luke 4:32).

A second recurrent feature in the passages examined in this chapter is Jesus' emphasis on faith and his condemnation of any lack of trust in God's power mediated by him. Pusillanimous men experienced the sharp edge of his tongue. In contrast to his imperious stance against evil, he displayed compassion towards the miserable and modesty, even self-effacement, after his efficacious action. He preferred to assign to the faith of the patient the miraculous cures and successful exorcisms. As has been noted earlier, belief in Jesus' healing power is depicted by the evangelists as the *conditio sine qua non* of any miraculous happening. Put bluntly, he who professed the possibility of miracles, and the ability of Jesus to perform miracles, was declared by him to be the real author of those miracles.

The third prominent theme is Jesus' insistence on secrecy regarding the healings and exorcisms performed by him. No explicit reason is given for such secrecy. In most cases the cure occurred before witnessing crowds, but even if it happened in private, like the healing of the deaf-mute, the extraordinary event was bound to attract attention. Acquaintances would have wondered how people previously blind, deaf, or smitten with leprosy had suddenly recovered their sight, hearing, or good health. Yet Jesus was against publicity. Two reasons may underlie this apparent shyness. Positively he held the view that the good news of the arrival of the Kingdom of God had to progress quietly like the growth of the seed in the ground. Negatively he did not wish to be hailed as the Christ, but he knew that active proclamation of his charismatic deeds would unavoidably place him in the context of the messianic age. Hence he decided to take preventive measures.

The discussion of several important doctrinal notions such as the concepts of the 'Son of man', the role of Scripture in the teaching of Jesus and his attitude to ritual law – topics which have been touched on in the foregoing pages – will receive fuller treatment in later chapters.

2

Controversy Stories

In common with the narratives and commands of the previous chapter, controversy reports fall within the category of story-telling, but they differ from the former in so far as they entail substantial portions of a didactic element. Polemics generally revolve around doctrines, beliefs, laws and customs. The nature of the stories which carry them may vary from the real to the fictional but many of them stand somewhere in between. They may be antedated from the age of the apostles and the evangelists in the mid to late first century AD to the lifetime of Jesus. Indeed, they often are. Rudolf Bultmann in his classic work *The History of the Synoptic Tradition* (Oxford, 1963) goes even further and asserts that *all* the controversy stories of the Gospels are imaginary and serve only as a literary frame for an action or saying around which the doctrinal polemic involving the early church develops. In reality, however, Bultmann himself was in two minds about the matter and declared that 'very probably' real words or deeds of Jesus inspired these accounts (op. cit., pp. 39–41).

I have counted seventeen polemical episodes in the Synoptic Gospels, which include sayings attributed to Jesus. Of these Mark and the triple tradition provide twelve, Q one, and the special sources of Matthew and Luke two each. The particular criticism aimed at the scribes and Pharisees figures in Mark, Q and Matthew's special tradition, but will be discussed on the basis of the conflated evidence garnered from all three sources. Sabbath observance was the most common and fertile topic for argument, and in particular the legality or otherwise of healing on the sacred day of rest (cf. nos. 3–6 below). Next to the Sabbath stood the issues of cleanness and uncleanness in the Law of Moses (nos. 8, 15), but we also encounter disputes about fasting, the grounds for divorce and the payment of tax to Rome (nos. 2, 9, 11). On the strictly theological level we have to consider the problem of forgiveness of sins (no. 1), the role and authority of Jesus (nos. 7, 10), and the part played by Scripture in religious faith and practice (nos. 12, 13). For the sake of clarity, the texts will be arranged according to the order in which they appear in Mark, with Q and the special material from Matthew and Luke inserted where appropriate. As a result, the seventeen polemical units will be examined under fifteen headings. The words ascribed to Jesus are always printed in italics (except in chapter 5).

1. Healing or forgiveness of sins (Mark 2:1–12; Matt. 9:1–8; Luke 5:17–26)

And when he returned to Capernaum . . . many were gathered together, so that there was no longer room for them, not even about the door . . . And they came, bringing to him a paralytic carried by four men. And when they could not get near him because of the crowd, they removed the roof above him; and when they had made an opening, they let down the pallet on which the paralytic lay. And when Jesus saw their faith, he said to the paralytic, *My son, your sins are forgiven.* Now some of the scribes [and the Pharisees (Luke)] were sitting there, questioning in their hearts, 'Why does this man speak thus? It is blasphemy! Who can forgive sins but God alone?' And immediately Jesus, perceiving in his spirit that they thus questioned within themselves, said to them, *Why do you question thus in your hearts? Which is easier, to say to the paralytic, 'Your sins are forgiven', or to say, 'Rise, take up your pallet and walk'? But that you may know that the Son of Man has authority on earth to forgive sins* – he said to the paralytic – *I say to you, rise, take up your pallet and go home.* And he rose, and immediately took up his pallet and went out before them all; so that they were all amazed and glorified God [who had given such authority to men (Matt.)].

All three Synoptic Gospels contain the account of the healing of a paralysed man in Capernaum, but Matthew has it in a slightly abbreviated form. Jesus is depicted as completely surrounded by a crowd in the house, so that the sick man could not be brought to him through the door. Therefore the stretcher-bearers opened the roof, and lowered the pallet in front of Jesus. The roof of ordinary village houses consisted of wooden planks nailed to beams or rafters and usually covered with mud, marl or clay. Josephus (*Antiquities* 14:459–60) reports that a group of Jewish soldiers attacked their opponents by opening the roof of the house in which their enemies were crowded together, and dropped large stones on them. The reference to tiles in Luke 5:19 seems inappropriate in a first-century Galilean village setting.[1]

Jesus' words to the paralysed man, 'My son, your sins are forgiven,'[2] require careful consideration. Unsympathetic bystanders – scribes (Mark, Matt.) or scribes and Pharisees (Luke) – considered the phrase a blasphemy, thinking that Jesus was arrogating to himself the privilege of pardoning sins which in their view was reserved for God alone. However, the expression attributed to Jesus is in the passive form ('your sins *are forgiven*', not '*I forgive* your sins'), and consequently has no such implication.[3] The same passive turn of phrase appears elsewhere, in the declaration pronounced by Jesus after a prostitute had anointed his feet (Luke 7:47–48; see chapter 8, no. 29), and when he spoke of the forgiveness of 'all sins' and 'blasphemies' (Mark 3:28; Matt. 12:31; Luke 12:10; see chapter 7, no. 3). It also occurs in the letter of James, a Judaeo-Christian document (Jas. 5:15): 'if [the sick man] has committed sins, *he will be forgiven*.'

In Jewish religious language this passive form, which by definition avoids the mention of the name of the forgiver, or alternatively a verb in the vague third person plural form (*they* forgive), can be employed

1. Tiles are attested four centuries later at Beth Shearim, the burial town of world Jewry in the Talmudic age; cf. Fanny Vitto, 'Byzantine Mosaics at Bet She'arim: New Evidence for the History of the Site', *Atiqot* 28 (1996), 119–20.
2. This is Mark's wording. Matthew prefaces it with 'Take heart', and Luke substitutes 'Man' for 'My son'. The latter is the customary form of address to a pupil by his teacher (see chapter 1, no. 9, n. 3). The phrase 'take heart' or 'have faith' is given as a usual exhortation preceding a miraculous event (Mark 6:50; 10:49; Matt. 9:22, 14:27).
3. The polemical riposte, 'the son of Man has authority . . . to forgive sins', while couched in a modest form, is nevertheless sharply provocative.

in Hebrew and Aramaic as a roundabout reference to God. If so, the words of Jesus were not tantamount to forgiveness of sins by him; he merely declared that pardon had already been granted (by God). In this context the phrase 'that you may know that the son of Man has authority on earth to forgive sins' should also be understood in the sense of declaring on earth a heavenly pardon. The Aramaic Prayer of Nabonidus, among the Dead Sea Scrolls, is couched in less careful language. There Nabonidus, the last Babylonian king, attributes his recent recovery from a long illness to the intervention of a Jewish exorcist who forgave his sins (4Q242). Granting pardon figures in the active form when it is done by God himself. Since metaphorically sins are debts, they can be *remitted* by God. The Lord's Prayer, using a mixed metaphor, requests God to 'forgive us our debts/sins' (Matt. 6:12; Luke 11:4). Strikingly, the active mode of the verb is used in the Gospels when in an ecclesiastical context the power to "loose or bind" or 'forgive or retain' sins is promised to Peter (Matt. 16:19), the apostles, and the church (Matt. 18:18; John 20:23). Jesus speaking of himself was more discreet.

Jesus did not enter into a linguistic argument with these country scribes, whom Josephus sarcastically designates as 'village lawyers' (*komogrammateis*). Their expertise was limited in practice to writing commercial contracts and marriage or divorce documents. Instead, Jesus took the bull by the horns and reading the minds of his opponents who were not brave enough to voice openly their complaint, he challenged them: is it easier to say to the paralysed man that his sins are forgiven, or command him to walk? (Mark 2:9). The evangelists paint Jesus as a dominant prophetic figure who, without waiting for an answer, uses his healing charisma to demonstrate that sins have been pardoned (Mark 2:10–11), without actually saying, 'I forgive your sins'.

The idea of interchangeability between healing and forgiveness of sins derives from an old popular form of the Jewish religion (see *The Changing Faces of Jesus*, 230–36). This Judaism in which the holy man rather than the priest, the Bible scholar or the rabbi plays the leading role, presents us with three connected concepts. The first is sin; the second is Satan, who causes sin; and the third is sickness, the consequence of sin. Seen from the opposite direction, healing follows forgiveness by way of repentance and results in liberation from the devil through exorcism. It was the charismatic holy man/exorcist who played the part of God's agent and was believed to bring about repentance, forgiveness, deliverance and healing.

While a fuller discussion of the idiom 'Son of Man' will follow later,[4] the specific mention of power to forgive sins *on earth* should be dealt with here. Forgiveness on earth implies a corresponding forgiveness in heaven. This is explicitly stated in the context of pardon granted in this world by the church: 'Whatever you loose on earth shall be loosed in heaven' (Matt. 16:19 and 18:18). The underlying imagery concerns an exact parallel between religion practised on earth and worship in the heavenly sanctuary. This notion is exemplified in the repeated assertion of the Dead Sea Scrolls that the divine service offered by the community at Qumran is the mirror image of the heavenly ceremonies enacted by the angels in the presence of God sitting on his throne (cf. *The Complete Dead Sea Scrolls in English* (London, 1998), 77–84). The peculiar religious calendar of the sect, 'issued from the mouth of God', ensured that their worship, and theirs alone, was the this-worldly copy of the celestial cult. Since the priests in the Temple of Jerusalem followed a different, hence incorrect, time reckoning, they celebrated their feasts and offered their sacrifices at the wrong moment so that their singing, clashing with the angelic choirs, produced cacophony.

The healing miracle is said to have filled the eyewitnesses with awe and amazement and they *all* glorified God. As no exception is mentioned, the evangelists appear to have included the scribes and Pharisees among the worshippers, implying that for a moment they had changed their mind about Jesus.

4. See chapter 7. Note, however, that Matthew (9:8), speaking of authority given to *men*, seems to understand the expression in a generic sense and not as applying to Jesus alone.

2. Debate about fasting (Mark 2:18–20; Matt. 9:14–15; Luke 5:33–35)

Now John's disciples and the Pharisees were fasting; and people came and said to him, 'Why do John's disciples and the disciples of the Pharisees fast [often and offer prayers (Luke)], but your disciples do not fast?' And Jesus said to them, *Can the wedding guests fast* [*mourn* (Matt.)] *while the bridegroom is with them? As long as they have the bridegroom with them, they cannot fast. The days will come, when the bridegroom is taken away from them, and then they will fast in that day.*

Ancient Jewish asceticism provides the context for this controversy story about fasting. The disciples of the hermit John the Baptist, whose regular diet was locusts and wild honey (Mark 1:6; Matt. 3:4), distinguished themselves by their frugality from the more easygoing Jesus and his circle.[5] Post-biblical sources mention, in addition to compulsory fasting (for instance on the Day of Atonement and during periods of drought with a view to soliciting rain), voluntary abstinence practised by the particularly pious. Luke's fictional Pharisee boasts of twice-weekly fasting (Luke 18:12) and we learn from the later rabbis that Mondays and Thursday were the usual private fast days. The Testaments of the Twelve Patriarchs allude to seven years of fasting by the Old Testament patriarch Reuben and two years by his brother Simeon, undertaken to atone for their sins (T. Reuben 1:10; T. Simeon 3:4). The heroine of the apocryphal Book of Judith similarly mortified herself every day after the death of her husband with the exception of Fridays and Saturdays (Judith 8:6). Ascetic rigour was in general foreign to Jesus' piety; in fact his slanderers called him 'a glutton and a drunkard' (Matt. 11:19; Luke 7:34; see chapter 8, no. 41), an exaggeration no doubt used to designate a non-puritanical kind of person.

5. The reference to the disciples of the Pharisees is almost certainly secondary since, unlike the disciples of the Baptist who were obviously part of the society in which Jesus moved in Galilee, the Pharisees belonged to the age and urban setting of the primitive church several decades after the time of Jesus. Neither were they renowned for their abstemiousness.

Jesus' riposte is metaphorical: 'Can the wedding guests fast while the bridegroom is with them?[6] . . . when the bridegroom is taken . . . then they will fast in that day.' The first of these two sentences is easy to interpret. A wedding feast with the bridegroom presiding over it is an occasion for eating, drinking and merry-making. Fasting would be totally out of place. The symbolism is generally, and correctly, understood as alluding to the messianic age and to Jesus as the person who ushers in this age. Similar imagery, timeless in character and patent in its significance, is explicitly identified in a later rabbinic Midrash with the Messiah's wedding feast (ExR 15:30). Hence the unsuitability of fasting while Jesus was engaged in proclaiming the instant arrival of the Kingdom of God and the lasting joy it would bring with it.

However, the second statement concerning fasting following the removal of the bridegroom clashes with the first both directly and metaphorically. The departure of the bridegroom at the end of the wedding dinner does not normally plunge the guests and relations into fasting, penance and gloom. Neither are fasting and mourning expected to succeed the messianic banquet; on the contrary those who have partaken of it are to experience everlasting bliss and rejoicing. For this reason one is prompted to conclude that the 'taking away' of the bridegroom-Messiah is not part of the original saying, but a later Christian gloss: the mystical marriage between Christ and the church (Eph. 5:22–33; Rev. 19:7–9) was to be preceded by the cross.

3. Debate about plucking grain on the Sabbath (Mark 2:23–28; Matt. 12:1–4, 8; Luke 6:1–5)

One sabbath he was going through the grainfields; and as they made their way his disciples began to pluck heads of grain. And the Pharisees said to him, 'Look, why are they doing what is not lawful on the sabbath?' And he said to them, *Have you never read what David did, when he was in need and was hungry, he*

6. The editor of Mark, suspecting that his readers might overlook the fact that the question is rhetorical, inserts here an explanatory gloss which is absent from Matthew and Luke 'As long as they have the bridegroom with them, they cannot fast.'

and those who were with him: how he entered the house of God, when Abiathar was high priest, and ate the bread of the Presence, which it is not lawful for any but the priests to eat, and also gave it to those who were with him? And he said to them, *The sabbath was made for man, not man for the sabbath; so the son of Man is lord even of the sabbath.*

The account of Jesus' hungry disciples plucking and eating ears of grain on the Sabbath supplies the material for this controversy story. Liberal-minded Jews of all ages would find the issue trivial. The action of the disciples certainly did not amount to theft (see Deut. 23:25). However, rabbinic and no doubt pre-rabbinic lawyers considered gleaning as a sub-category of harvesting, and the latter, together with thirty-eight further acts, was specifically forbidden on the Sabbath in the Mishnah (mShab 7:2). The excuse Jesus makes for his pupils rests on two grounds: the first is a biblical example or precedent, the second a general legal principle. The first alludes to the episode of David and his starving soldiers who ate the bread of the Presence in the temple at Nob which was reserved for priests only (1 Sam. 21:1–7). The unformulated reasoning is that if hunger overrules the Temple laws, it does likewise in the case of the Sabbath regulations. This is a sophisticated argument which is directly supported in Matthew 12:5 by Jesus' comment that the various acts involved in sacrificial worship in the Temple (butchery, cooking, etc.) also breach the rules relating to the sabbatical rest, yet priests perform them and remain guiltless. In the early second century AD, Rabbi Akiba reiterated the same rule, although by that time with the Temple in ruin it was devoid of practical significance. For a closer examination of this scriptural proof, see chapter 5, no. 1.

Apparently ignoring the previous reference to the biblical example, the evangelists continue with an absolute excuse in the form of a general rule enunciated by Jesus, namely that the Sabbath was made for man and not vice versa (Mark 2:27). The statement may sound perplexing, yet here again early second-century sayings echo the words attributed to Jesus. The Jew is not a slave of the Sabbath, announce the rabbis. On the contrary, 'The Sabbath is delivered up to you, and not you to the Sabbath' (Mekhilta de R. Ishmael on Exod. 31:14). In particular, the saving of life has always absolute priority and a man is permitted to profane one Sabbath in order to be able to observe many more (ibid. on Exod. 31:16).

Mark further specifies the general principle of the Sabbath's subordination to man with the assertion of the superiority of the Son of Man over the Sabbath (Mark 2:28; Matt. 12:8; Luke 6:5). See chapter 7, no. 2.

4. Debate about healing a man with a withered hand on the Sabbath (Mark 3:1–2, 4; Matt. 12:9–10, 12; Luke 6:6–7, 9)

Again he entered the synagogue, and a man was there who had a withered hand. And they [the scribes and the Pharisees (Luke)] watched him, to see whether he would heal him on the sabbath, so that they might accuse him . . . And he said to them, *Is it lawful on the sabbath to do good or to do harm, to save life or to kill?* But they were silent.

The narrative framework of this story has already been examined in chapter 1, no. 6.

Without specifying the locality, the evangelists present the cure of a man with a crippled hand in the typical setting of a synagogue gathering on the Sabbath. The curiosity of the opponents as to whether Jesus would heal on that day indicates that it was his habit to do so. In Mark's account, which appears the most natural, the initiative to bring the matter into the open is assigned to Jesus. He guesses what is in the minds of his critics.[7] Hence his challenging question, which is left unanswered by those present: 'Is it lawful on the sabbath to do good or to do harm, to save life or to kill?' (Mark 3:4; Matt. 12:12; Luke 6:9). A colourful Semitic idiom underlies the Greek phrase. The opposites, 'to do good – to do harm', and 'to save life – to kill', state the extreme limits of the suggested range of actions. However, since the negative alternative, 'to do harm' and 'to kill', is always unlawful and

7. Matthew, on the other hand, makes the hostile bystanders ask the question, 'Is it lawful to heal on the sabbath?' (Matt. 12:10).

not only on the Sabbath, the question is meant to focus exclusively on the positive aspects of doing good and saving life. In Luke's special tradition concerning the healing of a man suffering from dropsy, Jesus' question is presented in a simplified form: 'Is it lawful to heal on the sabbath, or not?' (Luke 14:3). The relevant polemical supplement attested by *Q* will be examined in connection with Luke 13:10–16 and 14:1–5 in nos. 5 and 6 below.

The basic principle, namely that the saving of life overrides the Sabbath, is crystal clear in rabbinic teaching (Mekh. Exod. 31:12; bYoma 85b); it is obviously integral to Jesus' outlook too. The rigorists among lawyers no doubt distinguished between life-threatening and less grave illnesses, but the more liberal wing of the rabbis classified any healing as ultimately belonging to life-saving. For instance they declared it permissible to treat someone with laryngitis even if it entailed 'work': 'If a man has a pain in his throat they may drop medicine into his mouth on the Sabbath, since there is doubt whether life is in danger, and whenever there is doubt whether life is in danger this overrides the Sabbath' (mYoma 8:6). A parallel teaching preserved in the *Q* tradition uses the common-sense *ad hominem* argument that, Sabbath or no Sabbath, a farmer would pull out of a well or a pit not only his son, but also his sheep (Matt. 12:11–12; Luke 14:5; see chapter 9, no. 1). The fact that Jesus and the later rabbis, especially the more generously-minded school of Hillel the Elder, represented the same doctrinal trend places a large question mark after the evangelists' statement (Mark 3:6; Matt. 12:14; Luke 6:11) that the Pharisees who had witnessed this healing were of the opinion that Jesus had committed a capital crime.

5. Healing a sick woman whose illness was attributed to a demon (Luke 13:10–16)

Now he was teaching in one of the synagogues on the sabbath. And there was a woman who had had a spirit of infirmity for eighteen years; she was bent over and could not fully straighten herself. And when Jesus saw her, he called her and said to her, *Woman, you are freed from your infirmity*. And he laid his hands upon her, and immediately she was made straight, and she praised God. But the ruler of the synagogue, indignant because Jesus had healed on the sabbath, said to the people, 'There are six days on which work ought to be done; come on those days and be healed, and not on the sabbath day.' Then the Lord answered him, *You hypocrites! Does not each of you on the sabbath untie his ox or his ass from the manger, and lead it away to water it? And ought not this woman, a daughter of Abraham whom Satan bound for eighteen years, be loosed from this bond on the sabbath day?*

Luke reports a typical Sabbath healing story, which is situated in an unnamed Galilean synagogue. The small-minded president of the congregation, forgetful of the woman's long illness, disapproved of Jesus' action despite the absence of any healing 'work' on his part. Indeed, all Jesus did was to lay his hands on the woman and declare her cured; neither of these acts amounted to a breach of the sabbatical rest. Afraid of reproving publicly the charismatic teacher, the president preferred to rebuke the congregation for soliciting healing on the one day when in his opinion it was prohibited. This provoked an angry rejoinder from Jesus. If it is permitted to untie a domestic animal in order to take it to a watering-place on the Sabbath, how much more should one be allowed figuratively to loosen the bond of a Jewish woman and free her from sickness?

Jesus addressed his reproach to 'hypocrites' in the plural; and not directly to the communal leader, hence the words reproduced may have had originally a more general destination similar to the criticism of scribes and Pharisees in Matthew 23 (see no. 15 below). The healing of the woman is represented as a liberation from the bond of Satan, the untying of his knots, an imagery that also underlies the power to bind and to loose sins referred to elsewhere (cf. no. 1 above and chapter 9, nos. 23–4). In Galilean rural society Jesus' stance against a rigid interpretation of the Sabbath law made common sense.[8] The Q supplements to the previous story concerning the rescue of son and

8. The Palestinian (i.e. Galilean) Talmud contains no regulations regarding agriculture, doubtless because rabbinic interference was deeply resented by the farming majority of Galilee.

sheep on the Sabbath (Mark 3:1–6 and parallels) add further support to this reasoning.

6. Healing a man with dropsy (Luke 14:1–5; Matt. 12:11–12)

One sabbath when he went to dine at the house of a ruler who belonged to the Pharisees, they were watching him. And behold, there was a man before him who had dropsy. And Jesus spoke to the lawyers and Pharisees, saying, *Is it lawful to heal on the sabbath or not?* But they were silent. Then he took him and healed him, and let him go. And he said to them, *Which of you, having a son* [*an ass* (variant reading)] *or an ox that has fallen into a well, will not immediately pull him out on a sabbath day?* (Luke).

What man of you, if he has one sheep and it falls into a pit on the sabbath, will not lay hold of it and lift it out? Of how much more value is a man than a sheep! (Matt.).

The story recounted in Luke resembles the Sabbath healing of a man with a withered hand (Mark 3:1–4; Matt. 12:9–12; Luke 6:6–9; see no. 4 above). As in Mark, Jesus asks a suspicious group of lawyers and Pharisees whether healing is permitted on the Sabbath. The question is less colourful here than in the accounts of Mark and Luke where Jesus speaks of doing good or harm and of saving or destroying life (Mark 3:4; Luke 6:9). In turn, Matthew makes Jesus positively and prosaically assert that one may do good on the Sabbath (Matt. 12:11). Here in Luke the audience remains silent (Luke 14:4; cf. also Mark 3:4). Jesus demonstrates the legitimacy of his action with a cogent *a fortiori* argument: they would all save without hesitation a child or a cow that had fallen into a well on the Sabbath (Luke 14:5). If – as seems likely – the reading 'a son' rather than 'an ass' is authentic, the issue of healing would definitely fall into the category of life-saving and as such would be patently legitimate on the Sabbath. But even if Jesus chose the animal simile and spoke of an ass, despite the disagreement among authorities concerning what one is allowed and what one is forbidden to do for sheep and cattle on the day of rest, it can hardly be doubted where the preference of small Galilean farmers lay. They certainly could not afford to obey the austere rule of the priestly legislators of the Qumran Damascus Document who decreed that no beast fallen into a cistern or a pit was to be rescued on the Sabbath (CD 11:13–14).

7. Dispute about demonic possession (Mark 3:22–26; Matt. 12:24–26; Luke 11:15–18)

And the scribes who came down from Jerusalem said, 'He [Jesus] is possessed by Beelzebul, and by the prince of demons he casts out the demons.' And he called them to him, and said to them in parables, *How can Satan cast out Satan? If a kingdom is divided against itself, that kingdom cannot stand. And if a house is divided against itself, that house will not be able to stand. And if Satan has risen up against himself and is divided, he cannot stand, but is coming to an end.*

The three Synoptic evangelists reproduce roughly in the same terms Jesus' riposte to the charge that his power over demons derived from his association with the prince of darkness, that is, he was in cahoots with Beelzebul. Mark links the argument to the charge levelled against Jesus in Nazareth by his family that he was insane (i.e. possessed by Satan) and that consequently he needed to be detained (Mark 3:21). The visiting Jerusalem scribes concurred with the family's assessment and considered his power to control evil spirits as itself the sign of a partnership with Satan.

The structure attested in Q (Matt. 12:22–24; Luke 11:14–16) is more plausible. Jesus had just exorcized a dumb (and blind (Matt.)) man and the astounded crowd wondered whether they were watching the Messiah at work. However, those who refused to think along those lines accused Jesus of complicity with the devil. Jesus gave a commonsensical reply: to imagine that the devil fights the devil (Mark 3:23) simply does not make sense. Internal division always leads to the collapse of any regime; yet as the many cases believed to be possessions proved, the empire of the prince of darkness was still flourishing. Therefore Jesus, its chief adversary, could hardly be a citizen of that empire. His authority came from God, not from Beelzebul (Matt. 12:27–28; Luke 8:18–20; see chapter 8, no. 43). The story illustrates the charismatic action of a holy man on the eve of the establishment of the Kingdom of God, which was believed to coincide with the collapse of the reign of Beelzebul.

8. Dispute about defilement (Mark 7:1–15; Matt. 15:1–11)

Now when the Pharisees gathered together to him, with some of the scribes, who had come from Jerusalem, they saw that some of his disciples ate with hands defiled, that is, unwashed. (For the Pharisees, and all the Jews, do not eat unless they wash their hands, observing the tradition of the elders; and when they come from the market place, they do not eat unless they purify themselves; and there are many other traditions which they observe, the washing of cups and pots and vessels of bronze.) And the Pharisees and the scribes asked him, 'Why do your disciples not live according to the tradition of the elders, but eat with hands defiled?' And he said to them, *Well did Isaiah prophesy of you hypocrites, as it is written, 'This people honours me with their lips, but their heart is far from me; in vain do they worship me, teaching as doctrines the precepts of men'* (Isa. 29:13). *You leave the commandment of God, and hold fast to the tradition of men.* And he said to them, *You have a fine way of rejecting the commandment of God, in order to keep your tradition! For Moses said, 'Honour your father and your mother'* (Exod. 20:12; Deut. 5:16)*; and, 'He who speaks evil of father or mother, let him surely die'* (Exod. 21:17; Lev. 20:9)*; but you say, 'If a man tells his father or his mother, What you would have gained from me is Corban'* (that is, given to God) – *then you no longer permit him to do anything for his father or mother, thus making void the word of God through your tradition which you hand on . . .* And he called the people to him again, and said to them, *Hear me, all of you, and understand: there is nothing* *outside a man which by going into him can defile him; but the things which come out of a man are what defile him.*

The debate about the causes of ritual defilement, told in different ways by Mark and Matthew, was provoked by visiting Torah experts from Jerusalem who, feeling superior to the locals, criticized the loose observance of religious customs among the Galilean followers of Jesus. The concrete opportunity for criticism was the failure of the disciples to wash their hands before a meal. Emphasis on the obligatory character of ancestral traditions, identified as the oral Law additional to the written Scripture, was the hallmark of the Pharisees and their rabbinic successors. Already Flavius Josephus made this clear when he wrote: 'The Pharisees have imposed on the people many laws from the tradition of the fathers not written in the Law of Moses' (*Antiquities* 13:297). Mark presented this essentially Jewish subject to a non-Jewish readership. This explains why he felt compelled to give a detailed list of Jewish purificatory regulations. Such a rehearsal of hand-washing, ritual baths, and washing of pots and pans (Mark 7:3–4) was hardly necessary for the original audience of Jesus.[9]

The answer of Jesus is developed in two stages. First he declares that his hypocritical opponents, fulfilling a prophecy of Isaiah, elevate their customs above the laws of God (Mark 7:6–8; Matt. 15:7–9). Next comes the illustration of this point by means of Bible interpretation. The Pharisees are accused of ranking ancestral customs higher than the laws of God; here in fact Jesus refers to one of the precepts of the Decalogue: 'Honour your father and your mother'. They are supposed to hold the view – intolerable to decent people – that if money earmarked for the support of parents was vowed as a gift to God, called Corban (offering), the vow had precedence even if it meant that father and mother had to suffer (Mark 7:9–13; Matt. 15:3–6; see also chapter 5, no. 5). Having thus demolished his opponents' argument, Jesus proclaims his own fundamental understanding of priorities in matters of purity. Internal values, such as filial piety, have priority over external details.

9. The reference to compulsory purification – 'baptism' or immersion in a ritual bath (*mikve*) – after a visit to the market reminds one of the daily ritual ablutions of the Essenes prior to meals (cf. Josephus, *War* 2:129, 132).

This anti-Pharisaic diatribe strikes the informed reader of the Gospel as out of true. The opponents are charged not with overvaluing man-made religious traditions, but with deliberately seeking to substitute them for the Mosaic Law given by God. Such a view is a gross distortion of what is known of the relationship between Scripture and tradition or written and oral Torah in the teaching of mainstream Judaism. The Gospel picture of the Pharisees' stance is not just exaggerated; it is unmistakably a caricature.

The biblical evidence supporting Jesus' criticism of the Pharisees consists in a free rendering of the Greek Septuagint translation of Isaiah 29:13: 'This people honours me with their lips', etc. But the second half of the quotation, 'in vain do they worship me, teaching as doctrines the precepts of men', substantially differs in meaning from the Hebrew Isaiah. In particular, the crucial phrase '*in vain do they worship me*' is based on a misreading or misinterpretation of the original by the Greek translator. In the Hebrew Isaiah the line translated by the Septuagint (LXX) 'in vain do they worship me, teaching as doctrines the precepts of men' is not a conclusion, but the continuation of the preceding series of causal sequences: because the people approach God only with their mouths and their lips without their heart being involved, *and because* their fear of God is inspired by precepts taught by men, *therefore* God will destroy their human wisdom. The opposition is between internal and external piety and not between divine and human commandments. However, since Jesus of Nazareth was a user of the Hebrew Bible and not of the Septuagint, he can in no way be made responsible for the fictitious scripture-based reasoning ascribed to him. In producing this proof, the evangelists had an eye on their Greek readership.

The accusation that the Pharisees would give precedence to a vow made in favour of the Temple over filial piety seems to be without foundation. This would have contravened the Ten Commandments, which they venerated as the summary of all the laws of God. Only rapacious priests might have advocated such an immoral practice, but they are not referred to in the story. In fact we have definite evidence both from Qumran and from rabbinic literature that in the case of a conflict between duties towards the sanctuary and towards parents, filial obligation was always made to prevail. The Dead Sea Damascus

Document explicitly states that 'No one shall consecrate the food of his house (i.e. family) to God' (CD 16:14–15). Likewise the Mishnah, using a more legalistic style, points out that both Pharisaic schools of the first century AD, those of Shammai and Hillel, ruled in favour of the family as against the Temple. 'If a man saw (from a distance) people eating his figs and said, "May they be Corban to you!"[10] and they were found to be his father and brothers and others with them, the School of Shammai say, "For them (father and brothers) the vow is not binding, but for the others with them it is binding." And the School of Hillel say, "For neither of them is the vow binding"' (mNedarim 3:2). Again the anti-Pharisee slant must come from a source later than Jesus.

In sum, the dilemma is resolved by Jesus' usual insistence on the superiority of morality over ritual duties. What renders man unclean is not what comes into him from outside; the real seeds of evil are internal (Mark 7:15; Matt. 15:11; see chapter 9, no. 4). In other words, defilement is caused not by the fact that something is intrinsically unclean, but by man's failure to obey God.

9. Debate about divorce (Mark 10:2–9; Matt. 19:3–8)

And Pharisees came up and in order to test him asked, 'Is it lawful for a man to divorce his wife [for any cause (Matt.)]?' He answered them, *What did Moses command you?* They said, 'Moses allowed a man to write a certificate of divorce, and to put her away.' But Jesus said to them, *For your hardness of heart he wrote you this commandment. But from the beginning of creation, 'God made them male and female.' 'For this reason a man shall leave his father and mother and be joined to his wife, and the two shall become one flesh.' So they are no longer two but one flesh. What therefore God has joined together, let no man put asunder.*

10. Josephus also cites Corban as a formula of vow and translates it into Greek as 'God's gift' (*Against Apion* 1:167).

Sayings of Jesus concerning marriage and divorce appear in the three Synoptics (cf. in addition to the present passage Matt. 5:32 and Luke 16:18), and indirectly in 1 Corinthians 7:10–11. This polemical statement was provoked by Judaean Pharisees.[11] Since divorce was an accepted fact in Jewish society, the Pharisees' testing question suggests that they knew that Jesus had disagreed with the common view on the subject. In Matthew's version the questioners have in mind the much-debated topic of grounds for divorce: Does a husband need specific reasons to put away his wife or can he do it *for any cause*? Since according to both evangelists a special answer is reserved for the disciples (remarriage after divorce is never permitted: Mark 10:10–12; see chapter 5, no. 6; or only in the case of the wife's adultery: Matt. 19:10–12; see chapter 9, no. 7), Mark's general question and Jesus' corresponding repartee must be dealt with first.

The Pharisees' inquiry about the lawfulness of divorce is answered by a counter-question regarding the teaching of the Law of Moses on the subject (Mark 10:3; cf. Matt. 19:7). They reply quoting Deuteronomy 24:1 by virtue of which the issuing of a *get*, or bill of divorce, licitly terminates a marriage. In the opinion of Jesus, however, divorce was not positively willed but only tolerated by God. It was granted by Moses in view of the fact that the fall of Adam and Eve corrupted the heart of man. When God originally planned human destiny in Paradise, he created a single man and a single woman. The two were destined to be so perfectly united as to become inseparable, or 'one flesh'. From this Jesus deduces that the primordial divine project did not include divorce and consequently it should not be imposed by men.

The matter seems rather confused, but an unformulated principle can reconcile the contradictions. Jesus' teaching was intended for the new messianic era in which the conditions of the golden age of the garden of Eden would be renewed. A similar argument based on

11. The geographical setting is confused in both Mark and Matthew. The evangelists envisage a journey from Galilee to Judaea, but Mark speaks of Jesus' entry into 'the region of Judaea and beyond the Jordan' whereas Matthew has 'the region of Judaea beyond the Jordan'. The most likely explanation is that Jesus arrived in Judaea through Transjordan, as attested by the majority of manuscripts, though not by the best ones. This would imply that Jesus travelled south from Galilee on the eastern side of the Jordan, thus avoiding the hostile Samaritan territory.

Genesis 1:27 ('male and female he created them') is used in one of the Dead Sea Scrolls to demonstrate the divine purpose of monogamous marriage, and possibly also of the prohibition of divorce (see CD 4:19–5:2). The immediacy of the Kingdom of God made for Jesus and his followers the restoration of the paradisiacal conditions of matrimonial morality (indissoluble marriage of one man and one woman) an absolute imperative. The novelty of this outlook is shown by the debate which continued in the brotherhood of the disciples of Jesus, who considered the indissolubility of marriage 'inexpedient' (Matt. 19:10) and thought divorce licit at least in some circumstances. The same outlook prevailed in the Pauline church (1 Cor. 7:10–15). The scriptural proof text on which the argument relies will be discussed in chapter 5, no. 32; see also chapter 9, no. 7.

10. Debate about the authority of Jesus (Mark 11:27–33; Matt. 21:23–27; Luke 20:1–8)

And they came again to Jerusalem. And as he was walking in the temple, the chief priests and the scribes and the elders came to him, and they said to him, 'By what authority are you doing these things, or who gave you this authority to do them?' Jesus said to them, *I will ask you a question; answer me, and I will tell you by what authority I do these things. Was the baptism of John from heaven or from men? Answer me.* And they argued with one another, 'If we say, "From heaven", he will say, "Why then did you not believe him?" But shall we say, "From men"?' – they were afraid of the people, for all held that John was a real prophet. So they answered Jesus, 'We do not know.' And Jesus said to them, *Neither will I tell you by what authority I do these things.*

The scene of this altercation was the Temple of Jerusalem where a semi-official deputation of the Jewish religious establishment, chief priests, scribes and elders, confronted Jesus. They wanted to know the source of the authority which qualified him to do 'these things'. 'These things', left unspecified, clearly did not refer to miraculous activity.

According to the evangelists no healing or exorcism was performed by Jesus in Jerusalem. The last charismatic cure recorded in the Gospels was the restoration of the sight of Bartimaeus in Jericho while Jesus was journeying to the holy city (Mark 10:46–52; Matt. 20:29–34; Luke 18:35–43; cf. chapter 1, no. 19). Consequently the only event which the delegation may have alluded to as 'these things' was Jesus' imperious behaviour in the Temple courtyard a day or so earlier when he caused a commotion in the merchants' and money-changers' quarter (Mark 11:15–19; Matt. 21:2–13; Luke 19:45–48; see chapter 5, no. 10). The fracas signalled danger in the politically unstable Jerusalem, and the guardians of law and order were duty bound to look into the matter. They would have been held responsible by the Roman authorities for any revolutionary breach of the peace. Also as custodians of the common good, they felt obliged to ensure that no foolish action of an irresponsible enthusiast should expose the Jewish people to Roman retaliation. Hence the precise formulation of the questions: Which institution authorized you and who in particular conferred on you this authority? If the episode has no foundation in reality, the evangelists must have been amazingly inventive story-tellers on this occasion.

Jesus, whose treatment of the merchants imitates the example of biblical prophets, was unimpressed by the high dignitaries and his reply took the form of a lofty counter-question: Will you answer me first? I will answer you afterwards (Mark 11:29; Matt. 21:24; Luke 20:3). With the moral superiority of a man of God, he then launched into an interrogation of the representatives of the Sanhedrin concerning their attitude to John the Baptist. Did they acknowledge his mission as divinely inspired? It is patent that they did not (cf. Matt. 21:32; Luke 7:29–30; see chapter 4, no. 24); officials representing the legal power of any religion rarely respect charismatic authority. According to the Gospel account preserved in *Q* (Matt. 3:7–10; Luke 3:7–9), the group of Pharisees and Sadducees, who out of curiosity or otherwise approached John, met with the rough side of the prophet's tongue. As one might expect, the answer of officialdom to Jesus was an evasive 'don't know', though the evangelists, unsympathetic to the envoys, present this noncommittal reply as a calculating escape from an insoluble quandary. If John's mission was ordained by God, they should have followed him, which they did not; if, on the other hand, they were to deny that John was an envoy of heaven, they ran the risk of being stoned by the crowd which venerated him as a prophet. So the officials were caught on the horns of a dilemma and kept silent. Hence the haughty refusal of Jesus to answer the authorities, a refusal which probably sealed his fate.

11. Debate about tax to be paid to the emperor (Mark 12:13–17; Matt. 22:15–22; Luke 20:20–26)

And they sent to him some of the Pharisees and some of the Herodians, to entrap him in his talk. And they came and said to him, 'Teacher, we know that you are true, and care for no man; for you do not regard the position of men, but truly teach the way of God. Is it lawful to pay taxes to Caesar, or not? Should we pay them, or should we not?' But knowing their hypocrisy, he said to them, *Why put me to the test? Bring me a denarius* (a coin), *and let me look at it*. And they brought one. And he said to them, *Whose likeness and inscription is this?* They said to him, 'Caesar's'. Jesus said to them, *Render to Caesar the things that are Caesar's, and to God the things that are God's*. And they were amazed at him.

The Synoptic Gospels intimate that the question about the legitimacy of paying tax to Rome, following the questions put to Jesus by the chief priests concerning his authority (cf. no. 10 above), represents a concerted effort by the clerical and lay powers (Pharisees and Herodians) in Jerusalem to discover grounds for his elimination. The issue of the imperial tax was a splendid opportunity for entrapment. Since the census of Quirinius in AD 6 the inhabitants of Judaea and Samaria had to pay tribute to Rome, and the members of the Council or Sanhedrin of Jerusalem were responsible for collecting the tribute and delivering it to Caesar (cf. Josephus, *War* 2:17). So if the fracas in the Temple made Jesus suspect as a potential revolutionary, the loaded question about the census money was a well-chosen means to compel him to reveal his true colours.

Jesus saw through their stratagem. He asked for a denarius and, pretending to be naive like a British judge, inquired about the identity of the person represented on it. Roman coins displayed the effigy and the name of the ruling emperor – Tiberius (AD 14–37) during the public life of Jesus. The account shows that Jesus was not a member of the revolutionary party which came into being in AD 6 precisely to protest against Jewish submission to Roman tax registration. If he had been, he would have protested against the sending of the denarius to the imperial treasury. Taking an apolitical stand, Jesus did not object: 'Render to Caesar the things that are Caesar's' (Mark 12:17; Matt. 22:21; Luke 20:25). The final clause – 'and to God the things that are God's' – indicates decisively that for the evangelists the orientation of Jesus was wholly religious.[12] The story has an air of authenticity and speaks against the theory of those New Testament scholars who picture Jesus as an anti-Roman rebel.

12. Debate concerning the resurrection of the dead (Mark 12:18–27; Matt. 22:23–32; Luke 20:27–38)

And Sadducees came to him, who say that there is no resurrection; and they asked him a question, saying, 'Teacher, Moses wrote for us that if a man's brother dies and leaves a wife, but leaves no child, the man must take the wife, and raise up children for his brother. There were seven brothers; the first took a wife, and when he died left no children; and the second took her, and died, leaving no children; and the third likewise; and the seven left no children. Last of all the woman also died. In the resurrection whose wife will she be? For the seven had her as wife' (Mark, Matt., Luke).

Jesus said to them, *Is not this why you are wrong, that you know neither the scriptures nor the power of God?* (Mark, Matt.).

The sons of this age marry and are given in marriage; but those who are accounted worthy to attain to that age and to the

12. In the Gospel of Thomas (no. 100) the saying is reproduced with the additional ending, 'and give me what is mine', which is totally alien to the logic of the polemic and is patently spurious.

resurrection from the dead neither marry nor are given in marriage (Luke).

... for they cannot die any more, because they are equal to angels, and are sons of God, being sons of the resurrection (Luke).

For when they rise from the dead, they neither marry nor are given in marriage, but are like angels in heaven (Mark, Matt.).

And as for the dead being raised, have you not read in the book of Moses, in the passage about the bush, how God said to him, 'I am the God of Abraham, and the God of Isaac, and the God of Jacob'? He is not God of the dead, but of the living; you are quite wrong.

The exchange with the Sadducees is not connected with the previous controversy stories, and is introduced into the Gospels at this juncture simply because the context is that of polemical questioning and also perhaps because an encounter of Jesus with the aristocratic Sadducees had to be located in Jerusalem. Unlike the two episodes about the authority of Jesus and the tax money (nos. 10 and 11), this teasing and sarcastic exchange looks completely artificial.[13] With tongue in cheek, the Sadducees are portrayed as poking fun at Jesus who for these upper-class Jerusalemites was a Galilean peasant. The background canvas is correct. The Sadducees, representing the top echelons of the Temple priesthood and their wealthy supporters, were traditionalists who spurned the idea of resurrection which they regarded as a Pharisee innovation. This is attested by the New Testament (here, and in Acts 23:8 and indirectly Acts 4:1–2) as well as by Josephus, according to whom the Sadducees denied any form of afterlife (*War* 2:165; *Antiquities* 18:16).[14] In this probably fictitious dispute they assumed, as no doubt many ordinary Jews did, that life after the resurrection

13. It would make better sense in the context of a later debate between Jewish-Christians and Sadducees.

14. The Essenes' doctrine, so Josephus tells us, constituted the in-between stage. They believed in spiritual survival, but rejected the reunification after death of matter and spirit, the essential requisite of the doctrine of bodily resurrection (cf. *War* 2:154–8).

would resemble present-day existence. On the basis of this assumption they cite the story of a woman who, in conformity with the law governing leviratic marriage (Deut. 25:5–6),[15] married successively seven brothers. Whose wife will this seven times widowed woman be after the resurrection? One can almost hear the Sadducee questioners' chuckle.

In reply to the challenge, the standard Pharisee teaching is put in the mouth of Jesus: in spite of body and soul being reunited, the risen men and women will be spiritual beings; they will no longer live as husbands and wives together. Already the Book of Enoch (1 Enoch 51:4), dating to the third/second century BC, uses the same language when it declares that all the resurrected righteous 'will become angels in heaven'. We hear a continuous echo of this conception. St Paul for example stresses, for the benefit of his theologically uneducated Corinthians, the difference between the physical body and the spiritual body which will follow the resurrection (1 Cor. 15:35–54). Two hundred years later Rab asserted in the Babylonian Talmud (bBer 17a): 'In the world to come there is no eating and drinking, no begetting children, no bargaining, no jealousy and hatred, and no strife; but the righteous shall sit with their crowns on their heads and enjoy the resplendence of the Shekhinah (divine Presence).'

Wishing to add more strength to the argument by supporting it from the Torah, the most sacred and authoritative part of the Bible, the editor of Mark, followed by Matthew and Luke, quotes words addressed by God to Moses (Exodus 3:6): 'I am the God of Abraham, and the God of Isaac, and the God of Jacob.' The proof is set out according to the Pharisee technique of Bible interpretation and will be analysed in chapter 5, no. 12. The tacit reasoning is that since God describes himself in the present tense as the God of the three patriarchs, Abraham, Isaac and Jacob are potentially alive, and will actually be revived at the time of the resurrection. However, this sort of scriptural proof would have been rejected out of hand by the Sadducees, who stood for the literal and not for the midrashic interpretation of the Bible.

15. According to this biblical law, if a husband dies without male issue, his brother is to marry the widow and the first-born son is legally considered as the child (and heir) of the deceased brother.

13. Debate about the son of David (Mark 12:35–37; Matt. 22:41–45; Luke 20:41–44)

And as Jesus taught in the temple, he said, *How can the scribes say that the Christ is the son of David?*

What do you think of the Christ? Whose son is he? They said to him, 'The son of David.' (Matt.).

David himself, inspired by the Holy Spirit, declared, 'The Lord said to my Lord, Sit at my right hand, till I put thy enemies under thy feet.' David himself calls him Lord, so how is he his son?

This is a polemical discussion directly centred on the interpretation of Psalm 110, a frequently cited messianic text in the New Testament and in rabbinic literature. In Mark (and Luke) there is no opponent in view; Jesus himself takes up a debating stand against the scribes concerning the relation between the Messiah and the Son of David, while Matthew makes Jesus put a provocative question to the Pharisees about the identity of the Christ. Jesus' answer consists in simply quoting Psalm 110:1.[16] That the Messiah was expected to be a descendant of king David was commonly held in ancient Judaism. Of course it is also taken for granted that the Psalms were written by David, inspired by the Holy Spirit, and the first-named Lord is God (the Hebrew text uses the Tetragram or YHWH), speaking to the second Lord mentioned by David, that is, the Messiah. We are faced here with a kind of quibbling biblical exegesis. If Jesus actually indulged in this sort of hair-splitting, its only possible aim would have been to embarrass the other party. It is more likely, however, that such an exegetical argument did not originate with him, but is evidence of subsequent Judaeo-Christian polemic with later Pharisees concerning the link between Christ and Lord, the two most commonly used titles

16. Luke, taking care of his non-Jewish readers, explicitly mentions that the citation derives from 'the Book of Psalms'. The other two evangelists assume that their readers would know.

of Jesus in the primitive church (cf. Acts 2:36). For further comments, see chapter 5, no. 14.

14. Warning against the leaven of the Pharisees (Mark 8:14–15; Matt. 16:5–6; Luke 12:1)

Now they had forgotten to bring bread; and they had only one loaf with them in the boat. And he cautioned them, saying, *Take heed, beware of the leaven of the Pharisees* [*which is hypocrisy* (Luke)] *and the leaven of Herod* [*the leaven of the Sadducees* (Matt.)].

The metaphor of the leaven has a twofold significance. It may be seen as an agent of life and strength, raising the dough and turning it to bread (Matt. 13:33; Luke 13:21; see chapter 4, no. 11). But it can also be understood as an agent of corruption, for instance when leavened bread is contrasted with the purity of unleavened bread. Here the symbol indicates false teaching issued primarily – or exclusively (Luke) – by the Pharisees, but also by the Sadducees and Herod or the Herodians. The original saying is more likely to be aimed at the Pharisee teaching alone, as in Luke. Since serious Pharisee presence in Galilee postdates the destruction of Jerusalem and the Jewish state in AD 70, the saying probably reflects the attitude of the apostolic church towards them. The other two parties are afterthoughts suggested to the evangelists by the debate about the tax money (Herodians) and the resurrection (Sadducees).

15. Polemics against Pharisees and lawyers (Mark 12:38–40; Matt. 23:1–33; Luke 20:45–47; 11:39–42, 44, 46–48)

The texts will be quoted below grouped under A, B, and C.

The following chain of rebukes and woes directed towards the representatives of the lay teaching authority in Judaism differs from the controversy stories treated so far and necessitates a different form of presentation. In his own way each of the Synoptic evangelists presents at this point an attack on Pharisees, scribes or lawyers. Mark and Matthew supply no real narrative framework, as for instance in the case of the reproach directed to 'hypocrites' in the story of the woman with 'a spirit of infirmity' in no. 5 above. Luke, on the other hand, places the bulk of his polemic in the context of a dinner attended by Jesus in the house of a Pharisee, where the host criticizes him for failing to purify himself before the meal (Luke 11:37–52).

Mark's concise quotation (Mark 12:38–40) is copied by Luke (20:46–47). The half-dozen sayings belonging to Q are reproduced by Matthew and Luke, each in his own way (Matt. 23:4 – Luke 11:46; Matt. 23:13 – Luke 11:52; Matt. 23:23–24 – Luke 11:42; Matt. 23:25–26 – Luke 11:39–41; Matt. 23:27–28 – Luke 11:44; Matt. 23:29–31 – Luke 11:47–48). Finally, Matthew further develops Q (23:5–11; 23:15–21), and prefaces the whole unit with a conciliatory introduction (Matt. 23:2–3) which to some extent removes the venom from the heated diatribe.

The composition as a whole consists of widely differing elements. To start with Mark's contribution (repeated by Luke), it is a warning against the pride and exhibitionism of the scribes, addressed to the listening crowd, but in Luke exclusively to the disciples of Jesus.

A. Polemics against scribes (Mark 12:38–40; Luke 20:46–47; Matt. 23:5–7)[17]

Beware of the scribes, who like to go about in long robes, and to have salutations in the market places and the best seats in the synagogues and the places of honour at feasts, who devour widows' houses and for a pretence make long prayers. They will receive the greater condemnation (Mark, Luke).

They do all their deeds to be seen by men; for they make their phylacteries broad and their fringes long,[18] *and they love the*

17. See also Matt. 23:14 in some manuscripts.

18. The fringes have already been discussed in chapter 1, no. 9. The phylacteries or tefillin consist of a selection of biblical texts written on leather strips and contained in a leather case. Several of the latter have been found in Qumran Cave 4; their length varies from 1.3 to 3.2 cm.

place of honour at feasts and the best seats in the synagogues, and salutations in the market places, and being called rabbi by men (Matt.).

The term 'scribe' (*sofer* in Hebrew, *safra* in Aramaic) is used, designating a 'book-man', an expert in the Bible, in particular in biblical and traditional law. On such men depended well-organized life, religious and secular. They were generally respected and no doubt often felt self-important; they dressed accordingly, wearing a long robe (*stole* or *talit*) and were used to being greeted with respect by all and sundry. In recognition of their dignity they were given choice seats in places of worship and at banquets, and the evangelists indicate that they expected such preferential treatment.

These allusions to professional pride carry with them a sting in the tail: the scribes are accused of mistreatment of widows and of making a public display of their religiousness. The charge that they exploited credulous and devout women is probably an exaggeration: it may simply mean that the scribes did not discourage donations to charity which in reality were beyond the means of the widow. As for publicly 'outpraying' the rest of the congregation because they thought it was expected of them, this may just have been a forgivable excess of zeal. In short, the scribes are portrayed as representatives of the ethos of the provincial *petite bourgeoisie*. Such a picture clashes with the modesty and sincerity of Jesus, the devout Hasid, whose eyes were fixed on the approaching Kingdom of God, and who advocated that acts of worship should be performed 'in secret' (cf. Matt. 6:5–8; cf. chapter 6, no. 7). Note that in Mark's warning against the behaviour of the scribes there is no hint at false teaching on their part; neither are they blamed for preventing ordinary Jews from serving God. It is for their misguided zeal, self-importance and exhibitionism that they are criticized.

B. The 'woes' in Q (Matt. 23:4 – Luke 11:46; Matt. 23:13 – Luke 11:52; Matt. 23:23–24 – Luke 11:42; Matt. 23:25–26 – Luke 11:39–41; Matt. 23:27–28 – Luke 11:44; Matt. 23:29–31 – Luke 11:47–48)

They [the scribes and the Pharisees] *bind heavy burdens, hard to bear, and lay them on men's shoulders; but they themselves will not move them with their finger* (Matt. 23:4).

Woe to you lawyers also! for you load men with burdens hard to bear, and you yourselves do not touch the burdens with one of your fingers (Luke 11:46).

But woe to you, scribes and Pharisees, hypocrites! because you shut the kingdom of heaven against men; for you neither enter yourselves, nor allow those who would enter to go in (Matt. 23:13).

Woe to you lawyers! for you have taken the key of knowledge; you did not enter yourselves and you hindered those who were entering (Luke 11:52).

Woe to you, [*scribes and* (Matt.)] *Pharisees, hypocrites! for you tithe the mint and* [*dill and cummin* (Matt.) – *and rue and every herb* (Luke)], *and have neglected the weightier matters of the law, justice and mercy and faith* [*and the love of God* (Luke)]; *these you ought to have done, without neglecting the others* (Matt. 23:23; Luke 11:42).

You blind guides, straining out a gnat and swallowing a camel! (Matt. 23:24).

Woe to you, scribes and Pharisees, hypocrites! for you cleanse the outside of the cup [*and of the plate* (Matt.) – *and of the dish* (Luke)], *but inside* [*they* (Matt.) – *you* (Luke)] *are full of extortion and* [*rapacity* (Matt.) – *wickedness* (Luke)]. *You blind Pharisee! first cleanse the inside of the cup and the plate, that the outside also may be clean* (Matt. 23:25–26). *You fools! Did not he who made the outside make the inside also? But give for alms those things which are within; and behold, everything is clean for you* (Luke 11:39–41).

Woe to you, scribes and Pharisees, hypocrites! for you are like whitewashed tombs, which outwardly appear beautiful, but within they are full of dead men's bones and all uncleanness. So you also outwardly appear righteous to men, but within you are full of hypocrisy and iniquity (Matt. 23:27–28).

. . . for you are like graves which are not seen, and men walk over them without knowing it (Luke 11:44).

Woe to you, scribes and Pharisees, hypocrites! for you build the tombs of the prophets and adorn the monuments of the righteous, saying, 'If we had lived in the days of our fathers, we would not have taken part with them in shedding the blood of the prophets.' Thus you witness against yourselves, that you are the sons of those who murdered the prophets (Matt. 23:29–31).

So you are witnesses and consent to the deeds of your fathers; for they killed them, and you build their tombs (Luke 11:48).

Most of the Q material adds up to a powerful prophetic censure of scribes, Pharisees or lawyers delivered in their presence. Compared with Mark, the Q criticism displays more violent hostility. It is no doubt the result of prolonged and embittered doctrinal conflict for which there is no evidence in the story recorded in the Synoptic Gospels. Couched in the form of woes,[19] it charges the professional teachers first with dishonesty in that they lay unbearable burdens on people while they themselves neglect the same duties (Luke 11:46; cf. Matt. 23:4). As a matter of fact, later rabbis regularly insisted on the opposite, namely that they themselves must carry the full weight of the commandments. Furthermore the scribes, Pharisees and lawyers failed in their duty of leading the community and in fact shut the gate of the Kingdom of God in their faces.[20] They placed obstacles in front of them in the form of everyday trivia. These obstacles were of their own creation and made people forget the greater issue at stake (Matt. 23:13; Luke 11:52).

19. Matthew 23:4, under the influence of Matthew 23:2, transforms into a warning to listeners and disciples the rebuke which in Luke 11:46 is addressed to the lawyers.
20. Luke speaks of the taking away of the key of knowledge, but the context suggests the key is that of the Kingdom of God. (See Matt. 16:19.)

A further reproach of Jesus to the Pharisees is provoked by their constant preoccupation with legal matters, such as tithing, in preference to the central issues of morality, justice, mercy and faith. According to Jesus, both should be observed (Matt. 23:23; cf. Luke 11:42). The petty legalistic mind, common in every age and religious setting, is pilloried here, but judging from the emphasis laid on the cardinal virtues of justice and love in rabbinic literature as well as in the Dead Sea Scrolls, the complaint in Q must be seen as a rhetorical exaggeration. The same failure to deal with matters in conformity with their real importance is stressed in the sarcastic hyperbole of filtering miniature insects out of liquids, yet overlooking the equally unclean camel (Matt. 23:24). A similar contrast between punctiliousness in observing external ritual customs and internal morality characterizes the woe on those who cleanse the outside of the cup and of the plate but ignore the (moral) filth inside (Matt. 23:25–26; cf. Luke 11:39–41). The protest recalls Mark 7:15, where Jesus claims that the source of uncleanness lies within man (see no. 8 above). Here, however, the treatment is more particular and technical. The argument is *ad hominem*; the Pharisees are accused of 'extortion and rapacity', charges which from the point of view of the available historical evidence are not applicable to them.

The meaning of the penultimate Matthean outburst concerning the image of a 'whitewashed' tomb is clear. It probably refers to a tomb made of stone and rendered with plaster. The scribes and Pharisees present themselves as outwardly immaculate and conceal their inward failings: hypocrisy and iniquity (Matt. 23:27–28). In Luke's version the opponents resemble unmarked graves which surreptitiously convey uncleanness without passers-by realizing it (Luke 11:44).

The tomb imagery introduces the last woe, addressed to the builders and decorators of the prophets' tombs (Matt. 23:29; cf. Luke 11:47). Jewish tradition identified and venerated the resting-places of many of the great men of the past.[21] But Matthew and Luke reproach the scribes and Pharisees for constructing these monuments and then pretending that they condemn their ancestors' behaviour towards the prophets (Matt. 23:30). This echoes the popular tradition, without scriptural

21. See Joachim Jeremias, *Heiliengräber im Jesu Umwelt* (Göttingen, 1958).

foundation, that many of the prophets suffered violent death as a result of their criticism of their contemporaries' behaviour. According to the apocryphal *Lives of the Prophets* (of the late first century AD), six of them, Isaiah, Jeremiah, Ezekiel, Micah, Amos and Zechariah the son of Jehoiada, were killed. The implication of the complaint is that by erecting monuments in their capacity as sons, the scribes and the Pharisees tacitly admitted their solidarity with their murderous fathers. Luke's briefer woe has the same meaning (Luke 11:47–48). Both woes castigate the same hypocritical attitude regularly attributed by Q to the scribes and Pharisees.

C. Matthew's supplements (Matt. 23:2–3, 8–12, 15, 16–22, 32–33)

The scribes and the Pharisees sit on Moses' seat; so practise and observe whatever they tell you, but not what they do; for they preach but do not practise (Matt. 23:2–3).

But you are not to be called rabbi, for you have one teacher, and you are all brethren. And call no man your father on earth, for you have one Father, who is in heaven. Neither be called masters, for you have one master, the Christ. He who is greatest among you shall be your servant; whoever exalts himself will be humbled, and whoever humbles himself will be exalted (Matt. 23:8–12).

Woe to you, scribes and Pharisees, hypocrites! for you traverse sea and land to make a single proselyte, and when he becomes a proselyte, you make him twice as much a child of Gehenna as yourselves (Matt. 23:15).

Woe to you, blind guides, who say, 'If any one swears by the temple, it is nothing; but if any one swears by the gold of the temple, he is bound by his oath.' You blind fools! For which is greater, the gold or the temple that has made the gold sacred? And you say, 'If any one swears by the altar, it is nothing; but if any one swears by the gift that is on the altar, he is bound by his oath.' You blind men! For which is greater, the gift or the altar that makes the gift sacred? So he who swears by the altar, swears by it and everything on it; and he who swears by the temple, swears by it and by him who dwells in it; and he who swears by heaven, swears by the throne of God and by him who sits upon it (Matt. 23:16–22).

Fill up, then, the measure of your fathers. You serpents, you brood of vipers, how are you to escape being sentenced to Gehenna? (Matt. 23:32–33).

Matthew's special material represents half-and-half critical remarks conveyed to the audience, including the disciples, and direct rebuke of the hypocritical Pharisees. The sayings as a whole are typically equivocal and exhibit the first evangelist's characteristic schizophrenia in his treatment of the Jewish religion of his age (cf. *The Changing Faces of Jesus*, 217). He emphasizes, perhaps even more strongly than Mark and Luke, the hypocrisy of those who are good at preaching but fall short in practice (Matt. 23:3). With an eye on the Christian community, Matthew elevates to the status of false doctrine the apparent Pharisee liking for flattery or for the honorific title *abba*, father (Matt. 23:7–10; cf. also chapter 9, no. 26).

He blames them for small-mindedness verging on silliness in their handling of details which do or do not render an oath or a vow binding. This is a fascinating subject for the wise and learned scribe, Matthew's ideal (see chapter 4, no. 21), but according to the rabbis it apparently lies outside the sphere of interest or knowledge of a Galilean. We are told that an oath on the Temple is invalid, but one on the gold of the Temple is binding (Matt. 23:16–19). For the benefit of the uneducated, Matthew (rather than Jesus) reveals the clue, namely that the general includes the particular (the Temple includes the gold of the Temple; the altar includes the gift placed on it), and perhaps also that 'altar', 'temple' and 'heaven' can be used as substitute names, in rabbinic jargon *kinuyyim*, for God (Matt. 23:20–22).

Perhaps the fiercest denunciation of the Pharisees is found in a supplement attached by Matthew to the last of his woes, regarding their phoney celebration of the prophets who were murdered by ancestors of the Pharisees. They are called 'serpents' and 'brood of vipers' who are doomed to Gehenna. The phrase 'brood of vipers' first appears on the sharp tongue of John the Baptist in his attack on Pharisees and Sadducees (Matt. 3:7; Luke 3:7). Since the expression is quite unusual, it would not be unreasonable to surmise that Matthew here echoes the Baptist. He also issues a sweeping condemnation of the Pharisees for ostentatiousness, for performing good deeds to be seen by men (Matt. 23:5; cf. chapter 6, no. 7).

Matthew's treatment of the Pharisees is not always wholly negative. His comment on their efforts to convert pagans to the Jewish religion is half criticism, half praise: they travel far afield to make a proselyte, but with their mistaken emphasis on certain duties they lead him to Gehenna (Matt. 23:15). To win Gentile converts to Judaism was the aim of the Pharisees of the House of Hillel who are depicted as keen to facilitate entry into the Jewish fold. For the anecdote according to which Hillel reduced the whole Torah to an all-inclusive single command to persuade a Gentile sympathizer, see chapter 5, no. 23. The missionary zeal of the Pharisees depicted here is highly commendable, even though Matthew is more than pessimistic about the future destiny of both converter and convert.[22]

However, Matthew's most eloquent appreciation of the Pharisees is largely positive. They are said to be the legitimate occupiers of the chair of Moses, that is to say, the presidential seat in the synagogue:[23] their teaching is valid even when their example does not correspond to it (Matt. 23:2–3). Leaving aside the general indictment for hypocrisy, the doctrine of the Pharisees meets here with wholesale approval. Directed towards Torah-observing Judaeo-Christians, the message is that all Pharisaic teaching is valid and must be strictly embraced. Such a positive statement constitutes a head-on clash with the accusation

22. I am unable to agree with Martin Goodman's interpretation, who sees in the Pharisees' effort an attempt to gain new Jewish adherents to their own religious party and not, as is generally understood, pagan neophytes for Judaism. Cf. *Mission and Conversion: Proselytizing in the religious history of the Roman Empire* (Oxford, 1994), 70–71.

23. Cf. Lee I. Levine, *The Ancient Synagogue* (New Haven, Conn., 1999), 323–7. A number of seats of Moses have been discovered by archaeologists. The earliest is from the island of Delos (first century BC); others are from Dura Europos, Hammat Tiberias and En Gedi, but the best known comes from the Roman–Byzantine synagogue of Chorazin that was constructed on the site of the building Jesus knew.

that they shut the Kingdom of heaven, annul legitimate vows, and especially that they neglect in their teaching the essential constituents of religion, justice, mercy, faith and love of God. In fact, by placing this declaration before all the incriminations, the editor of Matthew appears to have intended to offer a balanced picture: the reader had better remember this appraisal when confronted with the nasty jibes which follow.

A further consideration will help the general understanding of the anti-Pharisee polemic of the Synoptics. It concerns a noted passage of the Talmud which shows that rabbis also could be tough critics of their forerunners. The text lists seven types of Pharisee of whom six fail to meet with approval. The terminology is sarcastic. There is the *Sleeve Pharisee* who displays his good deeds on his sleeve (literally shoulder), followed by the *Hang-on Pharisee* who says, 'Hang on so that I can perform another good deed.' We encounter the *Book-keeping Pharisee* who, having committed a sin and done a good deed, sets one against the other in the debit and credit columns of his spiritual accounts. The *Parsimonious Pharisee* says, 'What can I set aside to perform a good deed?' The *Show me my sin and I will do something Pharisee* says, 'Show me what you claim to be my sin and I will quickly perform a good deed to cancel it.' Finally we see the *Pharisee of fear* who is like Job, and the *Pharisee of love* who resembles Abraham. Of them all, concludes the Talmud, only the Pharisee like Abraham found favour with God (ySotah 20c; bSotah 22b). The satirical tone of the passage reveals the redactor's awareness of the fact that the Pharisees of the past, while trying to appear immaculate, were not always paragons of virtue.

REFLECTIONS

As far as historicity is concerned the controversy stories in the Gospels range from the probably real to the almost certainly fictitious. Many of them are without anchor in time and space, but since the ultimate purpose of the narrators was to convey a teaching, the 'where and when' of the occasion is secondary. Nevertheless the primary doctrinal bias does not necessarily deprive them of a claim to reality unless we have additional evidence pointing to a date later than the time of Jesus. Thus the style of the argument with the Sadducees concerning resurrection, built on a Pharisee type of biblical proof, suggests that the polemic belongs to the age of the Jewish-Christian church's confrontation with the Sadducees. The same dating applies to the exegetical reasoning regarding the 'son of David' and most of the grievances against scribes and Pharisees. Again Jesus, the eschatological teacher, pronounced absolutely against divorce. However, as we shall see apropos the so-called 'antitheses' (chapter 5, no. 32 and chapter 9, no. 18), the issue of the dissolution of marriage continued to be debated among his followers as is manifest from the insertion of the clause 'except for unchastity' in Matthew (5:32; 19:9). This exception, together with the wording 'Is it lawful to divorce one's wife *for any cause*', reflects within the first-century church the debate between the strict school of Shammai, allowing divorce only for sexual misdemeanour, and the lenient school of Hillel, which tolerated it on any ground. In contrast, the arguments about the lawfulness of healing on the Sabbath, and purity rules like hand-washing, fit well in the parochial setting of rural Galilee.

The expectation of the imminent coming of the Kingdom of God furnishes the background for the debates concerning the role of Satan, the avoidance of fasting, and especially the all-pervading healing activity of Jesus. As his message to John the Baptist makes plain, the final age will be recognizable by the sudden recovery of the blind, the deaf, the lame and the lepers (Matt. 11:5; Luke 7:22).

The fifteen examples of dispute fall into two equal portions regarding their theoretical or practical nature: seven polemics turn on ideas, seven aim at practice, and the large anti-Pharisee unit can be split half-and-half. The ideas subject to debate concern the authority of Jesus, his alleged relation to Beelzebul, his power to pardon sins, and – less personally – the problems of resurrection, divorce, payment of tax to Rome and the meaning of 'son of David'.

Those discussions centred on practical commandments include Sabbath rules, mostly though not exclusively connected with healing and purification rites. But it is essential to bear in mind that frequently in the case of practical polemics the final solution is provided by a general principle, for instance that the saving of life overrules the

Sabbath law, or that the impurity of all external action derives from an internal source.

As a last reflection, it should be remarked apropos the nefarious part played by the woes against the Pharisees in the birth and development of Christian antisemitism that hypocrisy is a universal phenomenon in religious behaviour and not merely a characteristic of the Pharisees. After a detailed and penetrating study of the concept both in Greek and in the underlying Hebrew and Aramaic, the eminent linguist James Barr remarks: 'Hypocrisy isn't pretending to be good, it is self-righteousness . . . Christian hypocrisy . . . has not been absent from the scene of history. In the earliest times it was already there. Peter himself, and his associates, were according to St Paul implicated in *hypocrisis* (Gal. 2:13).'[24]

In fact, to point the finger at the Pharisees as though they were the only culprits in this domain is itself a signal act of hypocrisy.

24. 'The Hebrew/Aramaic Background of "Hypocrisy" in the Gospels', in *A Tribute to Geza Vermes*, ed. P. R. Davies and R. T. White (Sheffield, 1990), 321–3.

3

Words of Wisdom

After the controversy accounts which have been inserted into genuine or artificially created stories about Jesus, we now move to those sayings or logia which are attributed to him when he speaks as a teacher of wisdom. The Hebrew Bible contains collections of such utterances defining correct moral and religious behaviour, and so does the literature of ancient Mesopotamia and Egypt. In the Old Testament, the most important wisdom anthologies are the Books of Proverbs and Ecclesiastes. Among the Apocrypha the same genre is represented by the maxims of Jesus ben Sira, known also as the Book of Sirach or Ecclesiasticus, originally written in Hebrew, and by the Greek Wisdom of Solomon. We have a number of further compositions in the Pseudepigrapha and the Dead Sea Scrolls. Finally, sapiential teachings of the rabbis are dispersed in the Mishnah and the Talmud. The Mishnah tractate Abot, or Sayings of the Fathers, includes a special selection of words of rabbinic wisdom, revised and enlarged in the Sayings of Rabbi Nathan (Abot de-Rabbi Nathan).

This literary genre is mostly represented by brief, vivid and terse statements, that is to say in the form of proverbs and aphorisms. A fair number of those credited to Jesus, which fill the pages of the Gospels and in particular the Sermon on the Mount, are known outside the New Testament too, indicating that they may have had a secular or a religious extra-biblical origin before being appropriated by Jesus. Depending on the intention of the speaker and on the context in which it is used, an ordinary proverb can acquire a specific new meaning. Again, the same proverb may signify one thing in the mind of one teacher and quite another in the mind of the collector of sayings, who lived in a later age, pursued a different didactic aim, and addressed a different public. In the following pages, as well as in the next chapter on the parables, I will try to distinguish when possible the various levels of significance of a proverbial saying – its meaning before Jesus, on the lips of Jesus and in the formulation of the evangelists. I shall also try to indicate the special slants or twists which a maxim has acquired in the course of its development.

The reader will notice that many of the logia of the Gospels make good sense when they are seen in the framework of the imminent arrival of the Kingdom of God, i.e. the perspective which characterized the religious outlook of Jesus. However, the same sayings are also meaningful, though conveying a substantially different message, when understood from the spiritual and cultural standpoint of the primitive Palestinian or Hellenistic church

I. WISDOM SAYINGS IN MARK AND THE TRIPLE TRADITION

1. Who needs the physician? (Mark 2:17; Matt. 9:12–13; Luke 5:31–32)

Those who are well have no need of a physician, but those who are sick; I came not to call the righteous, but sinners [*to repentance* (Luke)].

This proverbial saying echoes the Galilean activity of Jesus as a charismatic healer. His interpretative comment, which identifies the sick with sinners, helps to clarify the general meaning. However, the narrative context in which the evangelists place the maxim is ill-chosen. It is not linked to Jesus' cures, but comments on his attitude to tax collectors, classified as sinners, with whom he was sitting at table (Mark 2:15–16; Matt. 9:10–11; Luke 5:29–30). The message conveyed epitomizes the mission of Jesus: as a healer, appointed by God, he is also the man commissioned to bring sinful Jews to repentance and set them on the way to the Kingdom of heaven.

The association between sin and sickness has already been considered in chapter 2, no. 1, and the link of physician with prophet will be discussed in no. 8 below.

2. The new and the old (Mark 2:21–22; Matt. 9:16–17; Luke 5:36–39; Gospel of Thos. 47:3–5)

No one sews a piece of unshrunk cloth on an old garment; if he does, the patch tears away from it, the new from the old, and a worse tear is made (Mark, Matt.).

No one tears a piece from a new garment and puts it upon an old garment; if he does, he will tear the new, and the piece from the new will not match the old (Luke).

And no one puts new wine into old wineskins; if he does, the [*new* (Luke)] *wine will burst the skins, and the wine is lost* [*will be spilled* (Matt., Luke)], *and so are the skins; but new wine is for fresh skins* (Mark, Matt., Luke).

And no one after drinking old wine desires new; for he says, 'The old is good' (Luke).

No one drinks old wine and immediately desires to drink new wine. And new wine is not put into old wineskins lest they burst; and old wine is not put into a new wineskin lest it spoil it. No one sews an old patch on a new garment because a rip will result (Gospel of Thos.).

These sayings are proverbs, which at one time probably circulated as maxims of secular wisdom. Luke introduces them as a parable told by Jesus. The Greek word *parabole* corresponds to the biblical and rabbinic *mashal* which in Hebrew also signifies proverb, wise saying or similitude.

The common theme is the contrast between new and old. In the first two sayings new is preferable to old, but in the additional proverb introduced by Luke 5:39 (which is missing from part of the manuscript tradition) the priorities are reversed, the old wine being better than the new. No historical or narrative setting is provided. The only possible guidance comes from the fact that the sayings follow the argument about fasting or not fasting, a subject which distinguishes Jesus' circle from that of John the Baptist. Assuming that the eschatological banquet alluded to in the preceding paragraph of Mark (Mark 2:18–20; Matt. 9:14–15; Luke 5:33–35) constitutes the background, and that the speaker continues to be Jesus expressing his own vision, the new cloth and the new wine should be seen as eschatological symbols. The old garment and old wineskin must therefore refer to the pre-messianic era, which is not condemned in itself, but is expected soon to vanish.

If the sayings transmitted by Mark and Matthew are understood in this sense, the new realities (cloth and wine) allude to Jesus' message about the Kingdom of God. It would be wrong therefore to attempt to patch up the old traditional religious practices with bits of fresh insight; the prophetic novelty of the proclamation of Jesus is to be embraced as a whole. The unused fabric of the patch would shrink at the first wash and would thus tear the old garment. Likewise the freshly pressed and still fermenting grape juice would attack and destroy the old worn wineskin. Jesus disapproved of compromises. However, it would be a mistake to see in this passage a rejection of traditional Judaism as such.

In Luke the proverb about mending a garment is re-edited in this latter sense. He speaks of tearing up the new dress to patch up – unsuccessfully – the old. By adding the final sentence about old wine versus new wine, Luke spoils the coherence of the original teaching. Gospel interpreters, unwilling to admit that Luke confused the issue, think that the person praising the old wine is a Jew who is opposed to the new message offered by Jesus. The Gospel of Thomas (47:3–5) also goes along with Luke and rearranges the order of the sayings. On the other hand, if Luke's statement about old wine being preferable to new is taken as a later addition by the church (see the story of the wedding feast in Cana in John 2:10), the old wine would designate the teaching of Jesus, and the new the false doctrines circulating in early Christianity which are hinted at in the letters of Paul and Peter, and in the Book of Revelation.

3. Overpowering a strong man (Mark 3:27; Matt. 12:29; Luke 11:21–22)

But no one can enter a strong man's house and plunder his goods, unless he first binds the strong man; then indeed he may plunder his house (Mark, Matt.).

When a strong man, fully armed, guards his own palace, his goods are in peace; but when one stronger than he assails him and overcomes him, he takes away his armour in which he trusted, and divides his spoil (Luke).

This logion is appended to the debate about the power of Jesus over satanic forces. His success has nothing to do with Beelzebul and receives no help from him. The reasoning goes like this: since Satan's empire still stands, it cannot be internally divided (cf. chapter 2, no. 7). The defeat of the prince of darkness and the plundering of his house cannot happen unless he, the strong man, is already tied up and imprisoned. Luke describes Beelzebul as a soldier wearing his trusted armour. Jesus is not explicitly named as his captor, but it is beyond any reasonable doubt that he is meant. It has been suggested by some interpreters that Jesus' triumph was due to God's prior victory over Satan. But the general Gospel picture of the fight against demonic powers points to an action initiated and performed by Jesus, albeit on God's behalf.

The imagery is not original, but derives from biblical and post-biblical literature where we read, 'Can his prey be taken from the strong man?' (Isa. 49:24, New English Bible), or 'For no one will take spoil from a mighty man' (Psalms of Solomon 5:3). The metaphor of binding Satan is also used both in the Apocrypha and in other intertestamental writings. In the Book of Tobit the angel Raphael ties up the demon Asmodeus hand and foot (Tobit 8:3). He deals in the same way with Azazel, leader of the fallen angels, whom he casts into the desert according to the Ethiopic Book of Enoch (1 Enoch 10:4).[1] When Satan is not overpowered he himself binds humans, as in the case of the sick woman whom Jesus delivered from demonic bonds which had lasted for eighteen years (Luke 13:16; cf. chapter 2, no. 5). This idea underlies the metaphor 'to bind and to loose' used in connection with sins (Matt. 16:19; 18:18; cf. chapter 2, no. 1; chapter 9, nos. 23 and 24). In short, the maxim is solidly planted in, and

1. The desert was thought to be the habitat of demons: 'When the unclean spirit has gone out of a man, he passes through waterless places seeking rest, but he finds none' (Matt. 12:43; Luke 11:24). Jesus' temptation by Satan is also placed in the wilderness (Mark 1:12–13; Matt. 4:1; Luke 4:1–2).

reflects, the apocalyptic–eschatological world of ideas of the age of Jesus.

4. The purpose of a lamp (Mark 4:21; Matt. 5:14–15; Luke 8:16; 11:33)

Is a lamp brought in to be put under a bushel, or under a bed, and not on a stand? (Mark).

You are the light of the world. A city set on a hill cannot be hid. Nor do men light a lamp and put it under a bushel, but on a stand, and it gives light to all the house (Matt.).

No one after lighting a lamp covers it with a vessel, or puts it under a bed, but puts it on a stand, that those who enter may see the light (Luke 8).

No one after lighting a lamp puts it in a cellar [literally 'a hidden place' (*eis krupten*)] *or under a bushel, but on a stand, that those who enter may see the light* (Luke 11).

Four sayings of Jesus have been assembled in chapter 4 of Mark, verses 21–22, 24–25 (see also nos. 5–7 below). Although they are presumed to belong together, they most likely have originated independently from one another. The proverb concerning the lamp is reproduced in four different forms in the Synoptics. The meaning of the saying as formulated in Mark is clear. Truth is there to be proclaimed, not to be concealed inside a container.[2] From the redactional point of view, this logion follows the parable of the sower, which according to the evangelists was intended to hide the message of Jesus from the listening crowd, though a special explanation is offered to the slow-witted disciples (Mark 4:1–20; see chapter 4, nos. 1a and 1b). In Mark the lamp logion corrects the misrepresentation of the purpose of teaching

2. The Greek (and Hebrew) loan word, *modios*, borrowed from the Latin (*modius*), and rendered as 'bushel' in English, is a sizeable measure of capacity for grain. The idea of camouflaging light in a jar by soldiers wishing to remain undetected figures also in the Bible (Judges 7:16) and Josephus (*Antiquities* 5:223).

in parables; the duty of the disciples is to facilitate understanding of the truth and not to hide it (cf. chapter 4, pp. 171–2]). The audience is not specified. Matthew (5:14) on the other hand, by adding that the light, symbol of the disciples as teachers,[3] is there for the benefit of all those who are in the house, gives a Jewish twist to the proverb. By implication the lamp is specifically for members of the house of Israel (cf. Matt. 10:5–6; 15:24). Luke, by contrast, stresses as usual the openness of the message for outsiders: the light is there for 'those who enter' the house from without (Luke 11:33). The text preserved in Mark appears the most genuine.

For further lamp symbolism, see Matthew 6:22, Luke 11:34, and no. 17 below.

5. All hidden things will be disclosed (Mark 4:22; cf. Luke 8:17; Matt. 10:26–27; Luke 12:2–3)

For there is nothing hid, except to be made manifest; nor is anything secret, except to come to light (Mark, Luke 8).

Nothing is covered that will not be revealed, or hidden that will not be known. What I tell you in the dark, utter in the light; and what you hear whispered, proclaim upon the house tops (Matt., Luke 12).

In the form of a general statement this saying proclaims that the time has come for all the secrets of God to be revealed. There is no reference to any limited group of addressees; Jesus teaches all and sundry. In this sense the proverb differs from the preceding parable of the sower, according to which 'the secret of the Kingdom' is made available only to the close followers of Jesus (Mark 4:11; Matt. 13:11; Luke 8:10; see chapter 4, no. 1a). Consequently, these words predate the stage when teaching in parables, a common didactic method among

3. The image of a town built on a hilltop implies visibility from afar. The Gospel of Thomas (3) takes it primarily to mean impregnability – an idea alien to the context – and only secondarily conspicuousness: 'A city that is built on a high mountain and fortified cannot fall, nor can it remain hidden.'

Palestinian Jews, was declared a means of concealment of the truth from Jesus' larger audience, its revelation being reserved only for the select few. The additional clause about proclaiming the message from the house tops, supplied in Matthew 10:27 and Luke 12:3, represents the later perspective of the apostolic age. It already presupposes the existence of a community of chosen initiates in the primitive church.

The privilege of receiving secret revelations recalls the world view of the esoteric Dead Sea/Essene sect. The 'mysteries' or *razim* entrusted by God to the Teacher of Righteousness of the Qumran community were first preached by him to wider circles. But when many refused to believe in his words, his message was strictly embargoed and made available only to fully enrolled members of the sect (cf. 1QpHab 2:1–3; 7:5–14; 1QS 9:18).

6. Measure for measure (Mark 4:24: Luke 8:18; Matt. 7:1–2; Luke 6:37–38)

Take heed what you hear; the measure you give will be the measure you get, and still more will be given you (Mark).

Judge not, that you be not judged. For with the judgement you pronounce you will be judged, and the measure you give will be the measure you get (Matt.).

Judge not, and you will not be judged; condemn not, and you will not be condemned; forgive, and you will be forgiven; give, and it will be given to you; good measure, pressed down, shaken together, running over, will be put into your lap. For the measure you give will be the measure you get back (Luke 6:37–38).

For with the judgement you pronounce you will be judged, and the measure you give will be the measure you get (Matt. 7; Luke 6).

Measure for measure (*middah keneged middah* in Hebrew; in Aramaic the word used is *mekhilta*) was a well-known and often-quoted Jewish proverb. The longer form is 'The measure with which a man measures, they [i.e. God and his heavenly family] will use to measure him in return' (cf. mSotah 1:7, etc.).[4] Usually the principle is quoted in connection with rewarding someone for his deeds.

The logion cited in the Sermon on the Mount and the corresponding passage in Luke are linked specifically to the concept of judgement (Matt. 7:1–2; Luke 6:38). The Gospel proverb enjoins magnanimity in dealing with other people, a rule that fits perfectly the religious inspiration of Jesus. These sayings acquire individual colouring from their context. So if Jesus uttered these words with an eye on the eschatological situation in which he believed he and his contemporaries lived, he was envisaging something more than simply being fair and generous. 'Take heed what you hear' and 'and still more will be given you' are meant to convey that a devoted listener to the mystery of the Kingdom would be rewarded by a fuller and deeper understanding of it.

The wording of the maxim in Matthew and Luke introduces the negative counterpart of the teaching: in order to escape judgement for one's misdeeds, one must abstain from judging others. This counsel is particularly apposite in the case of the conventionally pious who are sometimes only too apt to condemn their neighbours. Luke's proverb further insists positively on forgiveness and fairness. Both Matthew and Luke contemplate equality between giving and receiving; Mark and probably Jesus, who liked to provide old clichés with a new slant, promise a return which exceeds the deserts of human action.

7. Disproportionate remuneration (Mark 4:25; Matt. 13:12; Luke 8:18; Gospel of Thos. 41)

For to him who has will more be given; and from him who has not, even what he [*thinks that he* (Luke)] *has will be taken away* (Mark, Matt., Luke).

He who has something in his hand, to him will be given (more),

4. The Fragmentary Targum (Ms Paris), Gen. 38:26, makes the meaning plain: 'The measure with which a man measures on earth, they will measure for him in heaven'. See M. L. Klein, *The Fragment-Targums of the Pentateuch* I (Rome, 1980), 61.

and he who has nothing from him will be taken away even the little which he has (Gospel of Thos.).

This paradoxical maxim appears not only at this juncture, but also as the misapplied conclusion of the parable about the talents (Matt. 25:29; Luke 19:26; see chapter 4, no. 16). Judged by the rules of everyday morality, God's action may be qualified as unjust or at least capricious. However, by interpreting the saying at its surface value, one gets hold of the wrong end of the stick. It would seem that the underlying Semitic mode of thinking and speaking handles opposites in a peculiar manner. When Jesus asks whether it is lawful to do good or do harm, to save life or to kill on the Sabbath, he does not mean to suggest that doing harm or killing can be legitimately performed on the Sabbath, or on any other day (see chapter 2, no. 4). Attention is concentrated only on the positive side of the statement; the negative serves as contrast to bring the positive into greater relief. Likewise when power is granted to bind or to loose sins, exclusive emphasis lies on the authority to grant pardon. The same approach should be adopted in the explanation of the present saying. Therefore since the saying is reasonably assumed to be concerned with the secrets of the Kingdom, Jesus would insist more on the value of receptivity on the part of the well-disposed than on the disaster awaiting the unresponsive.

For a more prosaic version of the maxim, see chapter 4, no. 15.

8. No one is a prophet at home (Mark 6:4; Matt. 13:57; Luke 4:23–27; cf. John 4:44; Gospel of Thos. 31)

A prophet is not without honour, except in his own country, and among his own kin, and in his own house (Mark, Matt.).

Doubtless you will quote to me this proverb, 'Physician, heal yourself; what we have heard you did at Capernaum, do here also in your own country.' . . . Truly, I say to you, no prophet is acceptable in his own country. But in truth I tell you, there were many widows in Israel in the days of Elijah, when the heaven was shut up three years and six months, when came a great famine over all the land; and Elijah was sent to none of them but only to Zarephath, in the land of Sidon, to a woman who was a widow (1 Kings 17:1, 8–9; 18:1–2). *And there were many lepers in Israel in the days of the prophet Elisha; and none of them was cleansed, but only Naaman the Syrian* (2 Kings 5:14) (Luke).

For Jesus himself testified that a prophet has no honour in his own country (John).

No prophet is acceptable in his village; no physician works cures on those who know him (Gospel of Thos.).

The context indicates that the term 'prophet' must be understood not in the sense of a clairvoyant, but of a charismatic man of God. Indeed, in a Galilean setting the notion of prophet carries with it the concept of healing and vice versa. Since the members of his family and his fellow-citizens in Nazareth refused to recognize the prophetic status of Jesus, he was unable to perform cures in his home town (Mark 6:6; Matt. 13:58; Luke 4:23).

It is noteworthy, however, that when the subject of dispute is not charismatic activity but the teaching function, familiarity with a prophet is not a disadvantage but counts in his favour. Thus in the Old Testament the shepherd-prophet Amos was unwelcome in the northern sanctuary of Bethel because he was a Judaean; 'Go home and prophesy there!' he was firmly told by the high priest of Samaria (Amos 7:10–13). Similarly according to a Dead Sea Scroll a prophet could be treated as a teacher of falsehood by members of a different tribe while hailed as a herald of truth by members of his own clan (4Q375). Nevertheless, the situation is quite different in the context of faith-healing. The absolute trust required in this case does not come easily to relations and close acquaintances of the charismatic (cf. chapter 8, no. 4).

The logion about the prophet-physician is placed by Luke between two sayings concerned with healing (Luke 4:23 and 4:25–27). The first reads: 'Physician, heal yourself' (Luke 4:23). Sarcastic disparagement of doctors who pretend to heal the sick but are incapable of curing themselves was common in antiquity. An Aramaic maxim quoted in Genesis Rabbah 23:4 runs, 'Physician, physician, heal your lameness!' It echoes a line which goes back to Euripides in the ancient Greek world: 'A physician for others, but himself full of sores' (fragment 1080).

Luke does not seem to have fully grasped the sense and consequently the applicability of 'Physician, heal yourself.' For him and for the people from Nazareth as described by him, 'heal yourself' meant 'heal your own people' – and not the inhabitants of other places like Capernaum. Not surprisingly, the more perspicacious Mark and Matthew shy away from this proverb.

A second saying confirms that charismatic prophets, like Elijah and Elisha, had the habit of performing cures on 'foreigners' (the son of a Sidonian woman and the Syrian royal official, Naaman) and not on their nearest and dearest. The passage (Luke 4:25–27) plainly shows that Jesus was the heir of the miracle-working prophets of northern Israel, although apart from occasionally healing non-Jews he mostly exercised his therapeutic activity on his co-religionists, albeit outside his home environment.

9. Gaining the world but losing one's life (Mark 8:36–37; Matt. 16:26; Luke 9:25; cf. Matt. 10:39; Luke 17:33; John 12:25)

For what does it profit a man, to gain the whole world and forfeit his life? For what can a man give in return for his life? (Mark, Matt., Luke).

He who finds his life will lose it, and he who loses his life for my sake will find it (Matt. 10).

Whoever seeks to gain his life will lose it, but whoever loses his life will preserve it (Luke 17).

He who loves his life loses it, and he who hates his life in this world will keep it for eternal life (John).

Originally these proverbs were probably independent, but are joined here by the common theme of life. The first, the contrast between gaining wealth and losing one's life, is a familiar topic in wisdom literature. The most illuminating parallel comes from Ben Sira (Ecclesiasticus) 11:18–19, 'A man may grow rich by stinting and sparing, but what does he get for his pains? When he says, "I have earned my rest, now I can live on my savings", he does not know how long it will be before he must die and leave his wealth to others.' The theme recalls the parable of the rich and foolish farmer (Luke 12:16–20; cf. chapter 4, no. 30). The second proverb proclaims that no money can restore life to a dead man. The immediately preceding context is that of rules laid down for the disciples of Jesus concerning self-sacrifice (Mark 8:34–35; Matt. 16:24–25; Luke 9:23–24; cf. Matt. 10:39; Luke 17:33; see chapter 9, no. 5).

There are two possible settings for these maxims. The first represents the situation prevailing on the eve of the arrival of the Kingdom. There, because of the expected proximity of the 'day of the Lord', physical death is not the primary preoccupation. Losing one's life would rather be taken to signify symbolically the renunciation of secular values. The second setting is that of Christian discipleship within the primitive church, entailing suffering and persecution inflicted on members by outsiders. The foregoing maxim about self-denial and carrying one's cross (Mark 8:34; Matt. 16:24; Luke 9:23) implies that in its original sense the second proverb, 'What can a man give for the return of his life?', also belongs to the eschatological teaching of Jesus.

Matthew (10:39) and Luke (17:33) repeat the same theme and that in John (12:25) develops it further. By alluding to a disciple losing his life for the sake of Jesus, Luke speaks from the point of view of the persecuted early church.

10. Millstone around one's neck (Mark 9:42; Matt. 18:6; Luke 17:1–2)

Whoever causes one of these little ones who believe in me to sin, it would be better for him if a great millstone were hung round his neck and he were thrown into [*drowned in the depth of* (Matt.)] *the sea.*

Temptations to sin are sure to come; but woe to him by whom they come! (Luke 17:1).

The metaphor of the great millstone[5] fastened to the neck of a person guilty of leading the innocent astray has the appearance of a proverb, but no Jewish parallels are extant. In all three Gospels the seducer's guilt is absolute, as his victim is a 'little' believer. In Mark's (and Matthew's) setting the atmosphere is eschatological, with the Kingdom of God expressly mentioned a little later in Mark 9:47. The saying fits well into the context of the historical preaching of Jesus, but it could easily be adapted for later needs in the primitive church.

Compared with the solemn tone of the Gospel, the use of the millstone imagery in rabbinic literature is humorous. In connection with the precept that a father should find a wife for his son before sending him to study, with light-hearted male chauvinism Rabbi Yohanan remarks, 'With such a millstone around his neck, how can he occupy himself with the Torah?' (bKid 29b). If Jesus ever said anything humorous, the evangelists and the early church saw to it that no trace of wittiness would survive.

11. Salt without savour (Mark 9:49–50; Matt. 5:13; Luke 14:34–35)

For every one will be salted with fire.[6] *Salt is good; but if the salt has lost its saltness, how will you season it? Have salt in yourselves and be at peace with one another* (Mark).

You are the salt of the earth; but if salt has lost its taste, how shall its saltness be restored? It is no longer good for anything except to be thrown out and trodden underfoot by men (Matt.).

5. In the language of the rabbis the *great* millstone is literally a 'donkey stone' and refers to a mill powered by a donkey. The manually operated smaller version is called a 'man stone', mentioned in the Mishnah (mOholot 8:3).

6. The saying is extremely succinct and manuscript tradition tried to clarify it by adding: 'and every sacrifice will be salted with salt', or correct it to read: 'For every sacrifice will be salted with salt'. The allusion is to Leviticus 2:13.

Salt is good; but if salt has lost its taste, how shall its saltness be restored? It is fit neither for the land nor for the dunghill; men throw it away. He who has ears to hear, let him hear (Luke).

The main logion, 'Salt is good', etc. considers the eventuality of the salt ceasing to act as a preservative. In Mark it is preceded and followed by secondary proverbs. Being salted with fire is an eschatological–apocalyptic image of purification (cf. chapter 8, no. 56), and the reference to salt within a person alludes to a healthy state of the spirit which is conducive to peaceful coexistence among brothers.

Matthew and Luke further develop the image and describe what happens to the useless salt. The saying is attested also in rabbinic literature where it serves to illustrate something impossible. 'If salt rots, with what will it be salted?' (bBekh. 8b). The rabbis, tongue-in-cheek, explain this maxim by another impossibility. Rotten salt can be reactivated, they claim, with the help of the afterbirth produced by a (sterile) mule. Another rabbi, devoid of a sense of humour, earnestly remarks that salt cannot rot.

In sum, the meaning implied in the Gospels is that the followers of Jesus are instructed to cultivate the spiritual values represented by salt which, like fire, will keep them purified and enable them to be of one mind and live peacefully with one another. As for the allusion to being salted with *fire*, it points to the eschatological ministry of Jesus as the most natural context for this saying.

12. The camel and the eye of a needle (Mark 10:24–25; Matt. 19:24–25; Luke 18:25)

Children, how hard it is to enter the kingdom of God! It is easier for a camel to go through the eye of a needle than for a rich man to enter the kingdom of God.

In the opinion of Jesus the greatest obstacle before someone wishing to enter the Kingdom is constituted by attachment to worldly goods. This principle is illustrated in the story which precedes the present saying, that of the wealthy man who observes all the commandments, but is unwilling to part with his possessions on the eve of the arrival of the Kingdom (Mark 10:17–22; Matt. 19:16–22; Luke 18:18–23; cf. chapter 8, no. 14). The difficulty experienced by the rich is colourfully depicted in the metaphor of the camel and the eye of the needle.

A similar image is used in a light-hearted spirit in the Talmud. There an elephant, an even bigger animal, plays a part in a discussion of the nature of dreams. Apparently most ancient rabbis, innocent of Freudian psychoanalysis, were of the opinion that dreams sprang from rational thinking, and never contained figments of the imagination such as a golden palm leaf or an elephant passing through the eye of a needle. Only the rabbis from Pumbeditha, renowned for their hair-splitting acumen, could invent such impossibilities (bBer 55b).

See chapter 8, no. 14.

II. WISDOM SAYINGS IN *Q*

13. Out of court settlement (Matt. 5:25–26; cf. Luke 12:58–59)

Make friends quickly with your accuser, while you are going with him to court, lest your accuser hand you over to the judge, and the judge to the guard, and you be put in prison; truly, I say to you, you will never get out till you have paid the last penny (quadrans) (Matt.).

As you go with your accuser before the magistrate, make an effort to settle with him on the way, lest he drag you to the judge, and the judge hand you over to the officer, and the officer put you in prison. I tell you, you will never get out till you have paid the very last copper (leptos) (Luke).

In its basic message the saying encourages a debtor who is being brought before a judge to come quickly to an understanding with his creditor. Thus the danger of being found guilty and sent to jail will be avoided. Assuming that the outlook of the teacher is eschatological, the message is that those engaged in the cause of the Kingdom of God must seek reconciliation with their brethren before the ultimate Judge pronounces judgement (cf. chapter 9, no. 10). In determining the provenance of the saying, one should bear in mind, however, that imprisonment for debts was not part of the Jewish legal system (see chapter 4, no. 22). Hence the fully formulated precept is more likely to belong to the cultural and social framework of the Gentile church than to the authentic pronouncements of Jesus.

14. Generosity instead of retaliation (Matt. 5:38–42; Luke 6:29–30)

You have heard that it was said, 'An eye for an eye and a tooth for a tooth' (Exod. 21:24). *But I say to you, Do not resist one who is evil. But if any one strikes you on the right cheek, turn to him the other also; and if any one would sue you and take your coat, let him have your cloak as well; and if any one forces you to go one mile, go with him two miles. Give to him who begs from you, and do not refuse him who would borrow from you.*

Matthew's version of the saying entails a further refinement of the biblical law of retaliation. The meaning of the biblical quotation and its interpretation in ancient Jewish literature will be discussed in chapter 5, no. 21.

As usual Jesus gives hyperbolical advice, so it would be an error to take these words literally. When faced with ultimate choices, one must be ready to go, if necessary, to extremes. He is not content with prescribing passive resistance to wickedness, but demands a willingness to submit oneself to more injustice by 'offering the other cheek'. The other two counsels, to hand over one's coat to a robber as well as the shirt[7] he has demanded, and to be ready to walk a second mile with a man who has compelled one to walk one mile with him, suggest that Jesus sought to inculcate extreme generosity and goodwill towards opponents. This is how evil will be overcome by good (cf. Rom. 12:21).

7. Luke's highwayman demands the man's coat but in addition is given his shirt so that the victim is left naked.

15. Love your enemies (Matt. 5:43–48; Luke 6:27–28, 32–36)

You have heard that it was said, 'You shall love your neighbour (Lev. 19:18) *and hate your enemy.' But I say to you, Love your enemies and pray for those who persecute you, so that you may be the sons of your Father who is in heaven; for he makes his sun rise on the evil and on the good, and sends rain on the just and on the unjust. For if you love those who love you, what reward have you? Do not even the tax-collectors do the same? And if you salute only your brethren, what more are you doing than others? Do not even the Gentiles do the same? You, therefore, must be perfect, as your heavenly Father is perfect* (Matt.).

But I say to you that hear, Love your enemies, do good to those who hate you, bless those who curse you, pray for those who abuse you . . . If you love those who love you, what credit is that to you? For even sinners love those who love them. And if you do good to those who do good to you, what credit is that to you? For even sinners do the same. And if you lend to those from whom you hope to receive, what credit is that to you? Even sinners lend to sinners, to receive as much again. But love your enemies, and do good, and lend, expecting nothing in return; and your reward will be great, and you will be sons of the Most High; for he is kind to the ungrateful and the selfish. Be merciful, even as your Father is merciful (Luke).

Though their wording differs, Matthew and Luke hand down the same teaching of eschatological wisdom and sum up the message of Jesus in a single commandment: the disciples must be 'perfect' or 'merciful' as the Father in heaven is perfect and merciful. The contrast between the love of one's neighbour or brother and the love of an enemy is set up in the form of an antithesis between Leviticus 19:18 ('You shall love your neighbour') and Jesus' command. The formulation in Matthew has been the subject of much debate because the additional clause, 'and hate your enemy', has no equivalent in Leviticus. It has been correctly noted that the idea of hatred towards the wicked or towards enemies is frequently voiced in the Bible, but what we need is a direct juxtaposition of 'to love' and 'to hate'. The nearest example comes from the Qumran Community Rule 1:9–10 where the expressions 'to love all the sons of light' and 'to hate all the sons of darkness' are juxtaposed in the same sentence. But contrary to the teaching of Jesus, here the order to hate is expressly asserted. In my view, the phrase 'Love your neighbour and hate your enemy' needs to be treated in the same way as the contradictory alternatives earlier encountered: 'Is it lawful on the sabbath to do good or to do harm, to save life or to kill?' (Mark 3:4; Matt. 12:12; Luke 6:9; see no. 7 above). In other words, only the positive statement is intended for consideration; the negative aspect is there only to throw extra light on the positive half.

The true significance of the wisdom teaching of Jesus is crystallized in the final sentence enjoining the duty to imitate God in one's dealings with fellow humans. As divine love is all-embracing and extends over the good and the evil, the just and the unjust, so human love also must be universally disinterested and generous. The extreme illustration of this disinterestedness and generosity, the hyperbole exceeding all hyperboles, is love towards one's enemy given candidly without expecting anything in return.

As in general in the teaching of Jesus, the paramount insistence falls on the purity of intention in moral action. Love is pure if it is given to man and to God without counting on repayment of any sort. Hence the ideal model of unselfish love is that in which the partner is by definition unlikely to be well disposed towards one, i.e. an enemy. For parallels in ancient Judaism, see chapter 5, no. 22. The concrete examples of Matthew (tax-collectors and Gentiles) substituted for Luke's generic sinners are later editorial additions. Jesus was friendly towards the despised publicans.

16. Treasures in heaven (Matt. 6:19–21; Luke 12:33–34)

Do not lay up for yourselves treasures on earth, where moth and rust consume and where thieves break in and steal, but lay up for yourselves treasures in heaven, where neither moth nor rust consumes and where thieves do not break in and steal. For where your treasure is, there will your heart be also (Matt.).

Sell your possessions, and give alms; provide yourselves with purses that do not grow old, with a treasure in the heavens that does not fail, where no thief approaches and no moth destroys. For where your treasure is, there will your heart be also (Luke).

The conclusion in both Matthew and Luke is expressed by the same maxim, which specifies that a man's heart, or rather mind, is preoccupied with what he holds to be most valuable. Therefore one must ensure that the treasures will be spiritual and imperishable and not worldly goods which deteriorate and are in continuous danger of being stolen or destroyed. The teaching contains the usual emphasis on the absolute priority of the Kingdom of God.

17. The healthy eye (Matt. 6:22–23; Luke 11:34–36)

The eye is the lamp of the body. So if your eye is sound, your whole body will be full of light; but if your eye is not sound, your whole body will be full of darkness. If then the light in you is darkness, how great is the darkness!

Therefore be careful lest the light in you be darkness. If then your whole body is full of light, having no part dark, it will be wholly bright, as when a lamp with its rays gives you light (Luke 11:36).

Unlike the lamp simile discussed earlier (no. 4 above) which is concerned with light shed to illuminate the house, the eye, the symbolical lamp, is the source of light within man. If the eye is faultless, the spiritual light emanating from it will penetrate inside man and illumine his heart. But if the eye is not transparent, light will not pass through it, and darkness will reign inside man. No specific teaching attached to this proverb can be easily defined except that the seeker of God should hope and pray for the gift of enlightenment.

The saying presupposes the Jewish ethical – as opposed to magical

– imagery of the good eye and the evil eye, the source of virtue or wickedness. The saying attributed to the late first-century AD Rabbi Eliezer ben Hyrcanus identifies the 'good eye' with the 'good way' and the 'evil eye' with the 'evil way' (mAb 2:9). The concept of man being inwardly made up of light and/or darkness is rendered more intelligible by a Dead Sea Scroll (4Q186) according to which each human individual consists of nine parts of light or darkness, or a mixture of the two. The surviving fragment describes two persons; one is fairly good, with six parts of light against three parts of darkness, but the other is very wicked, having eight parts of darkness and only one part of light. Luke's wording, 'your whole body is full of light, having no part dark' (11:36), reminds one of this Qumran model.

18. God and mammon (Matt. 6:24; Luke 16:13; cf. Gospel of Thos. 47:2)

No one can serve two masters; for either he will hate the one and love the other, or he will be devoted to the one and despise the other. You cannot serve God and mammon.

No attestation of a proverb about the impossibility of serving two masters has been found in Jewish literature, yet the saying seems so natural that it would be unwise to imagine that it was invented by Jesus. The teaching requires hardly any comment: in the same way as a divided kingdom, including that of Satan, is bound to collapse (see chapter 2, no. 7), a man whose loyalties are split cannot render whole-hearted service to either of his two masters. Whether the illustration using God and mammon belongs to the original saying is debated, but the opposition between God and attachment to wealth is an integral part of Jesus' eschatological preaching as well as of non-eschatological Hasidic piety (see no. 12 above and chapter 8, no. 14).

The Hebrew term *mamon*, or more likely the Aramaic *mamona*, was commonly used in the age of Jesus. The Galilean holy man of the first century AD, Hanina ben Dosa, is said to have hated *mamon*, both his own and that which belonged to others (cf. Mekh on Exod. 18:21).

In fact, he is sometimes described as a man who lived in self-imposed poverty.

19. Trust in the heavenly Father (Matt. 6:25–34; Luke 12:22–32; cf. Gospel of Thos. 36)

Therefore I tell you, do not be anxious about your life, what you shall eat or what you shall drink, nor about your body, what you shall put on. Is not life more than food, and the body more than clothing? Look at the birds of the air: they neither sow nor reap nor gather into barns, and yet your heavenly Father feeds them. Are you not of more value than they? And which of you by being anxious can add one cubit to his span of life? And are you anxious about clothing? Consider the lilies of the field, how they grow; they neither toil nor spin; yet I tell you, even Solomon in all his glory was not arrayed like one of these. But if God so clothes the grass of the field, which today is alive and tomorrow is thrown into the oven, will he not much more clothe you, O men of little faith? Therefore do not be anxious, saying, 'What shall we eat?' or 'What shall we drink?' or 'What shall we wear?' For the Gentiles seek all these things; and your heavenly Father knows that you need them all. But seek first his kingdom and his righteousness, and all these things shall be yours as well.

Therefore do not be anxious about tomorrow, for tomorrow will be anxious for itself. Let the day's own trouble be sufficient for the day (Matt. 6:34).

Fear not, little flock, for it is your Father's good pleasure to give you the kingdom (Luke 12:32).

A series of counsels, reinforced by examples borrowed from rural life, stress the absolute need of faith or trust – the opposite of worry – and of the primacy of the present, ideas which are at the heart of the eschatological piety practised and preached by Jesus. Worldly concerns should not disturb total concentration on the spiritual task of the moment. The disciples' eyes must be fixed on the matters of today;

tomorrow will look after itself. The diverse elements of the passage form a coherent unity and it is meaningless to speculate whether some of them had a separate existence before they had been woven into this colourful tapestry. There is explicit reference to the Kingdom of God; hence the precept was primarily intended for Jesus himself and for his actual followers whom Luke calls the 'little flock'.

The idea that God looks after his creatures, the birds of the air and the lilies of the field, was part of Jewish religious thinking in the intertestamental and rabbinic period (see no. 29 below). R. Simeon ben Eleazar uses the same kind of *a fortiori* argument as Jesus: 'Have you ever seen a wild animal or a bird practising a craft? Yet they are provided for without any effort on their part although they were created only to serve me. But I was created to serve my Maker. How much more might not I be provided for without any effort on my part?' (mKid 4:14). The allusion to King Solomon as the prototype of a man living in luxury also belongs to folk ideology, but the extant sources speak about his sumptuous meals rather than his glorious garments (cf. Josephus, *Antiquities* 8:39–41; mBM 7:1). The latter twist is due to the imagination of Jesus. His complete trust in God and relentless focusing upon the task in hand reflect the core of his eschatological religion.

20. The chip and the beam (Matt. 7:3–5; Luke 6:41–42; Gospel of Thos. 26)

Why do you see the speck that is in your brother's eye, but do not notice the log that is in your own eye? Or how can you say to your brother, 'Let me take the speck out of your eye', when there is a log in your own eye? You hypocrite, take the log out of your own eye, and then you will see clearly to take the speck out of your brother's eye (Matt., Luke).

You see the speck that is in your brother's eye, but you do not see the beam that is in your own eye. When you take the beam out of your own eye, then you will see clearly to take the speck out of your brother's eye (Gospel of Thos.).

The metaphor of the speck, or more likely chip, and of the beam, illustrating the contrast between the insignificant and the monumental, is only loosely attached to the preceding topic of magnanimity in judgement (cf. no. 6 above), and belongs rather to the Q material of Jesus' diatribes against hypocrisy (cf. Matt. 23; see chapter 2, no. 15). The word 'hypocrite' appears only in the Sermon on the Mount in Q, and in Matthew 6:2, 5, 16 in *M*. The Gospel of Thomas gives an abridged and simplified version of Q. The same simile is encountered in the Talmud in the form of a dialogue between two quarrelling Jews: 'Take the chip out of your eye!' says one. 'Take the beam out of yours!' retorts the other (bArakh 16b; bBB 15b). With his usual inclination towards exaggeration, Jesus insists on genuine self-knowledge and self-correction instead of easy criticism of others. The counsel is applicable both in the eschatological situation and in the context of the primitive church; it is indeed timeless.

21. The Golden Rule (Matt. 7:12; Luke 6:31)

So whatever you wish that men would do to you, do so to them; [*for this is the law and the prophets* (Matt.)].

This aphoristic code of morality, expressed in a single sentence and designated since the sixteenth century as the Golden Rule, is inserted into the Sermon on the Mount by Matthew together with an additional comment on its relation to the Torah and the prophets. This subjective formulation of universal goodwill towards fellow beings is a teaching commonly attested in Jewish literary sources, too.

Sayings similar to the one attributed to Jesus circulated in various forms for centuries before the New Testament era and continued subsequently to be popular. They are always couched in a negative form – what you do not want to receive, do not give others – but apart from some badly disguised apologists of Christianity,[8] objective

8. For example, commenting on the principle attributed to Hillel (see below) G. B. Caird wrote: 'An ethical programme which consists in not-doing, especially when it has to be expounded in a vast commentary of rules and ceremonies, can hardly be compared with one which calls for positive and unlimited benevolence', in *Saint Luke. The Pelican Gospel Commentaries* (Harmondsworth, 1963), 104.

scholars deny a qualitative difference between the negative and positive formulation. In fact, both amount to the same. The earliest Jewish attestation comes from the apocryphal Book of Tobit 4:15, 'Do not do to anyone what you yourself would hate.' In fact, Tobit may have borrowed it from one of the Pseudepigrapha, the Sayings of Ahikar 8:88: 'Son, what seems evil to you, do not do to your companion!' Jesus ben Sira gives similar advice to his readers: 'Be as friendly to your neighbour as to yourself, and [in your behaviour towards him] be attentive to all that you yourself hate' (Ecclus. 31[34]:15). The same idea is voiced by Jesus' elder contemporary, the Alexandrian Jewish philosopher Philo: 'What someone would hate to suffer, he must not do to others' (*Hypothetica* 7:6).

Among the early rabbinic masters, Hillel, a contemporary of Philo, is reputed to have proclaimed, 'What is hateful to you, do not do to your fellow' (bShab 31a). The maxim has been preserved in an anecdotal context. An impatient Gentile, a would-be proselyte, wishing to be received quickly into Judaism, flippantly asked for a crash course in Torah study. He requested a mini-summary which he could learn while standing on one foot. The irascible Shammai threw him out, but the kindly Hillel condensed for him the Jewish religion in the famous sentence just cited. His additional comment, 'This is the whole Torah', closely resembles Matthew's concluding phrase, 'This is the law and the prophets' – that is to say, the saying provides the quintessence of all the teaching of the Bible. The story has of course no claim to historicity, but since the maxim was widely used, and its content is congruent with the ideas of Hillel, there is a good chance that he actually referred to it. The later midrash, Abot de-Rabbi Nathan (Recension B, 26), attributes the principle of Hillel to R. Akiba and removes from the anecdote the comic detail of standing on one foot while learning the whole Law. When asked to sum up the entire Torah in one sentence, Akiba replied, 'My son, our master Moses . . . spent forty days and forty nights on the mountain before learning it, and you say, "Teach me the whole Torah in one [sentence]." But, my son, this is the principle of the Torah: What you yourself hate, do not do it to your fellow.' The most interesting feature in both accounts is that the maxim is offered as a teacher's reply to a questioner. It is reasonable to suppose that Jesus' Golden Rule also came about in similar circumstances. Nevertheless his positive twist, compared with the negative formulation attested elsewhere, bears Jesus' hallmark.

22. The narrow gate (Matt. 7:13–14; Luke 13:24)

Enter by the narrow gate; for the gate is wide and the way is easy, that leads to destruction, and those who enter by it are many. For the gate is narrow and the way is hard, that leads to life, and those who find it are few (Matt.).

Strive to enter by the narrow door; for many, I tell you, will seek to enter and will not be able (Luke).

The image of the two gates, one wide and one narrow, can convey an equivocal message, but the history of the idea will help to solve the enigma. The idea of dualism of destiny goes back to biblical antiquity. Adam had to choose between good and evil in Paradise and the figure of the two ways can be traced to Jeremiah 21:8, 'Behold, I set before you the way of life and the way of death.' The instruction on the two spirits in the Community Rule of Qumran also speaks of the ways of the spirit of light and of those of the spirit of darkness (1QS 3–4). Likewise the tractate Abot of the Mishnah distinguishes the good way from the evil way (mAb 2:9).

The narrowness of the door and the difficulty of access are vividly described in the Fourth Book of Ezra (7:6–8): 'There is a city built and set on a plain, and it is full of good things, but the entrance to it is narrow and set in a precipitous place so that there is fire on the right and deep water on the left, and there is only one path lying between them.' In 4 Ezra, however, the narrow gate is not contrasted with a comfortable and easy way of access.

Matthew's presentation of the metaphor is more complex. The broad gate is the one that leads to perdition; it can be easily found and multitudes pass through it. By contrast, the approach to the gate leading to life is difficult and the opening is hard to find. Those who wish to cross the threshold of the Kingdom of God, that is to say the small company attached to Jesus, must listen attentively to his eschatological guidance pointing to the inconspicuous narrow gate. Luke seems to envisage a situation in which the message is preached more widely, i.e. the gospel is offered to the whole non-Jewish world, but owing to the narrowness of the entrance only a minority – the swiftest, keenest and most determined listeners – will be able to get through.

23. Houses built on rock and sand (Matt. 7:24–27; Luke 6:47–49)

Although this passage may be classified as a wisdom saying, it comes more appropriately under the umbrella heading of parable and will be discussed in chapter 4, no. 8.

24. The good tree and the bad tree (Matt. 7:16–20; cf. Matt. 12:33–35; Luke 6:43–45)

You will know them by their fruits. Are grapes gathered from thorns, or figs from thistles? So, every sound tree bears good fruit, but the bad tree bears evil fruit. A sound tree cannot bear evil fruit, nor can a bad tree bear good fruit. Every tree that does not bear good fruit is cut down and thrown into the fire. Thus you will know them by their fruits (Matt. 7).

Either make the tree good, and its fruit good; or make the tree bad, and its fruit bad; for the tree is known by its fruit. You brood of vipers! How can you speak good, when you are evil? For out of the abundance of the heart the mouth speaks. The good man out of his good treasure brings forth good, and the evil man out of his evil treasure brings forth evil (Matt. 12).

For no good tree bears bad fruit, nor again does a bad tree bear good fruit; for each tree is known by its own fruit. For figs are not gathered from thorns, nor grapes picked from a bramble bush. The good man out of the good treasure of his heart produces good, and the evil man out of his evil treasure produces evil; for out of the abundance of the heart his mouth speaks (Luke 6).

Luke's version is the simplest and is most likely the original. The imagery is eschatological. The impending fruit harvest – evoking the idea of the last judgement (see chapter 4, nos. 2, 5, 17) – will disclose the true nature of each tree. Hypocrisy will then be revealed to all. The picture differs from that known from the Bible which contrasts a tree standing next to a stream of water to one rooted in the dry land (Jer. 17:5–8; Ps. 1). The same idea is further developed at Qumran in one of the Thanksgiving Hymns, 1QH 16[formerly 8]:21–25: 'By my hand Thou hast opened for them a well-spring . . . that [their bough may become a beautiful] branch of glory . . . But if I take away my hand it shall be like a thistle [in the wilderness] . . .' In Jesus' logion both trees are productive but are distinguished by the quality of their fruit, whereas outside the New Testament a flourishing tree is set against one that is starving and fruitless. Once more we are faced with an individual slant given in the Gospels to a common Jewish idiom. The Q saying does not point to any particular setting in the life of Jesus. It simply and colourfully distinguishes the good teacher from the bad one.

To understand the proverb 'Out of the abundance of the heart the mouth speaks', it must be remembered that the heart in Semitic mentality is the symbolic seat of thinking rather than that of feeling. A rabbinic saying in Aramaic distinguishes someone who keeps in his heart what is in his heart from those who transfer their hearts' secrets to their mouths and thus divulge them (Genesis Rabbah 84:9). So 'out of the abundance of the heart the mouth speaks' recalls the image of the good heart filled with righteous ideas and contrasts it with the bad heart crammed with wicked thoughts.

25. The homeless Jesus (Matt. 8:20; Luke 9:58)

Foxes have holes, and birds of the air have nests; but the Son of Man has nowhere to lay his head.

This splendid pictorial answer was addressed by Jesus to a scribe who wished to join the fellowship of his disciples (Matt. 8:19). The evangelist implies that Jesus made an impression not only on simple folk, but also on some members of the provincial intelligentsia.[9] Luke, however, omits any reference to the status of the man and simply calls him 'someone'.

The wandering ministry in which Jesus and his close disciples were engaged removed them from the familiarity and security of the home fire. They were more deprived than any fox or bird which had an earth or a nest for shelter. The message is that those preaching the coming of the Kingdom are to embrace homeless existence with complete trust in divine Providence and are also to accept the insecurity that accompanies their calling. It makes the need for faith more tangible. The followers of Jesus are to put up with hardship and should need no encouragement, unlike those who require a reminder from him of God's benevolence towards the birds of the air and the lilies of the field. It would be hard to invent a saying more appropriate to the hazardous state in which Jesus and his apostles chose to live.

The saying is repeated in the Gospel of Thomas 86, with the addition 'lay his head *and rest*' in the sense of achieving Gnostic salvation.

26. Burying the dead (Matt. 8:22; Luke 9:60)

Follow me, and leave the dead to bury their own dead; [*but as for you, go and proclaim the kingdom of God* (Luke)].

Like the previous saying, this is also incidental advice. It was provoked according to Luke by an anonymous passer-by, and in Matthew by

9. For the function of rural scribes, see chapter 2, no. 1, above.

one of Jesus' disciples. The person in question planned to postpone his total commitment to the cause of Jesus until after he had laid his father to rest. Jesus declared that no procrastination could be tolerated when the issue was the Kingdom of God. He entrusted the 'dead' with the burial of the dead, that is to say, those who were not prepared to engage whole-heartedly in the cause of God. The term 'dead' is used metaphorically for the ungodly both in the New Testament (1 Tim. 5:6) and in rabbinic literature (yBer 4c).

The true meaning of this command seems to have been misunderstood by a good many New Testament scholars. They suggest that by uttering these words, Jesus contradicted one of Judaism's most sacred precepts, the one concerning filial piety. In fact burying the dead was held in biblical and rabbinic law to be a binding obligation. In order to have full freedom to arrange the funeral of a dead relative, the Jew is excused from all other religious duties, even from reciting the sacrosanct prayers of the *Shema* (Hear, O Israel) and the *Tefillah* (the Eighteen Benedictions). Taken in their literal sense, the words of Jesus meant that his interlocutor was to leave the burial of his father to other members of the family. This would be a simple reiteration of his principle that the Kingdom of God must be given top priority over all other religious commitments. In other words, in the case of conflicting duties the Kingdom of heaven had to take precedence. Luke's version of the saying makes this clear by adding, 'as for you, go and proclaim the kingdom of God'.

However, if we bear in mind the Jewish custom of almost instant burial of the body, with interment taking place on the day of death before sunset, the Gospel story becomes puzzling. This son on whose shoulders lay the responsibility for the arrangement of the burial of his father, a man who was no doubt in a state of ritual 'corpse' uncleanness, should have been busying himself with funeral matters. Yet we find him by the roadside, possibly (if Matthew is followed) as one of the disciples of Jesus! There is, however, another manner of reading the story. The father of the man whom Jesus had invited to join him was not yet dead. The son's answer to Jesus' invitation to follow him was an evasive 'not now, some time later, after the death of my father'. Such temporization would have provoked an indignant retort from Jesus who firmly believed in the supremacy of today, and in the imperative urgency of the task of the present moment (see also nos. 19 above and 36 below).

27. The harvest and the labourers (Matt. 9:37; Luke 10:2)

The harvest is plentiful, but the labourers are few; pray therefore the Lord of the harvest to send out labourers into his harvest.

The metaphor of the harvest is also used in rabbinic literature. According to Rabbi Tarfon, 'The day is short; the task is great; the labourers are idle; the wage is abundant; the master is pressing' (mAb 2:15). Here the stress is laid not just on the enormity of the task, but also on the lack of time, and the impatience of the master with his hired hands who in spite of their high pay showed themselves to be lazy. Compared with this, the parable of the vineyard (Matt. 20:1–16; cf. chapter 4, no. 23) underlines the generosity of the master and the greed and jealousy of the labourers who were first engaged.

Jesus' harvest simile appears in the context of his Galilean mission, more precisely when he first dispatched his disciples, two by two, according to Luke, to heal the sick and announce the nearness of God's Kingdom (Matt. 10:1, 7). Though their field of action was restricted, encompassing only a small corner of Galilee, the twelve missionaries were faced with a disproportionately large potential clientele. The harvest to bring in was plentiful and the workers few.

The originality of the point of view of Jesus is expressed in turning the harvest into a symbol of eschatological ingathering, or final judgement, at the inauguration of the Kingdom of God.

28. Sheep among wolves (Matt. 10:16; Luke 10:3; cf. Matt. 7:15)

Behold, I send you out as sheep [*lambs* (Luke)] *in the midst of wolves.*

Beware of false prophets, who come to you in sheep's clothing but inwardly are ravenous wolves (Matt. 7).

Jewish literature outside the New Testament includes a number of passages in which predators attack a flock of defenceless sheep. Thus in the Book of Enoch (1 Enoch 90:6–17) the good Jews, depicted as newly-born lambs, are ravaged by ravens, eagles, kites and vultures. The similitude survived until much later and is attested in the rabbinic Midrash Tanhuma (Toledot 5) where it reappears in a fictional exchange between Rabbi Joshua ben Hananiah and the emperor Hadrian. 'Great are the sheep (the Jews) which persist in the midst of seventy wolves (foreign nations)', remarked the emperor. To which Joshua answered, 'Great is the shepherd (God) who saves and protects the sheep and destroys the wolves before them.' In the rabbinic story the sheep are with the shepherd when they are set upon by a pack of wolves. Once more the Gospels manipulate the imagery: the sheep are not attacked by, but are sent among, the wolves. The dispatch of lambs among wolves is an exaggeration typical of the teaching style of Jesus, even though one requires a large dose of hyperbole to describe the unfriendly reception of the apostles in the course of their first mission as a bloody attack on them (cf. Mark 6:11; Matt. 10:14; Luke 9:5; 10:10–11). However, many New Testament scholars prefer to think that the situation corresponds to the hostile treatment met by the missionaries of the primitive church among Jews in the second half of the first century AD. The parallel saying in Matthew 7:15 about false prophets who are like wolves in sheep's clothing applies the imagery to the threat of the false messiahs of the pre-Parousia age (see Mark 13:5–6; Matt. 24:4–5; Luke 21:8 in chapter 8, no. 18).

29. Of sparrows and men (Matt. 10:28–31; Luke 12:4–7; cf. Luke 21:18)

And do not fear those who kill the body but cannot kill the soul; rather fear him who can destroy both soul and body in Gehenna. Are not two sparrows sold for a penny [five sparrows sold for two pennies (Luke)]*? And not one of them will fall to the ground without your Father's will [is forgotten before God* (Luke)]. *But even the hairs of your head are all numbered. Fear not, therefore; you are of more value than many sparrows.*

The main message is encouragement to fearlessness and limitless trust. God's care for birds and *a fortiori* for humans and its eschatological implications have already been considered in connection with 'Look at the birds of the air . . . your heavenly Father feeds them' (Matt. 6:26; Luke 12:24; cf. no. 19 above). Both sayings aim at fostering confident reliance on God, the chief virtue of the teaching of Jesus. The present passage is concerned with the commonest of birds, the sparrow, worth a halfpenny according to Matthew and even slightly less according to Luke. Yet each individual bird is specifically looked after by Providence. So is apparently each hair – counted by God – on every man's head. The latter image is biblical: 'As the Lord lives, there shall not one hair of his head fall to the ground' (1 Sam. 14:45).

Various rabbinic sources illustrate very vividly the same idea of divine concern for birds. They are associated with a legend whose hero is the renowned Rabbi Simeon ben Yohai of the first–second century AD. Emerging for the first time from a cave where he had been hiding for thirteen years during Hadrian's persecution after the second war of the Jews against Rome (AD 132–135), he watched a fowler hunting birds. Each time Simeon heard a heavenly voice decreeing (in Latin) 'escape' (*dimissio*), the fowler missed the bird, but when 'execution' (*specula*) was proclaimed from above, the bird was caught. Simeon ben Yohai's conclusion is similar to that of the Gospel: 'Not even a bird perishes without the will of heaven, how much less the son of man [i.e. "I"]?' (ySheb 38d; Genesis Rabbah 79:6, etc.).

30. Blind leading blind (Matt. 15:14; Luke 6:39)

And if a blind man leads a blind man, both will fall into a pit (Matt.).

Can a blind man lead a blind man? Will they not both fall into a pit? (Luke).

The maxim taken out of context has an obvious general meaning. If the teacher has no true knowledge, both he and his pupils will go astray. In Matthew, but not in Luke, the saying was aimed at the Pharisees, who found it offensive (cf. 15:12). It should be recalled that Matthew (23:16), too, qualifies the Pharisees as blind guides (cf. chapter 2, no. 15). So this saying also is part of the anti-Pharisee rhetoric of Matthew and of the primitive church. Note, however, that in Matthew 23:2–3 the teaching of the Pharisees is commended by Jesus (see chapter 2, no. 15).

31. The corpse and the vultures (Matt. 24:28; Luke 17:37)

Wherever the body is, there the vultures (eagles) will be gathered together.

There is no attestation for this saying in post-biblical literature, but similar images are contained in the Hebrew Bible, such as 'Where the slain are, there is (the vulture)' (Job 39:30). The saying concludes the Q account of the Parousia or coming of the Son of Man. The emphasis is on suddenness and on the destruction of many (Matt. 24:40–41; Luke 17:34–36) and the description concludes with the announcement of the instant arrival of carrion-eaters. The saying in its present form may come from the early church, but eschatological urgency is certainly part of Jesus' world view.

III. WISDOM SAYINGS IN *M*

32. Dogs and swine (Matt. 7:6; Gospel of Thos. 93)

Do not give dogs what is holy; and do not throw your pearls before swine, lest they trample them underfoot and turn to attack you (Matt).

Do not give what is holy to dogs, lest they cast them upon the dunghill (Gospel of Thos.).

This saying appears without a context in the Sermon on the Mount and has no direct parallel in Jewish sources. The dog–swine metaphor requires no elaborate explanation. Both have a pejorative meaning and appear together in the rabbinic proverb, 'Nothing is poorer than a dog and richer than a pig' (bShab 155b). The unclean swine are associated with non-Jewish territories (Mark 5:11; Matt. 8:30; Luke 8:32; 15:15); the wild boar symbolizes Edom (later Rome), and the dogs the Philistines in 1 Enoch 89:42. With the exception of the Latin version of Tobit (11:9) where the family dog is charmingly portrayed as joyfully wagging its tail on its young master's homecoming, dogs are disliked in Jewish literature. In the New Testament (Mark 7:27; Matt. 15:26) and in rabbinic literature they symbolize Gentiles (Midrash on Psalms 4:11) or Samaritans (Genesis Rabbah 81:3). Exceptionally they are associated with bad Jews whose countenance in the eschatological age is expected to resemble 'the face of a dog' (mSotah 9:15). In a similar vein, in the eyes of a late New Testament writer lapsed Christians fulfil the proverb, 'The dog turns back to his own vomit, and the sow is washed only to wallow in the mire' (2 Peter 2:22).

'Do not give dogs what is holy' may be a mistranslation from an Aramaic original. In Jesus' language the same group of consonants *q-d-sh* can be read either as *qedasha* (ring) or *qudsha* (holy thing). The Greek translator, some commentators argue, picked the wrong alternative – 'holy thing' instead of 'ring' – and in doing so spoilt the original parallelism which is thought to be: Do not give a ring to dogs and do not throw a pearl before swine.

Assuming that the saying was actually formulated in Aramaic, the maxim may represent a deliberate pun by Jesus. If so, we detect here an echo of his instruction that the Kingdom of God was to be preached exclusively to Jews (cf. Matt. 10:5–6; 15:24, 26; Mark 7:27; see chapter 8, no. 49). It would also imply that the precious secrets of the Kingdom were to be conveyed only to the Jewish followers of Jesus and denied to the Gentiles as well as unrepentant Jews. The end of the saying, 'lest they . . . turn to attack you', strikes one as secondary, inspired by the hostile reception of the apostolic preaching among Jews (represented as swine).[10]

33. Serpents and doves (Matt. 10:16; Gospel of Thos. 39)

Be wise as serpents and innocent as doves.

Matthew attached this independent logion to the Q saying concerning the sheep sent among the wolves (see no. 28 above). He thus created a truly mixed animal metaphor with lambs being advised to behave like crafty snakes and innocuous pigeons. The cleverness associated with a serpent derives from the Garden of Eden story, and the innocence of the dove is the result of a sympathetic exegesis of Hosea 7:11 in which the epithet 'silly pigeon' applied to the tribe of Ephraim is understood as meaning 'simple dove'. Centuries later the Midrash Rabbah still perpetuated the same images. We read in the Song of Songs Rabbah (2:14): 'God spoke thus of the Jews, "Towards me they are innocent like doves, but among the nations of the world they are as clever as serpents."' If the serpent–dove logion was meant in an eschatological sense, like those preceding it, cleverness and trustful simplicity would be presented – if I may be allowed to modernize and mix even further the metaphors – as necessary requisites for a safe crossing of the minefield leading to the Kingdom of God.

10. The form of the saying preserved in the Gospel of Thomas (93) cannot be original as it spoils the imagery: how do dogs throw holy things on the dunghill?

34. A shrub not planted by God (Matt. 15:13)

Every plant which my heavenly Father has not planted will be rooted up.

The imagery of a plant, tree or orchard is commonly used in the Bible, in the Dead Sea Scrolls and in the rest of Jewish literature to symbolize a living and growing human institution. Members of a community established by God are destined to survive and prosper in troublesome times. They are associated with the biblical 'remnant'. Often they represent the small faithful body of the chosen. By contrast, the shrubs which have taken root without the will of God will be pulled up and destroyed. Matthew's account identifies such a plant with the Pharisees (Matt. 15:12) and this probably reflects the period of conflict between this group and the primitive church in the final decades of the first century AD (see chapter 2, no. 15).

35. Exaltation – humiliation (Matt. 23:12)

Whoever exalts himself will be humbled, and whoever humbles himself will be exalted.

The sentence sounds like a proverb, though it is not one that is recorded in the extant literature. While it is obvious from where the reward and the punishment are expected, mention of God is avoided, as is sometimes the case also in rabbinic maxims. For instance, 'Whoever exalts himself over the words of the Torah, they will humble him ["they" being God and his heavenly court], but whoever humbles himself for the sake of the Torah, at the end they will exalt him' (Sayings of Rabbi Nathan, A 11). Matthew's saying cannot be linked to any particular context in the Gospels either, and serves rather as a multi-purpose concluding remark appended to various passages (cf. Matt. 18:4; Luke 14:11; 18:14). The tone is eschatological and the idea of self-humiliation fits the general outlook of Jesus. See for instance the episode in which Jesus rebuked James and John for requesting for themselves seats of honour (Mark 10:37; Matt. 20:21; see chapter 8, no. 15), or the parable of the marriage feast where guests are advised to occupy the lowest places (Luke 14:7–11; see chapter 4, no. 32).

IV. WISDOM SAYINGS IN *L*

36. The ploughman and the Kingdom (Luke 9:62)

No one who puts his hand to the plough and looks back is fit for the kingdom.

In addition to the need to act without delay when inspired to embrace the cause of those labouring for the Kingdom of God (see Matt. 8:22; Luke 9:59–60; cf. no. 26 above), the prospective seeker must also keep his gaze constantly fixed on the task. He must not hanker after the past like the man willing to follow Jesus only after he has said goodbye to his family. The maxim seems to be patterned on the story of the prophet Elisha, who was busily ploughing a field when he was asked by Elijah to follow him. Elisha first begged for permission to go and kiss his parents, but on second thoughts he changed his mind and ran after Elijah (1 Kings 19:19–21).

REFLECTIONS

Sapiential sayings and proverbs cannot usually be traced to individual authors but rather to popular wisdom. Their aim is to lay down basic rules of ethics and behaviour in colourful, often poetic images. Since the language used in them is figurative and metaphorical, the impact of the sayings depends to a large extent on the social, religious and cultural background of the listeners or readers. In consequence, the same formula is susceptible of multiple interpretation and can possess substantially different meanings depending on the specific slants given to it by various speakers; see the case of the lamp (no. 4), the narrow gate (no. 22), or the harvest (no. 27).

The thirty-six sayings or groups of sayings which have been surveyed represent a mixture of utterances ranging from commonplace wisdom to the most profound personal perception of the relationship between man and man, and man and God. The purpose of these general comments is to pinpoint the link between the maxims and aspects of the character of Jesus revealed in the Synoptic Gospels.

At the end of the previous chapter Jesus was portrayed as a first-century Galilean rural prophet, charismatic healer, exorcist and 'miracle-worker', intent on proclaiming the advent of the Kingdom of God. Do his wisdom sayings and proverbs substantiate this definition?

To start with the rural or village features, the wisdom sayings testify to a rich imagery borrowed from the life of the countryside: Jesus speaks of the birds of the air and the lilies of the field (no. 19); of sparrows (no. 29), foxes, sheep, wolves and snakes (nos. 25, 28, 33); of dogs and pigs (no. 32), of ploughing, harvest, and orchards (nos. 24, 27, 36). The chip and the beam and the house built on sand or rock also recall the life of a villager (nos. 20, 23).

The charismatic aspects of the life of Jesus are reflected in the proverbs relating to the physician (no. 1) and the prophet (no. 8), as well as to the overpowering of the forces of evil (no. 3).

As for the main topic of Jesus' message, the preparation of the disciples for the arrival of the Kingdom of heaven, directly or indirectly most of the wisdom sayings point in that direction (sees also chapters 8 and 9). Jesus' exclusive concern with the evangelization of the Jews is manifest in the proverb about dogs and swine (no. 32). Some of the logia could easily be adapted from their Kingdom of God setting to the later circumstances of early Christianity. For instance, the lamp is first meant to enlighten those within the house, the Jews to whom Jesus preached, but later it gives light to those who come from outside, the Gentiles (see no. 4 above). Likewise the narrow gate is big enough to allow the little flock of Jesus to enter the Kingdom, but it is hard to find, whereas in the perspective of the early church the stress is on the difficulty facing the larger non-Jewish crowds of squeezing through it (see no. 22 above). Nevertheless, it can safely be asserted that the majority of the wisdom sayings accord well with the eschatological message of Jesus.

The study of the parables in the next chapter will shed further light on the eschatological outlook of Jesus.

4

Teaching in Parables

A significant part of the religious message of Jesus has been handed down in the form of parables.[1] Compared with the succinct and vigorous proverbs and the slightly more elaborate, but still brief wisdom counsels, the parables or similitudes are more developed literary compositions. Their style is figurative and their purpose is either to convey a doctrinal instruction about the Kingdom of God or to make a moral point which may be with or without eschatological relevance.

Jesus was, according to Joseph Klausner, the greatest Jewish artist in parables, but was not the inventor of this literary form.[2] Known as *mashal* in Hebrew, the parable is a well-established literary category both in the Bible and in rabbinic writings. *Mashal* has a broader meaning in the Old Testament than in the Gospels, and covers all things sapiential from a brief maxim in the strict sense (the biblical book of Proverbs is called *Meshalim*, the plural of *mashal*) to a riddle or a fable. Perhaps the best-known scriptural riddle is Samson's teaser, 'Out of the eater came something to eat, and out of the strong something sweet' (Judges 14:14), alluding to the honey which Samson found in the carcass of a lion. Solving such riddles was a game played by clever kings and queens. Solomon and the queen of Sheba entertained themselves with them according to the Bible (1 Kings 10), and so did the same Solomon and Hiram, king of Tyre, according to Josephus (*Antiquities* 8:148–9).[3]

1. For the parable as a literary genre, see Frank Kermode, *The Genesis of Secrecy: On the interpretation of narrative* (Cambridge, Mass., 1979).
2. *Jesus of Nazareth: His life, times and teaching* (London, 1925), 414.
3. The deciphering of riddles was a kind of ancient game of gambling. Solomon and Hiram played for money, but what the queen of Sheba had to pay if she lost to the notorious womanizer Solomon is up to the reader to guess.

The biblical fable of the trees which look for a tree-king, but meeting with refusal from the noble olive tree, the fig tree and the vine are finally obliged to elect the worthless bramble (Judges 9:7–15), is set out without an interpretation. In fact the moral is that human kingship amounts to a rebellion against God's exclusive rule and only the wicked are ready to accept it. Other fables are followed by an explanation. The most famous Old Testament parable concerns the ewe-lamb belonging to a poor man which a rich man took by force and killed; it symbolizes King David's illegal union with Bathsheba, wife of one of his officers, Uriah the Hittite (2 Sam. 12:1–4). When David failed to realize that the story recited by Nathan was aimed at him, he was told by the prophet, 'Thou art the man!' (12:7). Isaiah's Song of the Vineyard (Isa. 5:1–7) also gives the clue, namely that the vineyard is Israel. Later Jewish parables which date from the first century AD, such as those in the eschatological Similitudes of Enoch (1 Enoch 37–71), the parable of the struggle between the forest and the sea in 4 Ezra 4:13–18, and the poetic parables of the fortified city and the plantation next to the spring of life in the Qumran Thanksgiving Hymns (cols. 15 and 16 [formerly cols. 7 and 8]), like most New Testament parables are not furnished with explication.

Closest to the parables of Jesus stand those of the rabbis.[4] They regularly follow a fixed pattern. They start with the heading, 'A parable', or 'I will tell you a parable'. Alternatively, they may begin with a question, 'To what can this thing be compared?', and continue with 'This thing can be compared to' (a king, or a man, etc.). The rabbis, unlike Jesus, frequently insert scriptural citations into their parables the meaning of which is clarified by the story. This may be illustrated by a sermon handed down in the name of the early second-century AD Rabbi Meir, the most famous of the parable-tellers (cf. mSot 9:15): 'What does Scripture understand by "For a hanged man is a curse of God" (Deut. 21:23)?[5] It is like twin brothers who resembled one another. One of them became the king of the whole world, the other a bandit. In time the bandit was captured and they hanged him on a

4. See David Stern, *Parables in Midrash: Narrative and exegesis in rabbinic literature* (Cambridge, Mass., 1991).

5. This unusual translation, instead of the customary 'For a hanged man is accursed by God', is given to justify the interpretation intended by Rabbi Meir.

cross. And all the passers-by remarked, "It seems that the king has been crucified." Therefore it is written, "For a hanged man is a curse of God"' (tSanh 9:7).[6]

The use of parables is common in post-biblical literature. The best-informed Christian in Jewish matters of his age, St Jerome, who settled in Bethlehem in the late fourth century AD and had a rabbi as his Hebrew teacher, left us the following telling remark: '[Jews,] Syrians and especially Palestinians are accustomed to add parables to all their discourses so that whatever cannot be fully grasped by the listeners from a simple statement should become intelligible through similitudes and examples' (Commentary on Matt. 18:23 in *Patrologia Latina* xxvi, 132C).

The forty parables contained in the Synoptic Gospels will have to be read in this wider context. I leave to the end their division according to subject matter – into parables based on episodes of daily life, countrymen's parables, social parables, legal parables and parables of marriage.

I. MARK AND THE TRIPLE TRADITION

1a. The parable of the sower (Mark 4:3–9; Matt. 13:3–9; Luke 8:5–8; Gospel of Thos. 9)

A sower went out to sow. And as he sowed, some seed fell along the path [*and was trodden under foot* (Luke)], *and the birds* [*of the air* (Luke)] *came and devoured it. Other seed fell on rocky ground, where it had not much soil, and immediately it sprang up, since it had no depth of soil; and when the sun rose it was scorched, and since it had no root* [*no moisture* (Luke)] *it withered away. Other seed fell among thorns and the thorns grew up and choked it, and it yielded no grain. And other seeds fell into good soil and brought forth grain, growing up and increasing and yielding thirtyfold and sixtyfold and a hundredfold . . . He who has ears to hear, let him hear.*

6. No explanation is supplied, but the message conveyed by the similarity of the twins points to Genesis 1:26–27, where man is said to be the image of God. So even the crucified criminal looks like the King. As a result, the possible confusion dishonours God.

The story of the sower is one of the two Gospel parables which is accompanied by a full interpretation (Mark 4:13–20; Matt. 13:18–23; Luke 8:11–15; see no. 1b below). The other is the tale about the weeds in Matthew 13:36–43 (see no. 17 below). The story describes an everyday happening in the lives of small farmers and agricultural workers in rural Palestine. Note, however, that the commentary, though attributed to Jesus, adopts a point of view different from that of the parable itself.

The parable recalls an account which has been incorporated in the Fourth Book of Ezra, a work dating from the late first century AD: 'For just as the farmer sows many seeds on the ground and plants a multitude of plants, yet not all that have been sown will sprout in due season, neither do all that have been planted take root, so not all those who have been sown in the world shall be saved' (4 Ezra 8:41). In 4 Ezra, the narrative is generic. The farmer does a good job, but as often happens, not every seed or seedling succeeds and grows. Those which do, owe their good fortune to the continued care of the farmer, who caters for their needs by watering them (8:42–45). In 4 Ezra a clearly formulated eschatological conclusion states that some people born into this world will be saved at the end; others will not.

The Gospel parable is enriched with more detail, and is also subtler. The story is not focused on the sower. Indeed, he is depicted as a not wholly efficient countryman who has wasted a good proportion of his seed corn in allowing it to land on the footpath, on rocky ground or among weeds, away from the fertile soil. The rich harvest (thirtyfold to a hundredfold) results not from the labour of the sower, but from the mysterious providentially arranged collaboration between the seed (i.e. the preaching) and the ground (that is, the God-inspired reaction of the listener). The message of the parable, identified by Jesus for his dull-witted disciples as 'the secret of the kingdom of God' (Mark 4:11),[7] is addressed not only to the elect, but to all listeners. If, as is likely, the sower/preacher is Jesus, he is not concentrating on his

7. On the notion of 'mystery', see chapter 3, no. 5, and the Qumran examples cited there. In itself the use of this word does not prove Paul's influence on this passage, as has been suggested by New Testament scholars. See C. H. Dodd, *The Parables of the Kingdom* (London, 1978), 14–15.

own role in spreading the good news, but on the part played by the good soil, namely the listeners ready to respond.

The alleged purpose of Jesus' use of parables will be examined later (cf. below, Reflections, 'The purpose of the parables', page 171), but the interpretation offered to the uncomprehending inner circle, which includes the twelve apostles, needs to be considered now.

1b. The explanation of the parable of the sower (Mark 4:13–20; Matt. 13:18–23; Luke 8:11–15)

And he said to them, *Do you not understand this parable? How then will you understand all the parables? The sower sows the word. And these are the ones along the path, where the word is sown; when they hear, Satan immediately comes and takes away the word which is sown in them* [*that they may not believe and be saved* (Luke)]. *And these in like manner are the ones sown upon rocky ground, who, when they hear the word, immediately receive it with joy; and they have no root in themselves, but endure for a while; then when tribulation or persecution arises on account of the word, immediately they fall away. And others are the ones sown among thorns; they are those who hear the word, but the cares of the world, and the delight in riches, and the desire for other things* [*and pleasures of life* (Luke)], *enter in and choke the word, and it proves unfruitful. But those that were sown upon the good soil are the ones who hear the word and accept it and bear fruit, thirtyfold and sixtyfold and a hundredfold.*

. . . they are those who, hearing the word, hold it fast in an honest and good heart, and bring forth fruit with patience (Luke).

The elements of the interpretation derive directly from the parable itself. There is not a word about the sower and the exegesis endeavours to describe the various reactions to the preaching (seed = word) by the hearers. The conditions of failure serve as a warning: the audience must resist the lures of Satan, persevere in the midst of difficulties and persecution, and make sure that wealth and pleasures do not deter them from obeying the word. On the contrary, they are to listen, consent and act promptly. The picture has the appearance of an eschatological canvas. In particular, tribulations, the obligatory renunciation of riches, worldly comfort and contentment are regular features in any portrayal of the eve of the arrival of the Kingdom. On the other hand, the many obstacles facing the believer, including persecution, may correspond to the situation prevailing in the early church. This is often suggested by commentators on the Gospels. Perhaps the strongest argument in favour of attributing the interpretation to the apostolic church rather than to Jesus is that his original Jewish followers, unlike the later Gentile adherents of Christianity, would not have required such a minute exposition of every single feature of the story. Since the parable is by no means a complex mystery, a general hint would have sufficed. It is noteworthy that more space is given and more effort deployed to account for the failures of the operation than to explain its success. Again, this seems to be the wisdom of hindsight stemming from the failure of the apostles' preaching among Palestinian Jews.

2. The parable of the secretly growing seed (Mark 4:26–29; Gospel of Thos. 21:9–10)

The kingdom of God is as if a man should scatter seed upon the ground, and should sleep and rise night and day, and the seed should sprout and grow, he knows not how. The earth produces of itself, first the blade, then the ear, then the full grain in the ear. But when the grain is ripe, at once he puts in the sickle, because the harvest has come.

After the fruit ripened, he came quickly with the sickle in his hand (and) reaped it. He who has ears to hear, let him hear (Gospel of Thos.).

This second parable of the sower is found only in Mark. Unlike the first, it mentions no failed seeds and dwells on the progressiveness and quasi imperceptibility of the growth of the seed into blade, ear and grain. It is explicitly stated that the spiritual reality symbolized is the Kingdom of God, whose arrival in its time is depicted as a harvest. Once the sowing has been completed, the farmer has only to wait and trust that the soil will, as it were automatically (*automatê* in Greek), produce the grain. The parable insinuates that once the proclamation has been made, progress – expected to be imperceptible – must be left to Providence. Some interpreters see here a concealed condemnation of Zealotism, the forcible promotion of the divine Kingdom of God by political means, as Jesus' revolutionary contemporaries tried to do. It is more likely, however, that the main message is that of faith-trust: one must totally rely on God, who will see to it that his cause triumphs. It is highly significant that the sower (Jesus) is also the harvester. The parable consequently assumes that he will be there to complete his mission.

3. The parable of the mustard seed (Mark 4:30–32; Matt. 13:31–32; Luke 13:18–19; Gospel of Thos. 20)

With what can we compare the kingdom of God, or what parable shall we use for it? It is like a grain of mustard seed, which, when sown upon the ground, is the smallest of all the seeds on earth; yet when it is sown it grows up and becomes the greatest of all shrubs, and puts forth large branches, so that the birds of the air can make nests in its shade.

. . . It is like a grain of mustard seed which a man took and sowed in his garden; and it grew and became a tree . . . (Luke).

'Tell us what the kingdom of heaven is like?' *It is like a grain of mustard seed, smaller than all seeds. But when it falls on the earth, which has been cultivated, it puts forth a great branch and becomes a shelter for the birds of heaven* (Gospel of Thos.).

The parable of the mustard seed continues the theme of the transformation of a seed by the soil. But whereas in the previous cases emphasis lay on the miraculous change taking place underground, here Mark and Matthew stress the incredible disproportion between the tiny seed and the size of the shrub that is produced. Luke discards the reference to the smallness of the seed; perhaps he and his readership were not familiar with it. The Gospel of Thomas offers an abbreviation of the Mark–Matthew version with an additional mention of the cultivated nature of the field. The great metamorphosis of the world into God's Kingdom has insignificant beginnings. Consisting first of Jesus and his small inner circle, the community of the elect is foreseen as expanding beyond all expectation.

To understand the metaphor, we have to bear in mind that in Jewish parlance the mustard seed symbolizes the smallest volume or quantity. When the rabbis speak of a tiny drop of blood they compare it to the size of a mustard seed (yBer 8d; bBer 31b). By contrast, the shrub into which it develops is the largest of its kind: grandiosely it is called a tree. The Galilean Rabbi Simeon ben Halafta of the late second century AD mentions that the mustard bush which he had climbed was as tall as a fig tree (yPeah 20b).

4. The parable of the wicked tenants of the vineyard (Mark 12:1–9; Matt. 21:33–40; Luke 20:9–16; cf. Gospel of Thos. 65)

A man planted a vineyard, and set a hedge around it, and dug a pit for the wine press, and built a tower, and let it out to tenants, and went into another country. When the time came, he sent a servant [*his servants* (Matt.)] *to the tenants, to get from them some of the fruit of the vineyard. And they took him* [*his servants* (Matt.)] *and beat him* [*beat one, killed another, and stoned another* (Matt.)], *and sent him away empty-handed. Again he sent to them another servant and they wounded him in the head and treated him shamefully. And he sent another, and him they killed; and so with many others, some they beat and some they killed. He had still one other, a beloved son; finally he sent him to them, saying, 'They will respect my son.' But those tenants said to one another, 'This is the heir; come, let us kill him, and the inheritance will be ours.' And they took him and killed him, and cast him out of the vineyard. What will the owner of the vineyard do? He will come and destroy the tenants, and give the vineyard to others* (Mark).

Again he sent other servants, more than the first; and they did the same to them (Matt.).

And he sent another servant; him also they beat and treated shamefully, and sent him away empty-handed. And he sent yet a third; this one they wounded and cast out (Luke).

The presumed chronological setting of the parable in the Gospels is Jerusalem in the days preceding the death of Jesus, when a number of controversy stories are also listed (see, for instance, chapter 2, nos. 10–13). All three Synoptic evangelists append to the narrative a biblical citation, 'The very stone which the builders rejected', etc. (Ps. 118:22–23). Although such an association of a parable with Scripture is quite common in rabbinic literature, here the biblical passage is not relevant, and its insertion in the parable is clearly secondary. It will be examined in the section devoted to scriptural interpretation attributed to Jesus (cf. chapter 5, no. 11), but in anticipation it should be pointed out that Psalm 118 was used as a proof text in early Christian debates with Jews (see Acts 4:11; 1 Peter 2:7).

The parable is a fictional account, inspired by the Song of the Vineyard in Isaiah 5:1–7. Some see in it a *pesher* type (i.e. fulfilment) interpretation of biblical history. For others it is an allegory in which each character has a symbolical identity. It typifies what the primitive church conceived as the infidelity and rejection of the Jews, and their replacement by a new (Christian) people of God. The vineyard is the Jewish people and the tenants are their leaders. The absentee landlord is God. The servant-messengers are the prophets represented as persecuted and murdered by the Jewish authorities (see chapter 2, no. 15B), and the beloved son, killed by the tenants, is Jesus. The tenants are destroyed (by the Romans in AD 70; see also the ending of the parable of the royal wedding banquet in Matthew 22:7 in no. 13 below), and the vineyard is inherited by the Gentile church. The meaning is made clear in Matthew's appended comment: 'Therefore

I tell you, the kingdom of God will be taken away from you and given to a nation producing the fruits of it' (Matt. 21:43; see chapter 8, nos. 37 and 49).

The general picture corresponds to the situation prevailing after the destruction of Jerusalem, with a perceived failure of the apostles' preaching to the Jews and the overall take-over of the Jesus movement by the church of the Gentiles. The theme of the Kingdom of God is lacking in this parable apart from the secondary mention of the phrase in Matthew's gloss (Matt. 21:43), quoted above.

5. The parable of the fig tree (Mark 13:28–29; Matt. 24:32–33; Luke 21:29–31)

From the fig tree learn its lesson: [*Look at the fig tree, and all the trees:* (*Luke*)] *as soon as its branch becomes tender and puts forth its leaves, you know that summer is near. So also, when you see these things taking place, you know that he is near, at the very gates* [*that the kingdom of God is near* (Luke)].

This brief parable is inserted by the redactors of the Gospels towards the end of the so-called Eschatological Discourse (Mark 13; Matt. 24; Luke 21). It immediately follows the announcement of the coming of the son of Man (see chapter 7, no. 19). Read in the latter perspective, the parable concludes with the assertion that the Parousia or Second Coming of Christ, a substitute for the impending inauguration of the Kingdom, is imminent. However, if the passage is taken separately, the conclusion chosen by Luke, namely that the Kingdom of God is near, can be maintained.[8] In a presumed Semitic original following the model of Amos 8:2, the terms 'summer' (*qayiz*) and 'end' (*qeyz*) would form a pun, but even without envisaging such a Hebrew play on words, summer indicates the closeness of harvest time, which in turn brings to mind the idea of the final judgement. Nevertheless, one should remember that the fig tree is said to be a sign which helps to foretell

8. The Greek phrase *engus estin*, usually rendered as '*he* is near', can just as well be understood, '*it* [i.e. the Kingdom] is near'.

the future and that Jesus, opposed to chronological speculation, was unwilling to provide such pointers.

For the cursing of the fig tree, see Mark 11:13–14; Matt. 21:19 in chapter 1, no. 21.

6. The parable of the doorkeeper (Mark 13:33–37; Matt. 25:14–15; 24:42; 25:13; Luke 19:12–13; 12:38)

Take heed, watch; for you do not know when the time will come. It is like a man going on a journey, when he leaves home and puts his servants in charge, each with his work, and commands the doorkeeper to be on the watch. Watch therefore – for you do not know when the master of the house will come, in the evening, or at midnight, or at cockcrow, or in the morning – lest he come suddenly and find you asleep. And what I say to you I say to all: Watch (Mark).

For it will be as when a man going on a journey called his servants and entrusted to them his property; . . . to each according to his ability. Then he went away (Matt. 25:14–15).

Watch therefore, for you do not know on what day your Lord is coming (Matt. 24).

Watch therefore, for you know neither the day nor the hour (Matt. 25:13).

A nobleman went into a far country to receive kingly power and then return. Calling ten of his servants, he gave them ten pounds . . . (Luke 19:12–13).

If he comes in the second watch, or in the third, and finds them so, blessed are those servants! (Luke 12:38).

The parable of the doorkeeper is used only by Mark to illustrate general admonitions to watchfulness in the final age while the master of the house is absent. Matthew and Luke also reproduce the same counsel to be alert, but insert it in different places (see no. 16 below).

The most likely ideological setting is once more the expectation of the Parousia, and probably of a greatly delayed Parousia, rather than that of the imminently awaited Kingdom which prevailed during the ministry of Jesus. The chief character of the story in Mark and Matthew is a merchant who departs on a long business trip; Luke in turn speaks of a nobleman invited to become king in a distant country. The intention of the traveller to return to his homeland is a tacit allusion to the Second Coming. The evangelists seem to have mixed two stories, one about a businessman and the other about a prince. As the precise moment of return of either was unknown to their servants, both accounts culminate in the customary admonition to continuous vigilance, a hallmark of the Parousia expectancy.

II. THE TRADITION OF MATTHEW AND LUKE (Q)

7. The parable of reconciliation before appearing in court (Matt. 5:25–26; Luke 12:58–59)

For the fragmentary simile advising a settlement out of court, see chapter 3, no. 13.

8. The parable of the two builders (Matt. 7:24–27; Luke 6:47–49)

Every one then who hears these words of mine and does them will be like a wise man who built his house upon the rock; and the rain fell, and the floods came, and the winds blew and beat upon that house, but it did not fall, because it had been founded on the rock. And every one who hears these words of mine and does not do them will be like a foolish man who built his house upon the sand; and the rain fell, and the floods came, and the winds blew and beat against that house, and it fell; and great was the fall of it (Matt.).

Every one who comes to me and hears my words and does them, I will show you what he is like: he is like a man building a house, who dug deep, and laid the foundation upon rock; and when a flood arose, the stream broke against the house, and could not shake it, because it had been well built. But he who hears and does not do them is like a man who built a house on the ground without a foundation; against which the stream broke, and immediately it fell, and the ruin of that house was great (Luke).

The simile of the house built by the righteous and by the wicked is familiar both from the Bible and from post-biblical Jewish literature. The wise man's house withstands the storm; that of the fool is blown over. The Book of Proverbs contains several examples of this kind. 'When the tempest passes the wicked is no more, but the righteous is established for ever' (Prov. 10:25). And again, 'The house of the wicked will be destroyed, but the tent of the upright will flourish' (Prov. 14:11). Two of the Thanksgiving Hymns from among the Dead Sea Scrolls also employ the appropriate architectural imagery. One speaks of a fortified city whose foundation is set on the rock and whose walls will be built with solidly laid tried stones (1QH 14[formerly 6]: 24–26). In the other we similarly encounter an edifice constructed on eternal foundations and fortified with a strong tower and high well-built walls which will never be shaken (1QH 15[formerly 7]:8–9). The same pictorial representation continues in rabbinic literature where the early second-century heretic rabbi, Elisha ben Abuyah, compares the virtuous wise man to a builder who 'first lays stones and then bricks. Even when much water rises and lies against them, they will not be dislodged' (Abot de-R. Nathan, A 24). The same teaching is formulated with the metaphor of a tree with strong roots substituted for the image of the house (cf. chapter 3, no. 24). It is developed as an answer by Rabbi Eleazar ben Azariah (late first century AD) to the question, 'He whose works are more abundant than his wisdom, to what is he likened?': 'To a tree whose branches are few, but whose roots are many; so that even if all the winds in the world come and blow against it, it cannot be stirred from its place' (mAb 3:18, commenting on Jer. 17:8).

The message of Jesus is that by accepting and putting into practice his teaching, his disciples erect a solid house which will survive and give shelter amid the calamities expected to signal the approaching

Kingdom of God. But the simile remains meaningful even when eschatological urgency is no longer felt.

For the church to be built on Peter, the Rock, see chapter 9, no. 23.

9. The parable of children playing (Matt. 11:16–19; Luke 7:31–35)

But to what shall I compare this generation? It is like children sitting in the market places and calling to their playmates, 'We piped to you, and you did not dance; we wailed, and you did not mourn.' For John came neither eating nor drinking, and they say, 'He has a demon'; the Son of Man came eating and drinking, and they say, 'Behold, a glutton and a drunkard, a friend of tax-collectors and sinners!' Yet wisdom is justified by her deeds [*by all her children* (Luke)].

The brief parable concerning spoilsport children is meant to illustrate reactions among Jews to the appeal to repentance at the approach of God's Kingdom made first by John the Baptist and then by Jesus. A group of children, urged by their friends to 'play' a burial game with them in a public square or to pretend to participate in a joyful festival, refuse in both cases. The Gospel accounts suggest that both messengers of the Kingdom, the ascetic John and the sociable Jesus, had substantial popular following in the country, but were given a cool or hostile reception by the leading classes of Jerusalem (cf. chapter 8, no. 41).

10. The parable of the demon returning to his former home (Matt. 12:43–45; Luke 11:24–26)

When the unclean spirit has gone out of a man, he passes through waterless places seeking rest, but he finds none. Then he says, 'I will return to my house from which I came.' And when he comes, he finds it empty, swept, and put in order. Then he goes and brings with him seven other spirits more evil than himself, and they enter and dwell there; and the last state of that man becomes worse than the first. [*So shall it be also with this evil generation* (Matt.).]

This parable-like saying is connected to the wisdom maxim examined in chapter 3, no. 3. It serves as a warning to 'this evil generation', presumably the last one dominated by satanic forces, that unless their repentance and faith, necessary for spiritual liberation, are profound and lasting, the old devil and fresh companions are likely to stage a homecoming from the desert of their exile.[9] The setting is in an era characterized by the practice of exorcism. It fits the ministry of Jesus, but also that of his immediate followers in the primitive church who continued his charismatic activity, as described in the Acts of the Apostles. The concluding sentence in Matthew suggests the former; its absence from Luke, the latter. In this regard, it should be borne in mind that Luke, worried by the delay of the Parousia, had a general tendency to dilute the eschatological content of Jesus' teaching (cf. *The Changing Faces of Jesus*, 219).

11. The parable of the leaven (Matt 13:33; Luke 13:20–21)

The kingdom of heaven is like leaven which a woman took and hid in three measures of flour, till it was all leavened.

To what shall I compare the kingdom of God? It is like leaven . . . (Luke).

After the agricultural similes cited in the parables of the sower, the secretly growing seed and the mustard seed (nos. 1, 2 and 3 above) which are intended to express the idea of a period of imperceptible gestation before the manifestation of the Kingdom of God, Q offers here a domestic version of the same teaching. This concept of a peaceful arrival of the Kingdom stands against another, less common representation in which it bursts violently into the world (Matt. 11:12; Luke 16:16; cf. chapter 8, no. 40).

The text speaks of three *seahs* of flour (a *seah* = *c.* 22 litres) mysteri-

9. For the return of an exorcized demon, see chapter 1, no. 17.

ously and powerfully raised by a small amount of leaven to produce a large quantity of bread. The tacit message addressed to the workers for the Kingdom of heaven concerns confidence in divine Providence, which will in time bring their labour to fruition. The same (positive) quality of the leaven is mentioned in 1 Corinthians 5:6, 'Do you not know that a little leaven leavens the whole lump [of dough]?'

But the leaven metaphor is frequently used to denote a trend towards corruption and doctrinal error, hence the warning against the leaven of the Pharisees, Sadducees and Herodians (Mark 8:15; Matt. 16:6; Luke 12:1; see chapter 2, no. 14). The negative idea is reflected in rabbinic literature, too, where it is linked to the notion of the evil inclination (*yezer ra'*). A Gentile barber-astrologer became a proselyte without purifying himself of all the old leaven still active in him. As a result he reverted to his ancestral paganism (yAZ 41a). In the Passover–Easter context it is the absence of leaven that represents perfection: 'Cleanse out the old leaven that you may be a new lump, as you really are unleavened' (1 Cor. 5:7).

12. The parable of the lost sheep (Matt. 18:12–14; Luke 15:4–7; Gospel of Thos. 107)

What do you think? If a man has a hundred sheep, and one of them has gone astray, does he not leave the ninety-nine on the mountains and go in search of the one that went astray? And if he finds it, truly, I say to you, he rejoices over it more than over the ninety-nine that never went astray. So it is not the will of my Father who is in heaven that one of these little ones should perish (Matt.).

What man of you, having a hundred sheep, if he has lost one of them, does not leave the ninety-nine in the wilderness and go after the one which is lost, until he finds it? And when he has found it, he lays it on his shoulders, rejoicing. And when he comes home, he calls together his friends and neighbours, saying to them, 'Rejoice with me, for I have found my sheep which was lost.' Just so, I tell you, there will be more joy in heaven over one sinner who repents than over ninety-nine righteous persons who need no repentance (Luke).

The kingdom is like a shepherd who had one hundred sheep. One of them went away, it was the largest. He left the ninety-nine and sought for the one until he found it. After he had exerted himself, he said to the sheep, 'I love you more than the ninety-nine' (Gospel of Thos.).

Matthew, Luke and the Gospel of Thomas offer three different versions of this famous parable. While he looks for the single lost sheep, the shepherd leaves his flock on the mountains in Matthew, or in the wilderness in Luke. The story ends with the emphasis laid on God's fatherly care for sheep, birds and animals symbolizing the simple and the innocent (see Matt. 6:26; Luke 12:24; Matt. 8:20; Luke 9:58; Matt. 10:29; Luke 12:6; cf. chapter 3, nos. 19, 25, 29). So the shepherd can be either God or, more likely, Jesus, seeking the lost sheep of Israel (Matt. 10:6; 15:24; cf. chapter 8, no. 49). In the latter case, the metaphor reflects the portrait of Jesus focusing on the lost, for example publicans and prostitutes. It is very different from the overstated image of Jesus dispatching his lambs among wolves (see chapter 3, no. 28). As for the Gospel of Thomas, its stance differs from both Matthew and Luke. Here the largest sheep goes astray, the one of which the shepherd is particularly fond. One would imagine that Jesus, with his liking for 'children', would have preferred the smallest one. Matthew and Luke echo here one of the most authentic teachings of Jesus which he may have formulated differently on successive occasions.

Rabbinic literature also refers to a man in charge of a dozen animals – symbols of the twelve Patriarchs of the Israelite tribes – who abandoned eleven of them in order to look for the missing twelfth. The drift of the tale is, however, quite different. The midrash speaks of beasts of burden owned by a merchant which were loaded with wine jars. So in order to ensure that no one could render the wine ritually unclean, and thus unfit for consumption by a Jew, the owner left the eleven animals in a public square where they were under constant observation, and set out to retrieve the missing one (Genesis Rabbah 86:4). The story is intended to explain why according to Genesis 39:2 the Lord had to protect the patriarch Joseph. He, the youngest of the sons of Jacob, was alone in Egypt while his eleven brothers lived in safety under the care of their father. As has been observed again and again, Jesus himself had a tendency to twist metaphors and folk tales to convey a fresh insight.

13. The parable of the wedding feast (Matt. 22:2–14; Luke 14:16–24; cf. Gospel of Thos. 64)

The kingdom of heaven may be compared to a king who gave a marriage feast for his son, and sent his servants to call those who were invited to the marriage feast; but they would not come. Again he sent other servants, saying, 'Tell those who are invited, Behold, I have made ready my dinner, my oxen and my fat calves are killed, and everything is ready; come to the marriage feast.' But they made light of it and went off, one to his farm, another to his business, while the rest seized his servants, treated them shamefully, and killed them. The king was angry, he sent his troops and destroyed those murderers and burned their city. Then he said to his servants, 'The wedding is ready, but those invited were not worthy. Go therefore to the thoroughfares and invite to the marriage feast as many as you find.' And those servants went out into the streets and gathered all whom they found, both bad and good; so the wedding hall was filled with guests. But when the king came in to look at the guests, he saw there a man who had no wedding garment; and he said to him, 'Friend, how did you get in here without a wedding garment?' And he was speechless. Then the king said to the attendants, 'Bind him hand and foot, and cast him into the outer darkness; there men will weep and gnash their teeth.' For many are called, but few are chosen (Matt.).

A man once gave a great banquet and invited many; and at the time for the banquet he sent his servant to say to those who had been invited, 'Come, for all is now ready.' But they all alike began to make excuses. The first said to him, 'I have bought a field, and I must go out and see it; I pray you, have me excused.' And another said, 'I have bought five yoke of oxen, and I go to examine them; I pray you, have me excused.' And another said, 'I have married a wife, and therefore I cannot come.' So the servant came and reported this to his master. Then the householder in anger said to his servant, 'Go out quickly to the streets and lanes of the city, and bring in the poor and maimed and blind and lame.' And the servant said, 'Sir, what you commanded has been done, and still there is room.' And the master said to the servant, 'Go out to the highways and hedges, and compel people to come in, that my house may be filled. For I tell you, none of those men who were invited shall taste my banquet' (Luke, Gospel of Thos.).

This long parable has been preserved in two forms, but even these two surviving literary units testify to a sequence of prior redactional changes. The basic scheme is that of a great dinner party to which numerous important guests have been invited. However, none of them turns up and all plead more pressing duties which could not have been foreseen. As a result, the host replaces them by outcasts or passers-by.

Luke's version is less complex than that of Matthew although it too shows signs of re-editing. It envisages a lavish dinner party (not a wedding feast) prepared by a rich man (not a king). An invitation is sent in advance to wealthy friends and on the day itself a servant is dispatched to remind each of them. When they all send their apologies, the same servant is ordered to bring along the poor and the physically disabled. Here comes an unexpected new development: there are not enough local beggars and cripples to fill the hall. As a result, others from beyond the city boundaries are forced to join in, and those on the original guest list are declared *personae non gratae* for ever.

Matthew's material reveals the hand of several editors. Originally it is a Kingdom of heaven parable. The chief character is a king and the occasion is the wedding of his son, to be celebrated with a great festive dinner. A group of servants (not just one) go out to call the invited guests. But these are so rude that they do not even send excuses but carry on with their business. Here the redactor of Matthew introduces an unexpected and inappropriate feature, the ill-treatment and murder of the servants by some of those invited, followed by the instant punishment of the criminals and the destruction of their city by fire. If we discard this supplement which is an unmistakable allusion to the end of Jerusalem in AD 70, the original story continues with the replacement of the unworthy by people found in the thoroughfares. Yet another remark spoils the narrative: the new dinner company consists, not of the worthy poor and sick, but of 'bad and good' people alike.

The mention of 'bad' guests joining the royal banquet serves as a stepping-stone for the additional parable of the wedding garment. Only those wearing the proper apparel (i.e. the good) are allowed to partake in the festal repast; the others are thrown into the outer darkness. Since it is unreasonable to expect that the people brought in from the highways and byways should wear their best clothes, we can take it for granted that this section of the story had an independent existence prior to its insertion in its present context.

Like the parable of the wise and foolish virgins in Matthew 25:1–13 (see no. 25 below), this tale is a warning to be ready when H-hour strikes on D-day. Rabbinic parallels can be cited to support this interpretation. A parable handed down in the name of Rabban Yohanan ben Zakkai of the first century AD describes a banquet organized by a king for his courtiers without telling them the day and the hour. The clever among them dressed up and continued to wait at the gate of the palace, while the improvident carried on with their business in working clothes, expecting to be informed in good time. All of a sudden the order to enter came, and the foolish ones were not allowed to sit down at table and had to watch the others eating and drinking (bShab 153a).

Without taking into account the secondary elements about the murderous prospective guests, Matthew's royal wedding feast or messianic banquet allegorizes the substitution of the Gentile church – the people collected from the thoroughfares – for the Jews who were unresponsive, first to the preaching of Jesus, and later to that of the apostles. It runs parallel with Matthew's clear statement that 'the sons of the kingdom will be thrown into the outer darkness' and their place will be taken by non-Jews (Matt. 8:11–12; cf. chapter 8, no. 37). The account is influenced, not to say contaminated, by the parable of the savage tenants of the vineyard (Matt. 21:33–40; cf. no. 4 above) from which the killing of the servants and the consequent punishment of the murderers derive.

As for the story about the dinner party told by Luke, in its original form it reflects the ministry of Jesus, who was turned down by the bourgeois Galilean leadership but gratefully welcomed by the Jewish social outcasts. However, since not enough of the latter could be found, the invitation was extended further. This is no doubt a revised version of the 'Jewish' parable. It recalls a rabbinic anecdote about a certain tax-collector by the name of Bar Ma'yan, who organized a dinner party for the city councillors. When they failed to turn up, the disappointed publican offered their places to the poor. This was his only good deed during his whole life, but he was rewarded for it by God when he died (ySanh 23c; yHag 77d). The introduction of the second set of dinner guests recruited from outside the city (the non-Jews) is an alteration introduced by Luke in conformity with his pro-Gentile interest.

In sum, the parable of the great banquet or wedding feast, when properly analysed, reveals three stages of development. The first presents the despised pariahs of Jewry as the new elect (Luke 1). The second includes also non-Jews (Luke 2). The third, the later common Christian understanding of the parable, substitutes the Gentiles for the ungrateful, indeed murderous Jews (Matthew).

14. The parable of the burglar (Matt. 24:43–44; Luke 12:39–40; cf. Gospel of Thos. 103)

But know this, that if the householder had known in what part of the night the thief was coming, he would have watched and would not have let his house be broken into. Therefore you also must be ready; for the Son of man is coming at an hour you do not expect.

The brief simile about the thief striking at an unforeseeable moment of the night represents the class of warnings which enjoin alertness and watchfulness (see the parable of the doorkeeper, no. 6 above; cf. also Matt. 25:13 at no. 25 below). The concluding comment concerning the unpredictability of the arrival of the Son of man[10] shows that the subject of the saying is the Parousia, the return of Christ. Perhaps the main difference between Jesus' teaching about the coming of the Kingdom and the church's preaching about the Parousia is that the former demands action whereas the latter consists in vigilant, yet passive, expectation. The same image of the burglar is used also by Paul in the First Letter to the Thessalonians, where he admonishes his followers: 'For you yourselves know well that the day of the Lord will come like a thief in the night' (5:2).

15. The faithful and wise servant (Matt. 24:45–51; Luke 12:42–46; cf. Luke 12:47–48)

Who then is the faithful and wise servant, whom his master has set over his household, to give them their food at the proper time? Blessed is that servant whom his master when he comes will find so doing. Truly, I say to you, he will set him over all his possessions. But if that [*wicked* (Matt.)] *servant says to himself, 'My master is delayed', and begins to beat his fellow servants* [*the menservants and the maidservants* (Luke)], *and eats and drinks with the drunken* [*and gets drunk* (Luke)], *the master of that servant will come on a day when he does not expect him and at an hour he does not know, and will punish him, and put him with the hypocrites* [*the unfaithful* (Luke)]; [*there men will weep and gnash their teeth* (Matt.)].

And that servant who knew his master's will, but did not make ready or act according to his will, shall receive a severe beating. But he who did not know, and did what deserved a beating, shall receive a light beating. Every one to whom much is given, of him will much be required; and of him to whom men commit much they will demand the more (Luke 12:47–48).

In its present form the parable, which is without narrative setting or application, is clear in its main message, but confused in its

10. For 'Son of man', see chapter 7, no. 23.

formulation. Does the parable-teller envisage one servant who can turn out either good or bad, or one good and one villainous servant? Be that as it may, the task of this estate manager is to care for the other servants during the absence of the master, the date of whose return is unknown. The behaviour of the wicked servant implies that the master is not urgently expected. The most likely message conveyed by the story is a warning to those church leaders in whom eschatological urgency was already on the wane. They should realize that their lord will appear one day to reward the faithful and punish the wicked. Repeated mention of drunkenness in the churches of St Paul may highlight the social background of this parable (1 Cor. 5:11; 11:20–21; 1 Tim. 3:3, 8; Tit. 1:7). The mention of 'hypocrites' in Matthew is seen by some interpreters as a possible original criticism of the scribes and Pharisees, but such an exegesis is much less natural than the one proposed here.

The supplement appended to this parable by the editor of Luke about severe and light punishment represents further speculation on the theme within the church. The conclusion is a proverb without the twist characterizing Jesus' saying on disproportionate remuneration in chapter 3, no. 7.

See also the parable of the servant's reward (Luke 17:7–10) in no. 38 below.

16. The parable of the talents (Matt. 25:14–30; Luke 19:11–27)

For it will be as when a man going on a journey called his servants and entrusted to them his property; to one he gave five talents, to another two, to another one, to each according to his ability. Then he went away. He who had received the five talents went at once and traded with them; and he made five talents more. So also, he who had the two talents made two talents more. But he who had received the one talent went and dug in the ground and hid his master's money. Now after a long time the master of those servants came and settled accounts with them. And he who had received the five talents came forward, bringing five talents more, saying, 'Master, you delivered to me five talents; here I have made five talents more.' His master said to him, 'Well done, good and faithful servant; you have been faithful over a little, I will set you over much; enter into the joy of your master.' And he also who had the two talents came forward, saying, 'Master, you delivered to me two talents; here I have made two talents more.' His master said to him, 'Well done, good and faithful servant; you have been faithful over a little, I will set you over much; enter into the joy of your master.' He also who had received the one talent came forward, saying, 'Master, I knew you to be a hard man, reaping where you did not sow, and gathering where you did not winnow; so I was afraid, and I went and hid your talent in the ground. Here you have what is yours.' But his master answered him, 'You wicked and slothful servant! You knew that I reap where I have not sowed, and gather where I have not winnowed? Then you ought to have invested my money with the bankers, and at my coming I should have received my own with interest. So take the talent from him and give it to him who has the ten talents. For to every one who has will more be given, and he will have abundance; but from him who has not, even what he has will be taken away. And cast the worthless servant into the outer darkness; there men will weep and gnash their teeth' (Matt.).

He proceeded to tell a parable, because he was near to Jerusalem, and because they supposed that the kingdom of God was to appear immediately. He said therefore, *A nobleman went into a far country to receive a kingdom and then return. Calling ten of his servants, he gave them ten minas, and said to them, 'Trade with these till I come.' But his citizens hated him and sent an embassy after him, saying, 'We do not want this man to reign over us.' When he returned, having received the kingdom, he commanded these servants, to whom he had given money, to be called to him, that he might know what they had gained by trading. The first came before him, saying, 'Lord, your mina has made ten minas more.' And he said to him, 'Well done, good servant! Because you have been faithful in a very little, you shall have authority over ten cities.' And the second came, saying, 'Lord, your mina has made five minas.' And he said to him, 'And you are to be over five cities.' Then another came, saying, 'Lord, here is your mina, which I kept laid away in a napkin; for I was afraid of you, because you are a severe man; you take up what you did not lay down, and reap what you did not sow.' He said to him, 'I will condemn you out of your own mouth, you wicked servant! You knew that I was a severe man, taking up what I did not lay down, and reaping what I did not sow? Why then did you not put my money into the bank, and at my coming I should have collected it with interest?' And he said to those who stood by, 'Take the mina from him, and give it to him who has ten minas.' (And they said to him, 'Lord, he has ten minas!') 'I tell you, that to every one who has will more be given; but from him who has not, even what he has will be taken away. But as for these enemies of mine, who did not want me to reign over them, bring them here and slay them before me'* (Luke).

The original parable has been handed down in two versions of which Matthew's is the more straightforward. A rich merchant, before setting off on a journey, entrusts varying sums of money to three of his servants with the instruction to use them for trading. Two do so successfully and double their capital, but the timid third one just hides his talent, the equivalent of 10,000 denarii or drachms,[11] and thus makes no profit. The first two are praised, rewarded and promoted by the master when he returns after a long absence, but the third is rebuked for not having invested the sum with the money merchants. He is dismissed, and the money which he did not use for profit-making is confiscated and handed over to the most enterprising and successful of them (see chapter 3, no. 7). The moral of the story is that in the context of the expectation of the Kingdom those who work for it must not fear taking risks to achieve success. Understood in this sense, the parable would not be alien to the outlook of Jesus. The two objections against attributing it to him arise from the urban, as against the usual

11. According to the parable of the hired hands for the vineyard (Matt. 20:2), one denarius was a day's wage for a hired labourer.

rural topic, and from the specific mention of the master's return 'after a long time', that is, at the Parousia.

The substance of Luke's account (19:13, 15–26) corresponds to Matthew's parable, but the monetary unit is the mina (=100 denarii), and the framework is totally different. It probably results from the amalgamation of a separate story with the present one. The leading character is not a merchant but a nobleman, and the purpose of his journey to a distant country is to be made king there. Quite unconnected with the commission of the ten servants (19:13), the storyteller alludes to a rebellion by the citizens against the ruler and to an embassy sent by them to warn him not to come back. Then follows inconsequentially the interview with the ten servants, and the execution of the traitors forms the abrupt ending of the account. Luke does not explicitly refer to a long absence. On the other hand, in an introductory phrase he states that the parable, that is the departure from home of the nobleman, was told in order to pour cold water on the expectation of the imminent arrival of the Kingdom of God (Luke 19:11). The story has no parallel in the teaching of Jesus and it is hard to see how the anecdote would fit within his perspective.

A prince's journey for royal appointment and its successful outcome make an unusual story. It has been suggested that the narrator was inspired by Herod Archelaus' efforts in Rome to obtain the title of king on the death of his father, Herod the Great, in 4 BC. Josephus reports that he was opposed there by a delegation of fifty Jews who petitioned Augustus for autonomy from the Herodian dynasty (*War* 2:80; *Antiquities* 17:299–300). Unlike the nobleman of the Gospel story, Archelaus was denied the royal dignity and had to put up with the title of ethnarch or national leader. How and for what purpose the evangelist could turn this episode into a parable of Jesus is hard to imagine. In any case, the whole of Luke 19:11–27 seems to be a shambles.

III. PARABLES IN MATTHEW (*M*)

17. The parable and interpretation of the weeds (Matt. 13:24–30, 36–43; cf. Gospel of Thos. 57)

The kingdom of heaven may be compared to a man who sowed good seed in his field; but while men were sleeping, his enemy came and sowed weeds among the wheat, and went away. So when the plants came up and bore grain, then the weeds appeared also. And the servants of the householder came and said to him, 'Sir, did you not sow good seed in your field? How then has it weeds?' He said to them, 'An enemy has done this.' The servants said to him, 'Then do you want us to go and gather them?' But he said, 'No; lest in gathering the weeds you root up the wheat along with them. Let both grow together until the harvest; and at harvest time I will tell the reapers, Gather the weeds first and bind them in bundles to be burned, but gather the wheat into my barn.' . . .

And his disciples came to him, saying, 'Explain to us the parable of the weeds of the field.' He answered, *He who sows the good seed is the Son of man; the field is the world, and the good seed means the sons of the kingdom; the weeds are the sons of the evil one, and the enemy who sowed them is the devil; the harvest is the close of the age, and the reapers are angels. Just as the weeds are gathered and burned with fire, so will it be at the close of the age. The Son of man will send out his angels, and they will gather out of his kingdom all causes of sin and all evildoers, and throw them into the furnace of fire; there men will weep and gnash their teeth. Then the righteous will shine like the sun in the kingdom of their Father. He who has ears, let him hear.*

The description of the field producing wheat and weeds, one sowed by the farmer, the other by his malevolent neighbour, is one of two Gospel parables which are furnished with a detailed interpretation. The other is the parable of the sower (see nos. 1a and 1b above). According to the commentary, the work of Matthew or one of his editors, the story is an allegory in which each feature of the parable has its precise equivalent: the sower is Jesus, the Son of Man; the field is the world; the good seeds are the righteous (the sons of the Kingdom) and the weeds, the sons of the devil; the enemy is Satan; the harvest is the end of the world and the reapers are the angels. We are shown in this allegory the destruction of the wicked and the salvation of the righteous at the final judgement presided over by the "Son of Man" (see chapter 7, no. 26). In short, this is a post-Parousia event sketched for or by the apostolic church.

One important feature of the parable is left untouched by the interpreter. The servants of the farmer volunteer to pull up the weeds, but are told to let them coexist with the wheat and wait for the time of the harvest to separate them. This may point to the original significance of the parable as conceived by Jesus. The workers for the Kingdom should devote themselves to positive action; they must leave judgement to God at the moment chosen by him, and known to him alone.

18. The parable of the hidden treasure (Matt. 13:44; Gospel of Thos. 109)

The kingdom of heaven is like a treasure hidden in a field, which a man found and covered up; then in his joy he goes and sells all that he has and buys that field (Matt.).

The kingdom is like a man who had a treasure hidden in his field, and did not know it. And when he died he left it to his son, who also knew nothing about it and accepted the field, and sold it. And the buyer went, and while he was ploughing he found the treasure. And he began to lend at interest to whomever he wished (Gospel of Thos.).

The message conveyed by Jesus' parable is simple: the Kingdom of heaven is worth everything one possesses. The man while ploughing someone else's field stumbles on a buried jar filled with money. He reburies it, and turning all his property into cash acquires the plot of land with, according to Jewish law, 'whatever is in it' (mBB 4:9). The moral of the parable is urgency combined with absolute readiness to sacrifice everything for the Kingdom of God.

The treatment of the hidden treasure in the Gospel of Thomas illustrates the general unreliability of this document as a source of the sayings of Jesus. The perfectly clear and deeply meaningful Gospel parable is completely distorted and the final outcome of the accidental find is that the discoverer becomes a greedy moneylender, an occupation forbidden by the Mosaic Law.

The story itself belongs to the saga of hidden treasures well known in oriental and Jewish folklore. The Copper Scroll from Qumran Cave 3, which may (though probably does not) refer to real treasure, is the latest addition to the list. It enumerates sixty-four different hoards concealed in as many hiding-places.

19. The parable of the precious pearl (Matt. 13:45–46)

Again, the kingdom of heaven is like a merchant in search of fine pearls, who, on finding one pearl of great value, went and sold all that he had and bought it.

The parable about the precious pearl is the twin sister of that concerning the hidden treasure and conveys the same doctrine. The difference, if any, between the two is that the purchase of the pearl entails commercial competitiveness and risk-taking, and as such stresses the deliberate and urgent character of the eschatological quest.

20. The parable of the net (Matt. 13:47–50)

Again, the kingdom of heaven is like a net which was thrown into the sea and gathered fish of every kind; when it was full, men drew it ashore and sat down and sorted the good into vessels but threw away the bad. So it will be at the close of the age. The angels will come out and separate the evil from the righteous, and throw them into the furnace of fire; there men will weep and gnash their teeth.

The parable of the net, or perhaps more exactly of the catch by means of a net, belongs to that class of eschatological similitudes which envisage a forensic denouement of religious history in the form of a final judgement. The fishermen first gather in their net all kinds of fish, then the catch is sorted out. The edible fish are set aside and the inedible thrown away. In this form the parable has no doctrine to inculcate apart from a banal warning to be good. But the meaningful message underlying it consists in an encouragement to the 'fishers of men' of the eschatological age to cast their net into the water in search of the good fish. The net and the catch imagery complete the Galilean country parables of the Gospels based on the work of the farmer, the shepherd and the fisherman.

21. The parable of the homeowner (Matt. 13:52)

Every scribe who has been trained for the kingdom of heaven is like a householder who brings out of his treasure what is new and what is old.

The parable portrays a Jewish-Christian teacher, a 'rabbi' of the Jesus party, perhaps the evangelist himself, who, as the many scriptural proof texts cited in Matthew's Gospel demonstrate, was well-versed in the old treasure of biblical doctrine and in the new eschatological message proclaimed by Jesus. The 'old' scribes were expert interpreters of Scripture (Matt. 7:29), whereas those of the Kingdom, the Jewish-Christian teachers, mastered novelty as well as traditional wisdom and were thus 'trained for the kingdom of heaven', that is, qualified to provide new teaching in the eschatological age.

22. The parable of the cruel servant (Matt. 18:23–35)

The kingdom of heaven may be compared to a king who wished to settle accounts with his servants. When he began the reckoning, one was brought to him who owed him ten thousand talents; and as he could not pay, his lord ordered him to be sold, with his wife and children and all that he had, and payment to be made. So the servant fell on his knees, imploring him, 'Lord, have patience with me, and I will pay you everything.' And out of pity for him the lord of that servant released him and forgave him the debt. But that same servant, as he went out, came upon one of his fellow servants who owed him a hundred denarii, and seizing him by the throat he said, 'Pay what you owe.' So his fellow servant fell down and besought him, 'Have patience with me, and I will pay you.' He refused and went and put him in prison till he should pay the debt. When his fellow servants saw what had taken place, they were greatly distressed, and they went and reported to their lord all that had taken place. Then his lord summoned him and said to him, 'You wicked servant! I forgave you all that debt because you besought me; and should not you have had mercy on your fellow servant, as I had mercy on you?' And in anger his lord delivered him to the jailers, till he should pay all his debt. So also my heavenly Father will do to every one of you, if you do not forgive your brother from your heart.

This parable takes us far away from Jesus' familiar Galilean countryside. The scene is set in a Gentile royal court and the customs referred to are totally non-Jewish. The servants are courtiers, or high officials. The money owed by the first is a colossal sum, 10,000 talents, one talent being the equivalent of 10,000 silver drachms or denarii.[12] This suggests that the 'servant' was either a provincial governor or a chief tax-farmer in charge of collecting the revenue from a whole province. The sale into slavery of the servant, his wife and children, as well as the imprisonment of a debtor, are contrary to Jewish law (see also chapter 3, no. 13). The king showed extreme generosity when he forgave the offending official who begged him for patience and pardon, but the latter failed to show similar pity to one of his comparatively petty debtors. (For forgiveness of sins described as remission of debts, see chapter 2, no. 1 and chapter 6, no. 5(f).) In short, the lesson taught

12. To appreciate the size of this sum, King Herod left to his patron Augustus 1,000 talents or 10,000,000 silver coins in his will (*Antiquities* 17:146, 190), i.e. one tenth of the amount quoted in the parable.

is the duty to imitate God's magnanimity towards one's fellows, an attitude central to the piety of Jesus. However, the story does not represent his mode of thinking as revealed in the other Gospel parables.

23. The parable of the labourers in the vineyard (Matt. 20:1–16)

The kingdom of heaven is like a householder who went out early in the morning to hire labourers for his vineyard. After agreeing with the labourers for a denarius a day, he sent them into his vineyard. And going out about the third hour he saw others standing idle in the market place; and to them he said, 'You go into the vineyard too, and whatever is right I will give you.' So they went. Going out again about the sixth hour and the ninth hour, he did the same. And about the eleventh hour he went out and found others standing; and he said to them, 'Why do you stand here idle all day?' They said to him, 'Because no one has hired us.' He said to them, 'You go into the vineyard too.' And when evening came, the owner of the vineyard said to his steward, 'Call the labourers and pay them their wages, beginning with the last, up to the first.' And when those hired about the eleventh hour came, each of them received a denarius. Now when the first came, they thought they would receive more; but each of them also received a denarius. And on receiving it they grumbled at the householder, saying, 'These last worked only one hour, and you have made them equal to us who have borne the burden of the day and scorching heat.' But he replied to one of them, 'Friend, I am doing you no wrong; did you not agree with me for a denarius? Take what belongs to you and go; I choose to give to this last as I give to you. Am I not allowed to do what I choose with what belongs to me? Or do you begrudge my generosity [literally, *is your eye evil because I am good*[13]]*?' So the last will be first, and the first last.*

13. See chapter 3, no. 17.

The central topic of this parable, namely equal payment for varying amounts of work, was part of Jewish folklore from Jesus to the rabbis of the Talmud. For example, the funeral sermon of a Palestinian sage, Rabbi Bun bar Hiyya, which was preached by Rabbi Zeira, consisted of a parable interpreting Ecclesiastes 5:12, 'Sweet is the sleep of a labourer' (yBer 5c). The homilist spoke of a king who employed many workers. One of these was very industrious and fast. Having observed this, the king invited him to keep him company for the best part of the day, and in the evening he paid the same wage to all of them. When the other labourers grumbled, they were told by the king that no injustice was done to them as the diligent workman achieved as much in two hours as they did in the whole day. Likewise, concluded the preacher, Rabbi Bun practised more piety in his short life of twenty-eight years than others who lived to a hundred.

Matthew's lesson drawn from the parable differs from Rabbi Zeira's commendation of total obedience to the Law. The generous master in Jesus' version is attracted to less meritorious late-comers, the tax-collectors and sinners. They are replaced by the Gentiles, as opposed to the Jews, in the perspective of the primitive non-Palestinian church. The concluding phrase, 'the last will be first, and the first last', alluding to a reversal of the hierarchical order, is a generally applicable cliché with no direct relevance to this parable (cf. Mark 10:31; Matt. 19:30; Luke 13:30).

For the teaching about the social outcasts overtaking the self-proclaimed virtuous, see no. 24 below.

24. The parable of the two sons (Matt. 21:28–32)

What do you think? A man had two sons; and he went to the first and said, 'Son, go and work in the vineyard today.' And he answered, 'I will not'; but afterward he repented and went. And he went to the second and said the same; and he answered, 'I go, sir',[14] *but did not go. Which of the two did the will of his father?*

14. The Greek textual tradition is confused, but the meaning as given here appears to be the best.

They said, 'The first.' Jesus said to them, *Truly, I say to you, the tax-collectors and harlots go into the kingdom of God before you. For John came to you in the way of righteousness, and you did not believe him, but the tax-collectors and the harlots believed him; and even when you saw it, you did not afterward repent and believe him.*

Although no exact parallel to this parable is extant in rabbinic literature, it seems to derive from folklore.[15] Its aim is to command the virtue of repentance. The son who had flatly said no to his father, but later changed his mind and obeyed him, is contrasted with the other son, who pretended to agree, but refused to act. The application to tax-collectors and prostitutes, attributed to Jesus, makes good eschatological sense. The link to John who baptized penitent publicans and harlots while the Pharisees and lawyers (Luke 7:29–30) failed to listen to him is a secondary supplement inspired by the earlier controversy story concerning the authority of Jesus and the baptism of John (Mark 11:27–33; Matt. 21:23–27; Luke 20:1–8; see chapter 2, no. 10). For the reversal of the hierarchical order, see no. 23 above.

25. The parable of the ten virgins (Matt. 25:1–13; cf. Luke 12:35–38; 13:25)

The kingdom of heaven shall be compared to ten maidens who took their lamps and went to meet the bridegroom. Five of them were foolish, and five were wise. For when the foolish took their lamps, they took no oil with them; but the wise took flasks of oil with their lamps. As the bridegroom was delayed, they all slumbered and slept. But at midnight there was a cry, 'Behold, the bridegroom! Come out to meet him.' Then all those maidens rose and trimmed their lamps. And the foolish said to the wise, 'Give us some of your oil, for our lamps are going out.' But the

15. The nearest story comes from the Midrash Exodus Rabbah 27:9 about a king wishing to let a field to tenants. One after another the men decline the proposal until the fifth says yes, but neglects to cultivate the field. The king is more dissatisfied with him than with those who have rejected his offer.

wise replied, 'Perhaps there will not be enough for us and for you; go rather to the dealers and buy for yourselves.' And while they went to buy, the bridegroom came, and those who were ready went in with him to the marriage feast; and the door was shut. Afterward the other maidens came also, saying, 'Lord, lord, open to us.' But he replied, 'Truly, I say to you, I do not know you.' Watch therefore, for you know neither the day nor the hour (Matt.).

Let your loins be girded and your lamps burning, and be like men who are waiting for their master to come home from the marriage feast, so that they may open to him at once when he comes and knocks. Blessed are those servants whom the master finds awake when he comes; truly, I say to you, he will gird himself and have them sit at table, and he will come and serve them. If he comes in the second watch, or in the third, and finds them so, blessed are those servants! (Luke 12).

When once the householder has risen up and shut the door, you will begin to stand outside and knock at the door, saying, 'Lord, open to us.' He will answer you, 'I do not know where you come from' (Luke 13).

When examined closely, this second of three wedding feast parables is very peculiar (see also Matt. 22:2–14; Luke 14:16–24 and Luke 14:8–11 in nos. 13 above and 32 below). The story is concerned with ten girls awaiting the bridegroom to accompany him to the marriage banquet. As he is expected to arrive late, each of them carries an oil lamp, but only the five clever ones bring extra oil for refilling their lamps. They all fall asleep, but are awakened at midnight when the bridegroom suddenly appears. The lamps of the wise maidens are in working order, but the foolish ones need fresh oil which their calculating sisters refuse to lend them. Instead they advise them to go to the market. The bridegroom welcomes those ready for the feast, then shuts the door and firmly turns away the late-comers (cf. also Luke 13:25). The concluding remark stresses the need for alertness. The parable is tailor-made for a community tired of waiting for a much delayed Parousia. The story emphasizes self-reliance in the harsh conditions of the final age. Nevertheless, the selfish wise virgins and the cold and heartless bridegroom do not reflect the ideas of kindness and benevolence which typify the piety taught by Jesus; rather they are a travesty of his teaching on generosity and confident prayer.

A similar story, though not in parable form, figures in Luke 12:35–38. Compared with the story of the ten virgins there are some changes of detail. The maidens are replaced by men servants, the master returns from the marriage feast instead of arriving at it, and while lamps are mentioned, no reference is made to oil supply or to refusal to help. On the other hand, unlike the hard-working servant of Luke 17:7–10 discussed in no. 38 below, the faithful and vigilant servants of the present story[16] are specially rewarded by the master, who serves them in person (cf. Mark 10:45; Matt. 20:28; Luke 22:27). The remark attached to the parable about the need for watchfulness in the increasingly long expectation of the Parousia applies here too.

26. The parable of the last judgement (Matt. 25:31–46)

When the Son of Man comes in his glory, and all the angels with him, then he will sit on his glorious throne. Before him will be gathered all the nations, and he will separate them one from another as a shepherd separates the sheep from the goats, and he will place the sheep at his right hand, but the goats at the left. Then the King will say to those at his right hand, 'Come, O blessed of my Father, inherit the kingdom prepared for you from the foundation of the world; for I was hungry and you gave me food, I was thirsty and you gave me drink, I was a stranger and you welcomed me, I was naked and you clothed me, I was sick and you visited me, I was in prison and you came to me.' Then the righteous will answer him, 'Lord, when did we see thee hungry and feed thee, or thirsty and give thee drink? And when did we see thee a stranger and welcome thee, or naked and clothe thee? And when did we see thee sick or in prison and

16. The second and third watches correspond respectively to 9 p.m. to midnight and midnight to 3 a.m.

visit thee?' And the King will answer them, 'Truly, I say to you, as you did it to one of the least of these my brethren, you did it to me.' Then he will say to those at his left hand, 'Depart from me, you cursed, into the eternal fire prepared for the devil and his angels; for I was hungry and you gave me no food, I was thirsty and you gave me no drink, I was a stranger and you did not welcome me, naked and you did not clothe me, sick and in prison and you did not visit me.' Then they also will answer, 'Lord, when did we see thee hungry or thirsty or a stranger or naked or sick or in prison, and did not minister to thee?' Then he will answer them, 'Truly, I say to you, as you did it not to one of the least of these, you did it not to me.' And they will go away into eternal punishment, but the righteous into eternal life.

This composite apocalyptic picture is akin to the judgement scene presided over by the Son of man in the Similitudes of Enoch, a book probably dating to the last decades of the first century AD, and thus roughly contemporaneous with, and possibly affecting, the redaction of the Gospel of Matthew. The end of the third similitude represents the Son of man, also called the Elect, sitting on the throne of glory and condemning sinners to destruction (1 Enoch 69:26–28), and concludes, 'From then on there will be nothing corruptible, for that Son of man has appeared and has sat on the throne of his glory, and everything evil will pass away' (1 Enoch 69:29). Matthew's parable, which stands on its own with no parallel in the New Testament, is also linked to the theme of the imitation of God. The doctrine relies on Leviticus 19:2, 'You shall be holy, for I the Lord your God am holy', and on Deuteronomy 11:22 where man's love towards God is identified as 'walking in all his ways'.

The concept of the imitation of God is encountered throughout the successive stages of rabbinic literature, but its most picturesque expression figures in a Talmud passage recommending Jews to follow the attributes of God. These are clothing the naked as God dressed Adam and Eve, visiting the sick as he visited Abraham after his circumcision, comforting mourners as he comforted and blessed Isaac after the death of his father, and burying the dead, as God buried Moses on Mount Nebo (bSotah 14a).

In Matthew's literary complex the parable structure incorporates the metaphor of the shepherd dividing the sheep from the goats. As he separates the two kinds, so will the royal judge set apart the righteous and the wicked. This seems to be the kernel of an original Jewish parable which subsequently underwent a twofold mutation. Following the model of Enoch the role of judge is played not by God the king, but by the Son of man, the human representative of the divine ruler. Secondly, under the influence of the doctrine of the imitation of God, which is an essential concept in the teaching of Jesus (cf. Matt. 5:48; Luke 6:36 in chapter 9, no. 12), man's behaviour towards his fellow man is employed as the moral yardstick by which good and evil actions are ultimately distinguished. The perspective is universal, with no specific reference to Jews or Gentiles: all the nations stand before the divine tribunal.

In its final form the parable is set in the context of the event of the Parousia and as such belongs to the ideology of the early church, with the son of Man, i.e. the returning Christ, empowered to be the final judge (cf. chapter 7, no. 26). However, the concept of the imitation of God is in full harmony with the religious ideas of Jesus, and this would work well in the hypothesis that before the Son of man became the hero of the account, judging the righteous and the wicked was believed to be the task of God. Beneath this earlier construct one can still perceive the simile of the divine shepherd and his decisive act of segregating the virtuous sheep from the evil goats.

IV. PARABLES IN LUKE (*L*)

27. The parable of the creditor and the two debtors (Luke 7:40–47)

Simon, I have something to say to you . . . A certain creditor had two debtors: one owed five hundred denarii, and the other fifty. When they could not pay, he forgave them both. Now which of them will love him more? Simon answered, 'The one, I suppose, to whom he forgave more.' And he said to him, *You have judged rightly.* Then turning to the woman, he said to Simon, *Do you see this woman? I entered your house, you gave me no water for my feet, but she wet my feet with her tears and wiped them with her hair. You gave me no kiss, but from the time I came in she has not ceased to kiss my feet. You did not anoint my head with oil, but she has anointed my feet with ointment. Therefore I tell you, her sins, which are many, are forgiven, for she loved much; but he who is forgiven little, loves little.*

The banal parable about a debtor whose large debt is generously written off, and who in consequence owes greater gratitude to his creditor than one whose insignificant debt is cancelled, is turned into a poignant story thanks to the wider context of the Gospel. There the behaviour of the man of bourgeois respectability is compared with that of the publicly despised whore (the woman who is a sinner). The emphasis of the parable lies on the thankfulness felt by him who has received forgiveness rather than on the generosity of the forgiver. The setting reflects Jesus' attitude to social outcasts and the story contains no element that would clash with his spiritual outlook.

For a parallel account of anointing Jesus, see chapter 8, no. 29.

28. The parable of the good Samaritan (Luke 10:30–36)

A man was going down from Jerusalem to Jericho, and he fell among robbers, who stripped him and beat him, and departed, leaving him half dead. Now by chance a priest was going down that road; and when he saw him, he passed by on the other side. So likewise a Levite, when he came to the place and saw him, passed by on the other side. But a Samaritan, as he journeyed, came to where he was; and when he saw him, he had compassion, and went to him and bound up his wounds, pouring on oil and wine; then he set him on his own beast and brought him to an inn, and took care of him. And the next day he took out two denarii and gave them to the innkeeper, saying, 'Take care of him, and whatever more you spend, I will repay you when I come back.' Which of these three, do you think, proved neighbour to the man who fell among the robbers?

The story seen from the redactional point of view serves to define the meaning of 'neighbour' in the commandment 'Love your neighbour as yourself' (Lev. 19:18), attached to Luke 10:27. The conclusion of the parable, namely that the neighbour is 'the one who showed mercy' (Luke 10:37), connects it with the initial question. But this connection is as superficial as it is misleading. If the primary object of brotherly love is the person who has done good to us, this attitude would clash with the principle of disinterested generosity which is the hallmark of the piety taught by Jesus (see chapter 3, no. 15). Responsibility for the link should therefore be credited to the redactor of the Gospel of Luke rather than to Jesus. Another possible misinterpretation envisages the parable itself as an attack on the classes associated with the Temple of Jerusalem. The priest and the Levite failed to take any notice of the man who lay by the wayside, conceivably because they imagined that he was truly dead. It was a foreigner, a despised Samaritan, who showed genuine humanity.[17]

It is not impossible that Luke actually intended to criticize the priest and the Levite. However, the original story may be read in a less hostile spirit. Jewish law and custom enjoined priests to avoid uncleanness resulting from contact with a corpse. So if the fictional priest thought that the body by the roadside was a cadaver, he was expected to give it a wide berth. According to the Qumran War Scroll, priests in charge of signalling the various phases of the eschatological combat with their trumpets had to stay at some distance from the battlefield 'lest they be defiled' (1QM 9:8). The Mishnah also stipulates that the High Priest should not take part in the funeral procession (mSanh 2:1).

The priest of the parable is said to be 'going down', that is, travelling away from Jerusalem, so the reason for not approaching a presumed dead body was obedience to the general rule which prescribes for priests the avoidance of defilement rather than concern for ritual cleanness in view of an impending participation in Temple worship. The case of the Levite is less clear as we are not told in which direction he was travelling, but the main issue is simple. Both are presumed to

17. Luke's fondness for Samaritans is shown also in his story of the ten lepers of whom only the one Samaritan thanked Jesus for healing them. See chapter 1, no. 36.

have thought that the motionless body was a corpse needing no further aid; hence they kept away from it as far as they could.

It was only the Samaritan, unbothered by ritual considerations, who took the trouble to investigate, and when he discovered that the man was still breathing he did what compassion and humanity demanded. The model for his action is provided by the Bible. In 2 Chronicles 28:8–15 Judaean prisoners of war were well treated by Samaritans: 'They clothed all that were naked among them; . . . provided them with food and drink, and anointed them; and carrying all the feeble among them on asses, they bought them to . . . Jericho.'

While the idea of loving care is typical of Jesus' piety, the Gospels do not depict him as particularly fond of Samaritans: 'Enter no town of the Samaritans!' he commanded his disciples.[18] So the parable is likely to be the creation of the early church. It is perhaps a Christian midrash in reverse on Jesus' teaching to love one's enemy. Here the 'enemy' is portrayed as showing love towards a Jew!

29. The parable of the unexpected guest (Luke 11:5–8)

Which of you who has a friend will go to him at midnight and say to him, 'Friend, lend me three loaves; for a friend of mine has arrived on a journey, and I have nothing to set before him'; and he will answer from within, 'Do not bother me; the door is now shut and my children are with me in bed; I cannot get up and give you anything'? I tell you, though he will not get up and give him anything because he is his friend, yet because of his importunity he will rise and give him whatever he needs.

This parable-like story uses the topic of oriental hospitality to describe the nature and efficiency of the prayer petition. A man must do everything possible, even make himself a nuisance to other friends, in order to obtain the wherewithal to show hospitality to an unexpected visitor in the middle of the night. The message is that a child's determination,

18. Hostility towards Samaritans was particularly virulent in the early decades of the first century AD after some Samaritans had desecrated the Temple at Passover by scattering human bones all over the sanctuary (Josephus, *Antiquities* 18:30).

motivated by the belief in paternal love, is bound to persuade the father – here God – to accede to the suppliant's request. This total trust is an essential part of the religion of Jesus; it is a necessary prerequisite in the case of healing miracles (cf. chapter 1, no. 9), but it also underlies the famous counsel to ask, seek and knock (Matt. 7:7–8; Luke 11:9–10; cf. chapter 8, no. 35).

Persistent demands addressed to God were seen as improper, indeed impudent, in the genteel and bourgeois society of the rabbis. Thus Honi the Circle-Drawer was accused of impertinence for threatening God with staying inside the circle which he drew around himself until his prayer was heard in heaven (mTaan 3:8). Likewise the pagan prophet Balaam, after God's refusal to grant him permission to curse the Jews, went on asking again and again until he was allowed to go (Num. 22:7–20). This story inspired the Talmudic saying, 'Chutzpah (audacity) affects even Heaven' (bSanh 105a). In the case of Honi, the seemingly disrespectful behaviour is excused on account of his particular proximity to God. He cannot be condemned because he is like a son in the heavenly household: 'Even though you importune God, he does what you wish in the same way as a father does whatever his persistent son asks him' (mTaan 3:8). The followers of Jesus, also children of God, are encouraged to display a similar familiarity towards the heavenly Father.

30. The parable of the rich farmer (Luke 12:16–20; cf. Gospel of Thos. 63)

The land of a rich man brought forth plentifully; and he thought to himself, 'What shall I do, for I have nowhere to store my crops?' And he said, 'I will do this: I will pull down my barns, and build larger ones; and there I will store all my grain and my goods. And I will say to my soul, Soul, you have ample goods laid up for many years; take your ease, eat, drink, be merry.' But God said to him, 'Fool! This night your soul is required of you; and the things you have prepared, whose will they be?'

The parable recounts the thoughts of a wealthy landowner who expects a particularly rich harvest. He makes arrangements in his mind for providing storage space for the massive quantity of grain that is far in excess of the capacity of his old barns. The one thing this careful planner fails to foresee is his sudden death during that very night.[19] The lesson confirms the fundamental precept of Jesus that one should not be anxious about the future and attention should focus instead on the needs of the present moment. Tomorrow will be taken care of by God in the final age.

The editor of Luke supplies for the parable an introductory dialogue and Jesus' reply at the end. Both are secondary and distort the meaning of the story. In the editorial introductory section a bystander invites Jesus to intervene in his quarrel with his brother about an inheritance. Jesus refuses. Dealing with property is not the business of an eschatological prophet: 'Man, who made me a judge or divider over you?' (Luke 12:14; see Gospel of Thos. 72:2–3). This evasive answer is accompanied by another extraneous editorial comment against acquisitiveness: 'Take heed, and beware of all covetousness; for a man's life does not consist in the abundance of his possessions' (Luke 12:15). Yet another, equally unconnected, explanation is stuck on to the genuine parable, contrasting the love of riches with a lack of generosity *vis-à-vis* the Father in heaven: 'So is he who lays up treasure for himself, and is not rich toward God' (Luke 12:21). As is often his habit, Luke tries to water down any appearance of eschatological urgency in the teaching of Jesus.

31. The parable of the fruitless fig tree (Luke 13:6–9)

A man had a fig tree planted in his vineyard; and he came seeking fruit on it and found none. And he said to the vinedresser, 'Lo, these three years I have come seeking fruit on this fig tree, and I find none. Cut it down; why should it use up the ground?' And he answered him, 'Let it alone, sir, this year also, till I dig about

19. The Gospel of Thomas abbreviates and reshapes the parable; the rich man plans to invest his money in agriculture so that he may sow, reap, plant and fill his storehouses with produce.

it and put on manure. And if it bears fruit next year, well and good; but if not, you can cut it down.'

This unusual parable dwells on the plans of the gardener regarding a fig tree which has failed to produce fruit three years running. The owner of the orchard-vineyard wanted to cut it down, but the gardener pleaded that special care might help it to become fruitful. The relatively long period envisaged – four years – does not fit well with Jesus' view of an imminent coming of the Kingdom. However, in the context of primitive Christianity it could be taken as an encouragement to church leaders to make an extra effort to save the unresponsive faithful. The Gospel version totally differs from the tale recorded in the story of Ahikar (8:35 [Syriac]; 8:30 [Arabic]) where the fruitless tree unsuccessfully pleads for one more year, but the adamant owner fells it.

32. The parable of choosing a seat at the wedding feast (Luke 14:8–11)

When you are invited by any one to a marriage feast, do not sit down in a place of honour, lest a more eminent man than you be invited by him; and he who invited you both will come and say to you, 'Give place to this man', and then you will begin with shame to take the lowest place. But when you are invited, go and sit in the lowest place, so that when your host comes he may say to you, 'Friend, go up higher'; then you will be honoured in the presence of all who sit at the table with you. For every one who exalts himself will be humbled, and he who humbles himself will be exalted.

The lesson of this third parable about a wedding feast (see nos. 13 and 25 above) is modesty and self-abasement. Guests should choose the humblest seats so as to be invited by the host to move to a higher place. The opposite would be embarrassing. The theme runs through Jewish literature from the Bible to the rabbinic midrash. The scene chosen by the Book of Proverbs is a royal banquet: 'Do not put yourself forward in the king's presence or stand in the place of the great; for it is better to be told, "Come up here", than to be put lower in the presence of the prince' (Prov. 25:6–7). The midrash like the Gospel envisages a less august social setting. 'Descend from your place two or three steps,' teaches Rabbi Simeon ben Azzai in the early second century AD. 'It is better for you to be told to go up than come down' (Exodus Rabbah 45:5; Leviticus Rabbah 1:5). Seeking for oneself pride of place in the synagogue or at feasts is condemned in connection with the scribes in Mark 12:38–39 and Luke 20:46 (see chapter 2, no. 15) and the apostles James and John are rebuked for requesting the seats next to Jesus at the banquet table in the Kingdom of God (Mark 10:37; see chapter 3, no. 35 and chapter 8, no. 15). So the original frame of the story was most likely eschatological but it could easily be generalized. The proverb regarding exaltation and humiliation, which is secondarily appended to this parable, has already been examined in chapter 3, no. 35.

33. The parable of the landowner and the king (Luke 14:28–33)

For which of you, desiring to build a tower, does not first sit down and count the cost, whether he has enough to complete it? Otherwise, when he has laid a foundation, and is not able to finish, all who see it begin to mock him, saying, 'This man began to build, and was not able to finish.' Or what king, going to encounter another king in war, will not sit down first and take counsel whether he is able with ten thousand to meet him who comes against him with twenty thousand? And if not, while the other is yet a great way off, he sends an embassy and asks terms of peace. So therefore, whoever of you does not renounce all that he has cannot be my disciple.

This double parable is inserted by Luke in a section giving instruction about discipleship, but even if the extraneous final exhortation to renounce earthly goods (cf. chapter 3, no. 12, and chapter 8, no. 14) is discarded, the stories do not fit the context. The message is that people should calculate and plan before they proceed to action. This attitude, disapproved of in the parable on the rich farmer (see no. 30 above), suits better the less frenzied circumstances of the life of the primitive church than the eschatological enthusiasm typical of the age of Jesus.

34. The parable of the lost drachm (Luke 15:8–10)

Or what woman, having ten silver drachms, if she loses one drachm, does not light a lamp and sweep the house and seek diligently until she finds it? And when she has found it, she calls together her friends and neighbours, saying, 'Rejoice with me, for I have found the drachm which I had lost.' Just so, I tell you, there is joy before the angels of God over one sinner who repents.

Supplementing the parable of the lost sheep (see no. 12 above) with a domestic parallel, Luke presents the story of a woman who painstakingly spring-cleans her house in search of a missing silver coin, and is delighted when she finds it. The message is identical to that of the lost sheep, namely that God is delighted when one lost soul turns back to him. The concluding remark concerning the angels' rejoicing over one repentant sinner repeats the lesson borrowed from the parable of the lost sheep, but it sounds less apposite here.

35. The parable of the prodigal son (Luke 15:11–32)

There was a man who had two sons; and the younger of them said to his father, 'Father, give me the share of the property that falls to me.' And he divided his living between them. Not many days later the younger son gathered all he had and took his journey into a far country, and there he squandered his property in loose living. And when he had spent everything, a great famine arose in that country, and he began to be in want. So he went and joined himself to one of the citizens of that country, who sent him into his fields to feed swine. And he would gladly have fed on the pods that the swine ate; and no one gave him anything. But when he came to himself he said, 'How many of my father's hired servants have bread enough to spare, but I perish here with hunger! I will arise and go to my father, and I will say to him, "Father, I have sinned against heaven and before you; I am no longer worthy to be called your son; treat me as one of your hired servants."' And he arose and came to his father. But while he was yet at a distance, his father saw him and had compassion, and ran and embraced him and kissed him. And the son said to him, 'Father, I have sinned against heaven and before you; I am no longer worthy to be called your son.' But the father said to his servants, 'Bring quickly the best robe, and put it on him; and put a ring on his hand, and shoes on his feet; and bring the fatted calf and kill it, and let us eat and make merry; for this my son was dead, and is alive again; he was lost, and is found.' And they began to make merry. Now the elder son was in the field; and as he came and drew near the house, he heard music and dancing. And he called one of the servants and asked what this meant. And he said to him, 'Your brother has come, and your father has killed the fatted calf, because he has received him safe and sound.' But he was angry and refused to go in. His father came out and entreated him, but he answered his father, 'Lo, these many years I have served you, and I never disobeyed your command; yet you never gave me a kid, that I might make merry with my friends. But when this son of yours came, who has devoured your living with harlots, you killed for him the fatted calf!' And he said to him, 'Son, you are always with me, and all that is mine is yours. It was fitting to make merry and be glad, for this your brother was dead, and is alive; he was lost, and is found.'

The main part of this well-known and much-loved parable deals with the theme of filial repentance and paternal forgiveness. The final section, which is likely to be secondary, confronts the apparent injustice between leniency towards the sinner and lack of special consideration for the constantly faithful. The story portrays the utmost degradation of the wayward younger son who in a foreign Gentile setting becomes a swineherd – a most un-Jewish way to earn a living – and in his hunger, longs for the food fed to pigs. His contrition, helped along by his misery, is depicted as genuine and sincere. He no longer considers himself worthy of being regarded as a son. Nevertheless his compassionate father treats him much better than he deserves or asks for, and welcomes him back with warmth and joy. The message of repentance belongs without any doubt to the central core of the teaching of Jesus.

Commentators dispute whether the leading actor is the son or the father, but in reality it is the young man who, with one exception, always takes the initiative. The exception consists in the father's forgiveness prior to the son's confession of sorrow. A similar repentance parable is told by Rabbi Meir, interpreting 'When you are in tribulation . . . you will return to the Lord your God' (Deut. 4:30): 'To what can this be compared? To a king's son who set out on the path of wickedness. The king dispatched his tutor to ask him to come home. The son replied that feeling unworthy and deeply embarrassed, he could not return. But a fresh message was brought to him by the pedagogue, "My son, can a son be ashamed of returning to his father? And if you return, is it not to your father that you return?"' (Deuteronomy Rabbah 2:3).

In the latter part of the story the conventionally good elder son enters the scene, filled with resentment on account of the father's generosity towards his wayward brother. He is reassured that his share of the heritage is safe; however, he should not begrudge the welcome offered by the father to a son who has been considered lost. The conclusion strikes an alien note. One would have expected from Jesus a word of criticism towards the jealous and unsympathetic elder son. The tone is rather that of early Christianity, protecting the rights of the well-behaved.

36. The parable of the crooked steward (Luke 16:1–9)

There was a rich man who had a steward, and charges were brought to him that this man was wasting his goods. And he called him and said to him, 'What is this that I hear about you?

Turn in the account of your stewardship, for you can no longer be steward.' And the steward said to himself, 'What shall I do, since my master is taking the stewardship away from me? I am not strong enough to dig, and I am ashamed to beg. I have decided what to do, so that people may receive me into their houses when I am put out of the stewardship.' So, summoning his master's debtors one by one, he said to the first, 'How much do you owe my master?' He said, 'A hundred baths [*c.* 4,000 litres] *of oil?' And he said to him, 'Take your bill, and sit down quickly and write fifty.' Then he said to another, 'And how much do you owe?' He said, 'A hundred kors* [*c.* 40,000 litres] *of wheat.' He said to him, 'Take your bill, and write eighty.' The master commended the dishonest steward for his shrewdness; for the sons of this world are more shrewd in dealing with their own generation than the sons of light. And I tell you, make friends for yourselves by means of unrighteous mammon, so when it fails they may receive you into the eternal habitations.*

This curious parable seeks to draw a positive lesson from the fraudulent action of the estate manager of a wealthy landowner. Foreseeing dismissal, he at once moves into action and advises his master's clients to falsify their bills of debt and reduce the sums they owe to the landowner. Thus the steward hoped to find himself in the good books of the debtors and receive some reward from them. The message seems to be that the just men, the 'sons of light',[20] should learn to be as prompt, decisive and clever in their approach to the Kingdom of God (i.e. the 'eternal habitations') as this crooked steward was in trying to save his skin (see the proverb about the wise serpent in chapter 3, no. 33). How this calculating approach fits the religious outlook of Jesus is hard to see; hence the parable is unlikely to be his.

The last two verses praising the behaviour of the steward and commending the good use of 'unrighteous mammon'[21] are probably

20. This is one of the three occurrences in the New Testament of the phrase familiar in the Community Rule from Qumran. The other two are John 12:36 and 1 Thessalonians 5:5.

21. This expression is the equivalent of 'wealth of wickedness' used in the Dead Sea Scrolls (cf. CD 6:15; 8:5; 19:17).

secondary. Such a counsel better suits the life out of a common purse practised in the early Jerusalem church described in the Acts than the poverty-inspired piety offered by Jesus to his fellow seekers after the Kingdom of God.

37. The parable of the rich man and the poor Lazarus (Luke 16:19–31)

There was a rich man who was clothed in purple and fine linen and who feasted sumptuously every day. And at his gate lay a poor man named Lazarus, full of sores, who desired to be fed with what fell from the rich man's table; moreover the dogs came and licked his sores. The poor man died and was carried by the angels to Abraham's bosom. The rich man also died and was buried; and in Hades [i.e. *Sheol*, the Jewish underworld], *being in torment, he lifted up his eyes, and saw Abraham far off and Lazarus in his bosom. And he called out, 'Father Abraham, have mercy upon me, and send Lazarus to dip the end of his finger in water and cool my tongue; for I am in anguish in this flame.' But Abraham said, 'Son, remember that you in your lifetime received your good things, and Lazarus in like manner evil things; but now he is comforted here, and you are in anguish. And besides all this, between us and you a great chasm has been fixed, in order that those who would pass from here to you may not be able, and none may cross from there to us.' And he said, 'Then I beg you, father, to send him to my father's house, for I have five brothers, so that he may warn them, lest they also come into this place of torment.' But Abraham said, 'They have Moses and the prophets; let them hear them.' And he said, 'No, father Abraham; but if someone goes to them from the dead, they will repent.' He said to him, 'If they do not hear Moses and the prophets, neither will they be convinced if some one should rise from the dead.'*

A folk-tale rather than a parable, the story of the wealthy man and the poor and sick Lazarus succinctly illustrates the popular representation propagated in the age of Jesus by the Pharisees of how earthly behaviour was rewarded and what were the forms of afterlife. At the end of a miserable life on earth Lazarus is allotted a blissful existence in the world to come: he dwells in Abraham's bosom, the resting-place of saintly Jews. The rabbinic writing Pesikta Rabbati (43:4) explicitly locates there the martyrs who fell victim to the persecution by the emperor Hadrian after the second war against Rome in AD 132–135. The wicked, on the other hand, are tormented by the flames of the netherworld whence they can look upwards and see Abraham and those with him, although no passage is possible between the two places. Neither can Abraham's protégés return to earth to warn the living. The reason given is that those who fail to obey the Law and the prophets will not listen to an otherworldly messenger either. The main doctrine conveyed contains no particular nuance recalling Jesus' preaching. The only aspect of the story that links it to the eschatological situation is the stress on the importance of listening to God's message mediated by Moses and the prophets and of acting on it in the present moment, the true place and time of salvation being here and now. It is not impossible therefore that an existing tale was given a special twist by Jewish Christianity.

38. The parable of the servant's reward (Luke 17:7–10; cf. Luke 12:37)

Will any one of you, who has a servant ploughing and keeping sheep, say to him when he has come in from the field, 'Come at once and sit down at table'? Will he not rather say to him, 'Prepare supper for me, and gird yourself and serve me, till I eat and drink; and afterward you shall eat and drink'? Does he thank the servant because he did what was commanded? So you also, when you have done all that is commanded you, say, 'We are unworthy servants; we have only done what was our duty.'

Blessed are those servants whom the master finds awake when he comes; truly, I say to you, he will gird himself and have them sit at the table, and he will come and serve them (Luke 12).

The purpose of this parable is to remind the servant of his status. After a full day's work doing two jobs, tilling the land and tending the flock, the exhausted man still has to attend and feed his master before he is allowed to sit down and have his own supper. He cannot even expect a word of thanks as he has simply been doing his job. The same thought is voiced by the saying attributed to Yohanan ben Zakkai, Jesus' younger contemporary: 'If you have performed much of the Torah, do not claim merit for yourself, for you were created for this purpose' (mAb 2:8). Those to whom the parable is addressed should adopt the same modest outlook. The parable of the servant's reward is probably modelled on a true saying of Jesus – the Master is ready to attend the faithful servant (see Luke 12:37; see no. 25 above) – but it is turned by the church upside down. The servant must never forget who he is.

39. The parable of the judge and the persistent widow (Luke 18:1–8)

And he told them a parable, to the effect that they ought always to pray and not lose heart. He said, *In a certain city there was a judge who neither feared God nor regarded man; and there was a widow in that city who kept coming to him and saying, 'Vindicate me against my adversary.' For a while he refused; but afterward he said to himself, 'Though I neither fear God nor regard man, yet because this widow bothers me, I will vindicate her, or she will wear me out by her continual coming.'* And the Lord said, *Hear what the unrighteous judge says. And will not God vindicate his elect, who cry to him day and night? Will he delay long over them? I tell you, he will vindicate them speedily. Nevertheless, when the Son of man comes, will he find faith on earth?*

The main thrust of this parable is the same as that of the unexpected guest (see no. 29 above): unceasing pressure produces fruit. The judge is wicked since he does not fear God, who commands the protection of widows, nor has he regard for this particular woman's just claim. But even so he gives in to her repeated badgering: *a fortiori* God, the just judge. As the introductory sentence indicates, the original teaching consists in an exhortation to unshakeable trust. However, the supplement from 'Will he delay long over them?' etc., attributable to Luke's editor, turns the parable into an intensified expectation of the delayed Parousia with watered down and weakened eschatological hope (see chapter 7, no. 28).

40. The parable of the Pharisee and the publican (Luke 18:9–14)

He also told this parable to some who trusted in themselves that they were righteous and despised others: *Two men went up into the temple to pray, one a Pharisee and the other a tax-collector. The Pharisee stood and prayed thus with himself, 'God, I thank thee that I am not like other men, extortioners, unjust, adulterers, or even like this tax-collector. I fast twice a week, I give tithes of all that I get.' But the tax-collector, standing far off, would not even lift up his eyes to heaven, but beat his breast, saying, 'God, be merciful to me a sinner!' I tell you, this man went down to his house justified rather than the other; for every one who exalts himself will be humbled, but he who humbles himself will be exalted.*

The parable contrasts two extreme religious attitudes, that of hypocritical self-satisfaction symbolized by the Pharisee, and that of sincere self-abasement typified by Jesus' favourite character, the tax-collector or publican. The Pharisee prides himself on doing everything that is compulsory and a great many optional acts of Jewish piety. There is no evidence attesting the solid presence of the Pharisees in the north of Palestine in the early first century AD. The role of the wicked in the story could belong originally to a scribe or lawyer. Whether the stereotype of the hypocritical Pharisee may have reached Galilee long before their heirs settled *en masse* in that province after the Hadrianic war in the second century AD[22] remains an open question. Be this as it may, since the ideas fit well in the mode of thinking of Jesus, the substance of the basic parable may well be authentic. For the concluding exhortation to humility against self-aggrandisement, see no. 32 above.

REFLECTIONS

1. *Classification of the parables*

The figurative style of the forty parables in the Synoptics enables us to gain valuable insight into the image world of the Gospels and, most likely, of Jesus himself. These parables may be arranged into seven groups according to their genres.

(a) The first and largest of them – thirteen units out of forty – elaborates on rural themes characteristic of the Galilean countryside. The farmer sows the seeds, waits for them to germinate and grow until they are ready to produce grain for the harvest . . . provided the seeds fall on fertile ground and are not eaten by birds, or suffocated by weeds (nos. 1, 2, 17). The tiny mustard seed develops into a large shrub (no. 3). At the prospect of a rich harvest, a farmer is preoccupied with plans to enlarge his insufficient storage space (no. 30). A lucky ploughman accidentally unearths a hidden treasure (no. 18). The

22. Traditional Christian anti-Judaism sees in the Pharisee of Luke the prototype of Judaism as opposed to the religion of Jesus. According to Joachim Jeremias, clear echoes of the sentiments of the Gospel Pharisee may be found in the prayer of Nehuniah ben ha-Kana quoted in the Talmud (bBer 28b): 'I thank thee, O Lord, that thou hast given me my lot with those who sit in the seat of learning, and not with those who sit at the street-corners . . . I am early to work on the words of the Torah, and they are early to work on things of no moment . . . I run towards the life of the Age to Come, and they run towards the pit of destruction' (*The Parables of Jesus* (London, 1978), 142). In reality, however, the two prayers are very different. That in Luke exudes conceit and self-satisfaction, while the other can be understood as expressing humility and gratitude. The same motivation characterizes the Qumran Thanksgiving Hymns, too. A sharp contrast between the righteous and the wicked often appears in the biblical Psalms, beginning with Psalm 1.

vineyard offers a good topic for meditation (no. 4), and the green shoots of the fig tree act as a calendar and announce the approach of summer (no. 5). A metaphorical message is conveyed by a barren tree which thanks to the use of manure is expected to become fruit-producing (no. 31). Further subjects include the fate of the hired hands in the vineyard (no. 23), and the story of a group of murderous tenants (no. 4). The inner secrets of the soul of two brothers are disclosed by their misleading first reaction to their father's command to go and work in the vineyard, followed by a change of mind (no. 24). The picture is completed by a shepherd's delight on finding his lost sheep (no. 12), and by the fishermen's landing of a large catch (no. 20).

(b) The second group of ten parables centres on domestic issues: the building of a house or a tower (nos. 8, 33), the behaviour of a wise homeowner (nos. 10, 14, 21, 29), the family banquet organized by a father on the return of his 'lost' son (no. 35), a woman preparing dough for the baking of bread, and spring-cleaning her house in search of a lost coin (nos. 11, 34), and finally children playing games in the street (no. 9).

(c) The third group of six parables takes us to the higher ranks of society with royal 'servants' (probably estate managers), a provincial governor and even kings playing the lead parts. Some servants perform their jobs faithfully and with competence in the absence of the master and are always ready to account for their stewardship; others abuse their power or display cool-headed craftiness and dishonesty to limit the damage caused by their irresponsibility and inefficiency (nos. 6, 15, 36, 38). A king shows first generosity and later justice to an unreliable and ungrateful official (no. 22) and another king reflects on the folly of waging war against a much stronger opponent (no. 33).

(d) The fourth category – three parables – is concerned not with rural and domestic matters, but with the business world of the big city. We are faced with the tough entrepreneur who expects his employees to make the capital entrusted to them produce interest (no. 16) and with the kind-hearted creditor (a contradiction in terms?) prepared to write off debts, large and small (no. 27). The go-ahead merchant unhesitatingly converts all his property into cash in order to acquire the pearl of his dreams (no. 19).

(e) The scene of the next three parables is the tribunal. In the first an out-of-court settlement is recommended to a man to avoid the danger of the arbitrator finding against him (no. 7). The second shows that it is worth importuning an unsympathetic judge if it results in the vindication of a just cause (no. 39). In the highest sphere of judicial activity the ultimate fate of mankind is decided by the royal judge (God) sitting on his throne on the judgement day (no. 26).

(f) The happenings at a solemn banquet, the symbol of the inauguration of the Kingdom, are the subject of the sixth group of three parables. A lesson is drawn from the conduct of the invited guests and the fate of their substitutes (nos. 13, 25), and the rules of etiquette relative to seating arrangements at the banquet table are illustrated by the misadventure experienced by a guest who chooses a place above his social standing (no. 32).

(g) Three miscellaneous parables have been left unclassified. The Pharisee and the publican in the Temple typify the two extreme religious attitudes of pride and humility (no. 40); the future destiny of the good and the wicked is acted out by the ungodly rich man and the poor Lazarus (no. 37); and the unexpected generosity of a Samaritan traveller is contrasted with the behaviour of members of the priestly clan (no. 28).

2. *The teaching of the parables*

One of the chief topics of the parables is the Kingdom of God or Kingdom of heaven (nos. 2, 3, 5, 11, 13, 17, 18, 19, 20, 22, 23, 24, 25).[23] It is symbolized by the imperceptibly growing seed and ultimately by the harvest (or the catch of fish). Throughout, the main lessons are typical of the teaching of Jesus: total and uncalculating trust in God combined with a wholehearted and devout commitment to paving the way of the Kingdom, together with repentance shown as the indispensable prerequisite for forgiveness. Other parables emphasize the necessity of mixing or not mixing old and new wisdom; constant vigilance and readiness for the imminent yet unpredictable hour of God's coming. Further necessary virtues are tenacity in prayer,

23. No. 1 (the sower) is also identified with the Kingdom in the appended comment of Jesus (Mark 4:11; Matt. 13:11; Luke 8:10).

strenuous and joyful effort in pursuing one's task, and courage empowering one to face up to risks. Watchfulness and perseverance are absolutely necessary as the absent master is often late and, like the burglar, arrives in the depths of the night. This theme is usually connected with a prolonged expectation of the Second Coming. In conflict with the faith–trust motive, some parables advise prudence, the careful weighing-up of pros and cons and the avoidance of risk, though in one case this is followed by Jesus' customary disapproval of precautionary measures: prudent plans misfire and sudden death demonstrates the futility of trying to ensure a safe future by shrewd calculation.

It is very remarkable that only one out of forty parables, that of the wicked tenants of the vineyard (no. 4), is directly meant to foreshadow the cross. This parable as a whole and the allusions to the role of the son of Man's delayed return are later additions to the original central message of Jesus.

3. *Distribution of the parables in the Gospels*

With the exception of the story of the doorkeeper (no. 6) set in the context of the Parousia, all the parables (nos. 1–5) included in Mark, the oldest of the Gospels, represent countrymen's stories close to the Galilean experience of Jesus. The nature of those preserved in Matthew and Luke (*Q*) is more general. They are mostly of the domestic kind (nos. 8, 11, 14), or deal with shepherds or servants (nos. 12, 15, 16). Matthew's special material contains five further genuine-sounding agricultural and fishing parables (nos. 17, 18, 20, 23, 24) and a mixture of imagery relating to household and family matters, but also to business and finance (nos. 19, 21, 22; see also no. 27 in *L*). The latter group represents alien territory as far as Jesus is concerned. To these we must add the parable of the last judgement (no. 26). Luke in turn had access to a collection of fourteen additional parables reflecting the whole range of topics found in the other sources, from the fruitless fig tree standing in the vineyard (no. 31) to the unjust judge misbehaving in the city (no. 39).

4. *The purpose of the parables*

As already wisely noted by Jerome, the aim of the Jewish parable is to make the message 'intelligible through similitudes and examples' (see above, p. 116). As far as the Gospel parables are concerned, unlike those of the rabbis, with the exception of two they are not of an exegetical nature, i.e. attached to biblical citations whose meaning they are expected to clarify. Two parables stand apart from the rest and contain Scripture excerpts: the parable of the wicked tenants (no. 4) associated with Isaiah 5:2 and Psalms 118:22–23, and to a lesser extent the story of the good Samaritan (no. 28), which, according to the attached editorial comment, expounds the significance of Leviticus 19:18, the definition of a neighbour. As far as the explication of the parables themselves is concerned, only those of the sower (no. 1) and of the weeds (no. 17) are furnished with systematic interpretation. The almost complete absence of exegesis is a clear indication that, allusive though they are by nature, the Gospel parables were expected to speak for themselves.

This surmise is contradicted, however, by one well-known New Testament passage. Between the parable of the sower and its exposition, all three evangelists insert a statement to the effect that the mysteries of the Kingdom of God were revealed only to the close disciples of Jesus (see chapter 3, nos. 4 and 5). Those who were not part of the inner circle were not meant to grasp them: 'To you has been given the secret of the kingdom of God, but for those outside everything is in parables; so that they may indeed see but not perceive, and may indeed hear but not understand; lest they should turn again, and be forgiven' (Mark 4:11–12; Matt. 13:11, 13; Luke 8:10). If this were true, Jesus, as esoteric teachers before and after him, would have used parables as riddles or enigmas to *conceal* from the general public the true meaning of his words. However, the truth is that preaching conveyed in parables had different effects on listeners or readers depending on whether they were Jews or Gentiles. The former, long since accustomed to this kind of didactic style, did not require pre-masticated nourishing. But the untrained Gentile Christians to whom the Greek Gospels were ultimately addressed were nonplussed by the strange language of the parables. For them, every *i* had to be dotted and every *t* crossed. In short, they required a detailed exegesis of the metaphorical imagery of Jesus. Reference to a lack of comprehension on the part of the apostles was probably intended to make non-Jewish Christians feel less ashamed.

When the whole collection of the parables is examined we realize that with the exception of the allegory of the tenants of the vineyard (no. 4) they all end up by focusing on a single religious or moral counsel, and colourfully exhort the addressees to embrace the attitude or perform the act commanded by the story.

5. *The multi-level significance of the parables*

In the course of this survey I have repeatedly pointed out that in their final form the parables of the Gospel may carry several meanings successively imposed on them. The first may have been perceived by the audience addressed by Jesus. This was replaced by another in the Palestinian Jewish church, which was preoccupied with the idea of the return of Christ. Non-Jewish Christianity, which had to cater for its special needs, adopted yet another. The parables of the wedding feast (no. 13), the labourers in the vineyard (no. 23), the Pharisee and the publican (no. 40) and the last judgement (no. 26) all belong to this class. The classification of the sayings of Jesus in the Appendix will distinguish between these various levels of significance.

5

Quoting or Interpreting Scripture

The Bible played a fundamental part in the religious and literary creativity of the Jews in the intertestamental era when the Apocrypha, Pseudepigrapha, the Dead Sea Scrolls and the earliest rabbinic writings were produced. In chronological terms we are talking of the period between *c.* 200 BC (roughly the end of the Old Testament literature) and AD 200 (the approximate completion of the Mishnah), with the career of Jesus falling almost exactly in the middle.

In their teaching and interpretative activity Jewish masters made use of the Bible, their Holy Scripture, in simple and complex ways. (1) Like some of the psalmists and wisdom poets of the later stages of the Old Testament, post-biblical and New Testament writers often borrowed familiar idioms from the sacred books in order to endow their own phrases with an aura of holiness and authority. Such an anthological style is frequently found in Jewish poetry and apocalyptic texts composed during the last centuries BC and the first century AD. (2) Other Jewish authors 're-write' the Bible, that is to say, they incorporate their exposition into an enlarged text of Scripture itself. This method is applied to Genesis in the Book of Jubilees and the Dead Sea Genesis Apocryphon, and to the whole Torah in the Qumran Reworked Pentateuch, the *Jewish Antiquities* of Josephus and in the Palestinian Aramaic paraphrases (Targums) of the Law. (3) Freshly developed doctrine may be supported by citing scriptural examples, or may itself be derived from the words of Moses and the prophets by laying specific emphasis on some of them or by contrasting one statement with another. (4) Again, both the Law and the prophetic works are often understood as foretelling the events of, and alluding to personalities of, the future eschatological age. (5) In the first few centuries of the Christian era the rabbis of the Midrash and Talmud continued and further developed interpretative methods. For instance they employed different biblical excerpts and conflated them to form the type of exegesis called *midrash*, which brings together two, three or more passages and produces a new meaning from this combination of texts. With the exception of the 're-written Bible', all these exegetical methods are attested in the Synoptic Gospels.

The books of the New Testament contain about nine hundred examples of Scripture quotations and interpretations, ranging from the allusive use of an Old Testament passage to an explicit citation. Well over two-thirds of this number figure in the letters of St Paul (including Hebrews) and the Book of Revelation. The Acts of the Apostles accounts for another hundred cases. The rest come from the Catholic Epistles (except the letters of John, which never cite the Bible), the Gospel of John and the narrative sections of the Synoptic Gospels. Use of the Bible directly attributed to Jesus in Mark, Matthew and Luke is relatively rare; if we discount the purely fictional and midrashic exegetical debate between him and the devil (Matt. 4:3–10; Luke 4:3–12), there are altogether forty instances, i.e. they amount to less than 5 per cent of the total.

I. MARK AND THE TRIPLE TRADITION

1. Plucking heads of grain (Mark 2:23–28; Matt. 12:1–6; Luke 6:1–5) [1 Sam. 21:1–7; Num. 28:9–10][1]

One sabbath he was going through the grainfields; and as they made their way his disciples began to pluck heads of grain. And the Pharisees said to him, 'Look, why are they doing what is not lawful on the sabbath?' And he said to them, *Have you never read what David did, when he was in need and was hungry, he and those who were with him: how he entered the house of God, when Abiathar was high priest, and ate the bread of the Presence, which it is not lawful for any but the priests to eat, and also gave it to those who were with him*? And he said to them, *The sabbath*

1. In this chapter, words printed in italics represent biblical quotations or allusions.

was made for man, not man for the sabbath; so the Son of man is lord even of the sabbath (Mark, Luke).

Or have you not read in the law how on the sabbath the priests profane the sabbath, and are guiltless? (Matt.)

The section has already been dealt with among controversy stories in chapter 2, no. 3. Here only its use of the Bible will be considered.

The scriptural allusion from 1 Samuel 21:1–7 is introduced as a precedent to justify the breach of ancestral custom by the disciples of Jesus. The issue is the interpretation of a legal rule which qualifies the plucking of heads of grain as harvesting, i.e. 'work' forbidden by Jewish law on the Sabbath (see mShab 7:2). The unformulated principle underlying the reasoning in the Gospels is that hunger is the first stage of a process which culminates in starvation. Starvation in turn is life-threatening, and as such entitles one to set aside the Sabbath observances. But Jesus of the Synoptics is not credited with this line of argument. Instead of analysing legal principles, he quotes the example of the great hero King David, referring to an event which happened in the temple of the city of Nob. According to the Bible, David transgressed, and permitted his famished soldiers to transgress, a law prohibiting lay Israelites to eat the sacred bread of the Presence reserved for priests.

Such an argument from precedent is not exclusive to the Gospel (or to Jesus). For instance, the precept of the Mishnah forbidding the Jewish king to participate in a funeral procession is questioned by Rabbi Judah b. Ilai (mid second century AD) on the grounds that according to 2 Samuel 3:31 David was allowed to follow the bier of Abner, the commander of his army (mSanh 2:3). Nevertheless, such a proof based on an example recorded outside the Law of Moses conflicted with rabbinic methodology, which considered the Pentateuch as the only authoritative source for legal rulings. The Dead Sea Damascus Document also stipulates that David's polygamy (cf. 2 Sam. 3:2–5) must not be invoked as a precedent to justify a breach of what the Qumran sectaries believed to be the biblical law of monogamous marriage (CD 5:2–5).

It is noteworthy, however, that Matthew, a 'scribe . . . trained for the kingdom of heaven' (Matt. 13:52), tried to improve the case by using a juridical precedent. He drew attention to butchery and cooking legitimately performed by priests in the course of sacrificial worship on the Sabbath, while slaughtering, dissecting, roasting, boiling or burning animals would have amounted to a breach of the Law if accomplished outside the Temple (see Matt. 12:5–6, alluding to Num. 28:9–10).[2] However, members of the original Galilean audience were less sophisticated than the rabbis of the Mishnah, or even Matthew. They were prepared to accept that what was good for David would be good for them, too.

2. Concealment of meaning through parables (Mark 4:11–12; Matt. 13:11–15; Luke 8:10) [Isa. 6:9–10]

To you has been given the secret of the kingdom of God (Mark, Luke) [kingdom of heaven, but to them it has not been given (Matt.)]. But for those outside everything is in parables, so that they may indeed *see* but not *perceive*, and may indeed *hear* but not *understand*; lest they should *turn* again, and be forgiven (Mark).

But for others they are in parables, so that *seeing* they may not see, and *hearing* they may not *understand* (Luke).

This is why I speak to them in parables, because *seeing* they do not see, and *hearing* they do not hear, nor do they *understand*. With them indeed is fulfilled the prophecy of Isaiah which says: '*You shall indeed hear but never understand, and you shall indeed see but never perceive. For this people's heart has grown dull, and their ears are heavy of hearing, and their eyes they have closed, lest they should perceive with their eyes, and hear with their ears, and understand with their heart, and turn for me to heal them*' (Matt.).

2. 'On the sabbath day two male lambs a year old without blemish, and two tenths of an ephah of fine flour for a cereal offering, mixed with oil, and its drink offering; this is the burnt offering of every sabbath, besides the continual burnt offering and its drink offering.'

Between the Gospel parable of the sower (Mark 4:3–9; Matt. 13:3–9; Luke 8:5–8; see chapter 4, no. 1a) and its interpretation (Mark 4:13–20; Matt. 13:18–23; Luke 8:11–15; see chapter 4, no. 1b) the evangelists introduce an explanation of the purpose of Jesus' teaching in parables and justify it from Isaiah 6:9–10. This text is cited allusively by Mark and Luke and fully by Matthew. The alleged aim is to prevent the listeners from grasping the message of Jesus which was reserved for initiates only. They were offered a special exegesis of the riddles (cf. chapter 4, p. 171).

Such an explication contradicts the nature of the many parables used in the Bible and in post-biblical Jewish literature, whose colourful metaphorical style is meant, not to obscure, but to facilitate understanding. Such an interpretation would make sense only if Jesus had been the teacher of an esoteric movement which restricted its message to select initiates as was the case in the Essene-Qumran community. There, members had to swear an oath never to disclose their secrets to outsiders (Josephus, *War* 2:141). According to the Dead Sea Community Rule full members had to conduct themselves towards non-members 'in a spirit of secrecy' (1QS 9:21) and hide 'the teaching of the Law from the men of falsehood' (1QS 9:16). The best explanation of the Gospel saying and its use of Isaiah 6 is that the evangelists antedated general Jewish unbelief to the time of Jesus and portrayed him as one who wished to hide the significance of his preaching from his compatriots. In later New Testament tradition Isaiah 6 is used as a proof text to demonstrate the blindness and obduracy of the Jews (Acts 28:23–28; John 12:37–41).

3. The parable of the secretly growing seed and the harvest (Mark 4:26–29) [Joel 3:13]

The kingdom of God is as if a man should scatter seed upon the ground, and should sleep and rise night and day, and the seed should sprout and grow, he knows not how. The earth produces of itself, first the blade, then the ear, then the full grain in the ear. But when the grain is *ripe*, at once he *puts in the sickle*, because *the harvest* has come.

The concluding phrase of the parable (see chapter 4, no. 2) describes the harvest, completing the process which started with sowing. Mark 4:29 borrows words from Joel 3:13 (Hebrew text 4:13): 'Put in the sickle, for the harvest is ripe.' Despite its somewhat cliché-like character and the lack of complete verbal identity with the Septuagint,[3] the terminology used by Mark is striking enough for it to be acknowledged as deriving from the Joel passage rather than representing common eschatological imagery. Nevertheless it should be observed that Joel was not such a popular book of the Bible for its knowledge to be assumed without further ado. Its insertion can therefore be more reasonably assigned to the editor of Mark than to the author of the parable, Jesus.

4. The parable of the mustard seed (Mark 4:30–32; Matt. 13:31–32; Luke 13:18–19) [Ezek. 17:23; 31:6; Dan. 4:10–12, 20–21]

With what can we compare the kingdom of God, or what parable shall we use for it? It is like a grain of mustard seed, which, when sown upon the ground, is the smallest of all the seeds on earth; yet when it is sown, *it grows up and becomes the greatest of all shrubs, and puts forth large branches, so that the birds of the air can make nests in its shade* [*branches* (Matt., Luke)].

The proverbial disproportion between the tiny mustard seed and the large shrub into which it develops has been discussed in chapter 4, no. 3. As far as the biblical background of the imagery is concerned, it is not a direct borrowing in its depiction of the mustard shrub but is inspired by the idea of the tall cedar (Ezek. 17:23 and 31:6), which in turn may have influenced the description of the huge tree in Nebuchadnezzar's dream (Dan. 4:10–12, 20–21). It should be observed that both passages envisage a tree of considerable height, and not a large bush.

It would seem likely, then, that the parable does not cite a particular

3. Mark replaces the noun 'vintage' (*trugê*) in the Septuagint translation of Joel by the more suitable Greek word *therismos*, 'harvest'.

biblical text, but rather uses a familiar scriptural motif. On the other hand, turning a mustard shrub into a large tree is an exaggeration typical of the teaching style of Jesus. The presence of birds is asserted in both Ezekiel and Daniel; hence the supposition advanced by some New Testament interpreters that these birds are deliberately introduced to allude allegorically to the admission of the Gentiles to the church appears unfounded.

5. Corban and filial respect (Mark 7:9–13; Matt. 15:3–6) [Exod. 20:12; Deut. 5:16; Exod. 21:17; Lev. 20:9]

You have a fine way of rejecting the commandment of God, in order to keep your tradition! For Moses said, *'Honour your father and your mother'*; and, *'He who speaks evil of father or mother, let him surely die'*; but you say, 'If a man tells his father or his mother, What you would have gained from me is Corban (that is, given to God) – then you no longer permit him to do anything for his father or mother, thus making void the word of God through your tradition which you hand on. And many such things you do.

The conflict between the demands of the commandment, 'Honour your father and your mother', and of a vow promising a donation to the Temple known as *Corban* or *Qorban* has been considered in connection with the debate on purity in chapter 2, no. 8. This Hebrew/ Aramaic term is used also by Josephus who renders it as 'gift to God' (*Against Apion* 1:167).

6. Prohibition of divorce (Mark 10:11–12; Matt. 5:31–32; 19:9; Luke 16:18) [Deut. 24:1]

Whoever divorces his wife and marries another, commits adultery against her; and if she divorces her husband and marries another, she commits adultery [and he who marries a woman divorced from her husband commits adultery (Mark, Luke)].

It was also said, '*Whoever divorces his wife, let him give her a certificate of divorce.*' But I say to you that every one who divorces his wife, except on the ground of unchastity, makes her an adulteress; and whoever marries a divorced woman commits adultery (Matt.).

The debate of Jesus with the Pharisees on divorce has been analysed, and his view that the conditions prevailing in Paradise are to be restored in the eschatological age has been explained, in chapter 2, no. 9.

The only Old Testament passage connected with the enactment of divorce through issuing a deed of separation (*sefer keritut*) is quoted by Jesus in his so-called antitheses, and by the rabbis in their relevant legal rulings. To understand the peculiarity of Jesus' stand, one must bear in mind that divorce and remarriage were legal and commonly practised in the Jewish world of his age; only the grounds for divorce were the subject of controversy among Pharisee teachers. The stricter jurist Shammai permitted the dissolution of marriage only for sexual misbehaviour by the wife, whereas the tolerant Hillel declared anything in the wife that caused the husband displeasure (for instance, if she was a bad cook) to be a sufficient reason for divorce (mGit 9:10). In the same spirit, Josephus writes that the Law of Moses permits divorce for 'whatever cause'. Indeed, this lax custom was generally the rule in Jewish society. For example, Josephus remarks that he divorced his wife, who had borne him three children, simply because he was dissatisfied with her (*Life* 426). Likewise the Pharisees in Matthew 19:3 inquire whether Jesus would approve of the granting of divorce on any ground.

The conflict between Jesus' and Paul's eschatological outlook (1 Cor. 7:10–11), advocating no change in personal status during the time of the final upheaval and thus hostile to divorce and remarriage,[4] and the light-hearted male Jewish attitude in regard to successive marital unions accounts for oscillating opinions in the primitive church, whose members were no longer animated by eschatological fever. For while the Jesus of Mark and Luke tolerates no second union, Matthew's

4. Even the married state is considered undesirable amid the eschatological woes: 'Alas for those who are with child and for those who give suck in those days!' (Mark 13:17; Matt. 24:19; Luke 21:23).

Jesus twice introduces into the passage the exception clause of unchastity (Matt. 5:32; 19:9). The reason for this is that the wife's sexual misbehaviour has already destroyed the unity of 'one flesh', the quasi-metaphysical bond holding together the original couple. Characteristically, even the eschatologically motivated Paul allowed the dissolution of marriage in one specific case: a newly-converted person was free to remarry if the pagan spouse was unwilling to go on living with the partner who had become a Christian (1 Cor. 7:15).

As for Mark's reference to a woman divorcing her husband, it envisages a legal context alien to the world of Jesus and his Jewish contemporaries in which a woman could not initiate divorce proceedings. Even when Salome, sister of Herod the Great, a royal princess, arrogated to herself the right to send a bill of divorce to her husband Costobarus, the action was declared illegal. Josephus explicitly states that only a man can issue such a document, and that without it no woman can enter into a new marriage bond (*Antiquities* 15:259).

Thus the Matthean antithesis on divorce reveals the complex religious and social conditions which affected Jesus, the Palestinian Jewish world of his time, and primitive Gentile Christianity.

See also chapter 9, no. 7.

7. The sign of Jonah and the queen of the South (Mark 8:12; Matt. 12:39–42 (16:4); Luke 11:29–32) [Jonah 1:17; 3:5; 1 Kings 10:1–10]

Why does this generation seek a sign? Truly I say to you, no sign shall be given to this generation (Mark 8:12).

An evil and adulterous generation seeks for a sign, but no sign shall be given to it except the sign of the prophet Jonah. *For as Jonah was three days and three nights in the belly of the whale*, so will the Son of man be three days and three nights in the heart of the earth (Matt. 12:39–40; cf. 16:4).

For as Jonah became a sign to the men of Nineveh, so will the Son of man be to this generation (Luke 11:30).

The men of Nineveh will arise at the judgement with this generation and condemn it; for they *repented at the preaching of Jonah*, and behold, something greater than Jonah is here. *The queen of the South* will arise at the judgement with [the men of (Luke)] this generation and condemn it; for she *came from the ends of the earth to hear the wisdom of Solomon*, and behold, something greater than Solomon is here (Matt., Luke).

The three Gospels supply three different answers of Jesus to those who ask him for a sign. These signs were expected to announce the timetable of the great events of the final age. In Mark 8:12 Jesus does not quote any biblical proof as he flatly refuses to provide a sign (see chapter 8, no. 7). The same unwillingness to accept or approve of premonitions is also expressed in Mark 13:21 and Matthew 24:23, 'And then if any one says to you, "Look, here is the Christ!" or "Look, there he is!" do not believe it.' And perhaps even more emphatically, 'The kingdom of God is not coming with signs to be observed; nor will they say, "Lo, here it is!" or "There!"' (Luke 17:20; cf. chapter 8, nos. 7 and 59). By contrast, in Matthew and Luke the answer is positive and entails the use of a biblical allusion. The quotations are differently interpreted by the two evangelists and both attach to the sign of Jonah a supplementary scriptural proof.

In Luke 11:30 Jesus refers to the sign of Jonah, the prophet who successfully preached repentance to the people of Nineveh (Jonah 3:5). He is presented as the prototype of Jesus who, like John the Baptist before him, was to call the Jews to repentance and thus prepare them for the arrival of the Kingdom of God (see Mark 1:15; Matt. 4:17 – Mark 1:4; Matt. 3:2; Luke 3:3). On the other hand, the appended comment about Jesus being greater than Jonah (or Solomon) in Matthew 12:41–42 and Luke 11:31–32 would sound boastful if uttered by Jesus himself; it is therefore more appropriately credited to the editor of the saying in Q (Matt., Luke).

The same Q passage supplements and reinforces the Jonah example with the story of the queen of the South who travelled from a far country to listen to the wisdom of Solomon (1 Kings 10:1–10). This is contrasted with the unwillingness of the 'evil and adulterous' contemporaries of Jesus who refused to hear the message of 'something greater than Solomon'. The expression 'queen of the South' differs from the Hebrew and the Greek text of Kings, both of which read 'queen of Sheba'. The Abyssinian tradition makes her the sovereign of Ethiopia. In Daniel 11 the 'king of the South' designates the Ptolemaic rulers of Egypt.

In Matthew 12:40 Jonah's stay in the belly of the 'great fish' (Jonah 1:17)[5] prefigures the three (incomplete) days during which the body of Jesus lay in the tomb. According to Jewish time reckoning attested in rabbinic literature, part of a day or night was accepted as a full day or night (yShab 12a; bPes 4a). This would allow us to count three days from Friday afternoon to Sunday morning, but no stretch of imagination could fit three nights into that period. The use of this biblical argument presupposes that Jesus has predicted his resurrection after *three* days. This question, together with the rabbinic theme of 'after three days', will be discussed later (see chapter 7, no. 14).

8. Punishment for making someone sin (Mark 9:47–48; Matt. 18:9) [Isa. 66:24]

And if your eye causes you to sin, pluck it out; it is better for you to enter the kingdom of God with one eye than with two eyes to be thrown into Gehenna, [*where their worm does not die and the fire is not quenched* (Mark)].

Following up the maxim about the great millstone (see chapter 3, no. 10), the colourful counsel of Jesus declares the sacrifice of one eye preferable to the destruction of the whole body in Gehenna or hell (cf. chapter 9, no. 6). The suffering in the underworld is described only in Mark, using words which correspond closely to the last verse in the Book of Isaiah (Isa. 66:24).

As in no. 2 above, the introduction of the scriptural verse serves as stylistic embellishment. Since the Isaiah text is missing from Matthew, who used Mark as his source, its insertion in Mark should probably be attributed to a later editor of that Gospel.

5. The Gospel's whale (*kêtos*) comes from the Septuagint, not from the Hebrew Bible.

9. How to gain eternal life (Mark 10:19; Matt. 19:17–19; Luke 18:20) [Exod. 20:12–16; Deut. 5:16–20; Lev. 19:18]

You know the commandments [If you would enter life, keep the commandments (Matt.)]: *'Do not kill, Do not commit adultery, Do not steal, Do not bear false witness,* [*Do not defraud* (Mark),] *Honour your father and mother.'*

. . . *and, You shall love your neighbour as yourself* (Matt.).

This is the longer version of the abbreviated religious itinerary to the Kingdom of God. (For two shorter versions, see nos. 13 and 23 below.) The ethical commands of the Decalogue are offered in answer to the question of how to gain eternal life (cf. chapter 8, no. 14). The main textual tradition of Mark includes the additional 'Do not defraud'. Absent from the Ten Commandments, it is taken from the Greek biblical manuscript, the Codex Alexandrinus, for Deuteronomy 24:14 (see also Ecclus. 4:1). Matthew, in turn, appends Leviticus 19:18, 'You shall love your neighbour', presented elsewhere as the quintessence of man's religious duties towards fellow humans (see no. 13 below).[6] By adopting such a shortcut, Jesus is in line here with the teaching that the Ten Commandments constitute the summary of the whole Torah and that they are holier than the rest of the laws of the Bible, having been proclaimed directly by God and not through Moses.[7] Such a simplification of religion is typical of Jesus and of other great Jewish moralists of his age, such as Philo of Alexandria.

6. St Paul fully embraces this moral principle. In Romans 13:8–9 he writes, 'He who loves his neighbour has fulfilled the law. The commandments, "You shall not commit adultery, You shall not kill, You shall not steal, You shall not covet", and any other commandment, are summed up in this sentence, "You shall love your neighbour as yourself."' Cf. also Galatians 5:14.

7. See Philo, *Special Laws* 1:1; *Decalogue* 175; Josephus, *Antiquities* 3:89.

10. The cleansing of the Temple (Mark 11:17; Matt. 21:13; Luke 19:46) [Isa. 56:7; Jer. 7:11]

And he taught and said to them, Is it not written, *'My house shall be called a house of prayer* [*for all the nations* (Mark)]'?[8] *But you have made it a den of robbers.*

The evangelists present the combined citation of Isaiah 56 and Jeremiah 7 as the biblical justification for Jesus' action when he overturned the merchants' and money-changers' stalls in the Temple. In fact, this is a *pesher*-type interpretation of prophetic texts. It is more likely to have stemmed from the primitive church than from Jesus, who was acting and teaching 'with authority' (Mark 1:27; Luke 4:36) and required no scriptural backing.

11. The parable of the wicked tenants of the vineyard (Mark 12:1–11; Matt. 21:33–42; Luke 20:9–18) [Isa. 5:1–2; Ps. 118:22–23]

A man planted *a vineyard*, and set a hedge around it, and *dug* a pit for the *wine press*, and *built a tower*, and let it out to tenants, and went into another country. When the time came, he sent a servant [his servants (Matt.)] to the tenants, to get from them some of the fruit of the vineyard. And they took and beat him, and sent him away empty-handed [beat one, killed another, and stoned another (Matt.)]. Again he sent to them another servant [other servants, more than the first (Matt.)], and they wounded him in the head and treated him shamefully [and they did the same to them (Matt.)] [him also they beat and treated shamefully, and sent him away empty-handed (Luke)]. And he sent another, and him they killed; and so with many others, some they beat and some they killed [And he sent yet a third; this one

8. Matthew and Luke omit 'for all the nations' as universalism is not part of their concern at this moment; Mark automatically quotes Isaiah 56:7 in full: 'My house shall be called a house of prayer for all peoples.'

they wounded and cast out (Luke)]. He had still one other, a beloved son; finally he sent him to them, saying, 'They will respect my son.' But those tenants said to one another, 'This is the heir; come, let us kill him, and the inheritance will be ours.' And they took him and killed him, and cast him out of the vineyard. What will the owner of the vineyard do? He will come and destroy the tenants and give the vineyard to others. Have you not read this scripture: *'The very stone which the builders rejected has become the head of the corner; this was the Lord's doing, and it is marvellous in our eyes'*?

Every one who falls on that stone will be broken to pieces; but when it falls on any one it will crush him (Luke).

The parable itself has been discussed and the biblical quotations noted in chapter 4, no. 4. It re-uses Isaiah's allegorical description of the people of Israel as a vineyard and applies it to the clash between Jesus and the Jewish religious leaders of his time. The free citation of Isaiah provides the story with a prophetic foundation. The situation in which Jesus found himself thus acquired the appearance of sad familiarity.

In contrast, the appended literal quotation of Psalm 118 carries with it a *pesher*-type apologetical message. The corner stone symbolizing the son of the owner of the vineyard typifies Jesus, the foundation stone of the church. The exposition supplied by Luke (20:18) indicates that the murderers will be avenged and destroyed by their victim.

Psalm 118:22 was a standard proof text used by the primitive church. It is quoted not only here, and indirectly in Mark 8:31 (the son of Man rejected by the elders, etc.), but also more fully in the Acts of the Apostles 4:11 and the First Letter of Peter 2:4–7. The lack of direct connection between the excerpt and the parable itself, and the fact that the Psalm citation is part of the debating arsenal of Jewish Christianity, strongly argues against a direct link between the quotation and the main body of the story, whereas the allusion to Isaiah 5 is part and parcel of the parable.

12. Proof of the resurrection of the dead (Mark 12:18–27; Matt. 22:23–32; Luke 20:27–38) [Exod. 3:6]

And Sadducees came to him, who say that there is no resurrection; and they asked him a question, saying, 'Teacher, Moses wrote for us that if a man's brother dies and leaves a wife, but leaves no child, the man must take the wife, and raise up children for his brother. There were seven brothers; the first took a wife, and when he died left no children; and the second took her, and died, leaving no children; and the third likewise; and the seven left no children. Last of all the woman also died. In the rsurrection whose wife will she be? For the seven had her as wife.' Jesus said to them, Is not this why you are wrong, that you know neither the scriptures nor the power of God? (Mark, Matt.).

The sons of this age marry and are given in marriage; but those who are accounted worthy to attain to that age and to the resurrection from the dead (Luke).

For when they rise from the dead, they neither marry nor are given in marriage, but are like angels in heaven (Mark, Matt.).

... for they cannot die any more, because they are equal to angels, and are sons of God, being sons of the resurrection (Luke).

And as for the dead being raised, have you not read in the book of Moses, in the passage about the bush, how God said to him, *'I am the God of Abraham, and the God of Isaac, and the God of Jacob'*? He is not God of the dead, but of the living; you are quite wrong (Mark, Matt., Luke).

For the debate with Sadducees in Jerusalem concerning the doctrine of the resurrection of the dead, understood as the reunification of body and soul, see chapter 2, no. 12. Here we are only concerned with the curious argument adduced from the 'book of Moses', i.e. Exodus 3:6, which at first sight has nothing to do with the raising of dead bodies. The demonstration is directed against the Sadducees, who rejected any form of afterlife. As a second thought, the editor of Mark attached this scriptural proof to the dispute. The reasoning reflects the technique of Bible interpretation championed by the Pharisees, protagonists of the doctrine of resurrection. The tacit thinking in this case is the following. Since God declares to Moses that he *is* (present tense) the God of Abraham, Isaac and Jacob, it is implied that the three (dead) patriarchs are already (potentially) alive, though they would actually be revived only at the time of the general resurrection of the dead at the end of time. A whole collection of Bible examples purporting to demonstrate from the Pentateuch the doctrine of the resurrection may be found in the Babylonian Talmud (Sanh 90). For instance the phrasing in Exodus 6:4 affirming that God would give the promised land to *them* (i.e. Abraham, Isaac and Jacob, long since deceased), and not to *you* (the later generations of Israelites), shows that the future resurrection of the patriarchs is assumed, and implicitly asserted there (bSanh 90b). However, this sort of scriptural proof would have made no impression on the Sadducees, as they stood for the literal exegesis of the Bible and shunned the intellectual acrobatics of the Pharisaic midrash.

13. The first and the second commandments (Mark 12:29–31; Matt. 22:37–40; cf. Luke 10:27–28) [Deut. 6:4–5; Lev. 19:18]

The first is, '*Hear, O Israel: The Lord our God, the Lord is one; and you shall love the Lord your God with all your heart, and with all your soul, and with all your mind, and with all your strength.*'

This is the great and first commandment. And a second is like it (Matt.).

The second is this, '*You shall love your neighbour as yourself.*' There is no other commandment greater than these.

On these two commandments depend all the law and the prophets (Matt.).

You shall love the Lord your God . . . and your neighbour as yourself. And he [Jesus] said to him, You have answered right; do this, and you will live (Luke).

Compared with the synopsis of religious obligations, based on the Decalogue (see no. 9 above), the present shorter summary continues to echo, as far as the 'neighbour' is concerned, the formula of Leviticus 19:18, 'and, You shall love your neighbour as yourself'. It was presented by Jesus to a well-intentioned scribe or lawyer. He declared on the one hand as one's primary duty the love of God, expressed in the words of the *Shema* or 'Hear, O Israel', the prayer repeated every day, and coupled it with the precept to love one's fellow, the single-phrase summary of man's moral duty towards man. We are thus confronted with the kernel of the Jewish religion. According to Matthew 22:40, the whole biblical revelation – the Torah and the prophets – is summed up in these two commandments.

In Luke 10:27, where the biblical text is recited not by Jesus, but by his interlocutor, the original two commands merge in a single one, the love of God *and* of the neighbour. This is the culmination of a tendency attempting to reduce the many laws of the Bible to one. The best rabbinic example may be read in the Talmud where the third-century Rabbi Simlai cuts down the 613 precepts of the Torah of Moses to one imperative, 'Seek me!', uttered by God in Amos 5:4 (bMak 24a).

For another one-sentence epitome of the Law and the prophets, formulated without biblical quotation, see the Golden Rule, 'So whatever you wish that men do to you, do so to them', in no. 23 below.

14. Debate about the son of David (Mark 12:35–37; Matt. 22:41–45; Luke 20:41–44) [Ps. 110:1]

And as Jesus taught in the temple, he said, [Now while the Pharisees were gathered together, Jesus asked them a question, saying, (Matt.)] How can the scribes say that the Christ is the son of David? [What do you think of the Christ? Whose son is he? They said to him, 'The son of David.' (Matt.)] David himself, inspired by the Holy Spirit, declared, *'The Lord said to my Lord, Sit at my right hand, till I put thy enemies under thy feet.'* David himself calls him Lord, so how is he his son?

In an argument with Pharisees about the meaning of Psalm 110:1 their customary verbal dexterity is skilfully turned against them. It goes without saying that the evangelist (impersonating Jesus) takes it for granted that David was a prophet,[9] the ancestor of the Messiah and the author of this Psalm. The final question – how can someone called by David his Lord be his son? – is rhetorical. It is not intended to produce an answer but rather to confuse the Pharisees. Biblical exegesis and anti-Pharisee argument of this kind are more likely to express the mentality of a Christian 'scribe' of the Palestinian church than the thinking of Jesus. For a more detailed examination see chapter 2, no. 13.

15. The return of the son of Man (Mark 13:24–27; Matt. 24:29–31; Luke 21:25–28) [Isa. 13:10; 34:4; Dan. 7:13–14; Ps. 65:7]

But in those days, after that tribulation, *the sun will be darkened, and the moon will not give its light, and the stars will be falling from heaven, and the powers in the heavens* will be shaken. And then they will *see the Son of man coming in* [*on the* (Matt.)] *clouds* [*of heaven* (Matt.)] with [great (Mark)] power and glory. And then he will send out the angels [with a loud trumpet call (Matt.)] and *gather* his elect *from the four winds, from the ends of the earth to the ends of heaven* [*from one end of heaven to the other* (Matt.)] (Mark, Matt.).

And there will be signs in sun and moon and stars, and upon the earth distress *of nations* in perplexity at the *roaring of the sea and the waves*, men fainting with fear and with foreboding of what is coming on the world; for *the powers of the heavens* will be shaken. And then they will see *the Son of man coming in a cloud* with power and great glory. Now when these things begin to take place, look up and raise your heads, because your redemption is drawing near (Luke).

9. For David as prophet, see the account of David's poems in the Qumran Psalms Scroll (11QPs 27:11; Acts 2:30).

Various eschatological images garnered from the Old Testament are used here to outline the circumstances of the return of Christ, the son of Man. The premonitory signs, borrowed from Isaiah in Mark and Matthew or from Psalm 65 in Luke, are combined with the crucial apocalyptic scene of 'one like a son of man' in Daniel 7 (see chapter 7, no. 19), and more freely with Deuteronomy 30:4, Isaiah 27:13 and Zechariah 2:6. For a similar description of the Parousia, see 1 Thessalonians 4:16–17: 'For the Lord himself will descend from heaven with a cry of command, with the archangel's call, and with the sound of the trumpet of God . . . then we who are alive, who are left, shall be caught up . . . in the clouds to meet the Lord in the air.'

Like the typology of Jonah mentioned earlier, this passage is intended for members of the primitive church, who looked for clues indicating the approach of Jesus' Second Coming. This typical concern of a community totally absorbed in the expectation of the imminent end-time stands in sharp contrast to the reluctance of Jesus to provide a timetable of the final happenings by means of premonitory signs (see no. 7 above).

16. The flight of the disciples (Mark 14:27; Matt. 26:31) [Zech. 13:7]

You will all fall away [because of me this night (Matt.)]; for it is written, *'I will strike the shepherd, and the sheep* [*of the flock* (Matt.)] *will be scattered.'*

The Zechariah quotation is employed in the form of a *pesher* to account for the abandonment of Jesus by all his disciples after he was arrested by the authorities. The same verse is cited in the Damascus Document from the Dead Sea Scrolls (CD 19:7–9). There, however, the 'scattered sheep' are understood as designating the wicked members of the Qumran sect opposed to the faithful who are called 'the little ones'. The followers of Jesus are also referred to as 'little ones' in the New Testament (see chapter 9, no. 24).

17. Words of sorrow in Gethsemane (Mark 14:34; Matt. 26:38) [Ps. 42:6]

My soul is very sorrowful, even to death; remain here, and watch [with me (Matt.)].

The distress felt by Jesus in the Garden of Gethsemane is conveyed to the three chosen apostles, Peter, James and John, through the words possibly taken from Psalms 42:5–6, 11 [12 in Hebrew], 43:5. The editor of Mark clarified the meaning of the citation by joining to it the non-biblical supplement, 'even to death'. Since it is not even certain that 'My soul is very sorrowful' is actually a quotation from Psalm 42 – it may be a sheer coincidence – there is no reason to postulate, as many Gospel interpreters do, that the whole refrain of Psalm 42:11 was borne in mind. They assume that in addition to the plaintive 'Why are you cast down, O my soul, and why are you disquieted within me?' Jesus was thinking also of its confident and happy ending, 'Hope in God; for I shall again praise him, my help and my God.'

18. Jesus' answer to the High Priest (Mark 14:61–62; Matt. 26:63–64; Luke 22:67–69) [Ps. 110:1; Dan. 7:13]

Again the high priest asked him, 'Are you the Christ, the Son of the Blessed?' And Jesus said, I am; and you will see *the Son of man seated at the right hand of Power, and coming with the clouds of heaven* (Mark).

Jesus said to him, You have said so. But I tell you, hereafter you will see *the Son of man seated at the right hand of Power, and coming on the clouds of heaven* (Matt.).

But he said to them, If I tell you, you will not believe; and if I ask you, you will not answer. But from now on *the Son of man shall be seated at the right hand of the power of God* (Luke).

To put the historicity of this reply of Jesus to Joseph Caiaphas in the right perspective, we must bear in mind the improbability of an interrogation of this sort within the framework of a formal meeting of the Jewish high court. The Sanhedrin was not permitted to meet at night, let alone during a night which was already part of a Sabbath or a festival.[10] (Note that the Jewish day starts with the appearance of the first star and finishes at sunset.) So *a priori* the genuineness of the dialogue is doubtful. As for the words themselves, they consist of an amalgam of Psalm 110:1 (the glorified Messiah, son of David, sitting at the right hand of God) and Daniel 7:13 (the son of Man arriving on the clouds). Luke, apt to dilute eschatological fervour, omits the reference to the Parousia in the clouds.

For the explanation of the Psalm excerpt see chapter 2, no. 13, and no. 14 above. It belongs to the basic proof texts of primitive Christianity (see, in addition to the texts already quoted, Acts 2:34–35; Rom. 8:34; 1 Cor. 15:25; Eph. 1:20; Col. 3:1; Heb. 1:3, 13; 8:1; 10:12–13). The 'son of Man' citations on which the Parousia doctrine is founded will be discussed in chapter 7, no. 20. The mention of 'thrones' in the plural in Daniel 7:9 and the granting of the everlasting kingship to the son of Man (Dan. 7:14) suggest an implicit relationship between Daniel 7 and Psalm 110.

19. The last cry of Jesus (Mark 15:34; Matt. 27:46) [Ps. 22:2]

And at the ninth hour Jesus cried with a loud voice, *Eloi, Eloi, lama sabachthani?* which means, 'My God, my God, why hast thou forsaken me?'

The last words of Jesus are reproduced in Aramaic, his mother tongue, which endows them with considerable psychological verisimilitude. In Hebrew (*'eli 'eli lamah 'azabtani*) they correspond to the opening words of Psalm 22:2. It is claimed by New Testament exegetes that when Jesus pronounced the first line of a Psalm which contains despair,

10. There is no reason to doubt the reliability of the relevant information contained in the Mishnah tractate Sanhedrin, especially mSanh 4:1.

he in fact was thinking of its happy ending; Psalm 22:31 speaks of deliverance of the oppressed (see also no. 17 above).

Two reasons militate against such a theologically inspired explanation. The first is that according to the evangelists the onlookers did not identify the cry as a quotation from a Psalm, but mistaking 'Eloi' or 'Eli' for 'Eliyah' (Elijah), wondered whether the dying man was asking the miracle-working prophet Elijah to take him down from the cross (Mark 15:35; Matt. 27:47). The second and more significant difficulty arises from the fact that the words of Jesus were uttered in Aramaic. Why should he quote a psalm in translation? The Bible was normally recited in Hebrew during the Sabbath service in the synagogue and it is reasonable to assume that worshippers knew the majority of the psalms by heart. The most likely interpretation of this phrase is that 'My God, my God, why hast thou forsaken me?' was a popular Aramaic exclamation of religious incomprehension. Johann Sebastian Bach in his St Matthew Passion appears to have best understood and expressed the deepest meaning of the cry of the dying Jesus. The attempts to substitute doctrinally unobjectionable words for this shocking exclamation indirectly argue for its authenticity.

II. THE Q TRADITION

20. Jesus' altercation with the devil (Matt. 4:3–10; Luke 4:3–11) [Deut. 8:3; Ps. 91:11–12; Deut. 6:16; 6:13]

And the tempter [the devil (Luke)] came and said to him, 'If you are the Son of God, command these stones to become [loaves of (Matt.)] bread.' But he answered, It is written, '*Man shall not live by bread alone* [*but by every word that proceeds from the mouth of God*' (Deut. 8:3) (Matt.)] (Matt., Luke).

Then the devil took him to the holy city [Jerusalem (Luke)], and set him on the pinnacle of the temple, and said to him, 'If you are the Son of God, throw yourself down; for it is written, "*He will give his angels charge of you*", and "*On their hands they will bear you up, lest you strike your foot against a stone*" (Ps. 91).'

Jesus said to him, Again it is written, *'You shall not tempt the Lord your God'* (Deut. 6:16) (Matt. 4:5–7; Luke 4:9–12).

Again, the devil took him [to a very high mountain, (Matt.)] and showed him all the kingdoms of the world and the glory of them [in a moment of time (Luke)]; and he said to him, 'All these I will give you, if you will fall down and worship me' (Matt.).

'To you I will give all this authority and their glory; for it has been delivered to me, and I give it to whom I will. If you, then, will worship me, it shall all be yours' (Luke).

Then Jesus said to him, ['Begone, Satan! for (Matt.)] it is written, '*You shall worship the Lord your God and him only shall you serve*' (Deut. 6:13) (Matt. Luke).

Mark simply refers to a forty-day period spent by Jesus in the desert before starting his public career, during which he was tempted by Satan (Mark 1:12–13); *Q* in turn supplies a detailed theological exchange between them based on Bible quotations by both parties. Most serious scholars consider this passage, not as historical reality, but pure Jewish midrash intended to demonstrate that Jesus, the 'Son of God', resisted tempting offers and showed himself totally subservient to God.

The nature of the scriptural polemic is typically rabbinic. It echoes the usual debating technique used by teachers of the Talmud and Midrash, with biblical argument and counter-argument succeeding one another (cf. bSanh 97b). The passage echoes or prefigures a particular kind of *haggadah* (theological or ethical elaboration of a biblical text where an Old Testament personality expertly manipulates the texts of Scripture).

The best illustration comes from a dialogue between Abraham and the devil in which Satan addresses Abraham: 'If one ventures a word with you, will you be offended? Yet who can keep from speaking? Behold, you have instructed many, and you have strengthened the weak hands. Your words have upheld him who was stumbling, and you have made firm the feeble knees. But now it has come to you, and you are impatient' (Job 4:2–5). Abraham replied: 'I will walk in my integrity' (Ps. 26:1). Satan retorted: 'Is not your fear of God your confidence?'

(Job 4:6). Abraham answered, 'Think now, who that was innocent ever perished?' (Job 4:7). Realizing that Abraham would not listen to him, Satan said, 'Now a word was brought to me stealthily' (Job 4:12), etc. (bSanh. 89b).

The Gospels include no other text of this sort and it is obvious that the exchange testifies to the theology of Q and has nothing to do with the teaching method of Jesus.

21. An eye for an eye and a tooth for a tooth (Matt. 5:38–42; Luke 6:29–30) [Exod. 21:24]

You have heard that it was said, '*An eye for an eye and a tooth for a tooth*'. But I say to you, Do not resist one who is evil (Matt.). But if any one strikes you on the right cheek, turn to him the other also; and if any one would sue you and take your coat, let him have your cloak as well; and if any one forces you to go one mile, go with him two miles. Give to him who begs from you, and do not refuse him who would borrow from you.

The scriptural law of Exodus 21:24 should itself be understood not as vindictive, but as restrictive. It lays down that the punishment must be proportionate to, and not exceed, the crime. Post-biblical Jewish legal tradition already specifically excluded the enactment of revenge in the case of wounding. The Mishnah (Baba Qamma 8:1) speaks of valuation, and the rabbinic commentary Mekhilta on Exodus 21:24 prescribes '(eye-) money' to compensate for the loss of an eye. The Palestinian Targum (Ps.-Jonathan on Exod. 21:24) is also quite specific: 'The price of an eye for an eye,' etc. The antiquity of the rule is attested by Josephus, who introduces the concept of financial compensation into his description of the Mosaic Law itself: 'He that maims a man shall undergo the like . . . unless indeed the maimed man be willing to accept money' (*Antiquities* 4:280). Jesus goes much further and advises boundless generosity. See also chapter 3, no. 14 and chapter 9, no. 11.

22. Love your neighbour and your enemy (Matt. 5:43–48; Luke 6:27–28, 32–36) [Lev. 19:18; Deut. 18:13]

You have heard that it was said, '*You shall love your neighbour* and hate your enemy.' But I say to you, Love your enemies and pray for those who persecute you, so that you may be the sons of your Father who is in heaven; for he makes his sun rise on the evil and on the good and sends rain on the just and on the unjust. For if you love those who love you, what reward have you? Do not even the tax-collectors do the same? And if you salute only your brethren, what more are you doing than others? Do not even the Gentiles do the same? You, therefore, must be perfect, as your heavenly Father is perfect.

The topic of the love of one's enemy has already been investigated in chapter 3, no. 15, and will be further discussed in chapter 9, no. 12. Here we focus exclusively on the biblical underpinning of this precept. Instead of perceiving love of the neighbour and hatred towards an enemy as contradictorily complementing one another, Jesus extends the concept of love to include the enemy and thus seeks to ensure that love is wholly unselfish.

This formulation of the perfect love is typical of Jesus, but similar though less neatly expressed ideas are attested outside the New Testament both in the Hebrew Bible and in post-biblical Jewish writings. The Old Testament enjoins the Jew to help an enemy to raise his donkey which has collapsed under its burden, or to bring back a stray domestic animal to its owner even if that owner is an enemy (Exod. 23:4–5). Elsewhere – negatively – the Israelites are commanded *not* to hate their traditional enemies, the Edomites and the Egyptians (Deut. 23:7). Closer to the time of Jesus, in the second century BC, the author of the Letter of Aristeas (227) prescribes 'liberal charity to our opponents so that in this manner we may convert them to what is proper and fitting to them'. A contemporary of Matthew and Luke, Flavius Josephus declares in his summary of the Law that Moses enjoined *epieikeia* (kindness, gentleness, graciousness) even towards avowed enemies (*Against Apion* 2:211). As so often the case, Jesus expressed with great power and simplicity ideas which were in the air and voiced in a less striking manner by other Jewish writers of his age.

23. The Golden Rule (Matt. 7:12; Luke 6:31) [Tobit 4:15; Ecclus. 31:15]

So whatever you wish that men would do to you, do so to them; [for *this is the law and the prophets* (Matt.)].

We have dealt with attempts at simplifying the Law in no. 9 above (Decalogue plus love of the neighbour) and no. 13 (first and second commandments, treated as one by Luke). Here we come to a single-precept summary of religion *without* biblical basis – unless of course the Apocrypha to which Tobit and Ben Sira belong are recognized as Scripture, as they were by the Jews of the Greek diaspora.

In fact the extra-biblical commandment, called in modern literature the Golden Rule, is attested in various forms in the works of Jewish and non-Jewish authors in Mediterranean antiquity. The subject has been examined in chapter 3, no. 21. A lot of ink has been spilt in arguing whether Jesus' positive formulation 'Do so to them' is superior to the negative 'Do not do to your fellow'. In fact, there is no qualitative difference between the two.

24. Bringing a sword (Matt. 10:34–36; Luke 12:51–53) [Mic. 7:6]

Do not think that I have come to bring peace on earth; I have not come to bring peace, but a sword. *For I have come to set a man against his father, and a daughter against her mother, and a daughter-in-law against her mother-in-law; and a man's foes will be those of his own household* (Matt.).

Do you think that I have come to give peace on earth? No, I tell you, but rather division; for henceforth in one house there will be five divided, three against two and two against three; they will be divided, father against son *and son against father, mother against daughter and daughter against her mother, mother-in-law against her daughter-in-law and daughter-in-law against her mother-in-law* (Luke).

This passage seems to clash with Jesus' praise of peacemakers (see Matt. 5:9; cf. chapter 8, no. 34). In fact, however, the two maxims envisage two different stages of the work for the Kingdom. Here we are faced with the decisive initial choice which is to be followed later by an effort aimed at reconciliation. The forecast that Jesus' appeal was to occasion family warfare, expressed by the hyperbolic contrast between peace and the sword, is reinforced by Micah's prediction about dissension within the household in the final age. The figurative 'sword' is replaced in Luke by its straight meaning, 'division'. Indeed the prophetic imagery is not about bloodshed but internal discord. The options facing those who were engaged in the search for the Kingdom of God often carried with them the necessity of painful decisions. The statement fits in well with Jesus' proclamation of the fundamental choice confronting his followers. Whether he himself backed up the teaching with a biblical citation is debatable.

For reference to the 'sword' in Luke 22:36, 38, see below, chapter 8, no. 52.

25. Jesus' answer to John the Baptist (Matt. 11:4–6; Luke 7:22–23) [Isa. 35:5–6; 61:1]

And Jesus answered them, Go and tell John what you hear and see: *the blind receive their sight and the lame walk, lepers are cleansed and the deaf hear, and the dead are raised up, and the poor have good news preached to them. And blessed is he who takes no offence at me.*

This famous dictum implicitly sums up the charismatic activity of Jesus through the combined use of two eschatological extracts from the Book of Isaiah. The cures performed by Jesus indicate to him and his followers the beginning of the messianic age (see chapter 8, no. 7). A similar coupling of passages from Isaiah and Psalm 146 figures in a fragment from Qumran Cave 4, the so-called 'Messianic Apocalypse': '. . . [the hea]vens and the earth will listen to his Messiah . . . He who liberates the captives, restores sight to the blind, straightens the b[ent] (Ps. 146:7–8) . . . He will heal the wounded, and revive the dead and bring good news to the poor' (4Q521 frag. 2, 2:1, 8, 12).[11] The association of prophetic texts describing the wonders of the final age seems to have been current in the time of Jesus.

26. The prophetic character of John the Baptist (Matt. 11:7–10; Luke 7:24–27) [Mal. 3:1]

What did you go out into the wilderness to behold? A reed shaken by the wind? Why then did you go out? To see a man clothed in soft raiment? Behold, those who wear soft raiment are in kings' houses [those who are gorgeously apparelled and live in luxury are in kings' courts (Luke)]. Why then did you go out? To see a prophet? Yes, I tell you, and more than a prophet. This is he of whom it is written, *'Behold, I send my messenger before thy face, who shall prepare thy way before thee.'*

Here we encounter the warm, loving and poetic description of the Baptist by Jesus. He recognizes him as the most outstanding prophet. The disparaging remarks attached to this eulogy represent the controversy among the disciples of Jesus and John (see Matt. 11:11–12; Luke 7:28; 16:16; cf. also Mark 1:7–8; Matt. 3:11; Luke 3:16; see also chapter 8, no. 40). The appended quotation from Malachi effects a compromise: John is the forerunner of Jesus in fulfilment of a prophetic prediction well integrated into the Gospel tradition (see Mark 1:2 in addition to the present passages). Jesus' praise of his master has an authentic sound. For other comments on John, see chapter 8, nos. 1, 7, 9 and 41.

11. E. Puech, *Discoveries in the Judaean Desert* XXV (Oxford, 1998), 10–11.

27. The fate of Capernaum (Matt. 11:23–24; Luke 10:15) [Isa. 14:13–15; Gen. 18–19]

And you, Capernaum, will you be *exalted to heaven*? You shall be *brought down to Hades* (Matt., Luke).

For if the mighty works done in you had been done in *Sodom*, it would have remained until this day. But I tell you, it shall be more tolerable on the day of judgement for the land of Sodom than for you (Matt.).

When pronouncing woes over the small towns of Galilee where many of his healings were performed without noticeable impact on their unrepentant inhabitants, Jesus singles out Capernaum, 'his own city', according to Matthew 9:1. The simile of being raised to heaven and lowered to Sheol, the Hebrew underworld (the Hades of Greek mythology) is thought to bear the stylistic influence of Isaiah 14:13–15, but the phrases may be part of the eschatological imagery current in the age of Jesus. Employing a scriptural example and displaying his customary habit of exaggeration, Jesus declares the people of Capernaum to be more guilty than the Sodomites, who together with the generation of the Flood represented evil personified to the Jewish mind in antiquity.

28. The sign of Jonah (Matt. 12:39–42; Luke 11:29–32) [Jonah 1:17; 3:5; 1 Kings 10:1–10]

See no. 7 above.

29. Persecution of messengers (Matt. 23:34–36; Luke 11:49–51) [Gen. 4:8; 2 Chron. 24:20–21]

Therefore I send you prophets and wise men and scribes, some of whom you will kill and crucify, and some you will scourge in your synagogues and persecute from town to town, that upon you may come all the righteous blood shed on earth, *from the blood of innocent Abel to the blood of Zechariah the son of Barachiah*, whom you murdered between the sanctuary and the altar. Truly, I say to you, all this will come upon this generation (Matt.).

Therefore also the Wisdom of God said, 'I will send them prophets and apostles, some of whom they will kill and persecute', that the blood of all the prophets, shed from the foundation of the world, may be required of this generation, *from the blood of Abel to the blood of Zechariah*, who perished between the altar and the sanctuary. Yes, I tell you, it will be required of this generation (Luke).

The ill-treatment by Jews of the Christian messengers of the apostolic age is presented as the continuation of the martyrdom of the righteous throughout biblical history, from the killing of Abel to the murder of a certain Zechariah in the Temple. The identity of this last individual is unclear. He can scarcely be the biblical Zechariah, the son of Barachiah, the son of Iddo, whose murder is nowhere recorded (Zech. 1:1). There was, it is true, another Zechariah, a priest (not a prophet), and the son of Jehoiada, who was stoned to death during the reign of the Judaean king Joash *circa* 800 BC, but this date is too early to mark the end of the present sequence of killings. To complicate matters further, the Old Testament itself does not testify to prophets being regularly murdered. Yet, as has already been remarked in chapter 2, no. 15B, the *Lives of the Prophets*, a late first-century AD Jewish work among the Pseudepigrapha, alleges that a number of them suffered violent deaths, and the *Ascension of Isaiah*, of approximately the same date, also ascribes martyrdom to the prophet Isaiah.

It has been argued that this saying derives from a pre-existent Jewish source, entitled 'the Wisdom of God', mentioned in Luke. The 'prophets, wise men and scribes' of Matthew represent the original Jewish terminology, which has been 'Christianized' by Luke to read 'prophets and apostles' instead. If this is true, the most apposite context for the passage is the late first century AD.

30. The coming of the Son of man prefigured by the age of Noah and Lot (Matt. 24:37–41; Luke 17:26–30, 32, 34–36) [Gen. 7:7; 19:1–26]

As were *the days of Noah*, so will be the coming of the Son of man. [For as in those days before the flood (Matt.)] they were eating and drinking, marrying and giving in marriage, until the day when Noah entered the ark, and [they did not know until (Matt.)] the flood came and swept them all away [destroyed them all (Luke)], so will be the coming of the Son of man (Matt. 24:37–39; Luke 17:26–27).

. . . on the day when the Son of man is revealed . . . I tell you, in that night there will be two in one bed; one will be taken and the other left (Luke 17:30, 34).

Then two men will be in the field; one is taken and one is left. Two women will be grinding at the mill [together (Luke)]; one is taken and one is left (Matt. 24:40–41; Luke 17:34–35).

Likewise as it was in *the days of Lot* – they ate, they drank, they bought, they sold, they planted, they built, but *on the day when Lot went out from Sodom fire and sulphur rained from heaven and destroyed them all* – so will it be on the day when the Son of man is revealed (Luke 17:28–30).

Remember *Lot's wife* (Luke 17:32).

The Son of man issue involved in this passage will be treated separately in chapter 7, no. 23. As far as this passage's use of Scripture is concerned, both Noah and Lot are cited as models or types. Their days are described as perfectly normal and ordinary, containing no premonition of any impending catastrophe caused by water or by fire. In other words, a quiet and settled situation is envisaged that is quite different from the eschatological frenzy characterizing the age of Jesus. The day of the Lord is not seen as imminent and the Parousia expectation of the post-AD 70 era is the most probable historical setting. The only possible hint at the imminence of the day of the Lord is the reference in Luke to Lot's wife, who was punished for glancing backwards while running from Sodom. This recalls Jesus' censure of the ploughman in the last days who looked back instead of firmly fixing his gaze in the direction of the coming Kingdom of God (Luke 9:62; see chapter 3, no. 36).

III. THE *M* TRADITION

31. You shall not kill (Matt. 5:21–23) [Exod. 20:13; Deut. 5:17]

You have heard that it was said to the men of old, '*You shall not kill*; and whoever kills shall be liable to judgement.' But I say to you that every one who is angry with his brother shall be liable to judgement; whoever insults his brother shall be liable to the council, and whoever says, 'You fool!' shall be liable to the Gehenna of fire.

This is the first of the six antitheses in which a scriptural precept is followed by what many New Testament interpreters consider as a new law. However, on closer examination it turns out to be Jesus' deeper grasp of the internal demands of the old commandment. The prohibition on killing, taken from the Decalogue, is accompanied by a supplementary comment noting that murder is liable to judgement. Paraphrastic developments of this sort characterize the rendering of the Ten Commandments in the Palestinian Aramaic Targums. So Jesus forbids anger towards a brother which may result in an insult, and thus become liable to judgement, although the threat of hell fire for calling someone a fool is a choice hyperbole. The underlying aim is the prevention of murder by eliminating its root cause, inward hostility. A rabbinic midrash reveals a similar reasoning. A person who stops loving may progress from not loving his fellow to hating and finally to murdering him (Sifre on Deut. 19:10–11). In sum, the antithesis is contradictory only in form, not in substance. This kind of antithetical teaching is attributed in the Synoptic Gospels to the Pharisees, too, in connection with the vow called *Corban*: 'For Moses said, "Honour your father", [etc.]; but you [Pharisees] say, "If a man tells his father or his mother, What you have gained from me is Corban" . . . then you no longer permit him to do anything for his father or mother' (Mark 7:10–12; Matt. 15:4–5; see chapter 2, no. 8). Those scholars who imagine that in the antitheses Jesus proclaims his unique superiority towards the Law should read their New Testament more carefully. In fact what we encounter here is not the abrogation but a reinterpretation of the Torah.

32. You shall not commit adultery (Matt. 5:27–30) [Exod. 20:14; Deut. 5:18]

You have heard that it was said, '*You shall not commit adultery.*' But I say to you that every one who looks at a woman lustfully has already committed adultery with her in his heart. If your right eye causes you to sin, pluck it out and throw it away; it is better that you lose one of your members than that your whole body be thrown into Gehenna. And if your right hand causes you to sin, cut it off and throw it away; it is better that you lose one of your members than that your whole body go into Gehenna.

Just as the control of anger will prevent murder, resisting lust at the stage of thought and desire is the prophylactic recommended by Jesus against adultery. His advice that it is better to pluck out one's eye if it constitutes an obstacle to entry into God's Kingdom is reminiscent of the imagery of the Dead Sea Scrolls. In Essene terminology, 'to follow after lustful eyes' is used both literally and figuratively for illegal sex and the betrayal of God (1QS 1:6; CD 2:16; 11QTS 59:14, etc.). The patriarch Issachar claims never to have fornicated 'by the uplifting of the eyes' (Test. of Iss. 7:2), and in the Book of Jubilees 20:4 Abraham commands that 'no woman is to commit fornication with her eyes or her heart'. For Josephus, too, wicked thought and evil intention are as sinful as the corresponding deeds (*Against Apion* 2:183, 217). In the language of the rabbis 'to follow your eyes' means to fornicate, and 'bawdy thoughts' carry heavier guilt than the resulting adultery (Sifre on Num. 15:39; bYoma 29a). The rhetorical exaggeration of plucking out an eye or cutting off a limb which may lead a man to sin in order to escape hell is typical of the vivid hyperbolical style frequently employed by Jesus (see Mark 9:43–48 and Matt. 18:8–9 in chapter 9, no. 6; cf. also chapter 9, no. 18).

33. You shall not swear falsely (Matt. 5:33–37) [Lev. 19:12]

Again you have heard that it was said to the men of old, '*You shall not swear falsely*, but shall perform to the Lord what you have sworn.' But I say to you, Do not swear at all, either by heaven, for it is the throne of God, or by the earth, for it is his footstool, or by Jerusalem, for it is the city of the great King. And do not swear by your head, for you cannot make one hair white or black. Let what you say be simply 'Yes' or 'No'; anything more than this comes from evil.

Among the various biblical commands relating to oaths and vows, Matthew's wording is closest to Leviticus 19:12 ('You shall not swear by my name falsely'), which is then further paraphrased on the model of other biblical texts, Deuteronomy 23:24 [English translation 23:23] ('You shall be careful to perform what has passed your lips') and Psalm 50:14 ('Pay your vows to the Most High').

The Old Testament passages stress the duty to keep an oath. Jesus goes further and enjoins complete abstention from oaths and vows, for two reasons. The first is that not carrying out a solemn undertaking would result in profaning the divine name. Not even the replacement of the name of God by a sobriquet, for instance heaven, earth, Jerusalem, etc., would weaken the obligatory force of the promise; its breach would still amount to perjury. The second reason for dispensing with oaths is that a person who is known for his reliability has his word as his bond.

The superfluousness of vows and oaths is also asserted by Philo at the beginning of the first century AD. According to the Alexandrian Jewish sage, a virtuous man's word should be considered as trustworthy as an oath: 'To swear not at all is the best course and most profitable to life, well suited to a rational nature which has been taught to speak the truth so well on each occasion that its words are regarded as oaths' (*Decalogue* 84). Elsewhere the Essenes are singled out by Philo as paragons of truthfulness. 'They show their love of God . . . by abstinence from oaths, by veracity' (*Every Good Man* 84). Josephus echoes him: 'Everything they [the Essenes] say is more certain than an oath. Indeed swearing is rejected by them as being more evil than perjury. For anyone who does not merit belief without calling on God is already condemned' (*War* 2:135). Similarly, according to the rabbinic midrash Mekhilta on Exodus 20:2, the Israelites accepted God as their king without swearing an oath of allegiance. All they needed to say was 'Yes, yes'. Jesus thus vigorously reasserts a trend deeply embedded in ancient Jewish piety.

See also chapter 9, no. 19.

34. Praying unobserved (Matt. 6:6) [Isa. 26:20]

When you pray, *go into your room and shut the door* and pray to your Father who is in secret; and your Father who sees in secret will reward you.

The larger unit of Matthew on prayer will be expounded in chapter 6, no. 7. As far as the scriptural allusion is concerned, it literally echoes a line from the apocalyptic chapter 26 of Isaiah. However, while the words are nearly identical, the sense in which they are used is quite different. In Isaiah God's people are advised to seek shelter behind closed doors during a period of danger, 'until the wrath is past'. In Jesus' teaching, the purpose of hiding behind closed doors is the safeguard of the purity of intention: a sincere act of piety should be observed only by God. No human witnesses are needed. The borrowing from Isaiah by the editor of Matthew has a purely stylistic value and purpose.

35. The annihilation of the wicked and the glorification of the just (Matt. 13:41–43) [Dan. 3:6; 12:3]

The Son of man will send his angels, and they will gather out of his kingdom all causes of sin and all evildoers, and *throw them into the furnace of fire*; there men will weep and gnash their teeth. Then *the righteous will shine* like the sun in the kingdom of their Father.

The interpretation of the parable of the weeds to which this excerpt belongs has been discussed in chapter 4, no. 17. The son of Man (see chapter 7, no. 25) directs the angelic harvesters to divide mankind in view of the final judgement. The destiny of the good and the evil is depicted in images taken from the Book of Daniel. The wicked are destined for the fiery furnace and the chosen will reflect the brilliance of the heavenly glory. The coincidence of terminology between Daniel and Matthew may be purely accidental and reflect commonly used imagery, or it may be due to the editor of the Gospel.

36. Rebuke to be administered before witnesses (Matt. 18:15–16) [Deut. 19:15]

If your brother sins against you, go and tell him his fault, between you and him alone. If he listens to you, you have gained your brother. But if he does not listen, take one or two others along with you, that every word may be confirmed *by the evidence of two or three witnesses*.

The full text dealing with a reproof to be administered to a brother (Matt. 18:15–20; cf. Luke 17:3) will be examined in chapter 9, no. 24. As for the biblical allusion, the application is indirect. Deuteronomy is concerned with determining the form of the testimony required in a criminal case. The Gospel in turn starts with an attempt to bring back an erring brother to the straight and narrow path. If he is unwilling to mend his ways, he is to be cautioned in the presence of one or two other persons before the matter can be handed over to the authorities of the church. Both the Dead Sea Scrolls and rabbinic law impose the obligation of a similar warning.

37. Jesus hailed in the Temple (Matt. 21:15–16) [Ps. 8:2]

But when the chief priests and the scribes saw the wonderful things that he did, and the children crying out in the temple, 'Hosanna to the Son of David!' they were indignant; and they said to him, 'Do you hear what these are saying?' And Jesus said to them, Yes; have you never read, *'Out of the mouth of babes and sucklings thou hast brought perfect praise'*?

This fulfilment interpretation is most probably the creation of the evangelist. In fact he seems to have manufactured the event to be thus interpreted, duplicating the 'Hosanna' song originally taking place, not in the Temple, but at Jesus' entry to Jerusalem (cf. Mark 11:9–10; 21:9; Luke 19:38).

IV. THE *L* TRADITION

38. Jesus interpreting Isaiah (Luke 4:16–21) [Isa. 61:1–2; 58:6]

And he came to Nazareth . . . and he went to the synagogue, as his custom was, on the sabbath day. And he stood up to read; and there was given to him the book of the prophet Isaiah. He opened the book, and found the place where it was written, *'The Spirit of the Lord is upon me, because he has anointed me to preach good news to the poor. He has sent me to proclaim release to the captives and recovering of sight to the blind, to set at liberty those who are oppressed, to proclaim the acceptable year of the Lord.'* And he closed the book and gave it back to the attendant, and sat down; and the eyes of all the synagogue were fixed on him. And he began to say to them, Today this scripture has been fulfilled in your hearing.

The setting of the episode, the reading and exposition of the prophetic section (*haftarah*) during a Sabbath worship in the synagogue of Nazareth, has been examined in chapter 1, no. 33. The passage quoted is an amalgam of Isaiah 61:1–2 and 58:6. It is given in the Greek Septuagint translation which on several points differs from the Hebrew Isaiah. The text read in a Galilean synagogue would have been the latter. Luke's citation is a midrashic combination of verses from Isaiah. It seeks to present a vigorous doctrinal statement summarizing the purpose of Jesus' mission as a charismatic prophet, healer and liberator. A similar composite citation (see no. 25 above) involving Isaiah 61:1 combined with Psalm 146:7–8 is inserted into a work known as a Messianic Apocalypse among the Dead Sea Scrolls (4Q521, fragment 2): '. . . the heavens and the earth will listen to his Messiah . . . He [God] will glorify the pious on the throne of the eternal Kingdom. He who liberates the captives, restores sight to the blind, straightens the bent (Ps. 146) . . . For he will heal the wounded, and revive the dead and bring good news to the poor' (Isa. 61:1). The re-worked biblical text is unlikely to have originated with Jesus, and should be attributed to Luke or his source. As for the blunt fulfilment interpretation that follows, it clashes with the style of Jesus evidenced elsewhere in the Synoptic Gospels (see chapter 1, no. 33).

39. Jesus alludes to his arrest (Luke 22:37) [Isa. 53:12]

For I tell you that this scripture must be fulfilled in me, '*And he was reckoned with transgressors*'; for what is written about me has its fulfilment.

The Deutero-Isaiah excerpt from the last Song of the Suffering Servant (for the interpretation see chapter 7, p. 250), placed immediately before the account concerning Jesus in Gethsemane, is used to announce his imminent arrest as 'a robber'. This type of fulfilment interpretation usually points to the early church. (See Mark 14:48; Matt. 26:55; Luke 22:52 in chapter 1, no. 25; cf. also chapter 8, no. 52.)

40. Jesus comforting the women of Jerusalem (Luke 23:28–31) [Hosea 10:8]

Daughters of Jerusalem, do not weep for me, but weep for yourselves and for your children. For behold, the days are coming when they will say, 'Blessed are the barren, and the wombs that never bore, and the breasts that never gave suck.' Then they will begin *to say to the mountains, 'Fall on us'; and to the hills, 'Cover us'*. For if they do this when the wood is green, what will happen when it is dry?

The lamentation over the fall of Jerusalem and the troubles which were to precede it is anticipated by women weeping at the sight of Jesus led to the cross. The fictional prophecy is strengthened by the quotation of the words of Hosea asking for the mountains and the hills to fall on and bury the women.[12] The passage, like the preceding one, represents the *pesher*-type interpretative method of early Jewish Christianity.

For Jesus' lament over Jerusalem, see chapter 8, no. 48.

41. The last cry of Jesus (Luke 23:46) [Ps. 31:5]

Then Jesus, crying with a loud voice, said, Father, *into thy hands I commit my spirit*!

The disturbing words, 'My God, my God, why hast thou forsaken me?', uttered by the dying Jesus according to Mark and Matthew (see above, no. 19), are eliminated here and replaced by a reassuring citation from Scripture. Luke's Jesus, to use freely a famous line from Dylan Thomas, goes 'gentle into that good night'. The alteration of

12. Luke or his editor cites the two halves of the words of the prophet in inverse order. Both the Hebrew text, including a surviving Dead Sea Scroll fragment (4QXIIg), and the Greek translation speak of mountains covering people and hills falling on them, and not the other way round as in Luke.

the words of the last cry seems to be deliberate and editorial, as are the words 'It is finished' in the Gospel of John (John 19:30).

REFLECTIONS

When one considers all the teaching which the Synoptic Gospels attribute to Jesus the most striking fact is the paucity of direct scriptural quotations and allusions. All in all we have encountered no more than forty separate cases. To put this finding in perspective, one should bear in mind that Paul's Letter to the Romans alone contains twice as many Bible citations as the sum total of those which Mark, Matthew and Luke associate with Jesus. The distribution of the quotations is worth noting. Nearly half of them (nineteen) figure in Mark and a quarter (ten) in *Q*. Seven occur in *M*, and four in *L*. Even before any critical analysis of these texts it becomes clear that the Old Testament did not play an important role in the preaching of Jesus: he did not argue his doctrine from the Bible. Compared with the Scripture-based teaching style of the Pharisees and the scribes this is quite remarkable.

The biblical material connected with Jesus in the Gospels can be arranged in six groups.

(1) From the point of view of doctrine the least significant are those allusions which have no substantive purpose, their role being simply stylistic, i.e. the literary embellishment of the narrative. Thus in the parable of the secretly growing seed (no. 3) the reference to Joel is a loose reproduction of the Greek Bible, introduced by the redactor of Mark. Again in the parable of the wicked tenants (no. 11) the allegory of the vineyard is sketched vaguely after Isaiah 5, but the accounts would be equally meaningful without those allusions. In the Gethsemane episode (no. 17) the words of Psalm 42, 'My soul is very sorrowful', required a paraphrastic addition, 'even to death', to become fully applicable to a prayer spoken by Jesus only a few hours before his crucifixion. As for the exaltation to heaven and lowering to hell of Capernaum (no. 27), it is a rhetorical exaggeration possibly inspired by Isaiah 14. The same assessment applies to the probable references to Daniel in the judgement scene describing the damned and the chosen (no. 35). As for the instruction to pray behind closed doors

(no. 34), it is true that the wording recalls Isaiah 26, but the significance of the image is of a totally different nature. It would be more correct to speak in these cases of the use of biblical language by Mark, Matthew and Luke than of scriptural citations proper.

(2) The same conclusion of uncertainty may apply to the Aramaic cry of the dying Jesus, 'My God, my God, why hast thou forsaken me?', reproduced by Mark and Matthew (no. 19), which is not necessarily a conscious reference to Psalm 22. In contrast, the revised version of it in Luke, 'into thy hands I commit my spirit' (no. 41), is not just a stylistic borrowing but has an actual message attached to it.

(3) Other sayings with biblical content belong to the category of example and typology. The majority of them are endowed with eschatological colouring. The model of David's behaviour (no. 1) serves as popular justification of the apparent Sabbath-breaking by the disciples of Jesus. The inhabitants of Sodom and the generation of the Flood who took no notice of warnings and became known as the greatest sinners of history are depicted as more amenable to conversion than the people of Capernaum who witnessed the many mighty deeds of Jesus (no. 27). Likewise the sinners of ancient Nineveh who were moved by Jonah's call to conversion would be in a position to put the unrepentant generation of Jesus to shame (no. 7). He saw the conflict faced by members of a family on account of the demands of God's Kingdom (no. 24) as foreshadowed by the words of the prophet Micah announcing division between parents, children and in-laws. These Old Testament texts are understood by Mark and *Q* not as fulfilled in and through Jesus, but as help for people to discover the meaning of the events and circumstances of the final age.

(4) Without anticipating the full interpretation of the 'Son of man' passages (nos. 7, 15, 18, 30, 35) it should be noted that they serve as the chief vehicles for the doctrine of the Parousia or Second Coming, a spiritual phenomenon that belongs to the post-Jesus age. In a similar vein, several Mark–*Q* quotations exemplify the interpretative technique of the early Jewish-Christian church. The argument which is meant to prove from Exodus 3:6 ('I am the God of Abraham', etc.) the doctrine of the resurrection (no. 12), the exegetical quibbling about the identity of the Messiah – was he the son or the Lord of David? (no. 14), and the idea of a serial persecution of the just since the murder of Abel

(no. 29), all these echo exchanges about the Bible between Palestinian Christians and Pharisees. As for the identification of Jesus as the corner stone of a new building in fulfilment of Psalm 118 (no. 11), it is also part of the apologetical weaponry of the early church.

Two types of Bible interpretation are of special significance for the understanding of the religion of Jesus.

(5) The first consists of various attempts to produce a progressively more succinct synopsis of the Torah. To begin with, the Decalogue, reducing the 613 precepts of Moses to ten, is offered as the quintessence of God's revelation to the Jews, playing the role of the key to the gate of the Kingdom of heaven (no. 9). Next we are told that all the Law and the prophets have to say is contained in the two precepts of the love of God and of one's neighbour, called the first and second commandments, or according to Luke just the one great commandment (no. 13). The same idea is expressed in the non-biblical Golden Rule, familiar to the Jews from the Apocrypha to Hillel and the later rabbis, where all the laws of Moses and the prophets are reduced to a single one (no. 23). In this way the religious and ethical message of Jesus appears as a vigorous summary of the most profound perception of Judaism.

(6) In a more particular form the six antitheses of Jesus and his controversial statement contrasting the rule about gifts vowed to God (Corban) with filial duties to parents (no. 5) bring into relief the inward significance of the commandments and the extended demands they impose (nos. 6, 21, 22, 31–33). Bearing in mind the central importance of the Decalogue, recited daily by every pious Jew in the days of Jesus, it is highly significant that three out of the seven precepts loosely classified as antitheses come from the Ten Commandments (nos. 5, 31, 32). If we add to them Leviticus 19:18 on the love of one's neighbour, a law of particularly high standing in Jewish thought (nos. 9, 13, 22), the kernel of the moral teaching of Jesus appears to be based on a very limited number of scriptural commandments or their interpretation.

Two important final comments need to be made. The first concerns the practical non-existence of concrete Scripture-based predictions attributed to, or made by, Jesus about his suffering and execution.[13]

13. The only exception is Luke 22:37 (see no. 39 above), where the secondary issue of Jesus' arrest *as a criminal* is superficially linked to Isaiah 53:12.

Bearing in mind that the crucifixion of Jesus was perhaps the greatest difficulty which the early church had to overcome in proclaiming him as the Messiah promised to the Jews, the absence of detailed biblical proof concerning this essential doctrine is astonishing. Though allegedly Jesus several times foretold his future suffering and death, vaguely hinting that they were fulfilling Scripture, he never backed these predictions with actual excerpts from the Bible. Remarkably, when St Paul later declared that Christ 'died in accordance with the scriptures' (1 Cor. 15:3), he did not give this as a message of the Lord, nor did he quote chapter and verse from the holy books to substantiate his claim.

The second comment relates to the flimsiness of the prophetic prediction of Jesus' resurrection, the other central belief of the church. Here all we are offered is the sign of Jonah, his stay in the belly of the giant fish for three days and nights, conceived as the typology of Christ remaining in the tomb until the third day, that of the resurrection (no. 7). But even in this case the interpretation is provided only by Matthew. Luke employs the Jonah symbolism as an allusion to the prophet's successful preaching of repentance in Nineveh foreshadowing Jesus' appeal to turn to God. Jews would have expected something more definite and conspicuous on a subject of such consequence, and from a master who is presented as one who repeatedly foretold his rising from the dead.

We shall return to this momentous subject in chapter 7, section II, and in chapter 10.

6

Prayers and Related Instructions

The presentation of the prayers of Jesus forms the shortest chapter of this book, but owing to the significance of the subject it may well turn out to be one of the most important. For a full grasp of what is to follow, readers will profit from a brief sketch of the place of prayer in intertestamental Judaism.

Jewish religion in the age of Jesus knew two categories of prayer: statutory and private.[1] The text of the statutory prayer was determined, and often revised, by religious authorities, and it reflected the basic concerns of the community as a social entity. The established wording was strictly to be followed during the recitation of these prayers at prescribed times. Among the daily prayers the *Shema*, 'Hear, O Israel', proclaiming the oneness of the Deity, and the Eighteen Benedictions were the most important. The *Shema*, which consists of three Scripture extracts – Deuteronomy 6:4–9, Deuteronomy 11:13–21 and Numbers 15:37–41 – was repeated twice, in the evening and in the morning. The Eighteen Benedictions were recited three times, morning, afternoon and evening. Known also as The Prayer *par excellence* (*Tefillah*), it celebrates God as the protector, healer and redeemer of his people, the source of holiness, repentance, forgiveness and peace, the provider of knowledge, the reviver of the dead, and the restorer through the Messiah of the kingship of David. These Benedictions have been preserved in two forms: the Palestinian, which is probably the older, and the Babylonian. In the Palestinian version the first benediction reads: 'Blessed art thou, Lord, God of our fathers, God of Abraham, God of Isaac and God of Jacob, great, mighty and fearful God, most high God

1. See Joseph Heinemann, *Prayer in the Talmud* (Berlin, 1977).

who createst heaven and earth, our shield and the shield of our fathers, our trust in every generation. Blessed art thou, Lord, shield of Abraham.' The liturgical use of both the *Shema* and the Eighteen Benedictions has continued to the present day.

The Gospels contain no positive evidence to indicate that Jesus actually rehearsed them several times daily, but as a pious Jew he was expected to observe all the rules relating to these prayers. Nevertheless, a well-known New Testament expert plainly overstates his case when claiming that the quotation of Deuteronomy 6:4–5, 'Hear, O Israel,' etc. in Mark 12:29–30 (see chapter 5, no. 13), and the inclusion of the phrase 'the God of Abraham, and the God of Isaac, and the God of Jacob' in Mark 12:26 (cf. chapter 5, no. 12), actually prove that Jesus was familiar with the liturgy of the *Shema* and the Eighteen Benedictions.[2]

The private prayer allowed freedom to the individual to choose the words which best expressed his sentiments and desires, and he could also decide the moment of his prayer. For instance, the first-century AD Galilean charismatic, Hanina ben Dosa, is said to have stopped with appropriate words a heavy downpour which was inconveniencing him in the countryside, but he then restarted the rain, after having reached the shelter of his home, for the benefit of nature and the satisfaction of the needs of his drought-stricken compatriots. His first prayer ran: 'Lord of the universe, the whole world is in comfort while Hanina is in discomfort', and the second continued: 'Lord of the universe, the whole world is in distress while Hanina is in comfort' (bTaan 24b).

The few relevant extracts from Jesus' prayers belong to the private class. They may be of considerable help in sketching his spiritual portrait since prayers often constitute the best expression of the religious turn of mind of an individual. Before considering the Gospel texts themselves which purport to convey the words of Jesus, two preliminary comments may be apposite. Negatively, the New Testament never mentions that Jesus prayed in the Temple, but testifies to the continued attendance of his apostles and of the members of the Jerusalem church at the prayer services of the Sanctuary (Acts 2:46; 3:1).

2. Joachim Jeremias, *The Prayers of Jesus* (London, 1967), 73–5.

Positively, we are told on the one hand that in a number of instances Jesus took part in synagogue worship (Mark 1:21; 1:39; Matt. 4:23; Luke 4:44; Mark 3:1; Matt. 12:9; Luke 6:6; Mark 6:2; Matt. 13:54; Luke 4:16), and on the other hand that several times he retired to remote places to engage in lengthy solitary prayer (see no. 7 below).

The nine relevant passages contained in the Synoptic Gospels which are discussed in this chapter can be divided into three groups: personal prayers of Jesus (nos. 3, 4, 6, 8, 9 below), a prayer, 'Our Father', taught by him to his disciples (no. 5), and instructions given by Jesus on how to pray or how not to pray (nos. 1, 2, 7).

I. MARK AND THE TRIPLE TRADITION

1. Effective prayer (Mark 11:23–24; Matt. 21:21–22; cf. Matt. 17:20; Luke 17:6)

Truly, I say to you, whoever says to this mountain, 'Be taken up and cast into the sea', and does not doubt in his heart, but believes that what he says will come to pass, it will be done for him (Mark).

Truly, I say to you, if you have faith and never doubt, you will not only do what has been done to the fig tree, but even if you say to this mountain 'Be taken up and cast into the sea', it will be done (Matt.).

Therefore I tell you, whatever you ask in prayer, believe that you have received it, and it will be yours [you will receive, if you have faith (Matt.)] (Mark, Matt.).

If you have faith as a grain of mustard seed, you will say to this mountain, 'Move from here to there', and it will move; and nothing will be impossible to you (Matt. 17, Luke 17).

According to Jesus, prayer in order to become effective must be inspired by limitless trust in God, just as no miracle can be performed without faith on the part of the blind, the leper or the demon-possessed in the charismatic power of the healer or the exorcist (see chapter 1, nos.

8–10, etc., and p. 50). In other words, the truly devoted person's prayer is said to be as powerful as the miracle-worker's command. As far as its context is concerned, this saying appears as a sequel to the story of the curse placed by Jesus on a fig tree which caused it instantaneously to wither (Mark 11:12–14; Matt. 21:18–19; see chapter 1, no. 21). The event was meant to illustrate the unfailing potency of Jesus' words and simultaneously the spiritual power bestowed on any man by his faith (Mark 11:23; Matt. 21:21; see chapter 8, no. 16).[3] The same metaphor of faith moving a mountain is quoted negatively to explain the disciples' inability to exorcize an epileptic boy (Matt. 17:20; Luke 17:6; see chapter 8, no. 46). The phraseology is typical of the hyperbolic language of Jesus (see chapter 3, nos. 14, 15; chapter 5, nos. 24, 25). It is quite different from the more modest style used by the Talmud and the Midrash in describing the prayer of miracle-working rabbis (see chapter 1, no. 9). It should also be noted that on one occasion Jesus lists prayer as the one and only means of achieving a successful exorcism: 'This kind [of demon] cannot be driven out by anything but prayer' (Mark 9:29). Leaving aside the vivid exaggerations, what Jesus stresses above all is the necessity of an approach to God based on absolute faith.

2. Forgiveness and prayer (Mark 11:25; Matt. 6:14–15; cf. 11:25–26)

And whenever you stand praying, forgive, if you have anything against any one; so that your Father also who is in heaven may forgive you your trespasses (Mark).

For if you forgive men their trespasses, your heavenly Father also will forgive you; but if you do not forgive men their trespasses, neither will your Father forgive your trespasses (Matt.).

3. The saying is also alluded to by Paul in 1 Corinthians 13:2, 'if I have all faith, so as to remove mountains'. Luke clumsily mixes the metaphor: 'You could say to this sycamine tree, "Be rooted up, and be planted in the sea".' The sycamine tree (in Hebrew *shiqmah*) is very deep-rooted and cannot easily be pulled up. But how can a tree be planted in the sea?

Next to absolute trust, Mark gives generous disposition towards people who have wronged or offended the person addressing God as the second precondition for an effective prayer. Matthew presents this saying as an enlargement on the petition 'Forgive us our debts' in the Lord's Prayer (6:12; cf. also 18:35), where it will be examined further (see no. 5 below). The message implies that since every sinful human being is in need of heavenly forgiveness, each must emulate the heavenly Father by pardoning his fellow. In short, in this saying Jesus brings into relief one of the most basic principles of his religious conduct: the imitation of God which enjoins one to do as God does (see chapter 9, no. 12).

3. The prayer of Jesus in Gethsemane (Mark 14:36; Matt. 26:39; Luke 22:42)

Abba, Father, all things are possible to thee; remove this cup from me; yet not what I will, but what thou wilt (Mark).

My Father, if it be possible, let this cup pass from me; nevertheless, not as I will, but as thou wilt (Matt.).

Father, if thou art willing, remove this cup from me; nevertheless, not my will, but thine, be done (Luke).

This is the first prayer uttered by Jesus himself which is reproduced in the Gospels. Both its form and its content suggest authenticity. In Mark, God is addressed as *Abba* in Aramaic, that is, in the mother tongue of Jesus which was presumably also the language of his private prayers. Instead of 'O Lord, our God, King of the universe', the standard Hebrew formula in Jewish prayers (see also no. 6 below), he uses in the vernacular the direct and familiar *Abba*, 'Father', or perhaps more correctly, 'My Father', as in Matthew. It must be noted, however, that *Abba* is not so familiar as to make it the equivalent of 'Daddy', as Joachim Jeremias[4] and some of his imprudent followers would have us believe. A more detailed discussion of the

4. Jeremias, *The Prayers of Jesus*, 57–66.

phrase will be given in connection with the Lord's Prayer (see no. 5 below).

The 'cup' to be removed is the biblical symbol of destiny (see also Mark 10:38; Matt. 20:22; see chapter 8, no. 15). This prayer asking God to take away the chalice of a threatening future suggests for the first time the possibility of doubt in the mind of Jesus concerning the successful outcome of his mission. But the request may represent a device introduced by Mark to prepare the reader for the shock of the cross. On the other hand, the authentic invocation and the whole-hearted acceptance of God's plan, 'not what I will, but what thou wilt', reflect total trust which is a genuine and essential part of the spirituality of Jesus. 'What thou wilt' echoes the clause 'Thy will be done' of the Lord's Prayer (see no. 5 below).

4. The last exclamation of Jesus (Mark 15:34; Matt. 27:46)

Eloi, Eloi [*Eli, Eli* (Matt.)], *lama sabachthani?* which means, '*My God, my God, why hast thou forsaken me?*'

This final address of Jesus to God, also uttered in Aramaic, has already been examined in chapter 5, no. 19. As it stands, it seems to be an expression of complete surprise, voiced by a man of limitless faith, in the sudden realization that there would be no heavenly intervention in his favour, as God – or his angel – intervened when Isaac was staring at the knife his father Abraham held ready to sacrifice him on Mount Moriah (Gen. 22:12). Indeed, this cry to God from the depths of bewilderment reveals the all-pervasive trust characteristic of Jesus.

For an alternative version of Jesus' last words in Luke's Gospel, see no. 9 below.

II. THE Q TRADITION

5. The Lord's Prayer (Matt. 6:9–13; Luke 11:2–4)

Pray then like this: Our Father who art in heaven, hallowed be thy name. Thy kingdom come, thy will be done, on earth as it is in heaven. Give us this day our daily bread; and forgive us our debts, as we also have forgiven our debtors; and lead us not into temptation, but deliver us from evil (Matt.).[5]

When you pray, say: Father, hallowed be thy name. Thy kingdom come. Give us each day our daily bread; and forgive us our sins, for we ourselves forgive everyone who is indebted to us; and lead us not into temptation (Luke).

'Our Father' is the prayer formula *par excellence* taught by Jesus to his disciples. It has been preserved in a shorter form in Luke and in a longer version in Matthew. The text is couched in collective terms of 'we', 'us', 'our' as opposed to the individual first person style of 'I', 'me', 'my'. The final doxology, 'For thine is the kingdom,' etc., is a later addition.[6] The majority of experts are correct in opting for Aramaic as the original language of 'Our Father', though some scholars argue (unconvincingly) in favour of Hebrew. The preference for Aramaic is based not only on the similarity of the Lord's Prayer to the *Qaddish*, an ancient Jewish prayer composed in Aramaic, but also on certain philological peculiarities in the Greek of Matthew which will be shown presently. Most students of the Lord's Prayer hold the shorter text of Luke to be original and attribute the supplements to Matthew or his editor, but the fact that Matthew's version is closer to Aramaic than Luke's, and that the parts of his version which are missing from Luke include genuine and fundamental ideas of Jesus, argue in favour of the opposite view. The dilemma may be resolved by advancing the theory that Jesus taught this prayer on more than one occasion to his disciples and each time in somewhat different wording.

The first three petitions, 'Hallowed be thy name', 'Thy kingdom come' and 'Thy will be done', all focus on God. They recall the *Qaddish*, the Aramaic prayer the shorter text of which runs: 'Magni-

5. A number of ancient codices, influenced by Matthew's version, read 'Our Father who art in heaven' in Luke, too.

6. The doxology, 'For thine is the kingdom and the power and the glory for ever. Amen', appearing in some manuscripts of Matthew, but absent from the oldest ones and from Luke, is in the view of the large majority of interpreters a later liturgical addition introduced by the early church, as shown by the Didache (see below).

fied and *sanctified be his great name* in the world which he created *according to his will. May he establish his Kingdom* during your life . . .'. In the enlarged form of the prayer, called the full *Qaddish*, one of the three additional paragraphs introduces the concept of the heavenly Father: 'May the prayers and supplication of all Israel be acceptable before *their Father who is in heaven*.' The most sensible conclusion is that the eschatological formula, requesting the coming of God's Kingdom in the present generation, was known to Jesus and that he was influenced and inspired by the *Qaddish* as a whole.

Though originally intended as a non-statutory group prayer, 'Our Father' was soon adopted by the primitive church as part of its formal communal worship. The Paternoster figures in the earliest liturgical manual of the church, the Didache (*circa* AD 100–150), where it ends with a doxology, 'For thine is the power and the glory for ever', and is followed by the injunction that it is to be recited thrice daily (Did. 8:2). Indeed, the Lord's Prayer has remained part of Christian worship up to the present day and offers in the form of an abstract the quintessence of the religion taught by Jesus.

Analysis of the Lord's Prayer

(a) Our Father who art in heaven

For a correct understanding of this phrase it should be recalled that the representation of the Deity as 'Father' is a basic element of Old Testament theology. Ancient biblical names like Abiel (God is my Father), Abijah (Yah [Yahweh/Jehovah] is my Father), Eliab (My God is Father), etc., all testify to this concept. They proclaim a parental relationship between God and individual members of the Jewish people. 'Is not he your father?' asks Deuteronomy 32:6. Inversely the Jews are designated God's children: 'Israel is my first-born son' (Exod. 4:22). In biblical books dating from after the Babylonian exile (i.e. roughly from the end of the sixth century to the end of the third century BC) we encounter the invocation 'Father', addressed to God: 'O Lord, you are our Father' (Isa. 63:16; 64:8; cf. Tobit 13:4), or 'You are my Father' (Ps. 89:26; cf. Ecclus. 51:1, 10). The initiates of the

Dead Sea community, too, called on God as 'Our Father' or 'My Father' (4Q502, frag. 39,3 and 4Q372, frag. 1,16), and in one of the Thanksgiving Hymns we read, 'Thou art the Father to all the sons of thy truth' (1QH 17 [formerly 9]:35). As for the rabbinic writings, they commonly employ the expression 'Our [my, thy, their] Father who art [is] in heaven'. The terminology of the appeal testifies to a close filial attitude towards God in all the sectors of ancient Judaism.[7] Jesus is simply depicted a follower of the established pattern current in his society, his age and his religion.

Instead of 'Our Father who art in heaven' Luke has simply 'Father'. The best explanation for the presence of the briefer form of address is that this is the formula regularly used by Luke (see Luke 10:21, 22:42 [against *Abba*, Father, in Mark 14:36 and 'My Father' in Matt. 26:39]; Luke 23:34, 46). His habit of employing 'Father' accounts for the shortening of the original 'Our Father who art in heaven'. Incidentally, the longer idiom is also recorded in a large number of ancient manuscripts of the third Gospel. It should further be borne in mind that while the formula 'Father' (or 'My Father') is perfectly suitable for a praying individual, 'Our Father' fits better a collective prayer. Indeed, note that even in Luke, the Lord's Prayer, headed with 'Father', is introduced as taught to a group: 'And he said to *them*' (Luke 11:2).

(b) Hallowed be thy name

The first petition endows the earthly and anthropomorphic father image with heavenly glory. The followers of Jesus are instructed, in fact, to imitate the cherubim whose choir proclaimed three times holy the supreme God enthroned on high (Isa. 6:3; see also Rev. 4:8). The disciples, like people reciting the *Qaddish*, are magnifying and *sanctifying* the great *Name* of the Lord. The idealized concept of Jewish worship which underlies the Lord's Prayer envisages strict correspondence, in words and timing, between earthly worship and the angelic praises of God in heaven (cf. chapter 2, no. 1; chapter 8, no. 53; chapter 9, nos. 23, 24, 26). It should be observed that in this

7. For a detailed list of references in biblical and post-biblical Jewish literature, see Emile Puech, 'Dieu le Père dans les écrits péritestamentaires et les manuscrits de la mer Morte', *Revue de Qumrân* 20/2 (2001), 287–310.

respect, too, Jesus, the Essenes and rabbinic Judaism speak with a single voice.[8]

(c) Thy Kingdom come

The call for eschatological fulfilment is the essential summary of the preaching of Jesus. It provides the Lord's Prayer with an aura of urgency similar to the *Qaddish*, which petitions for the establishment of God's reign in the present time, 'in your days'. The fact that the object of the supplication is to bring about the Kingdom of God, and not the return of Christ (the Parousia), clearly distinguishes Jesus' perspective from that of the early church. The first generations of Christians would have asked for the Second Coming of the crucified Jesus, who they believed had been resurrected and exalted in heaven, with a phrase like *Marana tha*, 'Our Lord, come!' (preserved in Aramaic in 1 Corinthians 16:22 and in Greek in Revelation 22:20).

(d) Thy will be done on earth as it is in heaven

This petition represents the practical response on the part of the disciples of Jesus to the call for the coming of the Kingdom. Obedience to God, that is to say, doing the will of the Father, is the principal duty of Jesus and his followers. It emerges from the parable of the father and the two sons and that of the prodigal son (see chapter 4, nos. 24, 35), and is the requirement to be accepted by anyone wishing to become a disciple of Jesus (Mark 3:35; Matt. 12:50; 7:21; cf. chapter 8, no. 3). The symmetry between divine will in heaven and human submission on earth is a theme known from rabbinic literature, too, where harmony of purpose is postulated between the heavenly and the earthly families of God (cf. tBer 3:7; bBer 17a, 29b). Jesus combines obedience to the Father's will with the eschatological realization of the Kingdom. Later rabbis de-eschatologized this complex and saw the metaphorical establishment of the Kingdom in the acceptance of the yoke of the

8. For Qumran, see in particular the Songs of the Holocaust of the Sabbath (4Q400–407). Rabbinic parallels will be listed below in connection with the petition, 'Thy will be done'.

Torah, that is to say, the faithful observance of all the laws of Moses (mBer 2:2; Mekhilta on Exod. 20:3).

In the second half of the Lord's Prayer the focus shifts from God and his Kingdom to the needs of the disciples of Jesus, to their bodily and spiritual well-being in the final age. All three petitions mirror central teachings of Jesus attested throughout the Gospels. The Greek adjective *epiousios* applied to the bread is the one particular concept which requires some explanation.

(e) Give us this day our daily bread

The two favoured interpretations of the adjective *epiousios* attached to 'bread' are either 'of the present day' or 'of the coming day', that is to say, of tomorrow. The latter option is backed by the formula discovered by Jerome in the Gospel according to the Hebrews. 'For *daily bread*, I found [there the Hebrew word] *mahar*, which signifies "of tomorrow". Hence the meaning is, "Give us today our bread of tomorrow", that is to say, our future bread' (*Commentary on Matthew* 6:11). But *pace* the author of the Vulgate, the guiding principle for a correct understanding and exposition of this phrase must be Jesus' emphasis on the supremacy of the present. Asking for today's bread is in harmony with 'Therefore do not be anxious about tomorrow, for tomorrow will be anxious for itself. Let the day's own trouble be sufficient for the day' (Matt. 6:34; see chapter 3, no. 19).[9]

(f) And forgive us our debts as we also have forgiven our debtors

The second 'we' petition combines the theme of a forgiving father and repentant son with man's duty to imitate God through generously pardoning the offences of his fellow humans. Once more these are essential features of the religious outlook of Jesus (see no. 2 above and

9. Nevertheless this stress on today does not necessarily exclude the idea of tomorrow in Western time reckoning. For whereas the Hebrew (lunar) day starts at sunset so that the twenty-four-hour period until the following sunset is 'today', in a solar day the hours after midnight would count as 'tomorrow'.

chapter 4, no. 22). Apropos the somewhat different wording of the shorter version, '*Forgive us our sins, for we ourselves forgive everyone who is indebted to us*', it should be noticed that Luke spoils the Aramaic metaphors of debt and debtor when he substitutes sin for debt, but still speaks of people who are 'indebted to us' instead of those who have 'sinned against us'. It would seem that those New Testament scholars who hold that Luke's version of the Lord's Prayer is the authentic one may need to do some serious rethinking.

(g) And lead us not into temptation, but deliver us from evil

The final double request is a direct corollary of the previous petition. The spiritually strong can face up to temptation. Abraham steadfastly withstood no less than ten ordeals (mAbot 5:3), the harshest of these being the divine demand that he should sacrifice his only son born to him in his old age. Jesus, too, is depicted as handling with ease the questions put to him by opponents, including the legendary temptations by Satan, which were intended to trip him up (see Mark 1:13; Matt. 4:1; Luke 4:2; Mark 8:11; Luke 11:16; Mark 12:15; Matt. 22:18). But those whose faith is less firm, 'the little ones' and 'the babes', are in need of protection. They had better ask for temptation to be removed and the tempter, Satan, be kept under control. Indeed, 'evil' in the last petition is best understood as 'the Evil One'.[10]

In sum, the themes of the Lord's Prayer – the fatherhood of God, his worship, the expectation of the arrival of his Kingdom, prayer restricted to the immediate necessities, repentance and forgiveness – reveal to the discerning observer the inner core of the gospel of Jesus.

10. See Matthew Black, 'The Doxology of the *Pater Noster*', in P. R. Davies and R. T. White (eds.), *A Tribute to Geza Vermes* (Sheffield, 1990), 333–6.

6. Jesus' thanksgiving prayer (Matt. 11:25–27; Luke 10:21–22; John 10:15)

I thank thee, Father, Lord of heaven and earth, that thou hast hidden these things from the wise and the understanding and revealed them to babes; yea, Father, for such was thy gracious will. All things have been delivered to me by my Father; and no one knows the Son [*who the Son is* (Luke)] *except the Father, and no one knows the Father* [*or who the Father is* (Luke)] *except the Son and any one to whom the Son chooses to reveal him.*

. . . as the Father knows me and I know the Father (John).

This thanksgiving hymn attributed to Jesus is artificially introduced in its present context by the editorial phrases, 'At that time Jesus declared' (Matt.) or 'In that same hour he rejoiced in the Holy Spirit and said' (Luke). The prayer vaguely refers to 'these things', concealed from the wise but disclosed to children. The allusion cannot aim at the lack of belief of the inhabitants of the Galilean towns of Chorazin, Bethsaida and Capernaum, which provoked the woe of Jesus (Matt. 11:20–24; Luke 10:13–15).[11] Nor does the epithet 'the wise and the understanding' apply to the Galileans (see chapter 5, no. 27). So the passage must stem from a separate source.

The main themes of the prayer are, first, the paradoxical decision of God to reveal his mysteries to the simple or to babes, rather than to the learned. This statement recalls Jesus' general teaching about the little ones and the children being the true heirs of the Kingdom of heaven (Mark 10:15; Matt. 18:3; Luke 18:17; Mark 10:14; Matt. 19:14; Luke 18:16). Secondly, the same general teaching includes the idea that God's secrets are revealed to and through Jesus (see Matt. 16:17). The latter feature is reminiscent of the Dead Sea Scrolls, where the Teacher of Righteousness conveys to the initiates of the Community

11. Luke further inserts a comment of Jesus about the charismatic powers given to his disciples, but it has no more relevance to this prayer than the unbelief of the Galileans (Luke 10:17–20).

(called 'the simple') the revelations granted him by God (1QpHab 12:4; 2:2–3; 7:5–6).

Despite these genuine elements, the present form of the passage (Matt. 11:25–27; Luke 10:21–22), preserved in Q or possibly in a separate source, is alien in spirit from all the other prayers or sayings of Jesus in the Synoptic Gospels. Indeed, we are faced here with a Synoptic section which most closely resembles the Fourth Gospel (see John 10:15; 17:25–26). Someone has recently, and perhaps not quite appropriately, referred to it as a 'Johannine thunderbolt'. Not surprisingly, the extant formulation of Matthew 11:25–27 and Luke 10:21–22 has been declared by most New Testament critics as foreign to the ideology of Jesus. Many classify it, in my opinion correctly, among the products of Gentile Hellenistic Christianity.

III. THE *M* TRADITION

7. How to pray and how not to pray according to Jesus (Matt. 6:5–8)

And when you pray, you must not be like the hypocrites; for they love to stand and pray in the synagogues and at the street corners, that they may be seen by men. Truly, I say to you, they have received their reward. But when you pray, go into your room and shut the door and pray to your Father who is in secret; and your Father who sees in secret will reward you. And in praying do not heap up empty phrases as the Gentiles do; for they think that they will be heard for their many words. Do not be like them, for your Father knows what you need before you ask him.

Jesus describes here both negatively and positively the behaviour to be adopted by a praying person and the form in which he should frame his supplication to God. Jesus is clearly envisaging here private prayer and condemns the hypocrites for performing their personal devotions in public so as to appear very pious. The indictment is the same as the one addressed to the scribes (Mark 12:38–40; Matt. 23:5–6; Luke 20:46; see chapter 2, no. 15A). Moreover the 'hypocrites' among Jews and all the Gentiles are blamed for being long-winded in their entreaties to God or the gods. This is contrary to biblical spirituality where prayer is praised for its brevity. 'Let your words be few,' we read in Ecclesiastes 5:2 (5:1 in Hebrew), and 'Do not repeat yourself in your prayer' echoes Ecclesiasticus 7:14. In the pagan Graeco-Roman world, Seneca ridiculed people for their tedious verbosity, which exhausted even the patience of the gods (Letter 31:5). Jesus' insistence on conciseness is in conformity with his teaching on the heavenly Father's foreknowledge of all the suppliant's needs (cf. Matt. 6:32; see chapter 3, no. 19).

Equally important is Jesus' emphasis on the privacy of prayer, which also has good biblical and Jewish antecedents. The miracle-working prophet Elisha addressed himself to God behind closed doors before reviving the son of the Shunammite woman (2 Kings 4:33). The patriarch Joseph withdrew to a hidden room before praying to God (Testament of Joseph 3:3), and the contemplative Essenes or Therapeutae closeted themselves in a consecrated room or 'monastery' where only the Bible was allowed and there they initiated themselves into the mysteries of the holy life (Philo, *On the Contemplative Life* 25). The ancient Hasidim retired to the rooftop or to an upper chamber in order to communicate with God (yBer 9d; bBer 34b; bTaan 23b). In short, a person inspired and motivated by deep trust does not need to spell out all his requirements, presenting as it were a shopping list to God, or to display his piety in public. In Jesus' view solitude assists concentration. The reference to God as one who dwells and sees 'in secret' will be dealt with at Matthew 6:4 concerning almsgiving (see chapter 9, no. 20).

According to the testimony of the Gospels Jesus applied these rules to his own spirituality and frequently chose solitary places, such as mountains and deserts, for meditation and prayer (see Mark 1:35; Luke 4:42; Mark 6:46; Matt. 14:23; Mark 14:35; Matt. 26:39; Luke 22:41; Luke 5:16; 6:12; 9:18, 28).

IV. THE *L* TRADITION

8. Jesus' prayer for forgiveness (Luke 23:33–34)

And when they came to the place which is called The Skull, there they crucified him . . . And Jesus said, *Father, forgive them; for they know not what they do.*

Half the oldest manuscript witnesses, among them a Bodmer papyrus, the Vaticanus and Beza's Codex, omit the sentence in verse 34 which contains the words of Jesus. Such uncertainty in the textual tradition suggests that the interpretation of the passage was the subject of serious debate in Christian antiquity. Put simply, according to half of the witnesses the crucified Jesus begged God's forgiveness for 'them', but the other half preferred to know nothing about the prayer. Who are 'they'? In the light of the context the pronoun points to the executioners, i.e. the Roman soldiers responsible for nailing Jesus to the cross (verse 33) and subsequently for casting lots for his clothes (verse 34). Against the silence of Mark and Matthew, the historicity of the utterance transmitted by Luke cannot be safely assumed. The wording itself also fills the mind of the critical reader with doubts. 'They know not what they do' could hardly refer to the legionaries. Their ignorance of Jesus' supernatural status was obvious. A specific prayer of forgiveness for the soldiers would also imply that the Romans were the chief culprits, a position contrary to the point of view adopted by early Christianity. As is well known, the evangelists, especially Matthew (27:24), sought to exculpate Pilate. So if Jesus did not mean the Romans, he must have prayed for the Jews. Such an interpretation of the words would be in harmony with the thought of the primitive Jewish church. The author of the Acts of the Apostles states that, while holding his compatriots responsible for the events leading to the crucifixion, Peter looked for, and found, mitigating circumstances. In his words, the inhabitants of Jerusalem and their rulers acted in ignorance (Acts 3:17). At a later stage, however, after the final fiasco of Christian preaching in Jewish Palestine, the main, indeed exclusive, blame for 'deicide' was laid on the shoulders of the Jews. By that time, the idea of an intervention by Jesus on behalf of his murderers was unthinkable. Therefore in order to exonerate the Romans by ensuring that the Jews alone were held culpable, "Father, forgive them; for they know not what they do" was excised from many manuscripts of the Gospel of Luke. The only pointer in this verse to the genuine message of Jesus is the centrality of the theme of forgiveness.

9. The last prayer of Jesus (Luke 23:46)

Then Jesus, crying with a loud voice, said, *Father, into thy hands I commit my spirit!*

'*Lama sabachthani?*', the heart-rending cry of incomprehension uttered by the dying Jesus according to the Gospels of Mark and Matthew (see chapter 5, no. 19), is replaced in Luke by pious words of resignation through citing Psalm 31:5 (see chapter 5, no. 41). This is the prayer of a textbook holy man and not of the fiery prophet from Galilee.[12]

REFLECTIONS

To summarize the contents of this chapter, five out of the nine literary units represent personal prayers pronounced by Jesus (cf. nos. 3, 4, 6, 8, 9). One of these, his last cry on the cross, is transmitted in two different versions (nos. 4 and 9). Another, the 'Our Father', is a communal prayer he taught his disciples when, according to Luke, one of them requested him to do so (no. 5). The remaining sections contain advice on the nature of genuine devotion. One of the prayers is headed by the Aramaic invocation *Abba* (no. 3). Another starts with *Eloi, Eloi*, etc. ('My God, my God'), and is entirely preserved in Aramaic (no. 4). The Lord's Prayer, which has been transmitted only in Greek, also reveals an Aramaic linguistic substratum. The last exclamation of Jesus in Luke ('Father, into thy hands', etc.) offers a theological

12. John's Jesus would not utter 'Why hast thou forsaken me?' either, but mixing the prosaic with the mysterious he simply says: 'It is finished' (John 19:30). 1 Peter 4:19 expresses common Christian piety: 'Let those who suffer according to God's will do right and entrust their souls to a faithful Creator.'

emendation of the final words of Jesus reproduced in Aramaic in Mark and Matthew in the form of a quotation from the Greek Psalms (no. 9).

Of the nine quotations, two appear to be inauthentic. It is hard to imagine that the quasi Johannine meditation in Matthew 11:25–27/ Luke 10:21–22 (no. 6), totally different from the rest of his prayers, can possibly belong to Jesus. The authenticity of the prayer for forgiveness and the last cry of Jesus in Luke (nos. 8 and 9) is also difficult to maintain. However, the other seven passages can be retraced to Jesus with a high degree of probability. The supplication in Gethsemane, with its Aramaic invocation *Abba* followed by a humble submission to the will of God, expresses without a shadow of doubt the authentic religiosity of Jesus (no. 3). The same favourable conclusion applies, as shown in our sentence-by-sentence commentary, to the Lord's Prayer (no. 5). God as Father, the sanctity of his name, the appeal for the instant coming of his Kingdom, the focus of prayer on immediate needs (the bread of today), the obligation to forgive in order to obtain forgiveness, and the hope in liberation from demonic powers: all these form a perfect synopsis of the doctrinal and moral message of Jesus.

Similarly, the counsels given by him to his praying disciples touch the heart of his teaching. The faith or trust in God of the charismatic almost miraculously brings about the fulfilment of what is expected of him. Faith is said to perform the miracles of healing. But there are conditions which must be observed. A person hoping to find God generous in regard to his offences must himself be generously forgiving to his neighbours. He must not display in public religious punctiliousness; on the contrary, he must address God in secret, one to one, and speak to him heart to heart. We are entitled to assume that the same lack of religious ostentation also applies to the followers of Jesus when they recite their communal prayers. As for '*Eloi, Eloi, lama sabachthani?*', the unexpectedness and disturbing character of these words militate in favour of their authenticity, with momentous consequences for our understanding of Jesus.

If, as has been pointed out, the ideas motivating a man's prayer are likely to allow a glimpse into the inner core of his religion, it follows that the elements contained in this chapter are likely to make a significant contribution to the main topic of this book, the quest of the authentic message of Jesus.

7

'Son of Man' Sayings

The phrase 'Son of man' is a key feature in the evangelists' portrayal of Jesus. To grasp the various shades of its meaning, the reader will require some familiarity with the wider employment of the idiom both in ancient Judaism and in the New Testament. In the Synoptic Gospels the expression 'Son of man' appears some sixty-five times if the parallels in Matthew, Mark and Luke are counted separately. In John we find eleven further instances. In the rest of the New Testament the part played by the phrase is insignificant. It figures only once in the Acts of the Apostles and twice in Revelation in direct quotations from the Old Testament, and never in Paul.

From the philological point of view it is generally accepted that the unusual Greek expression, *ho huios tou anthropou* ('the son of the man'), reflects the Aramaic phrase, *bar 'enash – bar nash* ('son of man') or *bar 'enasha – bar nasha* ('the son of man'). In the Gospels 'Son of man' is found exclusively on the lips of Jesus when he is speaking of himself. The idiom is easily intelligible to all and sundry: no one ever inquires about its significance. It is also perfectly acceptable to all listeners since nobody objects to its use by Jesus.

If the New Testament phrase, which is not a native Greek expression, is to make sense at all, it must be Aramaic sense. Therefore the vernacular Palestinian Aramaic use of *bar nash* or *bar nasha* must be considered first. Outside the Gospels, 'son of man' is most commonly employed in Jewish Aramaic (Targum, Midrash, Talmud) as the equivalent of 'a man' or 'the man'; it can also mean 'one' or 'someone', i.e. the indefinite pronoun. None of these usages sheds light on the terminology of the Synoptic Gospels. Furthermore, in the Galilean dialect of Aramaic, the mother tongue of Jesus, 'son of man' sometimes appears in direct speech, that is to say, in a monologue or a dialogue, as a roundabout reference to the speaker himself. It is not unlike the English 'yours truly' employed instead of 'I'. The purpose of such an oblique and generalizing style was to create a degree of obscurity and inclusiveness: in principle 'son of man' can relate to anybody. As a result it can camouflage something dreadful, or something that in plain speech would sound conceited. So in Aramaic parlance, it is *the son of man* rather than 'I' who is going to die ('to die' is a taboo phrase) or is about to be crowned king (a boastful assertion).[1] From the interpretative point of view it should be remembered that in the passages where 'son of man' is used as a circumlocution, the meaning of the statements is to be derived from the immediate or broader context and not from the idiom itself. 'Son of man' has no specific significance on its own.

We should furthermore bear in mind that the understanding of 'son of man' was influenced within and outside the New Testament by a well-known biblical Aramaic expression first attested in the Book of Daniel 7:13. There the sage Daniel dreams of four awesome beasts (a lion, a bear, a leopard and a monster), symbolizing the world empires of Babylonia, Media, Persia and Greece. He is then shown a scene of judgement in the heavenly court with God depicted as an old man, called 'the Ancient of days'. Death sentence is pronounced on the last of the four animals (the monster) and the other three are deprived of their dominion. The climax in verse 13 contrasts the beasts with a

1. See G. Vermes, 'The use of *bar nash/bar nasha* in Jewish Aramaic', a lecture originally delivered at a New Testament conference in Oxford in 1965, and published as Appendix E in *An Aramaic Approach to the Gospels and Acts* by Matthew Black (3rd edn., Oxford, 1967), 310–28. Reprinted in G. Vermes, *Post-biblical Jewish Studies* (Leiden, 1975), 147–65. Cf. further 'The Present State of the "Son of Man" Debate', *Journal of Jewish Studies* 29 (1978), 123–34. Reprinted in *Jesus and the World of Judaism* (London, 1983), 115–25, 175–80. See also G. Vermes, *Jesus the Jew* (London, 1973, 2001), 137–53, and *The Changing Faces of Jesus* (London, 2000), 38–41, 175–7.

Some scholars have objected to my interpretation of 'son of man' as an indirect self-reference to the speaker because they believe that the Aramaic idiom represents a general statement which includes the speaker, whereas in the Gospels 'son of man' points exclusively to the speaker. Their misunderstanding derives from a false conception of circumlocutional speech, which by nature demands an element of equivocation. If the speaker intends to be crystal clear, he can use plain language and need not to refer to himself in a roundabout way.

human figure, or in a literal translation of the Aramaic 'one like a son of man' (*kebar 'enash*). He is lifted up from the earth by the clouds, to be glorified and granted eternal kingship. According to the interpretation of the phrase given by the author of Daniel himself, 'one like a son of man' represents 'the saints of the Most High', that is to say, the Jewish people (Dan. 7:18, 22, 27). The oldest external parallel, the controversial first-century BC Aramaic Daniel Apocryphon from Qumran (4Q246), exhibits in my view the same collective meaning, 'one like a son of man' being the Israelite nation.

From the completion of the Book of Daniel in the 160s BC to the time of the destruction of Jerusalem in AD 70 the extant Jewish literature contains no evidence that the expression 'son of man' was used as a title, identifying the holder of a religious office (such as Messiah, Judge, etc.). However, in the decades following the end of the first Jewish war against Rome, which is also the period of the composition of the Synoptic Gospels (*c.* AD 70–100), we possess two independent literary attestations depicting a man-like figure either as a heavenly Messiah (4 Ezra 13), or as a celestial Judge (1 Enoch 37–71). A little later the famous Rabbi Akiba (died in AD 135) implicitly identified 'one like a son of man' of Daniel 7:13 with the Messiah, son of David, of the traditional Jewish expectation (bHagigah 14a; bSanhedrin 38b). In other words, according to the available documentation it was only after AD 70 that 'son of man' became the designation of an individual entrusted with an important messianic or judicial function. It is highly unlikely, therefore, that Jesus used 'son of man' as a title.

These preliminaries will provide a context for the presentation of the 'son of man' passages in the Synoptic Gospels. They will be examined under three headings:

1. 'Son of man' is simply a reference to the speaker (= Jesus), irrespective of the subject of the speech.

2. The 'son of man' is used when the speaker (= Jesus) predicts his suffering, death and resurrection.

3. The 'son of man', linked to Daniel 7, explicitly associates the speaker (= Jesus) with the last judgement.

I. 'SON OF MAN' A SELF-DESIGNATION OF THE SPEAKER

A. MARK AND THE TRIPLE TRADITION

1. The right of the 'Son of man' to forgive sins (Mark 2:9–11; Matt. 9:5–6; Luke 5:23–24)

Which is easier, to say to the paralytic, 'Your sins are forgiven', or to say, 'Rise, take up your pallet and walk'? But that you may know that the Son of man has authority on earth to forgive sins – he said to the paralytic – *I say to you, rise, take up your pallet and go home.*

The story itself has already been discussed in chapter 2, no. 1.

Here we are concerned only with the 'Son of man' idiom. Having established the symbolical synonymy of healing and forgiveness, Jesus asserts that healing is the equivalent of declaring sins pardoned, and demonstrates his charismatic power by curing the paralysed man.[2] The astonishment of the bystanders in Mark 2:12 and Luke 5:26 makes plain that 'Son of man' and Jesus were one and the same person. The underlying motive is modesty: it would have been unseemly to affirm bluntly, 'I can forgive sins' or 'I know that this man's sins have been pardoned.' In Matthew, however, the phrase 'Son of man' does not apply to Jesus alone, but is taken by the eyewitnesses in a generic sense. They praise God for having given such a power to 'men', implying that through healing the sick the charismatics were empowered to declare sins forgiven.

2. An identical order also appears in John 5:8 apropos the cure of a different paralytic, but with no mention of the phrase 'Son of man'.

2. The 'Son of man' is above the Sabbath (Mark 2:27–28; Matt. 12:8; Luke 6:5)

The sabbath was made for man, not man for the sabbath; so the Son of man is lord even of the sabbath (Mark).

For the Son of man is lord of the sabbath (Matt., Luke).

For the narrative to which the present passage is attached, see chapter 2, no. 3.

In Mark the general principle of man's superiority over the Sabbath precedes the statement about the 'Son of man'. Matthew and Luke have no knowledge of the general principle or, more likely, have deleted it from the text of Mark on which they depend, and reproduce only the remark concerning the pre-eminence of the 'Son of man' over the Sabbath. This complex saying may be explained in three different ways. (1) Many New Testament scholars, anticipating later developments of the Christian definition of Jesus, understand the phrase as a title referring to an eschatological figure with special superhuman powers. Jesus can overrule a Sabbath prohibition because he is the Messiah, indeed the Son of God. (2) For others, familiar with the meaning of the underlying Aramaic idiom, 'son of man' corresponds to a human being; thus the famous Julius Wellhausen in his Mark commentary of 1903. If so, the second clause would be an explanatory repetition of the first: the Sabbath was made for man, so he is above the Sabbath. (3) The phrase 'son of man' can be a circumlocutional reference by a modest speaker to himself.

3. Speaking against the 'Son of man' (Mark 3:28–29; Matt. 12:31–32; Luke 12:10)

Truly, I say to you, all sins will be forgiven the sons of men, and whatever blasphemies they utter; but whoever blasphemes against the Holy Spirit never has forgiveness, but is guilty of an eternal sin (Mark).

Therefore I tell you, every sin and blasphemy will be forgiven men, but the blasphemy against the Spirit will not be forgiven. And whoever says a word against the Son of man will be forgiven; but whoever speaks against the Holy Spirit will not be forgiven, either in this age or in the age to come (Matt.).

And everyone who speaks a word against the Son of man will be forgiven; but he who blasphemes against the Holy Spirit will not be forgiven (Luke).

This notoriously difficult passage starts with a saying contained in Mark and Matthew, expressing the teaching that all the sins of the 'sons of men' (Mark) or 'men' (Matt.) may be pardoned except blasphemy against the Holy Spirit. The Holy Spirit, or divine force, being the source of all virtuous actions, disrespect shown to it constitutes a very grave, indeed unforgivable sin. So far the matter is clear. The confusion arises when Matthew enlarges the statement by introducing the 'Son of man' and asserts that words spoken against him can be pardoned. (The supplement without the Marcan original figures in Luke, too.) This additional logion, borrowed from Q, asserts that criticism of the 'Son of man' (i.e. Jesus) is forgivable, but resistance to the Holy Spirit is not. Such an irreverent attitude to Jesus is unparalleled in the Gospels.

There are two possible solutions. The first may be expressed by paraphrasing the speaker (Jesus): 'You can contradict me, but you surely cannot disregard my (i.e., the son of man's) charismatic deeds performed through the spirit of God' (cf. Matt. 12:28; Luke 11:20; cf. chapter 8, no. 43). The second possible explanation would assume that Matthew 12:32 and Luke 12:10 form a doublet, in which the unusual plural, 'sons of men', 'men', of Mark 3:28 and Matthew 12:31, is automatically but erroneously corrected to read the customary singular 'Son of man'. This alteration naturally causes confusion by presenting criticism of Jesus as pardonable. In a number of similar sayings opposition to Jesus (the 'Son of man') is treated as an extremely serious matter: Jesus will reject the man who has denied him before God (see no. 18 below).

4. Question about the identity of the Son of man/Jesus (Mark 8:27; Matt. 16:13; Luke 9:18)

Who do men say that I am? (Mark, Luke).

Who do men say that the son of man is? (Matt.).

One of the clearest proofs of the interchangeability of 'son of man' and 'I' is supplied by Jesus' question addressed to his disciples at Caesarea Philippi. Some argue that the original formula included 'I' as in Mark and Luke, and that it was Matthew who substituted for it a secondary Aramaism, 'son of man'. However, since the question begins with 'men' (*beney nash*) and continues with 'son of man' (*bar nasha*), the underlying Aramaic phraseology sounds primary and authentic.

5. The 'Son of man' as servant (Mark 10:42–45; Matt. 20:25–28; Luke 22:25–27)

You know that those who are supposed to rule over the Gentiles lord it over them, and their great men exercise authority over them. But it shall not be so among you; but whoever would be great among you must be your servant, and whoever would be first among you must be slave of all. For the Son of man also came not to be served but to serve, and to give his life as a ransom for many (Mark, Matt.).

The kings of the Gentiles exercise lordship over them; and those in authority over them are called benefactors. But not so with you; rather let the greatest among you become as the youngest, and the leader as one who serves. For which is the greater, one who sits at table, or one who serves? Is it not the one who sits at table? But I am among you as one who serves (Luke).

The main aim of the saying is to display the contrast between secular behaviour exemplified by the Gentiles, whose kings and noblemen rule their subjects, and the way of life proposed by Jesus which consists in the reversal of the customary hierarchical order with the superior and the senior ministering to the inferior and the junior. The ultimate model of devotion and help is Jesus himself. In Luke 22:27 the speech is in the first person: 'I am among you as one who serves.' In Mark and Matthew the self-effacing 'son of man' is substituted for 'I'. The same idea is expressed in a parable where the master is waiting at table on his faithful servants (Luke 12:35–38; see chapter 4, no. 25).

The concluding words of Mark and Matthew, which define the aim of the mission of the 'Son of man' as giving 'his life as a ransom for many', disclose the point of view of high theology. This would make sense if it could be taken for granted and as historically proven that Jesus expected to die before the arrival of the Kingdom of God, and that he envisaged his future death as an atoning sacrifice. The texts analysed in section II below indicate that this was not the case. It is therefore reasonable to see in the sentence, 'the Son of man . . . came . . . to give his life as a ransom for many', words added by Mark and Matthew to the original logion preserved in Luke which reflect 'the redemption theories of Hellenistic Christianity'.[3]

6. The betrayal of the 'Son of man' (Mark 14:18, 20–21, 41; Matt. 26:21, 23–24, 45; Luke 22:21–22)

Truly, I say to you, one of you will betray me, one who is eating with me (Mark, Matt.).

It is one of the twelve, one who is dipping bread into the dish with me. For the Son of man goes as it is written of him [*as has been determined* (Luke)], *but woe to that man by whom the Son of man is betrayed . . .* (Mark, Matt., Luke).

It is enough; the hour has come; the Son of man is betrayed into the hands of sinners (Mark 14:41; Matt. 26:45)

The sayings are part of the Last Supper and of the account of the arrest of Jesus in the garden of Gethsemane (see chapter 1, no. 25). The 'Son

3. Rudolf Bultmann, *The History of the Synoptic Tradition* (London, 1963), 144.

of man' is unquestionably Jesus. Here as in other places the betrayal is claimed to have been predicted in the Bible ('it is written of him'), but as usual the Scripture passage is not cited.

B. THE Q TRADITION

7. Persecution on account of the 'Son of man' (Matt. 5:11; Luke 6:22)

Blessed are you when men revile you and persecute you and utter all kinds of evil against you falsely on my account (Matt.).

Blessed are you when men hate you, and when they exclude you and revile you, and cast out your name as evil, on account of the son of man! (Luke).

The Beatitudes, of which this is the concluding part, will be examined separately in chapter 8, no. 34. Here the focus is exclusively on the 'Son of man' idiom. Note that the circumlocutional language is adopted only by Luke; in Matthew Jesus speaks plainly in the first person.

8. The homelessness of the 'Son of man' (Matt. 8:20; Luke 9:58)

Foxes have holes, and birds of the air have nests; but the son of man has nowhere to lay his head.

The saying, already examined in chapter 3, no. 25, sketches in the usual hyperbolical style the Spartan existence of an itinerant preacher. Those who intend to follow Jesus in his campaign for the establishment of God's Kingdom must be prepared to imitate his way of life. Although the contrast between wild animals and man is proverbial and folkloric, the obvious primary meaning of 'son of man' is a modest 'I'.

9. The 'Son of man' accused of gluttony (Matt. 11:18–19; Luke 7:33–34)

For John came neither eating [*bread* (Luke)] *nor drinking* [*wine* (Luke)], *and they* [*you* (Luke)] say, 'He has a demon'; the Son of man came eating and drinking, and they [*you* (Luke)] *say, 'Behold, a glutton and a drunkard, a friend of tax-collectors and sinners!'*

For the parable of children playing in a public square to which the present saying is attached, see chapter 4, no. 9. The ascetic John the Baptist is contrasted with the more relaxed Jesus, the table companion of publicans and sinners (Mark 2:15; Matt. 9:10; Luke 5:29; Matt. 21:31–32; Luke 15:1; 18:10; 19:2, 5), who unassumingly refers to himself as the 'Son of man' (see also chapter 8, no. 41).

C. *THE* L *TRADITION*

10. The 'Son of man' came to seek the lost (Luke 19:9–10)

Today salvation has come to this house, since he also is a son of Abraham. For the Son of man came to seek and to save the lost.

This saying concludes the episode of Zacchaeus, sketched in chapter 1, no. 37. The chief tax-collector from Jericho, having met Jesus, repented and decided to mend his ways. He thus illustrated the purpose of the mission of Jesus (= the 'Son of man'), which was to call the lost to the Kingdom of God and thus save them.

11. The betrayal of the 'Son of man' (Luke 22:48)

Judas, would you betray the son of man with a kiss?

The account of the arrest of Jesus has been dealt with in chapter 1, no. 25. As customary in the circumstances, the question addressed to

Judas about his betrayal of Jesus is formulated in roundabout 'son of man' wording.

II. 'SON OF MAN' PREDICTIONS OF THE DEATH AND RESURRECTION OF JESUS

The Synoptic Gospels include six separate instances in which Jesus, always using the phrase 'Son of man' to indicate himself, foretells with more or less detail and clarity his suffering, death and, four times out of six cases, his resurrection. In order to avoid too much repetition, I will depart from my usual method, and will first present the quotations separately and follow them up by a general exposition.

A. MARK AND THE TRIPLE TRADITION

12. Mark 8:30–31; Matt. 16:20–21; Luke 9:21–22

And he charged them to tell no one about him. And he began to teach them that *the son of Man must suffer many things, and be rejected by the elders and the chief priests and the scribes, and be killed, and after three days rise again* (Mark).

Then he strictly charged the disciples to tell no one that he was the Christ. From that time Jesus began to show his disciples that *he must go to Jerusalem and suffer many things from the elders and chief priests and scribes, and be killed, and on the third day be raised* (Matt.).

But he charged and commanded them to tell this to no one, saying, *The Son of man must suffer many things, and be rejected by the elders and chief priests and scribes, and be killed, and on the third day be raised* (Luke).

13. Mark 9:9–10, 12; Matt. 17:9, 12

And as they were coming down the mountain, he charged them to tell no one what they had seen, until *the Son of man should have risen from the dead.* So they kept the matter to themselves, questioning what the rising from the dead meant . . . And he said to them, . . . *How is it written of the Son of man, that he should suffer many things and be treated with contempt?* (Mark).

And as they were coming down the mountain, Jesus commanded them, *Tell no one the vision, until the Son of man is raised from the dead* . . . He replied, . . . *So also the Son of man will suffer at their hands* (Matt.).

14. Mark 9:30–32; Matt. 17:22–23; Luke 9:43–45

They went on from there and passed through Galilee. And he would not have any one know it; for he was teaching his disciples, saying to them, *The Son of man will be delivered into the hands of men, and they will kill him; and when he is killed, after three days he will rise.* But they did not understand the saying, and they were afraid to ask him (Mark).

As they were gathering in Galilee, Jesus said to them, *The Son of man is to be delivered into the hands of men, and they will kill him, and he will be raised on the third day.* And they were greatly distressed (Matt.).

But while they were all marvelling at everything he did, he said to his disciples, *Let these words sink into your ears; for the Son of man is to be delivered into the hands of men.* But they did not understand this saying . . . and they were afraid to ask him about this saying (Luke).

15. Mark 10:32–34; Matt. 20:17–19; Luke 18:31–34; cf. Luke 24:44–47.

And they were on the road, going up to Jerusalem . . . And taking the twelve again, he began to tell them what was to happen to him, saying, *Behold, we are going up to Jerusalem; and the Son of man will be delivered to the chief priests and the scribes, and they will condemn him to death, and deliver him to the Gentiles; and they will mock him, and spit upon him, and scourge him, and kill him; and after three days he will rise* (Mark).

And as Jesus was going up to Jerusalem, he took the twelve disciples aside, and on the way he said to them, *Behold, we are going up to Jerusalem; and the Son of man will be delivered to the chief priests and scribes, and they will condemn him to death, and deliver him to the Gentiles to be mocked and scourged and crucified, and he will be raised on the third day* (Matt.).

And taking the twelve, he said to them, *Behold, we are going up to Jerusalem, and everything that is written of the Son of man by the prophets will be accomplished. For he will be delivered to the Gentiles, and will be mocked and shamefully treated and spit upon; they will scourge him and kill him, and on the third day he will rise.* But they understood none of these things; this saying was hid from them, and they did not grasp what was said (Luke).

These are my words which I spoke to you while I was still with you, that everything written about me in the law of Moses and the prophets and the psalms must be fulfilled . . . Thus it is written, that the Christ should suffer and on the third day rise from the dead, and that repentance and forgiveness of sins should be preached in his name to all the nations, beginning from Jerusalem (Luke 24).

B. THE M TRADITION

16. Matt. 12:40

For as Jonah was three days and three nights in the belly of the whale, so will the Son of man be three days and three nights in the heart of the earth.

See chapter 5, no. 7.

17. Matt. 26:1–2

When Jesus had finished all these sayings, he said to his disciples, *You know that after two days the Passover is coming, and the Son of man will be delivered up to be crucified.*

With the exception of Matthew's interpretation of the sign of Jonah (cf. no. 16) as the prophetic prefiguring of the time spent by the dead body of Jesus in his grave (see chapter 5, no. 7), all the various announcements of his final destiny were made, according to the evangelists, during the final period of his life. The first of them follows Peter's confession of his Messiahship at Caesarea Philippi (no. 12) and the last, uttered in Jerusalem, predates the fatal Passover only by two days (no. 17). The predictions are solemn, and their tone is emphatic, especially in Luke: 'Let these words sink into your ears', etc.; 'everything that is written of the Son of man by the prophets will be accomplished'; 'everything written about me in the law of Moses and the prophets and the psalms must be fulfilled' (nos. 14 and 15). Yet in the crucial period between the arrest and execution of Jesus, no one seems to have remembered the reiterated forewarnings concerning the events leading to the cross. Likewise all the apostles were at first reluctant to believe in the resurrection of Jesus. The evangelists had to provide some explanation to ensure credibility for their accounts; they all ended by laying the blame on the apostles for failing to grasp or simply forgetting the predictions of Jesus.

The least contorted is the account of Peter's outrage on hearing Jesus' announcement of his suffering and execution (see no. 12 above). The leader of the apostles, we are told, lost his temper and set out to rebuke Jesus, for which he was severely reprimanded: 'Get behind me, Satan!' (Mark 8:32–33; Matt. 16:22–23). Also, when informed after the Transfiguration of the coming resurrection of Jesus (cf. no. 13 above), Peter, James and John are all nonplussed: none of them had any idea of what rising from the dead meant (Mark 9:10)! Elsewhere the disciples are depicted as 'distressed' (Matt. 17:23) or as uncomprehending yet too frightened to inquire (Mark 9:32; Luke 9:45; see no. 14 above). Later, they are said to be unable to understand the words of Jesus (see no. 15; cf. also no. 17). At last the risen Jesus had to remind his apostles of the prophecies earlier conveyed to them concerning the suffering and resurrection of the Messiah (see no. 15 above).

It would appear, therefore, that the evangelists desperately tried to emphasize Jesus' wish to describe the cross and the resurrection as divinely predestined events foretold by the prophets and by Jesus himself, even though this made the uncomprehending apostles, who all abandoned and betrayed their Master at the moment of his ordeal, look silly, cowardly and undignified. Luke tries his best to manufacture an explanation. He remarks that at the prompting of their angelic informants, the female witnesses of the empty tomb finally remembered the announcement made by Jesus in Galilee that 'the Son of man must be delivered into the hands of sinful men, and be crucified, and on the third day rise' (Luke 24:6–7).

As far as the terms of the six alleged 'prophecies' of the final events of the life of Jesus are concerned, they do not fully agree with one another. The main accent lies on his forthcoming death (see nos. 12, 14), but only Matthew (20:19 and 26:2) explicitly refers to crucifixion (cf. nos. 15 and 17). The persons responsible for his killing are not clearly identified either. In four of the predictions they are either unnamed (see nos. 13, 16, 17), or vaguely alluded to as 'men' (no. 14). In the other two, the blame is placed on the Jewish leaders, 'the elders and the chief priests and the scribes' (cf. nos. 12 and 15). There is only one detailed statement relating to the death of Jesus. Mark 10:33–34 (no. 15), in the form of a prophecy after the fact, mentions the mocking, scourging and spitting on the accused by the executioners and identifies the judicial authorities as 'Gentiles', i.e. Romans (for the latter point see also Matt. 20:19).

With the exception of Luke 9:44 (cf. no. 14) and Matthew 26:2 (no. 17), which do not allude to the resurrection, the 'prophecies' summarily state that Jesus will rise from the dead 'after three days' or 'on the third day'. The figure of three days or the like (cf. chapter 5, no. 7), from the burial of Jesus to the discovery of the empty tomb, is clearly inspired by Matthew's interpretation of the sign of Jonah (no. 16 above): the three days and nights spent by the prophet in the belly of the great fish. The phrase 'on the third day' also recalls seven significant events in biblical history, which are all dated thus. The two most important of them are the first, 'On the third day Abraham lifted up his eyes and saw the place afar off' (Gen. 22:4), indicating Isaac's virtual 'resurrection' after the unaccomplished sacrifice, and the seventh and last, referring to the general revival of the dead: 'After two days he will revive us, on the third day he will raise us up' (Hos. 6:2).[4] These exegetical traditions seem to stand behind the belief in the resurrection of Jesus *on the third day*.

The general impression produced by these quotations is that they were meant to instruct the twelve apostles about the ultimate stages of the career of Jesus (cf. no. 15). It is possible to detect a slightly stronger emphasis on the prophetic announcement of the suffering and crucifixion. Mention of the resurrection is absent from two out of the six passages alluding to the execution and death of Jesus (see nos. 14 [Luke], 17).[5]

In addition to the various predictions by Jesus himself, Luke mentions emphatically, but without adducing details, that the whole destiny of the Messiah, his death and resurrection, were foretold by the prophets of the Old Testament: 'everything that is written of the Son of man by the prophets will be accomplished' (no. 15). Mark and Matthew allude to predictions relating to his betrayal and arrest: 'For

4. They are all listed in the Midrash Genesis Rabbah 56:1 (see my *The Religion of Jesus the Jew* (London, 1993), 58–9).

5. In the first announcement, which is followed by Peter's rebuke (no. 12), the reference to Jesus' rising is a secondary addition. If the original prophecy had included both his death and *resurrection*, Peter's indignation at hearing it would be hard to explain.

the Son of man goes as it is written of him, but woe to that man by whom the Son of man is betrayed' (Mark 14:21; Matt. 26:24), and 'Let the scriptures be fulfilled' (Mark 14:49), or 'But how then should the scriptures be fulfilled, that it must be so?' (Matt. 26:54). Again in an ambiguous way, Mark makes Jesus ask, 'How is it written of the Son of man, that he should suffer many things and be treated with contempt?' (Mark 9:12). In all these passages the evangelists deliberately introduce the argument of prophetic fulfilment, a familiar theme in the early church elaborated in the Acts of the Apostles and in the letters of St Paul.

To place the final events of the life of Jesus in proper perspective, it should be further borne in mind that mainstream Jewish tradition did not expect the Messiah to die, or afterwards to rise from the dead. The last poem of the Suffering Servant of the Lord (Isa. 53), which seems to be the most obvious text to be identified as foreshadowing the redemptive death of Jesus, is largely ignored in the Synoptic Gospels. The two passages in which it is quoted point in a different direction. In Matthew 8:17 the Servant's 'taking our infirmities and bearing our diseases' (Isa. 53:4) is literally applied to the healing activity of Jesus. Later, Luke (22:37) makes Jesus cite Isaiah 53:12, 'And he was reckoned with transgressors', to allude to his impending arrest as a criminal. The earliest New Testament attempt to associate the last song of the Servant of the Lord (Isa. 52:13 to 53:12) with the cross (the Servant is compared to a sheep led to the slaughter) is in Acts 8:32–35. There the deacon Philip, asked about the meaning of Isaiah 53:7–8, interprets it as alluding to Jesus. In 1 Peter 2:22 and 24 (probably dating to AD 100 at the earliest), the text of Isaiah 53 is twice used to describe Christ's passion, though without actually indicating that it comes from the Bible. It was the early church, not Jesus, that had occasional recourse to the Suffering Servant theme.[6]

6. The sensational claims by a few Qumran scholars asserting that Jews in the time of Jesus expected a dying Messiah are based on a fundamental misunderstanding of both the Gospels and some Scroll passages and have been justly disregarded by mainstream scholarship. See Robert Eisenman and Michael Wise, *The Dead Sea Scrolls Uncovered* (Shaftesbury, 1992), 27; Michael O. Wise, *The First Messiah: Investigating the Savior before Christ* (Berkeley, Calif., 1999); Israel Knohl, *The Messiah before Jesus: The Suffering Servant of the Dead Sea Scrolls* (Berkeley, Calif., 2000).

In short, no forecast of the cross and the resurrection had any impact on the members of the inner circle of Jesus. This is clear from the behaviour of the apostles during the last hours of his life. They all ran away and Peter went as far as to deny that he had ever known him. Even the first news of the resurrection is depicted as something coming out of the blue, and not as a forecast event. The whole series of forewarnings has the appearance of *vaticinium ex eventu*, a 'prophecy after the fact', introduced by the evangelists with later Christian generations in view. The members of the primitive church had to be persuaded that the disconcerting events of the crucifixion and resurrection were foreordained by God and were the fulfilment of the predictions made by Jesus and by the earlier prophetic visionaries of the Jewish people.

The relationship between the 'predictions' of the passion (and resurrection) of Jesus and the contrasting behaviour of the disciples during the crucial three days following the arrest of Jesus will be further examined and assessed in chapter 10, section I (3).

III. 'SON OF MAN' SAYINGS LINKED TO DANIEL 7 AND ATTRIBUTED TO JESUS

There are two ways in which the 'Son of man' concept of the Synoptic Gospels can be linked to Daniel 7:13. The connection can either be explicit by means of a direct quotation of the Old Testament text, or implicit with recognizable hints at the biblical passage which, however, fall short of actual citation. The Danielic colouring introduces heavy eschatological overtones in the portrayal of Jesus beyond the stage of his earthly activity coinciding with the dawn of the Kingdom of God. Indeed, the Synoptic 'Son of man' associated with Daniel reveals himself in mid-air, surrounded by the heavenly host of angels. He is outlined in the Gospels as involved in the final judgement of the righteous and the wicked following the pattern attested in the Fourth Book of Ezra and the First Book of Enoch, works representing Jewish ideology at the end of the first century AD. The date shows that we are dealing here not with the religious imagery of Jesus, but with that of the primitive church.

A. MARK AND THE TRIPLE TRADITION

18. The 'Son of man' coming in glory (Mark 8:38; Matt. 16:27; Luke 9:26; cf. Matt. 10:32–33; Luke 12:8–9)

For whoever is ashamed of me and of my words in this adulterous and sinful generation, of him will the Son of man also be ashamed, when he comes in the glory of his Father with the holy angels (Mark, Luke) [*and then he will repay every man for what he has done* (Matt.)].

Everyone who acknowledges me before men, I also [*the Son of man also* (Luke)] *will acknowledge before my Father who is in heaven* [*before the angels of God* (Luke)]; *but whoever denies me before men, I also will deny before my Father who is in heaven* [*will be denied before the angels of God* (Luke)] (Matt. 10; Luke 12).

The acknowledgement and denial of the 'Son of man' are said to follow his glorious apparition in the midst of an army of angels. This canvas recalls Daniel 7 and represents the world of the Second Coming, and as such is attributable to early Christianity. The concept of judgement, hinted at in Mark and Luke, with the angels playing the role of the judge's agents, is made explicit by the concluding phrase appended by Matthew: 'He will repay every man for what he has done'. It is equally possible, however, that Mark 8:38 is a reformulation of an earlier saying of Jesus: those who reject him during his ministry will be automatically condemned at the advent of the Kingdom of God.

19. The 'Son of man' coming to gather the elect (Mark 13:26–27; Matt. 24:30–31; Luke 21:27–28)

They will see the Son of man coming in clouds [*on the clouds of heaven* (Matt.)] *with great power and glory* (Mark, Matt., Luke).

And then he will send out the angels [*with a loud trumpet call, and they will gather* (Matt.)], *and gather his elect from the four winds, from the ends of the earth to the ends of heaven* (Mark, Matt.).

Now when these things begin to take place, look up and raise your heads, because your redemption is drawing near (Luke 21:28).

As has been explained in chapter 5, no. 15, the onset of wars (i.e. the Roman invasion of Judaea) and the forthcoming prophetic portents affecting the heavenly bodies will serve as a warning that the end has come. It will be marked by the Danielic image of the descent of the 'Son of man' on a cloud, that is, the return of Christ adorned with heavenly glory. The Eschatological Discourse (Mark 13; Matt. 24; Luke 21), which furnishes the context, was meant to admonish the followers of Jesus in the apostolic age to discern the premonitory signs and reject the many false prophets and pseudo-messiahs. These considerations and the strict parallel with Paul's conception of the Parousia clearly indicate that the perspective is not that of Jesus, but of primitive Christianity. Paul's words provide the proof: 'We . . . who are left until the coming of the Lord, will not precede those who have fallen asleep [i.e. died]. For the Lord himself will descend from heaven with a cry of command, with the archangel's call, and with the sound of the trumpet of God. And the dead in Christ will rise first; then we who are alive . . . shall be caught up together with them in the clouds to meet the Lord in the air' (1 Thess. 4:15–17). The closeness of Paul's image to the Eschatological Discourse of the Synoptics, especially of Matthew, is disclosed in the use of the term *parousia* (= coming) in Matthew 24:27, 37, 39 (see no. 23 below) and the occurrence of the same term eight times in 1 and 2 Thessalonians and 1 Corinthians in Paul. The universal outlook, viz. the ingathering of the elect from the four corners of the earth, corresponds to the vision of Gentile Christianity. But the original image is prophetic and envisages the eschatological reunion of the dispersed children of Israel (see Isa. 40–55).

20. The 'Son of man' sitting next to God (Mark 14:62; Matt. 26:64; Luke 22:69)

You will see the Son of man seated at the right hand of Power, and coming with [*on* (Matt.)] *the clouds of heaven* (Mark, Matt.).

But from now on the Son of man shall be seated at the right hand of the power of God (Luke).

The combined quotation of Psalm 110:1 (sitting at the right hand of God) and Daniel 7:13 (coming on the clouds) has already been discussed in chapter 5, no. 18. Both the heavenly exaltation of the risen Jesus and the Parousia of the 'Son of man' with the coming judgement implicitly threatening the High Priest, to whom these words are addressed, are part of the theological speculation of early Jewish Christianity. Note also that here as in the previous passage the 'Son of man' rides on the clouds in his earthbound journey from his celestial throne.

B. THE Q TRADITION

21. The 'Son of man' enthroned (Matt. 19:28; cf. Luke 22:28–30)

Truly, I say to you, in the new world (palingenesia), *when the Son of man shall sit on his glorious throne, you who have followed me will also sit on twelve thrones, judging the twelve tribes of Israel* (Matt.).

You are those who have continued with me in my trials; and I assign to you, as my Father assigned to me, a kingdom, that you may eat and drink at my table in my kingdom, and sit on thrones judging the twelve tribes of Israel (Luke).

On the face of it, both Matthew and Luke envisage the era following the Parousia and the ultimate elevation of the 'Son of man' to his throne in the 'new world'. The Greek *palingenesia* means renewal and corresponds to the Jewish concept of 'the world to come'. There the twelve apostles, the tribal chiefs of the new Israel, will share the glory of the exalted Christ as joint rulers and judges. In Luke's more complex version each apostle who has participated in Jesus' trials or temptations is rewarded with a place at the messianic banquet table as well as with a judicial seat.

In its final post-Parousia form the saying reflects the ideology of the early church. Nevertheless, if the promise to faithful followers is dated to the Galilean career of Jesus, and the sequence 'Son of man' – 'me' in Matthew – implies this, the recompense of the disciples may be envisaged as conferred by Jesus at the inauguration of the Kingdom of God which was expected to crown his historical mission.

22. The sudden arrival of the 'Son of man' (Matt. 24:26–27; Luke 17:22–24)

So if they say to you, 'Lo, he is in the wilderness', do not go out; if they say, 'Lo, he is in the inner rooms', do not believe it. For as the lightening comes from the east and shines as far as the west, so will be the coming of the Son of man (Matt.).

The days are coming when you will desire to see one of the days of the Son of man, and you will not see it. And they will say to you, 'Lo, there!' or 'Lo, here!' Do not go, do not follow them. For as the lightening flashes and lights up the sky from one side to the other, so will the Son of man be in his day (Luke).

These words ascribed to Jesus in the Eschatological Discourse, alluding to pseudo-messiahs, reflect the situation in Judaea during the years preceding the outbreak of the first Jewish rebellion against Rome in AD 66. According to Josephus, numerous revolutionaries, whom he calls 'impostors and deceivers', proclaimed themselves prophets and messiahs and led the credulous Jews to disaster, persuading their partisans to follow them to the desert.[7] The two most notorious

7. See *Antiquities* 20:97, 167–70; *War* 6:283–6.

individuals were Theudas and the man nicknamed 'the Egyptian'; both are mentioned in the New Testament too (Acts 5:36; 21:38). The Messiah hidden in the inner room (Matt. 24:26) alludes to someone who operates in conspiratorial secrecy. Jesus, or more exactly the primitive church a generation after Jesus in the late 60s AD, warns the faithful against these tricksters. The moment of the return of the 'Son of man' will be unpredictable; it will arrive suddenly like lightning. The aim of these admonitions is to maintain watchfulness, a typical feature of eschatologically inspired early Christianity.

23. The unexpected coming of the 'Son of man' (Matt. 24:37–44; Luke 17:26–27, 30, 34–35, 39–40)

As were the days of Noah, so will be the coming of the Son of man. For as in those days before the flood they were eating and drinking, marrying and giving in marriage, until the day when Noah entered the ark, and they did not know until the flood came and swept them all away, so will be the coming of the Son of man (Matt.).

As it was in the days of Noah, so will it be in the days of the Son of man. They ate, they drank, they married, they were given in marriage, until the day when Noah entered the ark, and the flood came and destroyed them all . . . so will it be on the day when the Son of man is revealed (Luke).

Then two men will be in the field (Matt.) [*I tell you, in that night there will be two in one bed* (Luke)]; *one is taken and one is left. Two women will be grinding at the mill; one is taken and one is left. Watch therefore, for you do not know on what day your Lord is coming. But know this, that if the householder had known in what part of the night the thief was coming, he would have watched and would not have let his house be broken into. Therefore you also must be ready; for the Son of man is coming at an hour you do not expect* (Matt., Luke).

The comparison of the flood and the Parousia has been examined in chapter 5, no. 30.

In this passage, which concludes the Eschatological Discourse in Matthew, the reference to the coming, or the day, of the 'Son of man' is intended to announce the abrupt onset of the final events.[8] The diversity of the fate of any two people symbolizes the unpredictability of the outcome of the last judgement. As in all the other similar passages, the moral lesson is the need for vigilance constantly stressed by the early church. Similar exhortations to watchfulness without any mention of the 'Son of man' figure also in the parable of the doorkeeper in Mark 13:35–36 and Matthew 25:13 (see chapter 4, no. 6).

C. THE M *TRADITION*

24. The programme of the disciples before the coming of the 'Son of man' (Matt. 10:23)

When they persecute you in one town, flee to the next; for truly, I say to you, you will not have gone through all the towns of Israel, before the Son of man comes.

The straightforward significance of this saying is that the largely unsuccessful initial mission of the disciples will almost immediately be followed by the triumph of Jesus, who self-effacingly calls himself the 'Son of man'. However, in the light of the immediate and the wider context and the general Parousia-related meaning of the coming of the 'Son of man', we realize that Matthew 10:23 has undergone editorial re-working.

The original story into which the saying is embedded is the first independent mission of the disciples of Jesus, dispatched in Galilee to preach the Kingdom of God and heal the sick (Mark 6:7; Matt. 10:1,

8. Luke's opening sentence, 'you will desire to see *one of the days* of the Son of man', is confusing. The plural, '*days* of the Son of man', in Luke 17:22 and 26 is unusual. The singular, '*day* of the Son of man' (Luke 17:24, 30, 31), modelled on the '*day* of the Lord' in the Old Testament, the equivalent of the 'coming (*parousia*) of the Son of man' in Matthew (24:27, 37, 39), is what one would expect. Luke's vacillation between the singular and the plural may be due to his customary unease when it comes to typically Jewish concepts. But the phrase 'one of the days' could mean also 'the first day', i.e. the onset of the era of the 'Son of man'. Moreover, the plural 'days of the Son of man' in Luke 17:26 may mechanically copy the preceding plural, 'the days of Noah'.

5–8; Luke 9:1–2; see chapter 8, no. 5). According to Matthew, they were to address Jews only, and were expressly forbidden to visit Gentiles or the Samaritans of the neighbourhood (cf. chapter 8, no. 49). Their ministry was successful and they did not meet with a hostile reception (Mark 6:12–13; Luke 9:6).

The editor of Matthew, however, anachronistically appended this 'Son of man' saying (Matt. 10:23) to an account of troubles – 'When they persecute you in one town, flee to the next' (Matt. 10:17–22) – which he had lifted from the much later setting of the Eschatological Discourse ending with the Parousia (see Mark 13:9–13 and Luke 21:12–17, 19; cf. chapter 8, nos. 19, 20). He thus changed the chronological framework from the earliest stages of the public career of Jesus to the time of the apostolic church during the first Jewish war against Rome (AD 66–70) and possibly beyond. By that period, in direct contradiction with the command of Jesus not to address non-Jews (Matt. 10:5), primitive Christian preachers had come into contact with Gentiles: 'You will be dragged before governors and kings . . . to bear testimony before them and the Gentiles' (see Matt. 10:18). Naturally, against this backdrop the advent of the 'Son of man' occurs, not in the initial phase of the preaching of Jesus and his followers in rural Galilee, but at the time of the Second Coming.

25. The 'Son of man' in the interpretation of the parable of the weeds (Matt. 13:37, 41–43)

He who sows the good seed is the Son of man . . . The Son of man will send his angels, and they will gather out of his kingdom all causes of sin and all evildoers, and throw them into the furnace of fire; there men will weep and gnash their teeth. Then the righteous will shine like the sun in the kingdom of their Father.

For the exposition of the parable, see chapter 4, no. 17, indicating both the later apocalyptic Parousia exegesis (the Son of man and his angels judging the wicked), and the original application to the imminent coming of the Kingdom of God.

Here in the opening sentence the 'Son of man' is best understood as a reference to the speaker, Jesus. But the second mention of the 'Son of man' reflects the ideology of the early church, as it definitely introduces the concepts of the return of Christ and the final judgement when the sinners will suffer fiery damnation while the righteous, like those of Daniel 12:3, will display the brilliance of the heavenly glory.

26. The 'Son of man' and the last judgement (Matt. 25:31–32)

When the Son of man comes in his glory, and all the angels with him, then he will sit on his glorious throne. Before him will be gathered all the nations, and he will separate them one from another as a shepherd separates the sheep from the goats.

For the interpretation of the parable of the last judgement, see chapter 4, no. 26.

Here the introduction of the 'Son of man' already enthroned as the final judge of mankind, resembling the heavenly 'Son of man' or 'Elect' of the Parables of Enoch, obviously presupposes the Parousia. The text thus represents, as all the similar passages previously discussed, the religious world view of the early church.

D. THE L *TRADITION*

27. The day of the 'Son of man' (Luke 17:22, 29–30)

The days are coming when you will desire to see one of the days of the Son of man and you will not see it . . . On the day when Lot went out from Sodom, fire and sulphur rained from heaven and destroyed them all – so will it be on the day when the Son of man is revealed.

For earlier treatments of these sayings, see nos. 22 and 23 above, and for the general context chapter 5, no. 30.

28. Faith at the coming of the 'Son of man' (Luke 18:6–8)

And the Lord said, *Hear what the unrighteous judge says. And will not God vindicate his elect, who cry to him day and night? Will he delay long over them? I tell you, he will vindicate them speedily. Nevertheless, when the Son of man comes, will he find faith on earth?*

This is a secondary interpretative supplement to the parable of the unrighteous judge and the persistent widow (see chapter 4, no. 39).

In the first two sentences Luke purports to quote Jesus' comment, emphasizing that if constant petition can compel a wicked judge to dispense justice, so *a fortiori* do repeated prayers influence a benevolent God. However, the general background, represented by the last three phrases, reflects the post-Jesus phenomenon of diminishing eschatological hope caused by the much delayed coming of the 'Son of man'.

29. Appearing before the 'Son of man' (Luke 21:34–36)

But take heed to yourselves lest your hearts be weighed down with dissipation and drunkenness and cares of this life, and that the day come upon you suddenly like a snare; for it will come upon all those who dwell upon the face of the whole earth. But watch at all times, praying that you may have strength to escape all these things that will take place, and to stand before the Son of man.

Luke's conclusion of the Discourse lacks the feverish atmosphere of the eschatological expectation of Jesus. The threat here is not approaching chaos, but vanishing enthusiasm. The great hope of the age of Jesus is replaced by mundane concerns about dissipation, self-indulgence and anxiety. Hence the customary early Christian insistence on vigilance, on staying awake while expecting the day of the Parousia to burst in suddenly. The speaker is the church, not Jesus.

For the social scourge of addiction to wine in the primitive church, see chapter 4, no. 15.

REFLECTIONS

My way of presenting the 'Son of man' passages of the Synoptic Gospels relies primarily on philological, exegetical and historical considerations which distinguish it from the theological approach adopted by the large majority of contemporary New Testament specialists. Surprisingly, before the nineteenth century, Christian Bible exegesis showed no interest in the 'Son of man' concept. Even among the Church Fathers little attention was paid to the subject, and when they referred to it they saw in the phrase 'Son of man' an assertion of the humanity of Christ neatly distinguished from the divine nature of the 'Son of God'. By contrast, most modern interpreters of the Gospels assume that the idiom 'the Son of man' was the title of an eschatological personality which was not framed by Jesus or the evangelists, but pre-existed in late Second Temple Jewish thought before being taken over and adapted by Jesus and the New Testament. The theory was clearly set out in the mid twentieth century by Rudolf Bultmann in his *Theology of the New Testament*.[9] He and many of his followers have classified the 'Son of man' sayings of the Gospels under three headings: (1) sayings referring to events during the earthly activity of Jesus; (2) references to the death and resurrection of Jesus; (3) matters pertaining to the future era of the return of the 'Son of man'. In Bultmann's opinion only the third category represents authentic sayings of Jesus, but for him the future 'Son of man' is a person distinct from Jesus. While generally agreeing that the 'Son of man' is an important theological concept, post-Bultmannian New Testament scholarship has displayed a great variety of views. They range from the thesis that the 'Son of man' is the most important self-designation of Jesus to the total scepticism of those who declare all the occurrences of the 'Son of man' to be the product of the church and consequently completely inauthentic as far as Jesus is concerned.

My own approach to the expression, as I have made clear in the opening pages, is first and foremost linguistic, based on the use of the

9. *Theologie des Neuen Testaments* (1948–1953) English translation: *The Theology of the New Testament* (London, 1952–1955).

idiom in Palestinian Jewish Aramaic. I consider the 'Son of man' instances in the first three Gospels primarily in a non-titular sense as a reference to the self by the subject of the sentence. Again and again the context and/or the Synoptic parallels make this absolutely plain. Take for example Jesus' words to a paralysed man, 'But that you may know that *the son of man* has authority on earth to forgive sins' followed by '*I* say to you, Rise' (Mark 2:10). Look again at Jesus' question to the apostles at Caesarea Philippi in Matthew's formulation, 'Who do men say that *the son of man* is?' (Matt. 16:13), and set it against Mark's and Luke's 'Who do men say that *I* am?' (Mark 8:27; Luke 9:18).

The eleven passages listed in section I simply reflect in the appropriate contexts the roundabout style used by the speaker when talking about himself. The employment of this idiom in sections II and III is also classified as self-reference in the first instance, but the meaning is specifically coloured by an indirect or direct association with the apocalyptic 'Son of man' verse in Daniel 7:13. As far as authenticity is concerned, here the main issue is to decide whether the scriptural connection was made by Jesus himself, or by either the evangelists or the later church. Bearing in mind the insignificant part played by Bible interpretation in the teaching technique of Jesus (see chapter 5, p. 212), there seems to be *prima facie* a good case for the church alternative.

Jesus is often made to address taboos or boastful subjects in direct speech in the Gospels. We have on the one hand, 'How is it written of the Son of man, that he should suffer many things and be treated with contempt?' (Mark 9:12; Matt. 17:12), and on the other, 'The Son of man has authority on earth to forgive sins' (Mark 2:10; Matt. 9:6; Luke 5:24). In both cases the use of circumlocution by means of substituting 'son of man' for 'I' is perfectly in place.

'Son of man' sayings which explicitly allude to Daniel 7:13 figure twice in the Synoptic Gospels. The first, 'They will see the Son of man coming in clouds with great power and glory' (Mark 13:26; Matt. 24:30; Luke 21:27), introduces the scene of eschatological judgement. The second, 'You will see the Son of man seated at the right hand of Power, and coming with the clouds of heaven' (Mark 14:62; Matt. 26:64; Luke 22:69), represents Jesus' answer to the High Priest's question whether he was the Messiah. In short, the expression 'Son of man', combined with Daniel 7:13, represents in the Synoptic Gospels an exegetical construct, often called an early church *midrash*, and in this capacity it acquires a definite messianic and eschatological significance. The same remark can also apply to the excerpts containing implicit references to Daniel 7, such as the mention of the coming of the Son of man with the angels to execute judgement (Mark 8:38; Matt. 16:27; Luke 9:26, etc.). A similar messianic interpretation of the Daniel passage appears, from the time of Rabbi Akiba onwards, in rabbinic literature too (see my *Jesus the Jew* (London, 1973), 171–2; 257–8).

To sum up, the chief contribution of the 'Son of man' passages to a deeper understanding of the Gospels is twofold:

1. The formula is the principal medium employed to present the belief of the early church concerning the predicted character of the death and resurrection of Jesus (see section II above).

2. The sayings inspired by Daniel 7, describing the arrival of the 'Son of man' on the clouds (see section III above), form the axis around which the church doctrine of the Parousia revolves.

Both these groups of texts mirror the early Christian interpretation of the Jesus phenomenon centred on the mystery of his death and resurrection and on the expectation of his Second Coming. The latter notion, the Parousia, was in turn substituted for Jesus' original proclamation of the imminent arrival of the Kingdom of God, the subject which will be scrutinized in the next chapter.

Appendix: 'Son of man' outside the Synoptic Gospels

To complete the picture, the Synoptic use of 'Son of man' should be compared with that of the Gospel of John and the rest of the New Testament writings.

As far as John is concerned, his eleven examples reflect the rich and fully developed messianic significance of the enthroned Danielic 'Son of man'. Nevertheless, all the instances in the Fourth Gospel are capable of being interpreted circumlocutionally in a way reminiscent of the Synoptics. Hence in John it is the 'Son of man' who gives eternal life, or will be 'lifted up', i.e. crucified for the redemption of the world, not 'I'.

The three central topics associated with he expression 'Son of man' in John's Gospel are:

1. The theological notion that faith in him bestows eternal life on the believer. For example, 'Do not labour for food which perishes, but for food which endures to *eternal life*, which the *Son of man* will give you' (John 6:27).

2. The gift of eternal life is specifically linked to the crucifixion of the 'Son of man'. For example, 'As Moses lifted up the serpent in the wilderness, so must *the Son of man* be lifted up, that whoever believes in him may have *eternal life*' (John 3:14–15). The image arises from the Old Testament story of the brazen serpent which Moses was ordered to fix to a pole. A glance at it was enough to provide protection against snake bites in the wilderness of Sinai (Num. 21:6–9). In John's interpretation, however, the raised-up serpent typified the 'lifted up' Jesus and the salvation promised to those who would look at the cross with faith. John gives here an interesting twist to the 'Son of man' imagery when he interprets 'to lift up' as crucifixion, and not in its normal figurative sense of exaltation (John 12:32–33).

3. The third and perhaps the most important aspect of the Johannine representation of the 'Son of man' concerns his journeys between heaven and earth. The idea of the descent and ascent of the 'Son of man' originated in Daniel 7 and was further developed in the Synoptic Gospels before reaching its climax in John. The cloud was envisaged from the Book of Daniel onwards as the vehicle of heavenly locomotion. 'Behold, with the clouds of heaven there came one like a son of man' (Dan. 7:13). Here the movement appears to be upward, as also in the account of Christ's ascension: 'He was lifted up, and a cloud took him out of their sight' (Acts 1:9), and in the description of the meeting in mid-air of the resurrected Christians and the still living faithful with Jesus at the moment of the Second Coming: 'For the Lord himself will descend from heaven . . . And the dead in Christ will rise first; then we who are alive . . . shall be caught up together with them in the clouds to meet the Lord in the air' (1 Thess. 4:16–17). On the other hand, in the Synoptic Gospels the return of the 'Son of man' on the clouds entails a descent from the heavenly regions (Matt. 24:30; Mark 13:26; Luke 21:27; Matt. 26:64; Mark 14:62). Finally, according to John the 'Son of man' travels in both directions: 'No one has

ascended into heaven but he who descended from heaven, *the Son of man*' (John 3:13). In the Fourth Gospel the eternal Word (*Logos*) is a heavenly traveller who is in temporary exile on earth, but longs to return to his real home.

The three New Testament 'Son of man' sayings outside the Gospels constitute separate categories. In the Book of Revelation when the visionary John describes an individual in the third person as 'one like a son of man' (Rev. 1:13; 14:14), he reproduces almost literally the text of Daniel 7:13. However, his style is completely different from the mode of self-identification by the speaker used in the Synoptics.

As for the last words uttered by the deacon Stephen, 'Behold, I see the heavens opened, and the Son of man standing at the right hand of God' (Acts 7:56), when he is stoned to death in Jerusalem for blasphemy, they simply repeat the answer of Jesus to the High Priest during his interrogation, 'You will see the Son of man seated at the right hand of Power' (Mark 14:62; Matt. 26:64; Luke 22:69). We can note two differences. The first is not greatly significant: Jesus speaks of the *sitting* and Stephen of the *standing* 'Son of man'. The second is important: in the Gospels 'Son of man' is a reference to the speaker, while in the Acts, in total contradiction to the Synoptic use, 'Son of man' serves as the title of a third person, Jesus.

8

Sayings about the Kingdom of God

Jesus was not a philosopher, nor a systematic theologian, so it is hardly surprising that he left no detailed exposition of the concept of the Kingdom of God in the Gospels. The subject has already been touched on earlier in the treatment of the twelve parables known as the parables of the Kingdom (see chapter 4, p. 169).[1] To facilitate general understanding, the incidental utterances of Jesus examined in this chapter will be set out thematically among the 'Reflections' at the end of this chapter (pp. 339–42). Before presenting the individual sayings, we must reflect on two essential problems arising from them. Both are bound to strike twenty-first-century Christian readers as disturbing. The first concerns the time of the arrival of the Kingdom, and the second its definition by national boundaries.

In regard to chronology, there seems to be solid evidence in the Gospels, confirmed by St Paul, which indicates that Jesus and the first generation of his followers expected the Kingdom of God to arrive during their lifetime. Its advent would be signalled according to the Eschatological Discourse (Mark 13; Matt. 24; Luke 21) by wars and a cataclysmic upheaval of the universe. This concept of a near-present end of time was not invented by Jesus or the primitive church. It was widely held in the Jewish world from the time of the biblical Book of Daniel onwards by the circles which produced the apocalyptic books such as Enoch, the Assumption of Moses, 2 Baruch and 4 Ezra, etc., as well as by the members of the Dead Sea community – in other words, between the second century BC and the first century AD.

1. Readers may find a fuller discussion of this topic in my earlier publications (*The Changing Faces of Jesus* (London, 2000), 201–9 and *The Religion of Jesus the Jew* (London, 1993), 119–51).

Seen in retrospect the forecast of an impending end occurring in the first century AD has proved erroneous: the Kingdom as foretold in the New Testament has never arrived. Such non-realization of the predictions confronted the followers of Jesus with a tough dilemma and demanded an alternative interpretation. The long and the short of it is that the Kingdom of God was perceived as already realized in the Christian church.

In the early 1990s a well-known English New Testament interpreter firmly asserted that any belief in the imminent consummation of the universe was 'inherently improbable' and formulated his claim in the form of a very western, indeed British, rhetorical question: 'Does any sane person ever quite believe that the world will end tomorrow?' In the light of such a challenge, Jesus' words relating to the Kingdom of God, and St Paul's statements about the Parousia or Second Coming of Christ in his own generation, will require close scrutiny. For if we follow the reasoning of the scholar in question, at stake is either the sanity of Jesus' and Paul's view of the future, or the sanity and reliability of objective New Testament criticism.

The Gospel evidence regarding the identity of the future citizens of God's Kingdom is equivocal, indeed self-contradictory. At one extreme stands the declaration, firmly attributed to Jesus, that the Kingdom of God is a Jewish preserve: Jesus was sent only to the lost sheep of the house of Israel and the good news was not to be spread among non-Jews. At the other extreme we find statements, also attributed to Jesus, to the effect that the gospel of the Kingdom was destined to all the nations and that Jesus himself commissioned his apostles to instruct and baptize not only the Jews, but also the entire non-Jewish world. In its most heightened form the pro-Gentile opinion, again purported as having stemmed from the mouth of Jesus, affirms that with the exception of the Old Testament patriarchs and prophets, and no doubt the relatively small number of his Jewish followers, the large majority of the participants of the great messianic banquet in the Kingdom of God will be non-Jews. These contradictory pronouncements do not appear in separate sources but are mingled in one and the same Gospel, in particular in Matthew.

Further basic matters which will be considered are the relationship between the Lord's Supper (the Christian eucharistic meal) and the

Kingdom of God, and the nature of the Beatitudes, i.e. the manifesto laid by Jesus before his disciples and all the prospective citizens of the Kingdom.

I. MARK AND THE TRIPLE TRADITION

1. The initial proclamation (Mark 1:15; Matt. 4:17)

The time is fulfilled, and the kingdom of God is at hand; repent, and believe in the gospel (Mark).

Repent, for the kingdom of heaven is at hand (Matt.).

Mark and Matthew preface their account of the ministry of Jesus with this short and incisive pronouncement. Its essence is that a new reality called the 'Kingdom of God/heaven' is close, that is to say, it is approaching or has already come, and that the audience, in order to become worthy of it, must perform a moral U-turn. Instead of walking away from God, they must change direction and go towards him.[2]

This is a familiar idea in the preaching of the Old Testament prophets, who sometimes also associate 'turning' with healing, as is manifest in Hosea 6:1, 'Come, let us *return* to the Lord; for he has torn, that he may *heal* us', or negatively in Isaiah 6:10, 'Make the heart of this people fat, . . . lest they . . . understand with their hearts, and turn and *be healed*.' In rabbinic literature the verb 'to turn' continues to signify 'to repent', but it is accompanied also by the noun 'repentance': 'Repentance (*teshuvah*) and good works are a shield against retribution' (mAb 4:11).

Repentance is the necessary preliminary for entry into the 'Kingdom of God'. This fundamental concept of Jewish eschatology envisages God's direct dominion over the righteous Jews and subsequently over the converted Gentiles.

Gospel tradition associates the call to return to God with the mission of John the Baptist. His mission consisted in inviting Jews to undergo

2. The Greek term *metanoia* substitutes for the Semitic metaphor of change of direction the more abstract concept of change of mind.

a baptism of repentance for the forgiveness of sins through immersing themselves in the river Jordan (Mark 1:4–5; Luke 3:3). Jesus subjected himself to John's baptism, considering it as a religious duty: 'Let it be so now; for thus it is fitting for us to fulfil all righteousness' (Matt. 3:15).[3] Matthew, in turn, makes Jesus repeat literally the brief appeal of John, 'Repent, for the kingdom of heaven is at hand' (Matt. 3:2). The powerful simplicity of the statement and its identity with the words of the Baptist, whose pupil Jesus was and whose work he set out to continue in Galilee (Mark 1:14–15; Matt. 4:12, 17), argue in favour of the short form of the proclamation without the supplementary words – 'and believe in the gospel' – attached to it by Mark.

The first part of this enlargement – 'The time is fulfilled' – is the theological definition of the moment of Jesus' appearance. His manifestation in public occurred at the divinely predestined instant. The idea is missing from the Gospel of Matthew, where the verb 'to fulfil' is used only in connection with the realization of biblical prophecies. In contrast, the description of Jesus' arrival in the fullness of time is typically Pauline: 'When the time had fully come, God sent forth his Son' (Gal. 4:4; cf. Eph. 1:9–10). Mark's concluding clause, 'and believe in the gospel' (i.e. the good news of salvation), is also most probably a church-inspired interpolation alluding to the preaching of Christian missionaries (see also Mark 8:35 in chapter 9, no. 5).[4] In short, the kernel of the saying concerning repentance and the nearness of the Kingdom is likely to belong to the authentic teaching of Jesus.

3. The Fourth Gospel ignores Jesus' baptism by John. Such an act of self-abasement was by that time considered incompatible with the dignity of the incarnate Word of God.

4. An alternative interpretation could be based on the variant reading 'preaching the gospel of the kingdom of God' instead of 'preaching the gospel of God' in Mark 1:14. In this case, 'believe in the gospel' in Mark 1:15 would be simply an explanatory gloss attached by Mark or his editor to the proclamation of Jesus, 'the kingdom of God is at hand'.

2. Healing and forgiveness of sins (Mark 2:9–11; Matt. 9:5–6; Luke 5:23–24)

Which is easier, to say to the paralytic, 'Your sins are forgiven', or to say, 'Rise, take up your pallet and walk'? But that you may know that the son of Man has authority on earth to forgive sins, . . . I say to you, rise, take up your pallet and go home.

The story of the paralytic has been investigated as a controversy narrative in chapter 2, no. 1.

From the eschatological vantage point of Jesus, all we need to underline here is the intrinsic coherence between sin and repentance/forgiveness on the one hand, and sickness and charismatic healing on the other, the latter being categorized as the external signal of the closeness or incipient presence of the Kingdom of God (see also no. 7 below).

3. New family ties (Mark 3:33–35; Matt. 12:48–50; Luke 8:21; cf. Luke 11:27–28; Gospel of Thos. 99:2; Matt. 10:37; Luke 14:26; cf. Mark 10:29–30; Matt. 19:28–29; Luke 18:29)

Who are my mother and my brothers? . . . Whoever does the will of God [of my Father in heaven (Matt.)] *is my brother, and sister, and mother* (Mark 3, Matt. 12).

My mother and my brothers are those who hear the word of God and do it (Luke 8).

A woman in the crowd raised her voice and said to him, 'Blessed is the womb that bore you, and the breasts that you sucked!' But he said, *Blessed rather are those who hear the word of God and keep it!* (Luke 11).

Those here who do the will of my Father are my brothers and my mother (Gospel of Thos.).

He who loves father and mother more than me is not worthy of me; and he who loves son or daughter more than me is not worthy of me (Matt. 10).

If any one comes to me and does not hate his own father and mother and wife and children and brothers and sisters, yes, and even his own life, he cannot be my disciple (Luke 14).

Truly, I say to you, there is no one who has left house or [wife or (Luke)] *brothers or sisters or mother or father or children or lands for my sake and for the gospel* (Mark) [*for my name's sake* (Matt.)] [*for the sake of the kingdom of God* (Luke)], *who will not receive a hundredfold now in this time, houses and brothers and sisters and mothers and children and lands, with persecutions, and in the age to come eternal life* (Mark 10, Matt. 19, Luke 18).

For family conflict in the final age, see chapter 5, no. 24.

In the period preceding the establishment of the Kingdom all personal links need to be reassessed and redefined. The new family of Jesus will be made up of those who listen to his preaching and do their freshly revealed duties to conform to the will of the heavenly Father. His blood relations did not fit this description; indeed some of them thought that he was out of his mind (Mark 3:21, 30–31; see also no. 4 below). The Gospel of John also echoes the Synoptics: 'For even his brothers did not believe in him' (John 7:5). From this point on, Mark, Matthew and Luke ignore the family of Jesus, including Mary. But she is treated with filial respect and love in the Gospel of John, and according to the author of the Acts the whole family, his mother and brothers, joined the apostles after Easter (Acts 1:14). Indeed, James the brother of the Lord (Gal. 1:19) was soon to lead the Jerusalem church, according to both Paul (Gal. 2:12) and the Acts of the Apostles (12:17; 15:13; 21:18). The fourth-century historian Eusebius of Caesarea reports that even the great-nephews of Jesus, grandsons of his brother Jude, were sufficiently famous at the end of the first century as members of the royal family of David to be placed on the political blacklist of potential revolutionary leaders by the emperor Domitian (*The History of the Church* 3:20–21). Luke (11:27–28) underlines the blessedness of those who listen to, and observe, the teaching of Jesus and declares them superior to Jesus' mother. This assertion is particularly noteworthy as it appears in a non-polemical context.

Whereas Mark 3:33–35 and parallels present the dilemma from the point of view of Jesus himself ('Who are my mother and my brothers?'), Matthew 10:37 and Luke 14:26 look at it through the eyes of the disciples of Jesus. The moral is the same. In case of a conflict between commitment to Jesus, the herald of the Kingdom, and attachment to one's family, Jesus and the Kingdom of God must come first. Using extreme verbal exaggeration, Jesus speaks of a need for a man to hate his parents, relatives, wife and children, and even himself, in order to become Jesus' disciple. While Jesus was among his disciples, the renunciation of family and possessions was demanded for his sake or his 'name's sake' (Mark 10, Matt. 19), phrases which Luke correctly replaces by 'for the sake of the kingdom of God' (Luke 18). The expressions 'for Jesus' sake' and 'for the sake of the Kingdom' are interchangeable. To follow Jesus is synonymous with devoting oneself to the Kingdom of God.

The omission of 'wife' in Mark 10 and Matthew 19 from the list of those to be left behind reflects the tradition of the primitive church formulated by Paul. According to him, missionaries – even the apostles, the brothers of Jesus, and Peter – could be accompanied on their journeys by their wives (see 1 Cor. 9:5). The mention of the 'gospel' is a supplement attributable to Mark (for other examples, see no. 1 above and chapter 9, no. 5). The distinction between this age and the age to come, a common Jewish concept, points to early Christianity. Jesus is unlikely to have promised recompense in this world *before* the imminently expected onset of the Kingdom. The same judgement applies to the gloss in Mark 10:30, which lists among the rewards houses, lands and family, and, most oddly, persecutions. The latter exhibits without any doubt the perspective of the nascent church.

Contrary to the Gospel of John, which grants a place of honour to the mother of Jesus at the wedding in Cana and at the cross (John 2:1–11; 19:26–27), the Synoptic evangelists intimate that there was coolness between him and his close relations. Their picture probably represents the historical truth.

4. No prophet is respected at home (Mark 6:4; Matt. 13:57; Luke 4:24; cf. John 4:44; Gospel of Thos. 31)

A prophet is not without honour, except in his own country, and among his own kin, and in his own house (Mark, Matt.).

Truly, I say to you, no prophet is acceptable in his own country (Luke).

For Jesus himself testified that *a prophet has no honour in his own country* (John).

No prophet is acceptable in his village; no physician works cures on those who know him (Gospel of Thos.).

The proverb on which this saying is built has been examined in chapter 3, no. 8.

'Prophet' is understood in these passages as a miracle-worker, and his role is naturally linked to the concept of charismatic healing. The stress is laid on the lack of success of Jesus *qua* prophet at home and in his own surroundings, or in Mark's words 'among his own kin, and in his own house', as against the warm reception given to him by strangers who were cured by him. Thus the old maxim, 'A prophet is not without honour . . .', illustrates the changed order of values and priorities in the eschatological age in which Jesus' activity takes place. In that context faith and trust in God's charismatic envoy have precedence over the claims of blood ties.

5. Rules for the missionaries of the Kingdom (Mark 6:8–11; Matt. 10:9–15; Luke 9:3–5; cf. Luke 10:4–11)

He charged them to take nothing for their journey except a staff; no bread, no bag, no money in their belts; but to wear sandals and not put on two tunics. And he said to them, *Where you enter a house, stay there until you leave the place. And if any place will not receive you and they refuse to hear you, when you leave, shake off the dust that is on your feet for a testimony against them* (Mark).

Take no gold, nor silver, nor copper in your belts, no bag for your journey, nor two tunics, nor sandals, nor a staff; for the labourer deserves his food. And whatever town or village you enter, find out who is worthy in it, and stay with him until you depart. As you enter the house, salute it. And if the house is worthy, let your peace come upon it; but if it is not worthy, let your peace return to you. And if any one will not receive you or listen to your words, shake off the dust from your feet as you leave that house or town. Truly, I say to you, it shall be more tolerable on the day of judgement for the land of Sodom and Gomorrah than for that town (Matt.).

Take nothing for your journey, no staff, nor bag, nor bread, nor money; and do not have two tunics. And whatever house you enter, stay there, and from there depart. And wherever they do not receive you, when you leave that town shake off the dust from your feet as a testimony against them (Luke).

Carry no purse, no bag, no sandals; and salute no one on the road. Whatever house you enter, first say, 'Peace be to this house!' And if a son of peace is there, your peace shall rest upon him; but if not, it shall return to you. And remain in the same house, eating and drinking what they provide, for the labourer deserves his wages; do not go from house to house. Whenever you enter a town and they receive you, eat what is set before you; heal the sick in it and say to them, 'The kingdom of God has come near to you.' But whenever you enter a town and they do not receive you, go into its streets and say, 'Even the dust of your town that clings to our feet, we wipe off against you; nevertheless know this, that the kingdom of God has come near.' I tell you, it shall be more tolerable on that day for Sodom than for that town (Luke 10).

These very significant instructions grouped together by the evangelists represent the basic regulations which Jesus gave to his twelve apostles

– or to the seventy or seventy-two disciples (Luke 10:1–12) – before dispatching them two by two (Mark 6:7; Luke 10:1) on a charismatic (i.e. exorcizing and healing) mission (Mark 6:7, 12–13; Matt. 10:1). Luke adds to curing and exorcism a third element: teaching, the preaching of the Kingdom of God (Luke 9:1–2).[5]

The stringent rules, enjoining total reliance on God's providential care, are typical of Jesus. They would be inappropriate to the organized and sedate missionary activity of the later church, in which ministers believed in their entitlement to be looked after by their congregations as set out by Paul in his address to members of the Corinthian church (1 Cor. 9:4–14). Matthew (10:10) and Luke (10:7) antedate the later custom to the age of Jesus, when he is made to declare that 'the labourer deserves his food/wages'.

The various accounts do not fully tally among themselves. Mark's report explicitly permits the envoys to carry a staff and wear sandals, whereas the texts of Matthew and Luke list both staff and sandals among the forbidden objects.[6] Mark's Jesus approves of the rod or staff; the Jesus of Matthew and Luke does not. Oddly, Mark forbids also the putting on of *two* tunics. The correct understanding of the precept is that Jesus' disciples should not take with them a *spare* tunic or a *second* pair of sandals, not even an extra ration of bread, and they should definitely not carry any money. Being equipped with a purse would be contrary to whole-hearted trust in God.

The messengers were to begin with wishing peace, a wish endowed with charismatic power capable of bringing blessings upon well-disposed recipients. Otherwise the greeting would revert to the 'peace-

5. Preaching and casting out demons are listed as the purpose of the future mission of the twelve in Mark 3:14–15.

6. Interpreters normally assume that the term refers to a traveller's staff which, when journeying on the unmade ancient Galilean and Judaean paths, provided a welcome and necessary support. But *rhabdos* can also designate a rod or stick which the traveller could use as a primitive protective weapon. St Paul offers the alternatives to the Corinthians of visiting them with a rod or with love (1 Cor. 4:21). In the insecure circumstances of first-century Palestine even the generally pacific Essenes were permitted, according to Josephus, to equip themselves with weapons against robbers (*War* 2:125). One of the followers of Jesus was armed and ready to use his sword in the garden of Gethsemane (see Mark 14:47; Matt. 26:51; Luke 22:49–50; cf. no. 52 below).

making' messengers. These were forbidden to be selective, and had to accept the first generous offer of shelter and stay there until the end of their short mission. While in the village, they were to cure the sick brought to them and proclaim the Kingdom of God, the nearness – indeed the presence – of which would be revealed by their success in healing and exorcizing. The express prohibition against going from house to house (Luke 10:7) may have been intended to prevent the exploitation of hospitality. Another even stronger possibility is that the pressure put on the missionaries to keep their stay brief would expedite the coming of the Kingdom. The ban in Luke 10:4 on saluting people on the road may also have been introduced for the same purpose. Cordial greetings could easily be followed by a long conversation. The prohibition could also have been motivated by the custom of the ancient Hasidim who constantly refused to allow social courtesies to break their mental concentration: 'Even if the king salutes him, he shall not return his greeting' (mBer 5:1).

Finally, the envoys of Jesus were instructed to turn their backs on unfriendly people. The mention of shaking dust from their feet recalls an old Jewish custom, which consisted in pilgrims and travellers cleansing themselves of the unclean dust of foreign lands before they entered the Holy Land. It is important to note that the envoys are depicted not as frightened and persecuted, but as dominant partners in command of the situation: if they are not listened to, they must show their displeasure by shaking the dust off their sandals and turning their backs on the unreceptive villagers.

The rules laid down are in harmony with the harsh conditions typical of the final age according to Jewish eschatology as well as in the New Testament. The various revisions introduced by the evangelists into the original instructions were meant to make these applicable to the circumstances prevalent in the early church. The most noteworthy of these is the declaration that the missionaries had the right to be looked after by their communities. These alterations suggest indirectly, but distinctly, the authenticity of the original words attributed to Jesus.

6. Jesus' attitude to Gentiles (Mark 7:27; Matt. 15:26)

And he said to her [the Syrophoenician woman], *Let the children first be fed, for it is not right to take the children's bread and throw it to the dogs.*

The metaphors of dog and swine applied to Gentiles in Matthew 7:6 have already been discussed in chapter 3, no. 32.

The words quoted from Mark and Matthew are taken from the episode of the healing of the daughter of a woman from the region of Tyre and Sidon. They depict Jesus as taking a chauvinistic Jewish stand. The story is set in southern Lebanon during one of the rare excursions of Jesus to foreign lands. There he was approached by a local Hellenized woman, described as Syrophoenician by Mark or Canaanite by Matthew, with the plea that he should exorcize and thus heal her sick child. The woman's confident prayer was first met with a sharp rebuke to the effect that charismatic marvels of the eschatological age were not intended for non-Jews. The spiritual bread destined for the children (of Israel) was not to be thrown to the dogs, symbolizing the Gentiles. The profound faith of the mother, who reminded Jesus that puppies were allowed to eat the crumbs which children had dropped from the table, compelled Jesus to depart from his rule of not treating non-Jews. 'For this saying you may go your way; the demon has left your daughter' (Mark 7:29), or 'O woman, great is your faith! Be it done for you as you desire' (Matt. 15:28), he is reported to have said.

The story clearly demonstrates that Jesus preached the way to the Kingdom of God only to Jews, the presumed 'sons of the kingdom' (Matt. 8:12). At the same time the account reveals that the appeal of a popular charismatic healer knew no national or religious boundaries.[7] It is amazing that the harshness attributed here to Jesus escaped

7. The rabbis tried to control such 'interdenominational' activities, but it is unclear how successful they were. According to a Tannaitic (second-century AD) story Rabbi Eleazar ben Dama, bitten by a snake, was keen to accept the services of the Jewish-Christian Jacob of Kefar Sama (or Sekhaniah) who offered to cure him in the name of Jesus. Rabbi Ishmael sought to stop him. Eleazar set out to argue the permissibility of such an intervention, but died before he was able to make out his case (tHul 2:22–24).

the notice of later editors. Against his usual trend, Matthew makes Jesus appear even more severe than in Mark's account. He first ignores the woman and when his disciples suggest that he should rid them of this nuisance, he takes no action: this Gentile person is not his problem (Matt. 15:23–24). The idea of a universal saving mission to every nation is not part of this picture. Jesus' intervention on this occasion was strictly an exception justified by the out-of-the-ordinary faith of the mother.

For further evidence, see no. 49 below.

7. Request for a sign (Mark 8:12; Matt. 16:4; 12:39; Luke 11:29; cf. Luke 17:20–21; Matt. 11:4–5; Luke 7:22)

Why does this generation seek a sign? Truly, I say to you, no sign shall be given to this generation (Mark).

An evil and adulterous generation seeks a sign, but no sign shall be given to it except the sign of Jonah (Matt. 16:4; 12:39; Luke 11:29).

The kingdom of God is not coming with signs to be observed; nor will they say, 'Lo, here it is!' or 'There!' for behold, the kingdom of God is in the midst of you (Luke 17:20–21).

Go and tell John what you hear and see: the blind receive their sight and the lame walk, lepers are cleansed and the deaf hear, and the dead are raised up, and the poor have good news preached to them (Matt. 11:4–5; Luke 7:22).

The passages, already examined in chapter 5, nos. 7 and 25 from the point of view of Old Testament interpretation, will now be approached from the angle of the expectation of signs in the final age. Signs, that is to say extraordinary phenomena believed to be of supernatural origin, can be understood in the Gospels as serving three different purposes. First, the ability to perform a sign on demand would demonstrate to unbelievers the supernatural power of a teacher. Secondly, signs taken as premonitory symbols may herald the approach of an expected supernatural event, for example the Second Coming of Christ. Thirdly, their occurrence in the form of charismatic cures could reveal that the person (a prophet, Jesus) who had performed them is approved by God, or that a divinely predestined period, for example the messianic age, has arrived.

The sayings represent Jesus' answer to opponents, variously tagged as Pharisees (Mark), Pharisees and Sadducees (or scribes) (Matt.), or crowds (Luke), who were demanding from him a supernatural proof of his mission. No self-respecting prophetic figure would have complied with such a request. Indeed, what seems to have been the authentic answer, a firm denial, is preserved in Mark in its simplest form, though Matthew and Luke are nearly as negative as Mark because the exceptional sign of Jonah awaiting fulfilment in the future (cf. chapter 5, no. 7) would not have satisfied the immediate need of the questioners for miraculous evidence.

Signs in the second sense are markers identifying the successive stages of events leading to the advent of the Kingdom of God (or the return of Christ). Here the Gospel testimony is equivocal. On the one hand, we encounter the negative attitude already attested in Mark 8:12, 'No sign shall be given'. Its clearest formulation comes in Luke 17:20–21: 'The kingdom of God is not coming with signs to be observed . . . for behold, the kingdom of God is in the midst of you.'[8] While eschatological fervour permeated a community, the arrival of the Kingdom was expected to be sudden and unpredictable. But when the prolonged delay of the Parousia defused the fervour, need for continuous vigilance was stressed (see the parables in chapter 4, nos. 6, 14, 25). Meanwhile comfort was sought in premonitory signs, which told observers how far they stood from the end. The revelation of such cataclysmic signs heralding the coming of the 'Son of man' is attributed to Jesus in the Eschatological Discourse (see nos. 17–28 below and chapter 5, no. 15). However, this message is flatly contradicted in Mark 8:12 ('No sign shall be given to this generation') and even more

8. The meaning of the Greek *entos* ('amid' rather than 'inside') is explicit in the corresponding passage of the Gospel of Thomas (113): 'It will not come when one expects it. They will not say, "Lo, here! Lo, there!". But the kingdom of the Father is spread out upon the earth, and men do not see it.'

staunchly in Luke 17:20–21, 'The kingdom of God is not coming with signs to be observed.'

Used in the third sense, signs are more generally connected to an era of miracles and are expected, in consequence, to characterize the messianic age. The most striking formulation appears in the response of Jesus to the envoys of John the Baptist who inquire whether he is the special messenger of God (Matt. 11:4–5; Luke 7:22). To the question of the followers of the Baptist – 'Are you he who is to come, or shall we look for another?' – the rejoinder attributed to Jesus consists of biblical verses alluding to the messianic era in the Book of Isaiah (Isa. 29:18; 35:5–6; 61:1; see chapter 5, no. 25). In this sense, Jesus did not object to being associated with signs (i.e. miracles) which were part of the general Jewish belief surrounding the advent of the reign of God. He indeed envisioned his healings and exorcisms, not as evidence of personal greatness, but as indicators of the nearness or presence of the Kingdom.

8. The coming of the Kingdom in Jesus' generation (Mark 9:1; Matt. 16:28; Luke 9:27)

Truly, I say to you, there are some standing here who will not taste death before they see that the kingdom of God has come with power [*before they see the Son of man coming in his kingdom* (Matt.)] [*before they see the kingdom of God* (Luke)].

Mark 9:1 is one of the most disputed passages in the Gospels. It is artificially appended to Mark 8:38 which alludes, not to the arrival of the Kingdom, but to the glorious return of the 'Son of man', i.e. the Second Coming of Christ impatiently awaited by the early church (see chapter 7, no. 18). However, if Mark 9:1 is taken independently – the parallels in Matthew and Luke support this reading of the texts – the verse becomes clear. It plainly states what is implicit throughout the whole eschatological preaching of Jesus, namely that he expected in his own generation the actual inauguration of the Kingdom. Mark's curious formulation, limiting the applicability of the forecast only to some of the onlookers ('some standing here'), is itself probably an attempt to extend the waiting period beyond the lifetime of Jesus until the Parousia or return of the 'Son of man' (cf. Mark 13:30; see no. 26 below).

Matthew reinterprets the words of Jesus about the advent of the Kingdom of God with power. For him they refer to the coming of the 'Son of man' in his kingdom. Thereby the maxim is transformed into a Parousia saying. This is all the more obvious since Matthew directly connects 'the Son of man coming in his kingdom' (Matt. 16:28) to the preceding verse, 'The Son of man is to come with his angels' (16:27), and thus assigns the return of the 'Son of man' to the later years of Jesus' generation (see also Matt. 10:23 in chapter 7, no. 24). As for Luke, he omits to mention both the 'Son of man' and the qualification that the Kingdom is coming 'with power'. In line with his general tendency to water down eschatological urgency in the teaching of Jesus (see Luke 22:69 compared with Mark 14:62 and Matt. 26:64; cf. chapter 5, no. 18), he prepares the way for a loose, non-eschatological exegesis of 'Kingdom of God' in the early church.

In sum, Mark 9:1 furnishes the clearest substantiation of the view that Jesus envisaged the coming of the Kingdom in his age, in the first century AD. It is not surprising therefore that we witness all kinds of exegetical acrobatics on the part of ecclesiastical interpreters of this passage. They seek to remove the possibility of 'error' from the lips of Jesus. Dennis Nineham's honest and courageous statement is no longer in print in the Penguin Gospel Commentaries, but it deserves to be kept on record: 'The difficulty that has been felt about this interpretation [viz. that the manifestation of the Kingdom of God in its full and final form lies in the very near future] is that it makes our Lord foreshorten the perspective drastically and sets definite bounds to the extent of his accurate foreknowledge in the days of his flesh. Nevertheless . . . the interpretation is to be accepted, and numerous writers have shown that admission of such ignorance, and even error, on the part of our Lord is fully compatible with belief in the Incarnation' (*The Gospel of Saint Mark* (Harmondsworth, 1963), 231–2).

9. The coming of Elijah (Mark 9:12–13; Matt. 17:11–12)

Elijah does come first to restore all things; and how is it written of the Son of man, that he should suffer many things and be treated with contempt? But I tell you that Elijah has come, and they did to him whatever they pleased, as it is written of him. [So also the Son of man will suffer at their hands (Matt.).]

The prophet Elijah was a familiar figure in Jewish religious thought in the age of Jesus. Since the time of Jesus ben Sira, the early second-century BC author of the Book of Ecclesiasticus, the role of agent of reconciliation and restoration of the tribes of Israel has been attributed to the returning Elijah (Ecclus. 48:10). According to the three Synoptic evangelists Jesus himself was identified by some of his contemporaries as a new Elijah (Mark 8:28; Matt. 16:14; Luke 9:19; cf. chapter 1, no. 16). For the 'Son of man' sayings, see chapter 7, no. 13.

In the circumstances it is quite normal to encounter Elijah in the teaching of an eschatological prophet like Jesus. Thus in the account of the events following the Transfiguration (Mark 9:2–8; Matt. 17:1–8; Luke 9:28–36) Jesus imposed silence on his three companions, Peter, James and John, 'until the son of Man should have risen from the dead' (Mark 9:9; Matt. 17:9), an event that would be preceded by the return of Elijah. He even asserted that Elijah had already come. The evangelists shared the traditional Jewish view that the prophet Elijah would reappear from heaven to be the precursor of the Messiah (see Mark 1:1–6; Matt. 3:1–6; Luke 3:1–6). The identification of Elijah with the Baptist is ascribed here, implicitly by Mark and explicitly by Matthew, to Jesus himself: 'The disciples understood that he [Jesus] was speaking to them of John the Baptist' (Matt. 17:13). Finally, it is worth noting that the figure of Elijah continued to enjoy popularity even in the non-eschatological context of rabbinic Judaism where it serves as the prototype of the ancient Hasidim. There is no doubt that the portrait of Honi or Onias the Righteous and of Hanina ben Dosa is modelled on Elijah (see my *Jesus the Jew* (London, 1973), 72, 77).

10. The children and the Kingdom of God (Mark 9:37; Matt. 18:5; Luke 9:48; cf. Mark 9:42; Matt. 18:6–7; Luke 17:1–2; Mark 10:15; Luke 18:17; Matt. 18:3–4; cf. John 3:3; Gospel of Thos. 22; Matt. 11:25; Luke 10:21)

Whoever receives one such child in my name receives me; and whoever receives me, receives not me but him who sent me (Mark 9:37; Matt. 18:5; Luke 9:48).

Whoever causes one of these little ones who believe in me, to sin, it would be better for him if a great millstone were hung round his neck and he were thrown into the sea (Mark 9:42; Matt. 18:6; Luke 17:2).

. . . and to be drowned in the depth of the sea (Matt. 18:6).

. . . than that he should cause one of these little ones to sin (Luke 17:2).

Woe to the world for temptations to sin! For it is necessary that temptations come, but woe to the man by whom the temptation comes! (Matt. 18:7).

Truly, I say to you, whoever does not receive the kingdom of God like a child shall not enter it (Mark 10:15; Luke 18:17).

. . . unless you turn and become like children, you will never enter the kingdom of heaven. Whoever humbles himself like this child, he is the greatest in the kingdom of heaven (Matt. 18:3–4).

. . . unless one is born anew, he cannot see the kingdom of God (John).

These children being suckled are like those who enter the kingdom (Gospel of Thos.).

I thank thee, Father, Lord of heaven and earth, that thou hast hidden these things from the wise and revealed them to babes (Matt. 11, Luke 10).

The proverbial aspect of the millstone metaphor has been considered in chapter 3, no. 10, and the privilege of the babes to receive the revelation of mysteries in chapter 6, no. 6.

Children, little ones and babes play a significant role in Jesus' description of the future citizenry of the Kingdom of God: only those who in some way resemble them qualify for admittance (cf. in particular Mark 9:37 and parallels, Mark 10:15 and parallels). Presumably the children's simple and total dependence on their parents provides the basis for Jesus' metaphorical imagery. The seekers of the Kingdom are advised to imitate the child's blind reliance and directness. A trusting son knows that his father would not give him a stone, a snake or a scorpion if he asked him for bread or a fish or an egg (Matt. 7:9–10; Luke 11:11–12). From the opposite viewpoint, the hopeful gaze of infants is preferred by God to the self-assurance of the wise (Matt. 11:25; Luke 10:21).

This reversal of the order of preference is typical of Jesus, but it demanded a corrective re-touch in some sectors of primitive Christianity. Hence the Gospel of Matthew praises the learned scribe 'trained for the kingdom of heaven' (Matt. 13:52; see chapter 4, no. 21). The central position granted to children in determining the right spiritual attitude in the quest for the Kingdom is typical of Jesus. From this point of view he stands apart both from the Bible and from later Jewish literature, where children play no significant part. The occasional allusion to the innocence of a one-day-old baby provides the nearest parallel in rabbinic literature to the teaching of Jesus. St Paul also compares the Corinthian Christians to babes inexperienced in evil (1 Cor. 14:20). Incidentally, Paul's attitude to children is in complete contrast to that of Jesus. The apostle prefers an adult mentality; he 'gave up childish ways' (1 Cor. 13:11), and recommends his followers to cease to be children in their thinking, and be of mature mind (1 Cor. 14:20). This is diametrically opposed to the thinking of Jesus.

11. An uncommissioned exorcist (Mark 9:39–41; Luke 9:50; cf. Matt. 12:30; Luke 11:23; Matt. 10:42)

Do not forbid him; for no one who does a mighty work in my name will be able soon after to speak evil of me. For he that is not against us [against you (Luke)] *is for us [for you* (Luke)].

He who is not with me is against me, and he who does not gather with me scatters (Matt. 12:30; Luke 11:23).

For truly, I say to you, whoever gives you a cup of water to drink because you bear the name of Christ, will by no means lose his reward (Mark 9:41).

And whoever gives to one of these little ones even a cup of cold water because he is a disciple, truly, I say to you, he shall not lose his reward (Matt. 10:42).

This saying attributed to Jesus is given as a comment on the apostle John's report (Mark 9:38) that he and his colleagues jealously tried to restrain a man who did not belong to their circle from exorcizing in the name of Jesus. The story shows that exorcistic activity was common and widespread, but also indirectly signals the peculiarity of Jesus' own charismatic style. Jesus himself is never depicted as one who expels demons in the name of somebody. Accused of casting out evil spirits in the name of Beelzebul (see chapter 2, no. 7), he asserted that the source of his spiritual power was 'the finger' or 'the Spirit' of God (Matt. 12:28; Luke 11:20; cf. no. 43 below). He recognized the uncommissioned but successful exorcist as an ally.[9] In fact, he quoted the proverb 'He who is not against me is for me/us/you' to reinforce his view that non-opponents should be counted as supporters. In a similar vein Jesus also declared that kindness shown by an outsider to someone simply because the latter was his disciple deserved particular reward.

The performance of exorcism in the name of someone raises an

9. The itinerant Jewish exorcists mentioned in Acts 19:13–16 also attempted to use the name of Jesus, but to no avail.

interesting historical question. The Book of the Acts of the Apostles clearly testifies that charismatic activity in the primitive church was regularly practised in the name of Jesus (Acts 3:6; 4:10; 16:18; cf. 19:13, 17). Likewise the seventy (or seventy-two) disciples are represented by Luke as joyfully informing Jesus on their return, 'Lord, even the demons are subject to us *in your name*!' (Luke 10:17). The latter detail, which is recorded only in Luke's Gospel, may well be due to this evangelist's tendency to adjust his account to the needs and customs of the churches for which he was writing. In fact the instruction given to the twelve apostles in Matthew 10:8, or even that to the seventy disciples earlier in Luke 10:9, contains no mention of healing or exorcizing 'in the name of Jesus'. It is therefore reasonable to consider the apostle John's complaint about the uncommissioned exorcist and Jesus' purported comment as a reflection of the situation prevailing in the primitive church and the consequent rivalries arising in it. The concluding saying in Mark 9:41 (indirectly paralleled in Matthew 10:42) about the merit earned by the gift of a glass of water to someone bearing 'the name of Christ' also suggests a setting in the early church.[10]

12. Leading children astray (Mark 9:42; Matt. 18:6–7; Luke 17:1–2)

See no. 10 above.

13. The children and the Kingdom of God (Mark 10:15; Matt. 18:3; Luke 18:17)

See no. 10 above.

10. Offering a drink to the thirsty is one of the good deeds listed in the parable of the last judgement in chapter 4, no. 26. It is well known from Acts 11:26 that the name 'Christians' was first borne by members of the church of Antioch in Syria, which was founded by Barnabas and Paul in the early to mid forties AD.

14. How to gain eternal life (Mark 10:18–19; cf. Mark 10:21; Matt. 19:17, 21; Luke 18:19–20, 22)

Why do you call me good? No one is good but God alone (Mark 10:18; Luke 18:19).

Why do you ask me about what is good? One there is who is good (Matt.).

You know the commandments (Mark, Luke).

If you would enter life, keep the commandments (Matt.).

You lack one thing; go, sell what you have, and give to the poor, and you will have treasure in heaven; and come, follow me (Mark 10:21; Matt. 19:21; Luke 18:22).

The context in which this saying is inserted is the encounter between Jesus, travelling from Galilee to Jerusalem, and a man described as a 'ruler' or synagogue leader in Luke 18:18. This pious Jew wanted to find out how to inherit eternal life, or in other words, the Kingdom of God (see Mark 9:43–47; Matt. 18:8–9; cf. chapter 9, no. 6). Jesus' succinct answer was a summary appeal to the Decalogue, the religious and moral kernel of the Jewish religion (Mark 10:19; Matt. 19:17; Luke 18:20; see chapter 5, no. 9). Its observance was to be followed by the surrender of worldly goods and entry into the company of those who were working under the leadership of Jesus for the Kingdom of God (Mark 10:21; Matt. 19:21; Luke 18:22).

The simple yet all-inclusive principle conveyed by Jesus here and in some of his parables (see chapter 4, nos. 18, 19) is absolute priority to be granted to the search for God, and the necessity to sever oneself from every attachment to wealth and all other secular values (Mark 10:23, 25; Matt. 19:23–24; Luke 18:24–25; see chapter 3, no. 12). Such attachment can be mastered by faith, the other basic norm constantly emphasized by Jesus: 'With men it is impossible, but not with God; for all things are possible with God' (Mark 10:27; Matt. 19:26; Luke 18:27; cf. also no. 10 above, nos. 16 and 35 below; chapter 1, nos. 8–10; chapter 3, nos. 19 and 29; chapter 4, no. 2; chapter 6, no. 1).

Jesus' objection to being called 'good' because God alone is entitled to be called good has provoked a great deal of comment among Christian interpreters. The reason for the unease lies in the neat distinction which the saying *prima facie* stipulates between Jesus and God. In fact, the texts under consideration are meant to bring into relief the absolute supremacy of God. In the hyperbolical language of Jesus, if God is called good, no one else is entitled to the same qualification. Nevertheless this exaggeration is no greater than the prohibition on addressing one's father as 'father' because God is the only legitimate bearer of this title (see Matt. 23:9; cf. chapter 9, no. 26). The overstatement is rather stretched to the limit, but the point is brilliantly made.

15. Seating in the Kingdom of God (Mark 10:35–45; Matt. 20:20–28; cf. Luke 22:27)

And James and John, the sons of Zebedee, came forward to him and said to him, 'Teacher, we want you to do for us whatever we ask of you.' [Then the mother of the sons of Zebedee came up to him, with her sons, and kneeling before him she asked him for something (Matt.)]. And he said to them [her (Matt.)], *What do you want me to do for you?* And they said to him, 'Grant us to sit, one at your right hand and one at your left, in your glory [in your kingdom (Matt.)]'. But Jesus said to them, *You do not know what you are asking. Are you able to drink the cup that I drink,* [*or to be baptized with the baptism with which I am baptized?* (Mark)] And they said to him, 'We are able.' And Jesus said to them, *The cup that I drink you will drink;* [*and with the baptism with which I am baptized, you will be baptized* (Mark)] *but to sit at my right hand or at my left is not mine to grant, but it is for those for whom it has been prepared* [*by my Father* (Matt.)]. And when the ten heard it, they began to be indignant at James and John. And Jesus called them to him and said to them, *You know that those who are supposed to rule over the Gentiles lord it over them, and their great men exercise authority over them. But it shall not be so among you; but whoever would be great among you must be your servant, and whoever would be first among you must be slave of all. For the Son of man also came not to be served but to serve, and to give his life as a ransom for many* (Mark, Matt.).

For which is the greater, one who sits at table, or one who serves? Is it not the one who sits at table? But I am among you as one who serves (Luke).

Various parts of this complex passage are discussed elsewhere. For Mark 10:42–45, about the 'Son of man' serving, see chapter 7, no. 5, and for Mark 10:43–44 on the contrast between lord and servant, see chapter 9, no. 26.

In Mark's account the context of Jesus' saying is a request addressed to him by the ambitious apostles James and John. Matthew's introduction of the mother, the wife of Zebedee, was intended to remove the blame from leading disciples of Jesus. Jesus' advice not to exalt oneself figures in Matthew 23:12 and Luke 14:11 (see also chapter 3, no. 35, and chapter 4, no. 32), but the inverse principle is laid down in Luke 9:48, 'He who is least among you all is the one who is great.'

In the repetitive answer of Jesus one element may be distinguished as belonging to the original setting, namely that the allocation of seats of honour in the Kingdom of God does not belong to Jesus, but is the exclusive privilege of the heavenly Father. The same inferior position is taken by Jesus when he denies any knowledge of the moment of the Parousia (see Mark 13:32; Matt. 24:36 in no. 26 below). The further elaboration of this basic answer, namely the mention of the Gentiles, and the reference to the acceptance of martyrdom,[11] reflect the situation and needs of the primitive church faced with hostility both in Palestine and in the diaspora. The allusion to the customs of the Gentiles, whom the disciples of Jesus were ordered to avoid (see no. 6 above and no. 49 below), also provides by anticipation an early Christian frame for the words allegedly spoken by Jesus to ten of his apostles (Mark 10:42–45; Matt. 20:25–28; Luke 22:25–27; see chapter 7, no. 5).

11. The 'cup' and the 'baptism' are symbols of tragic destiny.

16. The miraculously efficient prayer (Mark 11:22–24; Matt. 21:21–22)

Have faith in God. Truly, I say to you, whoever says to this mountain, 'Be taken up and cast into the sea', and does not doubt in his heart, but believes that what he says will come to pass, it will be done for him. Therefore I tell you, whatever you ask in prayer, believe that you have received it, and it will be yours (Mark).

Truly, I say to you, if you have faith and never doubt, you will not only do what has been done to the fig tree, but even if you say to the mountain, 'Be taken up and cast into the sea', it will be done. And whatever you ask in prayer, you will receive, if you have faith (Matt.).

As far as the Kingdom of God is concerned, we must underline the necessity of the limitless trust in God which, with the usual hyperbolic touch of Jesus, renders prayer instantaneously effective (see chapter 6, no. 1). For a similar emphasis on the omnipotence of faith, see the comment, 'for all things are possible with God' in no. 14 above (Mark 10:27; Matt. 19:26; Luke 18:27).

17. Prophecy of the destruction of the Temple (Mark 13:1–2; Matt. 24:1–2; Luke 21:5–6)

And as he came out of the temple, one of his disciples said to him . . . 'Do you see these great buildings!' And Jesus said to him, *There will not be left here one stone upon another that will not be thrown down.*

This text has already been dealt with in chapter 1, no. 22.

From the viewpoint of the advent of the Kingdom, the saying attributed to Jesus represents the opening of the Eschatological Discourse (nos. 18–28 below). The signs are associated with the destruction of

Jerusalem which is seen as the preparatory stage of the Parousia. In other words, the Discourse reflects the situation prevailing some forty years after the death of Jesus, and the evangelists voice the later ideas of the apostolic church.

The conflict between such a prophecy and Jesus' reluctance to provide premonitory signs is explained in no. 7 above; cf. also no. 45 below.

18. Warning about false messiahs (Mark 13:5–6; Matt. 24:4–5; Luke 21:8; cf. Mark 13:21–23; Matt. 24:23–25; cf. Matt. 24:26–27; Luke 17:22–24)

Take heed that no one leads you astray. Many will come in my name, saying, 'I am he!' [*'I am the Christ'* (Matt.)] *and they will lead many astray* (Mark, Matt.).

. . . *'I am he!' and, 'The time is at hand!' Do not go after them* (Luke 21:8).

And then if anyone says to you, 'Look, here is the Christ!' or 'Look, there he is!' do not believe it. False Christs and false prophets will arise and show signs and wonders, to lead astray, if possible, the elect. But take heed; I have told you all things beforehand (Mark 13:21–23; Matt. 24:23–25).

The days are coming when you will desire to see one of the days of the son of Man, and you will not see it (Luke 17:22). *So if they say to you, 'Lo, he is in the wilderness', do not go out; if they say, 'Lo, he is in the inner rooms', do not believe it. For as the lightening comes from the east and shines as far as the west,* [*For as the lightening flashes and lights up the sky from one side to the other* (Luke 17:24)], *so will be the coming of the Son of man* (Matt. 24:26–27; Luke 17:23–24).

The subject of the appearance of false messiahs immediately before the Parousia has already been mentioned in chapter 7, no. 22. In connection with the 'false prophets', it should be recalled that Josephus refers to a number of 'impostors and deceivers' who enticed credulous Jews to the desert with the promise of 'marvels and signs' (*Antiquities* 20:167–8). Phenomena such as those described in the Eschatological Discourse are typical of prophecies after the fact, fictitiously ascribed by the primitive church to Jesus.

19. Preliminaries of the approaching end (Mark 13:7–8; Matt. 24:6–8; Luke 21:9–11)

And when you hear of wars and rumours of wars, do not be alarmed; this must take place, but the end is not yet. For nation will rise against nation, and kingdom against kingdom; there will be earthquakes in various places; there will be famines; this is but the beginning of the birth-pangs.

. . . there will be great earthquakes, and in various places famines and pestilences; and there will be terrors and great signs from heaven (Luke 21:11).

The imagery of this passage is typical of Jewish apocalyptic literature, but significantly it is totally absent from the parables of Jesus. Already the prophet Ezekiel spoke of pestilence, famine and the sword characterizing the end of days (Ezek. 5:12), and the Fourth Book of Ezra of earthquakes and tumults of peoples, of wars of city against city and kingdom against kingdom (4 Ezra 9:3; 13:31). It is reasonable to suppose, as has been argued by some New Testament scholars, that the gospel tradition underlying the Eschatological Discourse derives from, and adapts, an otherwise unknown Jewish work composed in the final quarter of the first century AD. It should be noted that the expression 'birth-pangs' is part of the metaphors designating the troubles which signal the arrival of the Messiah (see bSanh 98b). The same image is also found in one of the Thanksgiving Hymns from Qumran, which describes in terms relating to childbearing the advent of a messianic figure: 'Like a woman in travail with her first-born child, upon whose belly pangs have come and grievous pains' (1QH 11: [formerly 3:] 7–8).

20. The persecution of the disciples as part of the preliminaries of the *eschaton* (Mark 13:9–11; Matt. 24:14; Matt. 24:9; Matt. 10:17–20; cf. Matt. 10:24–25; Luke 6:40; John 15:20; Luke 21:12–15)

But take heed to yourselves [*Beware of men* (Matt.)]; *for they will deliver you up* (Matt. 24:9) *to councils; and you will be beaten in synagogues; and you will stand before governors and kings for my sake, to bear testimony before them* [*and the Gentiles* (Matt.)] (Mark 13:9; Matt. 10:17–18).

And the gospel must first be preached to all nations (Mark 13:10). *And when they bring you to trial and deliver you up, do not be anxious beforehand what you are to say; but say whatever is given you in that hour, for it is not you who speak but the Holy Spirit* [*but the Spirit of your Father speaking through you* (Matt.)] (Mark 13:11; Matt. 10:19–20).

A disciple is not above his teacher, nor a servant above his master; [*but every one when he is fully taught will be like his teacher* (Luke 6:40)]; *it is enough for the disciple to be like his teacher, and the servant like his master. If they have called the master of the house Beelzebul, how much more will they malign those of his household* (Matt. 10:24–25).

And this gospel of the kingdom will be preached throughout the whole world, as a testimony to all nations; and then the end will come (Matt. 24:14).

But before all this, they will lay their hands on you and persecute you, delivering you up to the synagogues and prisons, and you will be brought before kings and governors for my name's sake. This will be a time for you to bear testimony. Settle it therefore in your minds, not to meditate beforehand how to answer; for I will give you a mouth and wisdom, which none of your adversaries will be able to withstand or contradict (Luke 21:12–15).

To the natural disasters and wars of Jewish apocalyptic imagery, the evangelists add a reference to the persecution of the followers of Jesus by Jews (councils and synagogues)[12] and Gentiles (governors and kings). The proclamation of the Christian message – the gospel – to all the nations is expected to precede the Day of the Lord (cf. nos. 33 and 53 below). The passage has a curiously Pauline flavour. Paul did indeed reminisce of his many imprisonments and beatings by Jews (2 Cor. 11:23–25), and the Acts of the Apostles mentions that he was arrested and corporal punishment was inflicted on him by Greek magistrates at Philippi (Acts 16:20–24). Again, he saw the successful preaching of the gospel to 'the full number of the Gentiles' as the climax of the process of evangelization leading to the Parousia (cf. Rom. 11:25). The same idea is repeated in Matthew 24:14. For a view of Jesus' opposition to a mission to non-Jews, see no. 6 above and no. 49 below.

The advice purportedly given by Jesus to his disciples that they should not worry about how to answer their interrogators because the Holy Spirit would put the right words into their mouths derives from a mixture of the genuine thought of Jesus (see chapter 3, no. 19) and Johannine mysticism: 'The Holy Spirit, whom the Father will send in my name, he will teach you all things' (John 14:26). The proverbial pronouncement on the master being superior to the pupil (Matt. 10:24–25; Luke 6:40) is loosely linked to the theme of persecution. In the same way as Jesus himself, accused of being an associate of Beelzebul (see chapter 2, no. 7, and no. 43 below), was the object of calumny and hostility, his followers must prepare themselves for a similar treatment.

21. Conflict within the family (Mark 13:12–13; Matt. 10:21–22; 24:9–13; Luke 21:16–17, 19)

And brother will deliver up brother to death, and the father his child, and children will rise against parents and have them put

12. See also Matthew 10:23, 'When they persecute you in one town, flee to the next; for truly, I say to you, you will not have gone through all the towns of Israel, before the son of Man comes': a passage already discussed in chapter 7, no. 24.

to death; and you will be hated by all [*nations* (Matt. 24:9)] *for my name's sake* (Mark 13:12–13; Matt. 10:21–22; 24:9; Luke 21:16–17))

And then many will fall away, and betray one another, and hate one another. And many false prophets will arise and lead many astray. And because wickedness is multiplied, most men's love will grow cold (Matt. 24:10–12).

But he who endures to the end will be saved (Mark 13:13; Matt. 24:13).

By your endurance you will gain your lives (Luke 21:19).

The final warfare opposing nations and kingdoms is brought closer to home. Prediction of disunity within the family in the final age has already been cited from the prophet Micah 7:6 (Matt. 10:34–36 and Luke 12:51–53; see chapter 5, no. 24). But the break-up of the family in the days preceding the arrival of the Kingdom corresponds to Jesus' own view of the events in the final age.

General hatred for Christians points to a late (second-century AD) date in the New Testament age. See, for instance, John 16:2, 'They will put you out of the synagogues; indeed, the hour is coming when whoever kills you will think he is offering service to God.' Likewise 1 Peter 4:14, written probably around AD 100, declares: 'If you are reproached for the name of Christ, you are blessed.' One should also recall Tacitus' famous description of the Christians of Rome as a class of men detested for their vices (*per flagitia invisi*, *Annals* 15:44, 2).

Encouragement to perseverance is a recurrent feature in societies motivated for an extended period by eschatological expectation. For typical examples see 2 Peter 3:9, 'The Lord is not slow about his promise . . . but is forbearing toward you . . . that all should reach repentance', and the Dead Sea Habakkuk Commentary speaking of the final age lasting beyond all the predictions of the prophets (1QpHab 7:9–14).

22. The apogee of the tribulation (Mark 13:14–20; Matt. 24:15–22; Luke 21:20–24; cf. Luke 17:31)

But when you see the desolating sacrilege set up where it ought not to be [*So when you see the desolating sacrilege spoken of by the prophet Daniel, standing in the holy place* (Matt.)] *(let the reader understand), then let those who are in Judaea flee to the mountains; let him who is on the housetop not go down, nor enter his house to take anything away; and let him who is in the field not turn back to take his mantle* (Mark, Matt.).

But when you see Jerusalem surrounded by armies, then know that its desolation has come near. Then let those who are in Judaea flee to the mountains, and let those who are inside the city depart, and let not those who are out in the country enter it; for these are days of vengeance, to fulfil all that is written (Luke 21:20–22).

And alas for those who are with child and for those who give suck in those days! (Mark, Matt., Luke).

Pray that it may not happen in winter (Mark, Matt.) *or on a sabbath* (Matt.).

For in those days there will be such tribulation as has not been from the beginning of the creation which God created [*from the beginning of the world* (Matt.)] *until now, and never will be. And if the Lord had not shortened the days, no human being would be saved; but for the sake of the elect,* [*whom he chose,* (Mark)] *he shortened the days* (Mark 13:19–20; Matt. 24:21–22).

For great distress shall be upon the earth and wrath upon this people; they will fall by the edge of the sword, and be led captive among all nations; and Jerusalem will be trodden down by the Gentiles, until the times of the Gentiles are fulfilled (Luke 21:23–24).

The final stage of the great eschatological upheaval is indicated by the desecration of the sanctuary in Jerusalem conceived on the pattern of the profanation of the Temple by Antiochus IV Epiphanes, who installed a statue of Olympian Zeus in the holy place in 167 BC (cf. Dan. 9:27; 12:11; 1 Macc. 1:54). The venue of the event is described in Mark allusively ('set up where it ought not to be') which necessitates and explains the appended rubric, 'let the reader understand'. Matthew, in turn, replaces Mark's vague words by a full explanation: 'spoken of by the prophet Daniel,[13] standing in the holy place', but abstains from deleting the rubric. Mark (13:19) and Matthew (24:21) attest a further near-citation of Daniel 12:1, 'There shall be a time of trouble, such as never has been since there was a nation till that time.' Luke, on the other hand, omits the Danielic image, and refers directly to the siege of Jerusalem (21:20), and even to a conquered city subjected to Roman rule. This state of affairs is to last until the completion of 'the times of the Gentiles', to be followed by the advent of the Parousia. The general atmosphere is that of fear, urgency, haste and rush. The hope is expressed that constraints imposed on fugitives by pregnancy, harsh weather or the Sabbath will not materialize. The miseries to be faced before the Parousia were forecast to be worse than any wretchedness previously experienced in history. Indeed, if these calamities were to run their full course, no one would be able to survive them.

The historical setting is obviously the siege of Jerusalem by the Romans between AD 67 and 70. Some interpreters who would like to date Mark from before the outbreak of the first Jewish rebellion against Rome (AD 66) propose to identify the 'abomination of desolation' with Gaius Caligula's edict to erect his statue in the Jewish Temple in AD 40 (Philo, *Embassy to Gaius* 30:203). However, since the edict failed to become effective and the statue of the emperor was never installed in Jerusalem, the story provides no basis for the Gospels. The Daniel account is best seen therefore as a prototype whose fulfilment was expected in the near future. In a way readers of the Gospels may have thought that it was realized in AD 70 when, surrounded by

13. Although in the Hebrew canon of the Bible Daniel is not among the prophets, but in the writings, late Jewish tradition, like Matthew, accords him the prophetic title. The Qumran 4QFlorilegium (4Q176) 2:3 also calls Daniel a prophet.

buildings on fire, the Roman legionaries constructed an altar and offered sacrifice to their military standards in the Temple court in Jerusalem (Josephus, *War* 6:316).

The idea of a tribulation so severe that, if its course were not shortened, it would become intolerable even to the righteous, is attested in the Bible and in later Jewish literature, where God is said to hasten the end (Isa. 60:22; 1QM 1:12; 2 Baruch 20:1–2; 83:1; Song of Songs Rabbah 8:14). Perhaps the most striking parallel comes from a contemporary source, Pseudo-Philo's *Book of Biblical Antiquities*: 'I will command the years and charge the times, and they shall be shortened, and the stars shall be hastened, and the light of the sun make speed to set, neither shall the light of the moon endure' (*Liber Antiquitatum Biblicarum* 19:13). The evangelists appear therefore to be treading on familiar paths.

23. Warning about false messiahs (Mark 13:21–23; Matt. 24:23–27; Luke 17:23–24)

See no. 18 above.

24. The return of the son of Man (Mark 13:24–27; Matt. 24:29–31; Luke 21:25–28)

See chapter 5, no. 15 and chapter 7, no. 19.

25. The parable of the fig tree (Mark 13:28–29; Matt. 24:32–33; Luke 21:29–31)

See chapter 4, no. 5.

26. The time of the Parousia (Mark 13:30–32; Matt. 24:34–36; Luke 21:32–33)

Truly, I say to you, this generation will not pass away before all these things take place. Heaven and earth will pass away, but my words will not pass away (Mark, Matt., Luke). *But of that day or that hour no one knows, not even the angels in heaven, nor the Son, but only the Father* (Mark, Matt.).

The three sayings grouped here seem to have originated independently from one another. The first, and possibly the second too, formed the original conclusion of the Eschatological Discourse. The belief that the Second Coming would occur during the lifetime of the contemporaries of Jesus was part of the expectation of the early church. This belief was founded on the teaching of Jesus announcing, not the Parousia, but the immediate advent of the Kingdom (see no. 8 above). The permanence of the words of Jesus, like those of the Law of Moses (cf. Matt. 5:18), guarantees for as long as is necessary the trustworthiness of the prophecy (see chapter 9, no. 16). As for the caveat concerning eschatological chronologies and premonitory signs, it also belongs to the kernel of the authentic message of Jesus. In his view, matters relating to the Kingdom of God are unpredictable and must remain in the hand of God alone, and consequently it is improper to engage in guesswork about them.

27. Exhortation to watchfulness (Mark 13:33–37; Matt. 25:14–15; 24:42; 25:13; Luke 19:12–13; 12:38)

See chapter 4, no. 6.

28. Appearing before the 'Son of man' (Luke 21:34–36)

See chapter 7, no. 29.

29. The anointing in Bethany (Mark 14:6–9; Matt. 26:10–13; cf. Luke 7:41–50; John 12:7–8)

Let her alone; why do you trouble her? She has done a beautiful thing to me. For you always have the poor with you, and whenever you will, you can do good to them; but you will not always have me. She has done what she could; she has anointed my body beforehand for burying. And truly, I say to you, wherever the gospel is preached in the whole world, what she has done will be told in memory of her.

The unexpected anointing of Jesus by a woman is a well-known story recounted in different contexts. Here it is located in Bethany, in the house of Simon surnamed the Leper, two days before Passover (Mark 14:1; Matt. 26:2). The person responsible for it was an unknown woman who generously poured a flask of pure nard – an expensive ointment – on the head of Jesus. In John's Gospel, too, the venue is Bethany, but the date is six days before Passover, and the woman is Mary, the sister of Lazarus (John 12:1–3). Luke, on the other hand, places the episode in Galilee at an earlier stage in Jesus' career, where in the house of a Pharisee also called Simon the act is performed by a whore ('a woman of the city, who was a sinner', Luke 7:37, 39). This prostitute, or Mary, the sister of Lazarus, in John's Gospel, anointed the feet of Jesus after wiping them with her hair. Jesus gave a twofold answer to the complaint of some of the witnesses (Mark) or the disciples (Matt.) or Judas Iscariot (John) about wasting the precious substance instead of selling it to help the poor: the poor would be with them always, but Jesus only for a short time, and the anointing was to anticipate his burial rites, which would not be performed prior to the placing of his body in the grave.

The Mark–Matthew–John accounts re-use the original story, best preserved in Luke, which reveals Jesus' known sympathy for social outcasts, such as whores, and emphasizes forgiveness, another major theme of his teaching, which can be gained through an action inspired by love. The re-worked narrative, which foresees the situation of the poor in a distant future and the preaching of the gospel to the whole world, represents the outlook of the no longer eschatologically-minded primitive church.

30. The words of Jesus during the Last Supper (Mark 14:22–25; Matt. 26:26–29; Luke 22:15–20; 1 Cor. 11:23–26)

And as they were eating, he took bread, and blessed, and broke it, and gave it to them, and said, *Take; this is my body*. And he took a cup, and when he had given thanks he gave it to them, and they all drank of it. And he said to them, *This is my blood of the covenant, which is poured out for many. Truly, I say to you, I shall not drink again of the fruit of the vine until that day when I shall drink it new in the kingdom of God* (Mark).

Now as they were eating, Jesus took bread, and blessed, and broke it, and gave it to the disciples and said, *Take, eat; this is my body*. And he took a cup, and when he had given thanks he gave it to them, saying, *Drink of it, all of you; for this is my blood of the covenant, which is poured out for many for the forgiveness of sins. I tell you I shall not drink again of this fruit of the vine until that day when I drink it new with you in my Father's kingdom* (Matt.).

And he said to them, *I have earnestly desired to eat this passover with you before I suffer; for I tell you I shall not eat it until it is fulfilled in the kingdom of God*. And he took a cup, and when he had given thanks he said, *Take this, and divide it among yourselves; for I tell you that from now on I shall not drink of the fruit of the vine until the kingdom of God comes*. And he took bread, and when he had given thanks he broke it and gave it to them, saying, *This is my body which is given for you. Do this in remembrance of me*. And likewise the cup after supper, saying, *This cup which is poured out for you is the new covenant in my blood* (Luke).

The Lord Jesus on the night when he was betrayed took bread, and when he had given thanks, he broke it, and said, *This is my body which is for you. Do this in remembrance of me.* In the same way also the cup, after supper, saying, *This cup is the new covenant in my blood. Do this, as often as you drink it, in remembrance of me.* For as often as you eat this bread and drink this cup, you proclaim the Lord's death until he comes (1 Cor.).

Four accounts of the Last Supper have survived in the New Testament. They agree among themselves on several essential points, but they also display substantial variations. It is also remarkable that the Gospel of John contains no report of a Passover meal shared by Jesus with his apostles. This is no doubt due to the fact that according to the Fourth Gospel the arrest and crucifixion of Jesus took place the day before the feast, and consequently there could not be any question of Jesus partaking in a real paschal dinner. John specifies that the Jewish dignitaries who handed over Jesus to Pilate refused to enter his palace, the *praetorium*, so as to remain ritually clean so that they 'might eat the passover' (see John 18:28). There is general consensus among New Testament interpreters that the narrative of the Last Supper, with its paucity of concrete details, was first and foremost written as a record of what the early church understood from the outset as the institution of a significant religious ritual, that of the Eucharist. This ecclesiastical view in retrospect affects willy-nilly the meaning of the words presumed to have come from the lips of Jesus. Of course, if the chronology given by John is correct, the meal which Jesus had on the evening before his death was not a *Passover* supper.[14] Consequently the words allegedly spoken during it were uttered by him in different circumstances on another occasion, or are largely the product of the early church.

Let us begin with Paul's account. The First Letter to the Corinthians,

14. Some scholars have recently surmised that Jesus followed the custom of the Essenes, whose Passover always fell on a Wednesday, with the preparatory meal on Tuesday evening. However, bearing in mind the essentially non-Essene (non-legal) character of the religion of Jesus, the hypothesis of his adoption of the Essene liturgical calendar appears not just dubious, but quasi impossible.

which antedates the Synoptic Gospels by fifteen to forty-five years, clearly attests that at the time of its writing, in *circa* AD 55, the institution of the Lord's Supper was already an established custom in Corinth and that it was not observed properly. 'When you meet together,' writes Paul, 'it is not the Lord's supper that you eat' (1 Cor. 11:20). He further reports that the ritual act of eating bread and drinking wine, ordained by Jesus, was specifically intended to serve as a reminder of his death until 'he comes', i.e. until the day of the Parousia. The death of Jesus, represented by the broken bread, symbol of his body, and the cup of wine, symbol of his blood, was seen as the figurative enactment of a new covenant of atonement for the believers. It was substituted for Judaism's sacrifice of the paschal lambs which were slaughtered in their thousands on the eve of the great feast of liberation in the Temple in Jerusalem. A similar view is also expressed earlier in the same First Letter to the Corinthians: 'The cup of blessing which we bless, is it not a participation in the blood of Christ? The bread which we break, is it not a participation in the body of Christ? Because there is one bread, we who are many are one body, for we all partake of the one bread' (1 Cor. 10:16–17). These two texts testify to the conviction of the first generation of Christians in Corinth, and in other churches of Paul, of being in communion with Christ and mystically having a share in his redeeming death.

In the opening section of the present passage (1 Cor. 11:23–24), St Paul conveys to his Gentile readers his theological concept of the cross, which – as he states elsewhere – is the centrepiece of the Christian mystery: 'We preach Christ crucified' (1 Cor. 1:22). Though writing to Gentiles, Paul sets this concept primarily in a Jewish Passover framework: 'Christ, our paschal lamb, has been sacrificed' (1 Cor. 5:7). Indeed, the Lord's Supper took place, according to Paul, in the course of the Jewish *seder* (or Passover) meal, and the 'eucharistic' words, or words of blessing, over the cup were pronounced 'after supper' (1 Cor. 11:25). This no doubt refers to the benediction after the fourth and final cup of wine of the traditional *seder*.[15]

Though steeped in Jewish ideas, Paul's account is addressed, as I have

15. The drinking of four cups of wine in the course of the Passover meal is mentioned already as an established tradition in the age of the Mishnah (mPes 10:1).

observed, to the non-Jewish Corinthians, who were not accustomed to the age-old Israelite taboo according to which blood, belonging exclusively to God, was never allowed to be consumed by men. Even Gentile converts to Christianity were obliged to abstain from it by virtue of the decree issued by the Council of the apostles in Jerusalem, chaired by James the brother of the Lord (Acts 15:29). Among Corinthian Greeks, however, Paul had no need to watch his words and could speak, without facing a particular taboo, about a new Passover entailing the drinking of the sacrificial blood of Jesus, an idea which would have been intolerable in a traditional Jewish setting. The Gospel of John furnishes a perfect illustration (John 6:52–60). When Jesus provocatively equates his teaching on the 'bread of life' with eating his flesh and drinking his blood, not only the hostile 'Jews' but even many of his disciples declared themselves scandalized and abandoned him (John 6:66).

How then did Paul's teaching about the Lord's Supper come into being? The generally held scholarly opinion is that he inherited the relevant tradition from those who preceded him in the faith in the same way as his teaching about the resurrection of Christ was passed on to him by the church (1 Cor. 15:3). There he explicitly lists particular apparitions of the risen Jesus to specific individuals, to Peter, James, the twelve apostles, to over five hundred brethren and finally to himself. Paul obviously learned these stories from his seniors by word of mouth (1 Cor. 15:5–7). On the other hand, he seems to attribute his knowledge of the institution of the Lord's Supper explicitly and exclusively to Jesus himself: 'For I received from the Lord what I also delivered to you' (1 Cor. 11:23). If so, he obtained it from revelation and not from tradition just as he asserts that he acquired by means of direct supernatural communication from God his understanding of the mystery of Christ: 'But when he who had set me apart before I was born, and had called me through his grace, was pleased to reveal his Son to me . . . I did not confer with flesh and blood, nor did I go up to Jerusalem to those who were apostles before me' (Gal. 1:15–17). If this exegesis is accepted, it would be reasonable to assume that the eucharistic interpretation of what seems to have been the ordinary and repeated communal meal of the church comes from Paul, who is certainly the earliest witness of it. It would then follow that the later evidence of Mark, Matthew and Luke is likely to bear the mark of the influence of Paul and, if so, it will have to be interpreted in the light of 1 Corinthians 11:23–26. Therefore there are good reasons to consider Paul as the primary source of the paschal interpretation of the institution of the Eucharist, a ritual which was to be reiterated 'in remembrance' of Jesus.

Of the three Gospel reports on the Lord's Supper the one nearest to Paul's is that of Luke (Luke 22:15–20). This would hardly be surprising if Luke was, as many scholars think, one of Paul's disciples, travel companions and fellow workers (Philem. 24; Col. 4:14; 2 Tim. 4:11). Three particular points are noteworthy. Like Paul, Luke presents the Lord's Supper as a *remembrance* ceremony, regularly to be repeated. Like Paul, he expressly speaks of the 'cup after supper', and calls this cup containing the wine, symbol of the blood of Jesus, the cup of the *new* covenant.[16] Since none of these significant details appears in Mark and Matthew, and since the temporal priority of 1 Corinthians over the Gospel of Luke is unquestionable, the only logical conclusion is that Luke is here positively under the influence of Paul. It should be pointed out, however, that the Pauline tradition is not the only one handed down by Luke. In his Gospel it is preceded by another saying of Jesus, attested also by Mark and Matthew, which Luke has no doubt borrowed from the older Gospel of Mark. It connects the eating of the Passover and the drinking of the wine with the imminent coming of the Kingdom of God (Luke 22:16, 18). In short, Luke echoes Paul, but combines his teaching with the eschatological tradition relating to the Kingdom, which he has in common with the other Synoptic evangelists.

Contrary to Luke, Mark and Matthew place Jesus' statement about the Kingdom not before, but after the blessing of the bread and the cup. Neither of them suggests in any way that the mystical communion typified by the apostles' sharing the food and drink with Jesus was the institution of a rite intended to be perpetuated in the form of a liturgy. Neither Mark nor Matthew mentions Jesus' command: 'Do this in remembrance of me.' For them the dinner in question was a single,

16. The phrase 'new covenant' is not peculiar to the Gospels or to Paul. It goes back to Jeremiah 31:34 and is found several times in the Dead Sea Scrolls in connection with the community of Qumran.

special event. It makes full sense without any sacrificial *Passover* colouring and without any link to the *death* of Jesus. Mark and Matthew attach nothing to the phrase 'this is my body',[17] but their words relating to the cup carry the supplementary Passover allusion to 'my blood of the covenant, which is poured out for many'. To this Matthew adds, 'for the forgiveness of sins'. Luke in turn writes, 'This cup which is poured out for you is the new covenant in my blood.'

The variations in recording a saying of such crucial importance for the Christian church are indicative of a process of re-wording and re-editing. This is all the easier to understand if it is accepted that the Passover supper tradition is devoid of any historical basis. If Jesus was crucified the day before the Passover, he could not have taken part in a *seder* meal; he was dead by then, and consequently the story must be a later creation of the church.

The concluding remark in Mark and Matthew further confirms that in its most obvious sense Jesus' declaration that he will not drink wine until the arrival of the Kingdom of God implies that partaking in the bread and wine was not for him a dramatization of his death. On the contrary, it would appear that he looked forward to continuing his work for a while until he witnessed in the company of his disciples the advent of the Kingdom of God.

The diverse literary descriptions of the Last Supper represent complex variations in the tradition of the early church concerning its central religious ritual. In an attempt to clarify the conundrum, I will supply here a tentative reconstruction of the development of the eucharistic teaching as it is reflected in the New Testament.

At the last communal supper, which Jesus shared with his apostles *before* the feast of Passover, he recited the customary blessings over the bread and the wine.[18] This meal was no doubt the one referred to in John 13:1–2, 21–30; the betrayal of Jesus by Judas is mentioned there, but without any indication that it was a *seder* or Passover meal. In his prayer Jesus dramatically conveyed to his table companions that eating the same bread, symbolically his body, and drinking wine,

17. Luke follows it with 'which is given for you' (cf. Paul: 'which is for you').
18. See, for instance, the rule relating to the communal meal in the Dead Sea sect: 'When the table has been prepared, . . . the priest shall be the first . . . to bless the first fruit of the bread and new wine' (1QS 6:5–6).

symbolically his blood, from the same cup, represented a spiritual and mystical union between teacher and disciples. In this eschatological, but definitely *non-paschal*, account Jesus made a vow not to touch the fruit of the vine until he and all the members of his fellowship would participate in the great banquet in the Kingdom promised to the elect at the impending consummation of the age.

This religious drama of the last meal was set by Paul against the forthcoming death of Jesus and turned into a revised Passover liturgy. It became a supertemporal mystery play about the sacrificial redemption of mankind. Its paschal and eschatological aspects, that is, its connection with the Jewish liberation festival on the one hand and with the advent of the Kingdom of God on the other, were amalgamated when the reshaped story was incorporated into the three Synoptic Gospels. The mixed character of the account is most clearly visible in the Gospel of Luke. He first gives Paul's Passover version: 'I have earnestly desired to *eat this passover* with you before I suffer' (Luke 22:15). Then immediately he follows it up by the eschatological conclusion of the other Synoptics traceable to Jesus, but bereft of any Passover reference: 'for I tell you I shall not eat it *until it is fulfilled in the kingdom of God* ... I tell you that from now on I shall not drink of the fruit of the vine *until the kingdom of God comes*' (Luke 22:16, 18). So the Gospels contain two representations of the Last Supper. One of these is an optimistic picture in which Jesus firmly looks forward to the inauguration of the Kingdom already looming on the horizon. The other is the Pauline mystical enactment of the redemption of mankind through the Passover tragedy of Jesus celebrated in the form of a symbolical Passover meal.

31. The forsaking of Jesus by his disciples and his denial by Peter (Mark 14:27–28, 30; Matt. 26:31–32, 34; Luke 22:31–32, 34)

You will all fall away [*because of me this night* (Matt.)]; *for it is written, 'I will strike the shepherd and the sheep* [*of the flock* (Matt.)] *will be scattered.' But after I am raised up, I will go before you to Galilee ... Truly, I say to you, this very night, before the cock crows twice, you* [Peter] *will deny me three times* (Mark, Matt.).

Simon, Simon, behold, Satan demanded to have you, that he might sift you like wheat, but I have prayed for you that your faith may not fail; and when you have turned again, strengthen your brethren . . . I tell you, Peter, the cock will not crow this day, until you three times deny that you know me (Luke).

The disgraceful desertion of Jesus by all his close disciples is presented as the fulfilment of the prophecy of Zechariah (13:7) about the dispersal of the sheep following the removal of the shepherd (see chapter 5, no. 16). Even the sanguine Peter, leader of the group, is forewarned, without effect, that he would repeatedly betray his master. In both cases some attempt is made to mitigate the odium of the treachery. The disciples and Peter were predestined to act as they did in order to fulfil an ancient prophecy or a prediction of Jesus.[19]

The mention of Jesus' post-resurrection appearance in Galilee (Mark 14:28) is introduced abruptly.[20] Mark 14:28 ('I will go before you to Galilee') is thought to represent an editorial 'prophetic' preliminary to Mark 16:7, where an anonymous messenger in the empty tomb announces that Jesus will arrive in Galilee ahead of the apostles and meet them there (see no. 53 below).

32. Hearsay prophecy about the destruction and rebuilding of the Temple (Mark 14:58; Matt. 26:61; cf. Mark 15:29; Matt. 27:40; John 2:19)

'We heard him say, "*I will destroy this temple that is made with hands, and in three days I will build another, not made with hands*"' (Mark).

19. Note that Luke comes to the rescue of the principal apostle by introducing a special prayer of Jesus intended to enable him to perform better in the future.
20. The verse is absent from a Fayyumic Coptic fragment, but whether this is significant or is merely accidental is impossible to ascertain.

'This fellow said, "*I am able to destroy the temple of God and to build it in three days*"' (Matt.).

Destroy this temple and in three days I will raise it up (John).

In John's formulation alone does the saying come directly from Jesus, who claims miraculous power to reconstruct the Temple in three days if it is destroyed by his Jewish opponents. In the other two quotations the saying takes the form of an accusation levelled against Jesus for uttering these words. In Acts 6:14 the same charge is laid against the protomartyr Stephen for using them on a later occasion. The symbol of three days recalls the sign of Jonah relative to the three days spent by the body of Jesus in the grave (chapter 5, no. 7) and to his resurrection on the third day (chapter 7, no. 14). We are facing here a figurative Christian interpretation. Indeed, John states this explicitly when he explains that the destruction of the Temple and its restoration after three days does not refer to a building but to the death of Jesus and his rising from the tomb (John 2:21).

These sayings seem to be motivated explicitly or implicitly by the critical attitude of the Hellenistic Jewish members of the Palestinian church towards the Temple of Jerusalem, chief symbol of the religion of Palestinian Judaism. The protomartyr Stephen, one of the leaders of the Hellenistic Jewish Christians, further infuriated his already hostile Jewish audience by denying that God ever dwelt in 'houses made with hands' (Acts 7:48) and by repeating Jesus' reported words about the forthcoming destruction of the Temple (Acts 6:14). One of the serious Jewish charges against Paul was also that he preached against the Law and the Sanctuary (Acts 25:7–8). All the extant evidence seems to suggest that the hostile utterances against the house of God vaguely attributed to Jesus in the New Testament were meant to provide antinomian Gentile Christianity with verbal ammunition traceable to Jesus himself. The only event showing Jesus at odds with something linked to the Temple system is his outburst against the merchants and money-changers plying their trade in the courtyard of the Sanctuary (cf. chapter 2, no. 10, and chapter 5, no. 10). In fact, John links the saying mentioned to his account of the 'cleansing' of the house of God (John 2:14–21). While the historical Jesus displayed no particular interest in the Temple, the Gospels contain no solid evidence indicating any theological hostility on his part towards the Temple of Jerusalem.

33. The commission of the apostles in the longer ending of Mark (Mark 16:15–18)

Go into all the world and preach the gospel to the whole creation. He who believes and is baptized will be saved; but he who does not believe will be condemned. And these signs will accompany those who believe: in my name they will cast out demons; they will speak in new tongues; they will pick up serpents, and if they drink any deadly thing, it will not hurt them; they will lay their hands on the sick, and they will recover.

Since the longer ending of Mark (Mark 16:9–20) is missing from the Sinaiticus and the Vaticanus, i.e. the oldest and most authoritative New Testament manuscripts, its authenticity is generally rejected by scholars. The contents of this section largely duplicate sayings attested elsewhere in the genuine Gospels. The worldwide mission of the apostles is discussed in no. 20 above and in no. 53 below (Matt. 28:18–20). The signs accompanying believers are dealt with in no. 7 above and no. 54 below (Luke 10:19–20). Only speaking in tongues (Mark 16:17) is not alluded to in the Gospels; however, it is depicted elsewhere in the New Testament as a not uncommon charismatic phenomenon, known as glossolalia, in the primitive church. In Acts 2:4–11 the apostles are reported to have spoken in tongues on the first Pentecost in Jerusalem and to have been understood by foreigners. Paul, on the other hand, refers to the spiritual gift of speaking in tongues as incomprehensible without a competent interpreter (1 Cor. 14:2–6). To this category most probably belonged the charismatic speech attributed to the Roman centurion Cornelius and his household after they were seized by the Holy Spirit (Acts 10:44, 46), as were Paul's converts in Ephesus (Acts 19:6).

The remark on glossolalia in Mark 16:17 clearly shows that we are dealing here with ideas of the early church backdated to Jesus.

II. THE Q TRADITION

34. The Beatitudes and Woes: manifesto for the seekers of the Kingdom (Matt. 5:3–12; Luke 6:20–26; Gospel of Thos. 69)

Blessed are the poor in spirit, for theirs is the kingdom of heaven.
Blessed are those who mourn, for they shall be comforted.
Blessed are the meek, for they shall inherit the earth.
Blessed are those who hunger and thirst for righteousness, for they shall be satisfied.
Blessed are the merciful, for they shall obtain mercy.
Blessed are the pure in heart, for they shall see God.
Blessed are the peacemakers, for they shall be called sons of God.
Blessed are those who are persecuted for righteousness' sake, for theirs is the kingdom of heaven.
Blessed are you when men revile you and persecute you and utter all kinds of evil against you falsely on my account. Rejoice and be glad, for your reward is great in heaven, for so men persecuted the prophets who were before you (Matt.).

Blessed are you poor, for yours is the kingdom of God.
Blessed are you that hunger now, for you shall be satisfied.[21]
Blessed are you that weep now, for you shall laugh.
Blessed are you when men hate you, and when they exclude you and revile you, and cast out your name as evil, on account of the son of man! Rejoice in that day, and leap for joy, for behold, your reward is great in heaven; for so their fathers did to the prophets.
But woe to you that are rich, for you have received your consolation.
Woe to you that are full now, for you shall hunger.
Woe to you that laugh now, for you shall mourn and weep.

21. The Gospel of Thomas (69) presents the substance of the saying in a form which has nothing in common with the style of the other Beatitudes: 'Blessed are they who are hungry, that the belly of him who desires may be satisfied.'

Woe to you, when all men speak well of you, for so their fathers did to the false prophets (Luke).

The Beatitudes are precious pearls in the teaching of Jesus from the point of view of both piety and poetry. They have been preserved in Matthew and Luke in two separate forms. Luke's shorter version is generally held in higher esteem by New Testament scholars as far as authenticity is concerned, but the more reasonable view is that at least in part Luke and Matthew may reflect two versions both of which originated with Jesus. A perfunctory reading will suffice to make plain that the inspiration and the literary construction of the final two verses (Matt. 5:11–12 and Luke 6:22–23) differ from the rest. Only three out of the first eight Beatitudes of Matthew are paralleled in Luke.

The purpose of the composition is obvious: it is centred on the Kingdom of God, the entry into which constitutes the reward in the first and the last Beatitudes. Hence it is fair to conclude that this concept of the Kingdom is the axis around which the whole complex turns. In other words, we are faced here with what one might call the manifesto of Jesus addressed to those who wished to embark with him on his great eschatological mission. Those who accepted the conditions described in the Beatitudes, and possessed the appropriate virtues, were promised access to the final bliss.

The eight Beatitudes of Matthew are reduced to four in the version of Luke, but here they are contrasted with four Woes which are absent from Matthew. So Luke's account is no longer just a programme for those engaged on the quest for God, but serves at the same time as a warning to those who resist the appeal of Jesus and choose to walk in the path of wickedness. The other noticeable difference between the two lists of Beatitudes lies in the spiritualization of qualities in Matthew: Luke's 'poor' become the 'poor in spirit', and while the hungry of Luke long for food, those of Matthew yearn for 'righteousness'.

The spiritual features which are proclaimed by Jesus as worthy of blessing and required of the seekers of the Kingdom are common virtues of Jewish piety. They are prominent in the books of the Old Testament, attested in the Dead Sea Scrolls, and again and again praised by Jesus elsewhere in the Gospels. It has often been pointed out that the Beatitudes resemble the opening verses of chapter 61 of Isaiah. Isaiah (61:1–2) mentions the good tidings to the poor, the care of the broken-hearted, the liberation of the captives, the proclamation of God's mercy and the comforting of mourners. Similar ideas, including the mention of the 'eternal Kingdom', are also displayed in the Qumran wisdom work known as a Messianic Apocalypse: 'For the Lord will consider the pious and call the righteous by name. Over the poor his spirit will hover and will renew the faithful with his power. And he will glorify the pious with the throne of the eternal Kingdom . . . He who liberates the captives, restores sight to the blind, straightens the bent . . . He will heal the wounded, and revive the dead, and bring good news to the poor' (4Q521 2:4–12). The phrase 'poor in spirit' of Matthew 5:3 is echoed in the War Scroll from Qumran, where the author speaks of the defeat of the 'hard of heart' by the 'poor in spirit' (1QM 14:7).

Matthew's opening Beatitude concerning poverty in spirit constitutes the first qualification for entitlement to a share in the Kingdom. Poverty is one of the top virtues in the Gospels. Jesus preaches the good news to the poor (Matt. 11:5; Luke 7:22), and in his teaching as well as in his parables the poor are the chief guests invited to the great banquets (Luke 14:13; see chapter 4, no. 13). The stressful preparation for the Kingdom, after requiring the severance of family ties, is comparable to mourning (Matt. 5:4), but the subsequent eschatological rejoicing will provide comfort. Jesus exhorts his disciples to imitate his meekness (Matt. 11:29; see no. 51 below), a virtue to be rewarded by the possession of the land (Matt. 5:5), which once more designates not the possession of this-worldly goods, but that of the Kingdom of God in the near future. The phrase recalls extracts from Psalm 37: 'Those who wait for the Lord shall possess the land' (Ps. 37:9); 'The meek shall possess the land' (Ps. 37:11); 'The righteous shall possess the land' (Ps. 37:29). Feeding the hungry and giving drink to the thirsty appear among the righteous acts remembered at the final judgement (Matt. 25:35), and those who went hungry while listening to Jesus' words of righteousness could count on being miraculously fed in the wilderness (see chapter 1, nos. 11, 14). But hunger and thirst for righteousness (Matt. 5:6) remind one of the idea of God's 'kingdom and his righteousness' which will ensure, according to the Sermon on the Mount, that the disciples of Jesus will be provided with all their earthly needs (Matt. 6:33; Luke 12:31; see chapter 3, no. 19).

As for the virtue of mercy, the whole career of Jesus, healer of the sick and friend of the despised, exemplifies compassion. Furthermore, although a different yet synonymous Greek term (*eleêmôn*) is used here, the virtue advocated is the same as in the counsel to be merciful (*oiktirmôn*) in imitation of God (Luke 6:36). Again, the purity of heart (Matt. 5:8), i.e. simplicity and integrity, is an essential constituent of the religion preached by Jesus. His followers were exhorted to learn from him how to be humble of heart (Matt. 11:29; see no. 51 below) and how to concentrate their minds on the heavenly treasures (Matt. 6:21; see chapter 3, no. 16). In connection with the first Gentile converts of the primitive church, the Council of Jerusalem declared that their hearts were cleansed by faith through the Holy Spirit (Acts 15:9).

The idea of making peace is the equivalent of reconciliation, the creation of a common thinking. Matthew's word, 'peacemaker', is unparalleled in the New Testament, but peace itself is a central notion in Jewish religious thinking. In the Bible God is the author of peace (Isa. 45:7), and the famous teacher Hillel, an older contemporary of Jesus, exhorted his students to become disciples of Aaron, 'peace lovers and peace makers' (mAb 1:12). According to the teaching of Jesus, his followers, kept healthy by spiritual salt, must live peacefully among themselves (Mark. 9:50; see chapter 3, no. 11). The peacemakers are entitled to be called 'sons of God'. The honorific title 'sons of God', when applied to a group in the Bible and in post-biblical Jewish literature, designates either the members of God's heavenly court (the angels), or the Jews in general, or particularly saintly people totally devoted to the affairs of their Father in heaven (see *The Changing Faces of Jesus*, 32–4). Here they are the people engaged in the work of eschatological reconciliation while expecting the instant arrival of God's Kingdom.

The last Beatitude in Matthew (5:10), on the blessedness of the persecuted, sounds a dissonant note both in its present literary context and in the light of the tradition concerning the early mission of the disciples of Jesus. Unless the idea of persecution is treated as another hyperbole, an exaggeration for an unfriendly reception (cf. no. 5 above), it clashes with the rest of the Beatitudes and alludes rather to the conflict between the apostolic church and unsympathetic Jews in Palestine and in the diaspora. In fact, the disciples are encouraged by Jesus to take up a tough stand and show their displeasure when they are not warmly welcomed (Mark 6:11, etc.). Inhospitable Jews are compared to the evil inhabitants of Sodom, representing the most wicked generation in history, that of the flood (see no. 5 above). The apostles James and John, true Galilean fanatics, apparently took Jesus' simile about the Sodomites literally, and wished to bring down fire from heaven on the Samaritan village which was unwilling to receive them (Luke 9:54). There is no hint at actual persecution while Jesus was among his followers. Hence the notion of martyrdom alluded to in Matthew 5:10, though incontestably a Jewish concept, had better be associated not with the apostles in the time of Jesus, but with the ill-treatment suffered by Christian missionaries in the later decades of the first century (see nos. 20 and 21 above; cf. also chapter 5, no. 24 and chapter 7, no. 24).

The concluding part of the Beatitudes in Matthew (Matt. 5:11–12) further develops the motive of persecution. The passage is easily distinguishable from the preceding eight verses. The 'Blessed are *you*' in Luke is substituted for Matthew's usual third-person formula, 'Blessed are those', and Jesus is presented as the cause of the violent treatment meted out to his followers, along the lines of the theme developed in other persecution passages (Matt. 10:18; Mark 13:9; Luke 21:12 ['for my name's sake']; Matt. 10:39; 16:25; Mark 8:35; Luke 9:24; see chapter 9, no. 5). Moreover a definite Jewish context is introduced through linking the suffering Christians to their biblical prophetic predecessors. It should also be observed that in 'your reward is great in heaven' (Matt. 5:12), 'heaven' replaces the twice-quoted 'kingdom of heaven' (Matt. 5:3, 10). The implied celestial reward after afflictions on earth belongs to a different thought category from the entry into the Kingdom of the poor in spirit. Recompense on high following earthly suffering indicates a total contrast between this world and the next, as is commonly attested in rabbinic literature. In contrast, the continuity is hinted at in Jesus' parables on the growing seed (cf. chapter 4, nos. 1, 2).

Despite some notable differences, the Beatitudes and the corresponding Woes preserved in Luke (Luke 6:20–23, 6:24–26) add little in substance to the teaching transmitted in Matthew. The poor are materially poor without a spiritualization of the concept, but anyone familiar with Jewish biblical and post-biblical religious ideas knows that absence of possessions is seen there as conducive to trust in God and thus to piety. Access to the Kingdom is presented as very hard for the well-off (Mark 10:23–25; Matt. 19:23–24; Luke 18:24–25; see no. 14 above and chapter 3, no. 12). Luke's second Beatitude speaks of physical hunger (6:21) as against hunger and thirst for righteousness in Matthew, but in the corresponding Woe (Luke 6:25) the hunger is almost certainly figurative. Matthew's mourning is replaced by weeping and the corresponding comfort by laughter (Luke 6:21). It is noteworthy that in all the Gospels the verb 'to laugh' is found only in Luke's third Beatitude and his third Woe. Jesus himself is nowhere described as laughing in the Gospels. He does not seem to have possessed the rabbis' sense of humour. One further small comment: Luke's expression 'on account of *the son of man*' patently does not add anything to Matthew's 'on *my* account'; it is a circumlocution for 'I', as has been shown in chapter 7, no. 7.

While the Beatitudes convey genuine religious ideas of Jesus, the literary form is not of his own making. Several Old Testament psalms, starting with Psalm 1, begin with 'Blessed is', and in six of them the formula is reiterated (Ps. 32:1–2; 84:4–5; 119:1–2; 128:1–2; 137:8–9; 144:15). However, the most striking parallel to the Gospels' Beatitudes comes from the Dead Sea Scrolls where a Hebrew poem, unfortunately badly damaged, repeats three times 'Blessed is' or 'Blessed are'. It is known as 4QBeatitudes or (4Q525).[22] And the relevant section reads: '[Blessed is the man] . . . with a pure heart and who does not slander with his tongue. Blessed are those who hold to [Wisdom's] precepts and do not hold to the ways of iniquity. Blessed are those who rejoice in her, and do not burst forth in ways of folly. Blessed are those who seek her with pure hands, and do not pursue her with a treacherous heart.' The Qumran wisdom poem provides us with a good insight into the literary structure of the Beatitudes of Matthew and Luke. In Matthew, each praiseworthy virtue is accompanied by the appropriate reward: 'Blessed are the poor in spirit, for theirs is the kingdom of

22. See E. Puech, *Discoveries in the Judaean Desert* XXV (1998), 122–3.

heaven'. Luke's Beatitudes also reveal the same pattern, but in the Woes they are followed by the list of vices and their punishments: 'Woe to you that laugh now, for you shall mourn and weep.' The Scrolls' Beatitudes are a kind of halfway house; they bless the practitioners of a virtue who do not indulge in the contrasting vice. Exposition by antithesis is a well-chosen means for moral instruction, but if the aim of the preacher is to recommend a way of life and place a manifesto before prospective followers, the style preserved in Matthew is clearly more efficient.

Did Jesus compose the Beatitudes of Matthew, or Luke, or both? No simple answer is possible. As has been shown, taken separately each statement can be ascribed to him on the basis of similar teachings elsewhere in the Gospels. On the other hand, the Beatitudes, apart from the supplementary verses mentioning the preacher himself and his Jewish (prophetic) background (Matt. 5:11–12; Luke 6:22–23), lack the personal and local colouring typical of the language of Jesus. So we cannot be sure that Jesus ever presented his prospective followers with a neat manifesto of eight or four points. It is more likely that the Beatitudes are a faithful synopsis of his preaching produced by the early tradition and framed so as to appeal to believers both inside and outside the Jewish fold.

For further Beatitudes, see Luke 11:28 in no. 3 above; Matthew 13:16 and Luke 10:23 in no. 44 below; and Matthew 23:39; Luke 13:35 in no. 48 below.

35. The power of prayer addressed to the heavenly Father (Matt. 7:7–11; Luke 11:9–13; Matt. 26:53–54; Gospel of Thos. 2)

Ask, and it will be given you; seek, and you will find; knock, and it will be opened to you (Matt., Luke).

He who seeks must not stop seeking until he finds (Gospel of Thos.).

For everyone who asks receives, and he who seeks finds, and to him who knocks it will be opened. Or what man of you [What father among you (Luke)], *if his son asks him for bread, will give him a stone? Or if he asks for a fish, will give him a serpent?* [*Or if he asks for an egg, will give him a scorpion?* (Luke)] *If you then, who are evil, know how to give good gifts to your children, how much more will your Father who is in heaven give good things* [*give the Holy Spirit* (Luke)] *to those who ask him!* (Matt., Luke).

Do you think that I cannot appeal to my Father, and he will at once send me more than twelve legions of angels? But how then would the scriptures be fulfilled, that it must be so? (Matt. 26).

The religious principle underlying this famous passage is that unconditional trust in a loving heavenly Father is all-powerful and able to obtain anything. The necessity of such trust is strongly underlined in connection with charismatic healing. Without absolute faith no cure can ever take place (see chapter 1, no. 9). The same idea is brought into relief in the parable of the unexpected guest (see chapter 4, no. 29), and in the metaphor of faith moving mountains (see no. 46 below, and chapter 6, no. 1).

A similar hyperbolical reference to the immediate efficacy of prayer is put by Matthew on the lips of Jesus in the garden of Gethsemane. Had he prayed for the dispatch of a whole army of angels to help him to escape capture by the Temple police, God would have intervened (Matt. 26:53). The reason for not requesting such spectacular help was Jesus' presumed desire to ensure that the relevant prophecies reached their fulfilment (Matt. 26:54). On the lack of authenticity of prophecies relating to the passion, see chapter 7, pp. 249–51.

36. The condition of entry into the Kingdom (Matt. 7:21–23; Luke 6:46; 13:26–27)

Not everyone who says to me, 'Lord, Lord', shall enter the kingdom of heaven, but he who does the will of my Father who is in heaven. On that day many will say to me, 'Lord, Lord, did we not prophesy in your name, and cast out demons in your name, and do many mighty works in your name?' And then will I declare to them, 'I never knew you; depart from me, you evildoers' (Matt.).

Why do you call me 'Lord, Lord', and not do what I tell you? (Luke 6).

Then you will begin to say, 'We ate and drank in your presence, and you taught in our streets.' But he will say, 'I tell you, I do not know where you come from; depart from me, all you workers of iniquity!' (Luke 13).

The two halves of the saying are distinct, as is indicated both by their content and by the fact that they are presented in separate chapters in Luke. Their coupling is the result of Matthew's editorial work. The maxim calling Jesus 'Lord, Lord' is a distinct unit which neither evangelist could properly accommodate. In Luke it is attached to the saying, 'The evil man out of his evil treasure produces evil' (Luke 6:45; see chapter 3, no. 24) and applies to insincere followers of Jesus in his own time. Matthew on the other hand uses the phrase as a preface to a post-Parousia dialogue between the final Judge and the failed disciples of Jesus and recalls the parables of the ten virgins and of the last judgement (Matt. 25:12 and 25:44–45; see chapter 4, nos. 25, 26). The self-defence pronounced by the guilty and the Judge's words of rejection are linked in Luke quite naturally to a scene of the ultimate reckoning. It is hard to decide whether Luke or Matthew represents the more original form of the saying, 'Lord, Lord'. However, Matthew's statement about obeying the will of the heavenly Father is undoubtedly a genuine Jewish formula (see mAb 5:20) which is one of the fundamental requirements of the piety of Jesus (see no. 3 above; cf. also chapter 6, nos. 3 and 5). Hence it can be acknowledged as an argument favouring authenticity.

37. Jews replaced by Gentiles in the Kingdom (Matt. 8:10–12; Luke 7:9; 13:28–29; cf. Matt. 21:43)

Truly, I say to you, not even in Israel have I found such faith. I tell you, many will come from east and west and sit at table with Abraham, Isaac, and Jacob in the kingdom of heaven, while the sons of the kingdom will be thrown into the outer darkness; there men will weep and gnash their teeth (Matt.).

I tell you, not even in Israel have I found such faith (Luke 7).

There you will weep and gnash your teeth, when you see Abraham and Isaac and Jacob and all the prophets in the kingdom of God and you yourselves thrust out. And men will come from east and west, and from north and south, and sit at table in the kingdom of God (Luke 13).

Therefore I tell you, the kingdom of God will be taken away from you and given to a nation producing the fruits of it (Matt. 21).

The prediction concerning the exclusion of the Jews from the great banquet, except the patriarchs (so Matthew) and the prophets (according to Luke), is attached to the story of the healing of the centurion's servant in Matthew (Matt. 8:5–13; Luke 7:1–10; see chapter 1, no. 28), and to the conditions of entry into the Kingdom in Luke. An identical comment is appended in Matthew to the parable of the wicked tenants of the vineyard (Matt. 21:43). The idea of the rejection of the Jews and preference given to the Gentiles gathered from the four winds clashes with Jesus' assertion that the gospel was intended only for Jews (see no. 6 above and no. 49 below). The general gist of the teaching of Jesus excludes the possibility of a wholesale damnation by him of the Jewish people. The most likely explanation is that the saying was put in the mouth of Jesus after the general failure of the apostolic preaching among Jews, or that the insertion was the work of a later editor of the Gospel who represented the thought of the Gentile church.

38. Hostile audiences (Matt. 10:16; Luke 10:3)

Behold, I send you out as sheep [*lambs* (Luke)] *in the midst of wolves.*

This is an exaggerated description of the conditions which the apostles of Jesus were to face, since none of them is said to have perished while Jesus was alive. For further comments see chapter 3, no. 28.

39. Acknowledgement or denial of Jesus (Matt. 10:32–33; Luke 12:8–9)

So every one who acknowledges me before men, I also will acknowledge before my Father who is in heaven; but whoever denies me before men, I also will deny before my Father who is in heaven (Matt.).

And I tell you, every one who acknowledges me before men, the Son of man also will acknowledge before the angels of God; but he who denies me before men will be denied before the angels of God (Luke).

This maxim resembles the sayings which deal with lapsed disciples who speak against the 'Son of man' or are ashamed of Jesus (see chapter 7, nos. 3 and 18). In both Matthew and Luke the setting is the final judgement in the presence of God the Father and the angels. Acknowledging Jesus before men is the equivalent of the primitive Christian confession of faith, such as Jesus is Lord, Jesus is the Christ, Jesus is the Son of God (see Acts 2:36; 9:20; Rom. 10:9; 1 Cor. 12:3; 2 Cor. 4:5; Phil. 2:11). The passage must therefore have been introduced into the Gospels by the early church.

40. Jesus on John the Baptist (Matt. 11:11–15; Luke 7:28; 16:16)

Truly, I say to you, among those born of women there has risen no one greater than John the Baptist; yet he who is least in the kingdom of heaven is greater than he (Matt., Luke 7). From the days of John the Baptist until now the kingdom of heaven has suffered violence, and men of violence take it by force. For all the prophets and the law prophesied until John; and if you are willing to accept it, he is Elijah who is to come. He who has ears to hear, let him hear (Matt.).

The law and the prophets were until John; since then the good news of the kingdom of God is preached, and everyone enters it violently (Luke 16).

For the eulogy of John by Jesus, see chapter 5, no. 26, and for his identification with the returning Elijah, see no. 9 above.

The unreserved praise heaped by Jesus on the Baptist (Matt. 11:7–10; Luke 7:24–27; see chapter 5, no. 26), which ends with John's proclamation as the greatest of all the prophets, is continued here: John is the most eminent of all human beings! Nevertheless qualifications begin to creep in which reduce him to the status of 'yesterday's man'. Every follower of Jesus will outrank John in the Kingdom. He belongs to the ancient regime of the Law and the prophets; with Jesus the novelty of the Kingdom of God has started. These derogatory remarks are unlikely to derive from the person who has just designated John as the most outstanding of men. They must reflect polemics between the followers of Jesus and those disciples of the Baptist who venerated him as the Messiah (Luke 3:15). Another line of the polemic made John himself confess that he was inferior to the one who was to succeed him and whose sandals he was unworthy to untie or carry (Mark 1:7; Matt. 3:11; Luke 3:16). Such a sharp critical attitude is later replaced by a compromise in which John is identified as the new Elijah, the precursor and herald of Jesus (see also no. 9 above).

In both Matthew and Luke the arrival of the Kingdom is said to generate violence among those who seek to enter, something at first sight contrary to the irenical behaviour of the future 'sons of God', the blessed peacemakers (Matt. 5:9; see no. 34 above). Most commentators interpret the sayings on violence in a pejorative sense as alluding to bellicose Jewish revolutionaries (Zealots or Sicarii) whose continuous agitation until the fall of Jerusalem in AD 70 hindered the tranquil progress towards the reign of God. The image can, however, also be understood as describing the popular success of Jesus with excited and noisy Jewish crowds elbowing their way towards him. With the customary hyperbolical penchant of Jesus, the scene can be compared with one in which fighting men surge forward in an effort to reach the Kingdom of heaven.

41. The ascetic John and the convivial Jesus (Matt. 11:16–19; Luke 7:31–35)

But to what shall I compare this generation? It is like children sitting in the market places and calling to their playmates, 'We piped to you, and you did not dance; we wailed, and you did not mourn.' For John came neither eating nor drinking, and they say, 'He has a demon'; the son of Man came eating and drinking, and they say, 'Behold, a glutton and a drunkard, a friend of tax-collectors and sinners!' Yet wisdom is justified by her deeds [*by all her children* (Luke)].

The parable on the children playing in the street to which the comment on John and Jesus is appended has already been dealt with in chapter 4, no. 9. The implied message is that while proclaiming the impending arrival of the Kingdom of heaven, neither the Baptist's harsh asceticism nor Jesus' liberal attitude to public sinners – eating and drinking with them – made a great impression on their contemporaries. The story makes better sense in retrospect, the primitive church comparing John and Jesus, than on the lips of Jesus. It was not his habit to speak disparagingly of himself as a glutton and a drunkard. On the other hand, the equal ranking of the two, instead of Jesus being placed above John, argues against the attribution of this passage to the primitive church.

42. Failure of charisma in Galilean villages (Matt. 11:21–23; Luke 10:13–15)

Woe to you, Chorazin! woe to you, Bethsaida! for if the mighty works done in you had been done in Tyre and Sidon, they would have repented long ago in sackcloth and ashes. But I tell you, it shall be more tolerable on the day of judgement for Tyre and Sidon than for you. And you, Capernaum, will you be exalted to heaven? You shall be brought down to Hades.

Jesus is presented as lamenting the lack of lasting impact of his charismatic activity on the inhabitants of localities of the Galilean lakeside. Chorazin is nowhere else mentioned in the Gospels, but Bethsaida (literally 'house of the fishermen') was a place where Jesus had a following (Luke 9:10–11). It was the home town, according to the Fourth Gospel, of the senior apostles Peter, Andrew and Philip (John 1:44; for Capernaum, see chapter 5, no. 27). The picture sketched here is very different from the portrayal of the friendly Galilean villages, where Jesus was surrounded by sympathetic crowds, found elsewhere in the Gospels. Capernaum, for instance, is once called Jesus' own town (Mark 2:1; Matt. 9:1). The harsh judgement on these localities is more likely to mirror the resistance of the Galileans to the later Christian missionaries preaching that Jesus was the Messiah. All the extant evidence proves that Jesus, the charismatic healer, was warmly welcomed by them. What we hear are the woes of the Jewish church, antedated to the time of Jesus.

43. The charismatic nature of exorcism (Matt. 12:27–28; Luke 11:18–20)

[*For you say that I cast out demons by Beelzebul* (Luke).] *And if I cast out demons by Beelzebul, by whom do your sons cast them out? Therefore they shall be your judges. But if it is by the Spirit* [*by the finger* (Luke)] *of God that I cast out demons, then the kingdom of God has come upon you.*

This is the concluding part of the polemic on the nature of exorcism described in chapter 2, no. 7.

Jesus did not cast out demons in the name of someone, as his disciples and other exorcists did (see no. 11 above), but by means of a spiritual power believed to be of divine origin. Thus the conquest of the reign of Satan was perceived as already in progress and reciprocally the establishment of God's Kingdom as an incipient reality (see no. 8 above).

44. The blessedness of the disciples (Matt. 13:16–17; Luke 10:23–24)

Blessed are your eyes, for they see, and your ears, for they hear. Truly, I say to you, many prophets and righteous men [many prophets and kings (Luke)] *longed to see what you see, and did not see it, and to hear what you hear, and did not hear it.*

This Beatitude pronounced on the disciples of Jesus is placed by Matthew after the charge of blindness, deafness and incomprehension levelled against the hostile Jews (see chapter 5, no. 2). Originally it was probably transmitted as an independent unit, and Luke reproduces it unattached to any context. The message is that the close associates of Jesus are fortunate to witness the charismatic events of the final age, which their prophetic predecessors could only hope to observe. The linking of prophets and the righteous is customary in Matthew (see Matt. 10:41; 23:29); Luke's 'prophets and kings' is probably the original form of the saying. There is no reason to doubt the substantial authenticity of the words attributed to Jesus.

45. Interpreting signs (Matt. 16:2–3; Luke 12:54–56)

When it is evening, you say, 'It will be fair weather; for the sky is red.' And in the morning, 'It will be stormy today, for the sky is red and threatening.' You know how to interpret the appearance of the sky, but you cannot interpret the signs of the times (Matt.).

When you see a cloud rising in the west, you say at once, 'A shower is coming'; and so it happens. And when you see the south wind blowing, you say, 'There will be scorching heat'; and it happens. You hypocrites! You know how to interpret the appearance of earth and sky; but why do you not know how to interpret the present time? (Luke).

The two texts belong to the issue of Jesus' attitude to signs (see no. 7 above). The genuineness of Matthew's formula is doubtful as it is absent from the oldest codices, the Sinaiticus and the Vaticanus. The version in Luke recalls the style of the rabbinic texts on weather. The import of the saying, namely that people possessing a countryman's wisdom are capable of forecasting the weather of the day yet are unable to recognize the signs of God's plan for the future, can be interpreted in different ways. If the signs are taken to be premonitory clues concerning the advent of the Kingdom or the Parousia, they are unlikely to have proceeded from Jesus, who disapproved of giving advance notification (see Mark 8:12; Luke 17:20). But if they are related to the charismatic manifestations of Jesus' ministry or the messianic age, the passage conveying them may well be authentic (cf. Matt. 11:4–5; Luke 7:22).

46. The power of faith (Matt. 17:20; Luke 17:6)

For truly, I say to you, if you have faith as a grain of mustard seed, you will say to this mountain, 'Move from here to there', and it will move; and nothing will be impossible to you.

. . . you could say to this sycamine tree, 'Be rooted up, and be planted in the sea', and it would obey you (Luke).

The maxim stresses the limitless efficacy of faith/trust in the eschatological age. The details have been discussed in chapter 6, no. 1; cf. also no. 16 above.

47. Persecution of messengers (Matt. 23:34–36; Luke 11:49–51)

Therefore I send you prophets and wise men and scribes, some of whom you will kill and crucify, and some you will scourge in your synagogues and persecute from town to town, that upon you may come all the righteous blood shed on earth, from the blood of innocent Abel to the blood of Zechariah the son of Barachiah, whom you murdered between the sanctuary and the altar. Truly, I say to you, all this will come upon this generation (Matt.).

Therefore also the Wisdom of God said, 'I will send them prophets and apostles, some of whom they will kill and persecute', that the blood of all the prophets, shed from the foundation of the world, may be required of this generation, from the blood of Abel to the blood of Zechariah, who perished between the altar and the sanctuary. Yes, I tell you, it will be required of this generation (Luke).

The saying has already been discussed in chapter 5, no. 29. For further mention of persecution, see nos. 20 and 34 above. In conformity with the eschatological perspective of Jesus, the present generation is identified as the last one.

48. Lament over Jerusalem (Matt. 23:37–39; Luke 13:34–35)

O Jerusalem, Jerusalem, killing the prophets and stoning those who are sent to you! How often would I have gathered your children together as a hen gathers her brood under her wings, and you would not! Behold, your house is forsaken and desolate. For I tell you, you will not see me again until you say, 'Blessed is he who comes in the name of the Lord.'

The main problem with this lament arises from the mention of frequent attempts by Jesus to save the children of Jerusalem. If the chronology and the story line of the Synoptic Gospels are accepted, Jesus had only one short period of public activity in Jerusalem. Hence this moving poem of grief, which ends with a Beatitude, probably alludes to the Parousia, i.e. the arrival of one 'who comes in the name of the Lord'. It is therefore a composition most likely post-dating the time of the living Jesus and should be taken as a product of the early church.

On the other hand, some commentators advance the hypothesis that this text comes from a Jewish composition in which the speaker is the divine Wisdom (see Luke 11:49; chapter 5, no. 29). Assuming that this supposition is correct, the phrase, 'How often would I have gathered your children together', addressed to Jerusalem, would no longer constitute a problem since Jewish sapiential tradition holds that Lady Wisdom was continuously trying to advise and safeguard her children. The metaphor of the mother bird protecting the chicks under her wings is biblical (cf. Ps. 17:8; 36:7; 57:1, etc.) as well as rabbinic ('under the wings of the divine Presence (Shekhinah)').

For another lament on the women of Jerusalem and their children, see Luke 19:41–44 (cf. no. 60 below) and Luke 23:28–31 (cf. chapter 5, no. 40).

III. THE *M* TRADITION

49. Mission to Jews alone (Matt. 10:5–8; 15:24)

Go nowhere among the Gentiles, and enter no town of the Samaritans, but go rather to the lost sheep of the house of Israel. And preach as you go, saying, 'The kingdom of heaven is at hand.' Heal the sick, raise the dead, cleanse lepers, cast out demons. You received without paying, give without pay (Matt. 10).

I was sent only to the lost sheep of the house of Israel (Matt. 15).

Matthew attached to the account of the dispatch of the apostles on their first missionary journey a clause limiting their activity to Jews only, and expressly forbidding them to approach non-Jews, even Samaritans. The same restriction applied to the activity of Jesus himself; his mission was exclusively to the house of Israel (Matt. 15:24). As we have seen in the story of the Syrophoenician woman (Mark 7:27; cf. no. 6 above), charismatic healing outside the boundaries of the Holy Land was not part of his task as Jesus understood it. In 'I was sent', the sender is without any doubt God. Moreover, in the maxim outlawing the gift of holy things to dogs or the throwing of a pearl before swine (Matt. 7:6; see chapter 3, no. 32), by common consent the animals are recognized as symbols of the Gentiles.

Matthew explicitly and Mark implicitly assert (see Mark 7:27, the story of the Syrophoenician woman) that the missionary work of Jesus and of his envoys was meant only for Jews, with the explicit exclusion of Gentiles and Samaritans. This claim is in sharp contrast with the frequent assertion found elsewhere that the gospel was to be preached to all the nations of the world (Mark 14:9; 16:15; Matt. 24:14; 28:19; see nos. 20, 33 above, and 53 below). Indeed Matthew once goes so far as to declare that the Gentiles would occupy almost all the seats originally destined for the (Jewish) 'sons' at the eschatological banquet in God's Kingdom. The only Jews to be found there would be the patriarchs and the prophets of the Old Testament (Matt. 8:11–12; 21:43; Luke 13:28 in no. 37 above).

It can, then, be taken for granted that the activity of Jesus himself and of his disciples during his life was solely focused on Palestinian Jews, excluding pagans and Samaritans. Even on the rare occasions when he ventured outside Jewish territory, to the district of Tyre and Sidon and the area of the Decapolis beyond the river Jordan, he is never reported to have taught there. Nor do the Gospels include any hint that at some later stage he intended to broaden his appeal. In the circumstances the presence of diametrically opposite viewpoints in Mark and especially in Matthew demand an explanation.[23] For a full discussion of the issue, see chapter 10, pp. 376–80.

23. The issue does not present itself in the work of Luke, who was himself a Gentile and wrote from the point of view of non-Jewish Christianity.

50. The messengers represent Jesus (Matt. 10:40–41; cf. Luke 10:16)

He who receives you receives me, and he who receives me receives him who sent me. He who receives a prophet because he is a prophet shall receive a prophet's reward, and he who receives a righteous man because he is a righteous man shall receive a righteous man's reward (Matt.).

He who hears you hears me, and he who rejects you rejects me, and he who rejects me rejects him who sent me (Luke).

The account of the sending of the twelve apostles in Matthew and of the seventy disciples in Luke (Matt. 10:5–15; Luke 10:1–12; see no. 5 above) is followed and concluded by Jesus' statement that the envoys are his ambassadors. Friendly reception given to them amounts to welcoming Jesus himself, and beyond Jesus, God, whose messengers they are. No negative reaction is anticipated, which implies that Jesus foresaw a largely successful mission. The saying resembles Jesus' maxim that welcoming children is the equivalent of welcoming him (see Mark 9:37; Matt. 18:5; Luke 9:48 in no. 10 above).

51. The yoke of Jesus (Matt. 11:28–30)

Come to me, all who labour and are heavy laden, and I will give you rest. Take my yoke upon you, and learn from me; for I am gentle and lowly in heart, and you will find rest for your souls. For my yoke is easy and my burden is light.

This poignant maxim recalls Jesus ben Sira, the second-century BC author of the Book of Ecclesiasticus. According to this sage, Lady Wisdom invites people to come to her, find rest and accept her yoke (Ecclus. 6:26, 28, 30 [Hebrew]; 24:19; 51:26). A substantial scholarly opinion holds that Matthew 11:28–30 does not stem from Jesus, but is an excerpt from an otherwise unknown Jewish sapiential book. The term 'yoke', a common expression in rabbinic literature, is used only here in the Gospels and Jesus is nowhere else called 'lowly' (*tapeinos*). But the strongest argument against associating this saying with him is that much of his moral message was neither easy nor light. See chapter 9, nos. 5, 6, 12, 25.

52. Jesus on the use of force (Matt. 26:52; cf. Luke 22:35–38)

Put your sword back into its place; for all who take the sword, will perish by the sword (Matt.).

When I sent you out with no purse or bag or sandals, did you lack anything? . . . But now, let him who has a purse take it, and likewise a bag. And let him who has no sword sell his mantle and buy one. For I tell you that this scripture must be fulfilled in me, 'And he was reckoned with transgressors'; for what is written about me has its fulfilment. And they said, 'Look, Lord, here are two swords.' And he said to them, *It is enough* (Luke).

We are faced here with the controversial issue of Jesus' approach to the use of physical force. The disciple, unnamed in the Synoptics but identified as Peter in John 18:10, who had menacingly drawn his sword to defend his master was stopped by Jesus from using it. The saying as preserved in Matthew 26:52, 'all who take the sword, will perish by the sword', hands down a precept of non-violence which is in harmony with the well-known commands of Jesus, 'Do not resist one who is evil. But if anyone strikes you on the right cheek, turn to him the other also', and 'Love your enemies' (Matt. 5:39; Luke 6:29; Matt. 5:44; Luke 6:27; see chapter 3, no. 15; chapter 5, no. 21 and chapter 9, no. 12). A somewhat more equivocal use of 'sword' appears in the warning, 'I have not come to bring peace, but a sword' in Matthew 10:34 (see chapter 5, no. 24).

The real difficulty facing the interpreter arises from Luke's attempt to link the present saying with Luke 10:4, 'Carry no purse, no bag,' etc. (see no. 5 above). This suggests that just before his arrest, Jesus reversed the rules he earlier gave to his messengers and advised them to trade their mantle for a sword. As a result his apostles would from then on be the associates of someone considered a criminal in fulfilment of Isaiah 53:12, 'He was reckoned with transgressors' (see chapter 5, no. 39). When Jesus was informed that two of his disciples were already armed, he declared that to be enough.

Two main types of interpretation have been advanced, but I find neither of them very convincing. Luke 22:36 (the buying of a sword), together with Matthew 10:34 (Jesus brings not peace but a sword) and the actual act of violence by an apostle recorded in the Gethsemane story (Mark 14:47; Matt. 26:51; Luke 22:50; John 18:10), are cited as the New Testament basis of a theory which turns Jesus into a violent revolutionary, that is to say, a messianic pretender ready to lead an armed struggle against the Romans. Three arguments confute such a view. First and foremost, as has just been underlined, there is strong and almost unequivocal emphasis in Jesus' teaching on non-resistance and non-violence. Secondly, we must not forget the curious fact that in Luke's version of Matthew's 'I have not come to bring peace, but a sword' (Matt. 10:34), the word 'sword' is understood figuratively and replaced by 'division' (Luke 12:51). Thirdly, some interpreters consider the purchasing of a sword as one of those violent metaphors of which Jesus was fond. In that case, the words 'It is enough' signify, not Jesus' approval of the disciples' military preparedness, but his firm dismissal of the subject.

As a tentative solution of the conundrum created by Luke, I would consider the whole passage (Luke 22:35–38) ending with the mention of two swords as a preparation for the unexpected question put by the disciples to Jesus in Gethsemane, 'Lord, shall *we* strike with the sword?' (Luke 22:49). The question set by Luke in the plural presupposes that more than one apostle is armed. For a similar anticipation of an unexpected event, the arrangement by the risen Jesus for a rendezvous with his apostles in Galilee, compare Mark 14:28 with Mark 16:7 (cf. no. 31 above).

53. The universal mission of the apostles (Matt. 28:18–20; cf. Mark 16:15–16)

All authority in heaven and on earth has been given to me. Go therefore and make disciples of all nations, baptizing them in the name of the Father and of the Son and of the Holy Spirit, teaching them to observe all that I have commanded you; and lo, I am with you always, to the close of the age (Matt.).

Go into all the world and preach the gospel to the whole creation. He who believes and is baptized will be saved; but he who does not believe will be condemned (Mark).

For Mark 16:15–16, see no. 33 above.

The saying is ascribed to the risen Jesus appearing on a Galilean mountain, an event foretold in Mark (see no. 31 above), but attested exclusively in Matthew. The main message, viz. a worldwide mission of the envoys of Jesus, contradicts his prohibition on approaching non-Jews (see no. 49 above). In fact, the passage contains further ideas unrecorded elsewhere in the New Testament. Here Jesus claims all authority in heaven and on earth. Previously he is said to be endowed only with authority *on earth* to forgive sins (see chapter 2, no. 1).[24] In the earlier missionary programmes there was no question of baptism, let alone of baptizing all the nations. Moreover, baptism administered in the name of the Father, the Son and the Holy Spirit is unheard of not just in the Gospels but anywhere in the whole New Testament. The formula occurring in the Acts of the Apostles is baptism 'into' or 'in the name of' Jesus (Acts 2:38; 8:16; 10:48; 19:5), and baptism 'into Christ' in Paul (Rom. 6:3; Gal. 3:27). Outside Matthew, the trinitarian formula, Father, Son and Holy Spirit, first occurs in the early church manual entitled the Didache or Teaching of the Twelve Apostles, which is dated to the first half of the second century AD. All this points

24. The Messianic Apocalypse of Qumran may furnish a parallel when God's Messiah is described as one to whom heaven and earth listen (4Q521 fr. 2, line 1). However, the beginning of the line is missing and the lacuna may contain the subjects who in heaven and on earth are listening.

to a late Gentile-Christian origin for Matthew 28:18–20. Eschatological enthusiasm had already cooled down and the declaration 'I am with you always, to the close of the age' envisages, not an imminent Parousia, but a long-term future for the church and for its members initiated through baptism.

IV. THE *L* TRADITION

54. Power over the forces of evil (Luke 10:18–20)

I saw Satan fall like lightning from heaven. Behold, I have given you authority to tread upon serpents and scorpions, and over all the power of the enemy; and nothing shall hurt you. Nevertheless do not rejoice in this, that the spirits are subject to you; but rejoice that your names are written in heaven.

For an earlier treatment of the subject, see no. 33 above.

This paragraph forms the conclusion of the account of the mission successfully accomplished by the seventy/seventy-two disciples (see Luke 10:1–17; see also no. 5 above). Power over poisonous reptiles is thought to go hand-in-hand with the idea of dominion over wickedness, evil being typified by the serpent of Paradise in Genesis 3.

The childish pride of the apprentice healers and exorcists (Luke 10:17) demanded correction; if they felt happy, it had to be not on account of their victory over evil but because their names appear on God's heavenly register (cf. Exod. 32:32–33). To put their triumph in perspective, it was to be contemplated against the picture of Jesus beholding the fall of Satan from heaven. Note, however, that Jesus is not portrayed as the direct cause of Satan's downfall.

The passage is inspired by Isaiah 14:12, a dirge on the fall of the day star or Lucifer, and the image is fully developed in the Book of Revelation 12:9: 'And the great dragon was thrown down, that ancient serpent, who is called the Devil and Satan, the deceiver of the whole world.'

There is no need to interpret Jesus' statement as a claim to actual visionary experience. To shed further light on Luke 10:18–20, it should be mentioned that in popular Jewish religious tradition immunity to a snake bite was considered the supernatural privilege of charismatic holy men. Hanina ben Dosa, the first-century AD Galilean Hasid, was bitten by a snake while praying, but it was the snake, and not Hanina, that died at once (tBer 3:20; yBer 9a). In the New Testament St Paul's story provides a good illustration. When after his shipwreck he landed in Malta, all of a sudden a viper fastened on his hand. The onlookers expected him to drop dead, but he shook off the snake into the fire and remained unharmed. The Maltese bystanders immediately took him for a god (Acts 28:3–6).

55. Making the good choice (Luke 10:41–42)

Martha, Martha, you are anxious and troubled about many things; one thing is needful. Mary has chosen the good portion, which shall not be taken away from her.

This doctrine – the superiority of the Kingdom over mundane matters – is in harmony with Jesus' counsel not to be anxious as far as ordinary needs are concerned (Matt. 6:25; Luke 12:22; cf. chapter 3, no. 19). The story may be fictional, but the basic ideas expressed in the words of Jesus belong to the authentic kernel of his message.

56. Fire and baptism (Luke 12:49–50; Gospel of Thos. 10)

I came to cast fire upon the earth; and would that it were already kindled! I have a baptism to be baptized with; and how I am constrained until it is accomplished! (Luke).

I have cast fire upon the world, and behold I guard it until it is ablaze (Gospel of Thos.).

Two maxims have been placed by Luke before Jesus' announcement that family strife would follow his proclamation of the approaching Kingdom (see no. 21 above and chapter 5, no. 24). The link seems artificial and the connection between the sayings about fire and baptism requires some explanation. The two notions appear together in one of John the Baptist's predictions, namely that he who was to follow him would baptize with the Holy Spirit and fire (Matt. 3:11; Luke 3:16) or with the Holy Spirit (Mark 1:8). Since John's baptism with water aimed at producing repentance, baptism with fire is obviously understood to be a more powerful means of spiritual cleansing. Like a furnace, it would separate the dross and produce pure metal. Salting with fire is another metaphor to indicate eschatological purification (see Mark 9:49; Matt. 5:13; Luke 14:34; cf. chapter 3, no. 11). It is most likely therefore that in their original meaning the sayings represented a yearning for the prompt arrival of the great catharsis of the end-time. At a later stage, probably after the crucifixion, baptism became the symbol of self-sacrifice. It is in this sense that the phrase is used in Mark 10:38, 'Are you able to drink the cup that I drink, or to be baptized with the baptism with which I am baptized?' (see no. 15 above).

57. Lesson to be drawn from bloodshed and disaster (Luke 13:2–5)

Do you think that these Galileans were worse sinners than all the other Galileans, because they suffered thus? I tell you, No; but unless you repent, you will all likewise perish. Or those eighteen upon whom the tower in Siloam fell and killed them, do you think they were worse offenders than all the others who dwelt in Jerusalem? I tell you, No; but unless you repent you will all likewise perish.

Two events, an act of cruelty inflicted by Pontius Pilate on Galileans and the catastrophe resulting from the accidental collapse of a tower killing eighteen people in Jerusalem, are used by Jesus as a basis for drawing a moral lesson. The disasters did not affect particularly guilty people; but for the grace of God, anyone of Jesus' audience might have suffered the same fate. So they must turn away from sin at once, repentance must not be delayed. Neither the massacre of pilgrims from Galilee by the Roman governor nor the Siloam disaster is recorded outside Luke, but the brutality of Pilate is well known from Josephus (*War* 2:175–7; *Antiquities* 18:60–62). Note that the *Antiquities* passage listing Pilate's misdeeds[25] immediately precedes the *Testimonium Flavianum*, Josephus' short reference to Jesus (*Antiquities* 18:63–4).

58. The self-definition of Jesus (Luke 13:31–33)

Some Pharisees came, and said to him, 'Get away from here, for Herod wants to kill you.' And he said to them, *Go and tell that fox, 'Behold, I cast out demons and perform cures today and tomorrow, and on the third day I finish my course. Nevertheless, I must go on my way today and tomorrow and the day following; for it cannot be that a prophet should perish away from Jerusalem.'*

The passage is Luke's composition. It is inserted immediately before the lament on Jerusalem, murderess of prophets (see Luke 13:34–35; cf. no. 48 above). According to the evangelist some Pharisees warned Jesus that Herod Antipas, ruler of Galilee, was threatening his life. The purpose of the notice he is given is to explain why Jesus left Galilee and to present his departure as a deliberate step towards prophetic martyrdom in Jerusalem. This story contradicts what Luke writes elsewhere, namely that Antipas had entertained no animosity towards Jesus; on the contrary, he was curious to meet the famous healer (Luke 9:9; 23:8). Some interpreters of Luke wonder whether the threat signalled by the Pharisee messengers had any real basis, or whether it was a stratagem intended to frighten Jesus away from Herod's territory.

Some of the prophetic words attributed here to Jesus concerning his fate – the mention of three days and his death in Jerusalem – belong not to history, but to New Testament apologetics, as has been argued earlier (see chapter 7, nos. 12, 14–16). However, the contemptuous reference to the tetrarch of Galilee as 'that fox' could easily reflect the

25. The others are the introduction of the statue of the emperor into Jerusalem; the use of money from the Temple treasure for building an aqueduct; and the slaying of Jewish protesters (*Antiquities* 18:60–62).

sharp tongue of Jesus. The phrase could be completed to read something like 'that fox who imagines himself to be a lion', i.e. king.[26] Likewise the summing-up of his mission as 'casting out demons and performing cures' genuinely summarizes the quintessence of his Galilean activity.

59. The Kingdom comes without premonitory signs (Luke 17:20–21)

The kingdom of God is not coming with signs to be observed; nor will they say, 'Lo, here it is!' or 'There!' for behold, the kingdom of God is in the midst of you.

The question of signs has been discussed in no. 7 above, where it was noted that the expression 'in the midst of' (*entos*) should be understood as 'amid' rather than 'inside' you. As Jesus is not addressing his followers, he would hardly announce that the Kingdom of God was *within* unrepentant outsiders.

For the corresponding passage in the Gospel of Thomas 113, see no. 7, note 8 above.

60. Prophetic lament over the fall of Jerusalem (Luke 19:41–44)

And when he drew near and saw the city he wept over it, saying, *Would that even today you knew the things that make for peace! But now they are hid from your eyes. For the days shall come upon you, when your enemies will cast up a bank about you and surround you, and hem you in on every side, and dash you to the ground, you and your children within you, and they will not leave one stone upon another in you; because you did not know the time of your visitation.*

26. The metaphor is well known in rabbinic Hebrew: 'Be the tail of lions and be not the head of foxes' (mAb 4:15); 'Lion son of a fox' designates an outstanding person of lowly origin (yShab 12c).

Luke anticipates here, by means of a *vaticinium ex eventu* or prophecy after the fact, the situation which is fully developed in the Eschatological Discourse (see nos. 18–28 above). Luke and the Gentile church conceive of the destruction of Jerusalem as the divine punishment inflicted on the Jews for their refusal to recognize their 'visitation' by Jesus.

REFLECTIONS

In the comments that follow, the sayings attributed to Jesus on the subject of the Kingdom of God, the central topic of his teaching, are arranged under four headings. As I have observed at the beginning of this chapter, the Gospels contain no detailed description, let alone a proper definition, of what Jesus understood by the concept of the Kingdom of God. Instead he presents us in his customary existential fashion with an outline of the path leading to that Kingdom, also called now and again 'eternal life'. Nothing in the picture drawn by Jesus clashes with the culture and religion of the Judaism of his age. In fact all the features it contains fit perfectly in the canvas of late biblical and intertestamental eschatology preserved in Jewish literature between 200 BC and AD 100.

The sayings fall into four categories: (1) Jesus and the Kingdom; (2) Jesus' disciples and the Kingdom; (3) the arrival of the Kingdom; and (4) the citizens of the Kingdom.

1. Jesus and the Kingdom

Jesus is portrayed by the evangelists as God's ultimate herald of the Kingdom, who was assisted in his preaching mission by a small group of chosen disciples. His own teaching was accompanied and validated by charismatic acts, mostly healing and exorcism. The same activities were also performed by his apostles (nos. 2, 5, 11, 33, 43, 44, 54, 58). The immediate task of his mission was eschatological purification designated on one occasion as 'baptism of fire' (no. 56). The various accounts concerning the Lord's Supper are also connected with the Kingdom of God either in announcing its imminent coming or as an institutional reminder of Jesus' Passover 'sacrifice' (no. 30). A final significant indicator makes plain that while Jesus is recognized as the person empowered to usher in the Kingdom, it is God who will be in charge of it after its inauguration. Hence Jesus confessed that he had no say in the allocation of seats at the eschatological banquet (no. 15), nor did he know when H-hour would strike on the final D-day. It should also be made clear that this first group of texts includes no reference to the Second Coming of the crucified and risen Christ prior to the establishment of the Kingdom. The Parousia idea represents a later stage of doctrinal development in the early church.

2. *Jesus' disciples and the Kingdom*

Two roles, one positive, one negative, are assigned to the apostles and disciples recruited by Jesus to act as his assistants in the implementation of his God-given eschatological mandate.

Positively, the first move had to be repentance since Jesus and his circle followed in the footsteps of John the Baptist, the preacher of penitence (no. 1). Without repentance no progress towards the Kingdom was conceivable (no. 57). The next spiritual attribute they had to possess was complete trust in God, allowing charisma to flow and endowing prayer with efficacy (nos. 7, 16, 35, 46). The principal virtues they had to acquire were the simplicity and confidence of a child, the ideal heir of the Kingdom of God (no. 10). Envoys dispatched on a preaching and healing mission were instructed to rely completely on God; they should carry no money or supplies, and had to entrust themselves to the generosity of sympathetic listeners (no. 5, revised in no. 52). They were to be warmly received and well treated as ambassadors of Jesus (no. 50). The spiritual manifesto of the Beatitudes constituted their guide towards the Kingdom (no. 34). Insincere followers of Jesus together with those who actually denied him would be unmasked and rejected at the final judgement or after the Parousia (nos. 36, 39).

Negatively, the disciples of Jesus were expected to sever all bonds, including family ties, which might hinder them from following their master (nos. 14, 21). In this they had to imitate the example of Jesus, who distanced himself from his relations (nos. 3, 4). A further negative aspect of the disciples' destiny consisted in a constant threat of persecution by synagogues and councils, governors and kings (nos. 15, 20, 34, 47). They were like sheep sent among wolves (no. 38). This gloomy picture reflects the life of the early church in conflict with Gentiles and Jews rather than the circumstances in which Jesus and his companions found themselves. Indeed, the New Testament mentions neither any ill-treatment of the apostles during his life, nor their persecution by the Romans after the crucifixion.

3. The arrival of the Kingdom

The chronology of the advent of the Kingdom is a major issue in New Testament interpretation. A double picture emerges from the sources. On the one hand the arrival of the Kingdom was envisioned in the lifetime of Jesus and his contemporaries. On the other hand, the full realization of the reign of God was expected to take place after the Parousia or the return of Christ and the subsequent final judgement. The first alternative is expressed in sayings asserting that the Kingdom was 'at hand' and would be experienced by members of the living generation (nos. 1, 8, 27). It will follow close on the death of John the Baptist (nos. 9, 40, 41). In regard to premonitory signs, the sayings are divided. Some reject altogether the idea of signs (no. 7). Others, no doubt resulting from a prolonged period of waiting, and reflecting the need for comfort and reassurance, supply detailed indications to impatient believers concerning the nearness of the Second Coming. These signs reach their climax with the siege of Jerusalem and the destruction of the Temple in AD 70 (nos. 17, 18, 19, 32, 45, 48, 60), which were mistakenly thought to signal the immediate coming of the Kingdom.

Later Christian theology identified the arrival of the Kingdom of God with the establishment of the church. The Gospels themselves provide no basis for this idea which was first fully formulated in the time of St Augustine (354–430).

4. *The citizens of the Kingdom*

We are faced with two discrepant pictures regarding the identity of those who were to be admitted into the Kingdom. In the first representation, Jesus and his apostles address the gospel only to Jews; it is expressly forbidden to evangelize Gentiles and Samaritans (nos. 6, 49). The sayings of the second group, which reflect the circumstances of the early church, not only include non-Jews among the clientele of the apostles (but not of Jesus), but make them the main, indeed the sole, beneficiaries of the Christian preaching. At the royal banquet in the Kingdom only Gentile guests will sit at the table, with the exception of the saints of the Old Testament and, implicitly, the Jewish followers of Jesus, although by that time this Judaeo-Christian minority would no longer be counted as Jews (nos. 20, 29, 33, 37, 53).

This sketch of the eschatological message of the Synoptic Gospels will be supplemented in the next chapter by an account of the special rules of conduct laid down by Jesus for those who intended to follow the arduous path towards the Kingdom of God.

A final glance must be cast on the distribution of the Kingdom references in the sources of the Synoptic Gospels. They appear across the whole spectrum. The bulk, thirty-three out of sixty, are found in Mark, followed by Matthew–Luke (*Q*) with fifteen items. The special material of Matthew (*M*) and Luke (*L*) exhibit respectively five and seven attestations. The general conclusion is that the Kingdom of God concept is solidly embedded in all the layers of the gospel tradition. It is at the heart of the message of Jesus.

9

Eschatological Rules of Behaviour

To complete the picture of the eschatological teaching of Jesus we must cast a final glance at the special instructions on ethical and social conduct which according to the Synoptic evangelists Jesus gave to his close followers. These rules were meant to guide them during the crucial period leading to the establishment of the Kingdom of God. They represent Jesus' particular understanding and interpretation of Jewish law and morality. Contemporary New Testament scholars, especially Rudolf Bultmann and his followers, assign most of these sayings to the early church and see in them regulations concerned with the life of the first Christian communities, who were anxiously awaiting the impending return of Christ at the Parousia. It is possible, however, to envisage these precepts and commandments as primarily relating to the generation of Jesus himself. Some of the topics are directly connected with the Torah, such as its permanent validity, the question of healing on the Sabbath, the meaning of uncleanness, etc. Other sayings either reinterpret and internalize the Law of Moses on divorce, adultery, sexual abstinence and oaths, or determine Jesus' favourite path to true piety consisting in the practice of humility and in the avoidance of violence, ostentatiousness and conceit.

Maxims already discussed under different headings in the course of the previous chapters will now be treated succinctly and only in an eschatological perspective.

I. MARK AND THE TRIPLE TRADITION

1. Man is superior to the Sabbath (Mark 2:27–28; Matt. 12:8; Luke 6:5; cf. Matt. 12:11–12; Luke 14:5; 13:15)

The sabbath was made for man, not man for the sabbath (Mark); *so the son of Man is lord even of the sabbath.*

What man of you, if he has one sheep and it falls into a pit on the sabbath, will not lay hold of it and lift it out? Of how much more value is a man than a sheep! (Matt.).

Which of you, having a son or an ox that has fallen into a well, will not immediately pull him out on a sabbath day? (Luke 14).

Does not each of you on the sabbath untie his ox or his ass from the manger, and lead it away to water it? (Luke 13).

These sayings have been examined in the context of polemics in the light of parallel Jewish traditions in chapter 2, no. 3, and in association with the 'son of man' topic in chapter 7, no. 2. The parallels in Matthew 12:11–12 and Luke 14:5 have been dealt with in chapter 2, no. 6, and the passage of Luke 13:15 in chapter 2, no. 5.

In addition to what has already been said in the earlier sections, it should be noted that by elevating man with his corporeal and spiritual needs, and even domestic animals, above the rules of an unenlightened and servile observance of ritual laws, Jesus stressed the necessity for the right order of priorities in the search for the Kingdom. At a later stage in the Gentile church, this reassessment of religious obligations was mistaken for a deliberate condemnation of the practices of the Jewish religion. But such was not the intention of Jesus.

2. Performing acts of healing on the Sabbath (Mark 3:4; Matt. 12:12; Luke 6:9)

Is it lawful on the sabbath to do good or to do harm, to save life or to kill?

For an examination of this question in Mark and Luke – in Matthew it is transformed into a statement – see chapter 2, no. 4, and chapter 3, no. 15.

The essence of the teaching emphasizes the precedence of charismatic healing over ordinary Sabbath observance. To those of Jesus' followers and sympathizers who shared his eschatological outlook the claim made obvious sense, but it sounded shocking to some conventionally-minded Jews and even to later Jewish Christians in a period when the expectation of the Kingdom of God was no longer an urgent issue.

3. Rules for missionaries (Mark 6:8–11; Matt. 10:9–15; Luke 9:3–5; cf. Luke 10:4–11)

See chapter 8, no. 5.

4. The source of uncleanness (Mark 7:15, 18–23; Matt. 15:11, 17–20)

There is nothing outside a man which by going into him can defile him, but the things which come out of a man are what defile him (Mark).

Not what goes into the mouth defiles a man, but what comes out of the mouth, this defiles a man (Matt.).

Do you not see that whatever goes into a man from outside cannot defile him, since it enters, not his heart but his stomach, and so passes on? . . . What comes out of a man is what defiles a man. For from within, out of the heart of a man, come evil thoughts [*murder, adultery* (Matt.)], *fornication, theft, murder, adultery* [*false witness, slander* (Matt.)], *coveting, wickedness, deceit, licentiousness, envy, slander, pride, foolishness. All these evil things come from within and they defile a man* [*but to eat with unwashed hands does not defile a man* (Matt.)] (Mark, Matt.).

The beginning of the account, 'Why do your disciples ... eat with hands defiled' (Mark 7:5) and Matthew's final clause (Matt. 15:20) form the conclusion of the debate about hand-washing, and have already been examined in chapter 2, no. 8.

The main part of the saying represents a hyperbolical internalization of impurity, the real cause of which is declared to be primarily moral and only secondarily ceremonial. Ritually unclean food which enters through the mouth, let alone pure food touched by unwashed hands, cannot according to Jesus lastingly affect a person's condition because everything that enters through the mouth is soon evacuated from the body. On the other hand, the various kinds of moral evil listed by him proceed from the depth of the heart. They contaminate the person who harbours them as well as anyone influenced by this person. We are witnessing here the general moralizing tendency which Jesus adopted in continuity with the prophets of the Hebrew Bible. The same line was often embraced by the later rabbis (see Vermes, *The Religion of Jesus the Jew*, 44–5). It follows from these remarks that the interpretation of the text offered by a good many New Testament scholars, namely that Jesus formally spoke against and rejected the dietary laws of Judaism, is misconceived. The words of Mark (7:19), 'Thus he [Jesus] declared all foods clean', did not come from Jesus, but were inserted as a gloss by the editor of the Gospel. His aim was to overcome Gentile Christian worries about the compulsory character of the Jewish dietary laws. The earliest history of the Palestinian Jesus movement shows that the apostles and all the Jewish disciples remained faithful observers of the traditional food regulations. In the Acts of the Apostles we hear Peter declare, 'I have never eaten anything that is common or unclean' (Acts 10:14). The same Peter, having adopted a more elastic attitude towards non-kosher meals in the mixed Jewish-Gentile church of Antioch, reverted to ancestral practice in the presence of a delegation sent to Syria by the rigorously traditionalist James, the brother of the Lord. As a result, Peter was accused by Paul of hypocrisy (Gal. 2:11–14). Needless to say, this Gospel passage must not be read in the light of the freedom from ceremonial laws of the Old Testament preached by Paul to his non-Jewish audiences in the diaspora.

5. The doctrine of self-sacrifice (Mark 8:34–37; Matt. 16:24–26; Luke 9:23–25; cf. Matt. 10:38; Luke 14:27)

If any man would come after me, let him deny himself and take up his cross [*daily* (Luke)] *and follow me. For whoever would save his life will lose it; and whoever loses his life for my sake and the gospel's will save it* [*find it* (Luke)]. *For what does it profit a man, to gain the whole world and forfeit* [*loses or forfeits* (Luke)] *his life?* [*For what can a man give in return of his life?* (Mark, Matt.).]

He who does not take his cross and follow me is not worthy of me (Matt. 10).

Whoever does not bear his own cross and come after me cannot be my disciple (Luke 14).

The appended proverb, 'For what does it profit a man, to gain the whole world and forfeit his life?' (Mark 8:36–37; Matt. 16:26; Luke 9:25) has been dealt with in chapter 3, no. 9.

The saying about taking up the cross sums up Jesus' teaching about the need to surrender everything in the interest of the Kingdom of God. (For the same doctrine, see the parables of the hidden treasure and the precious pearl in chapter 4, nos. 18 and 19, and no. 6 below.) Carrying one's cross is a metaphor symbolizing readiness for total self-sacrifice. The message is addressed to the immediate followers of Jesus. The life saved is the life which is to be enjoyed in the Kingdom, life and Kingdom being synonyms (see no. 6 below). Later the saying was understood as applying to the moral behaviour of Christians in the church. Linked to this is the gloss in Mark concerning losing one's life for the sake of *the gospel*, i.e. the proclamation of the good news by church missionaries, which is absent from both Matthew and Luke.

The mention of taking up one's cross does not allude exclusively to Jesus' own fate; crucifixion occurred frequently in Roman Palestine. For example, Publius Quinctilius Varus, governor of Syria, executed by crucifixion 2,000 Jewish revolutionaries caught in the country after the rebellion which followed the death of Herod the Great in 4 BC (Josephus, *War* 2:75). Earlier, in 88 BC, the Hasmonaean priest-king Alexander Jannaeus crucified in Jerusalem 800 Pharisees (*War* 1:96–8; *Antiquities* 13:380–83). The Qumran Temple Scroll (11QTemple 64:6–13) and the Nahum Commentary (4QpNah 1:7–8) most probably allude to crucifixion when they speak of hanging alive on the tree the traitors of the Jewish nation. The midrash Genesis Rabbah 56:3 describes Isaac carrying wood for the sacrifice which Abraham was to offer on Mount Moriah (Gen. 22:6) as someone bearing his cross on his shoulder.

6. The doctrine of self-mutilation (Mark 9:43–48; Matt. 18:8–9; cf. Matt. 5:29–30)

And if your hand [*or your foot* (Matt.)] *causes you to sin, cut it off* [*and throw it away* (Matt.)]; *it is better for you to enter life maimed* [*or lame* (Matt.)] *than with two hands* [*or two feet* (Matt.)] *to go to Gehenna, to the unquenchable fire. And if your foot causes you to sin, cut it off; it is better for you to enter life lame than with two feet to be thrown into Gehenna. And if your eye causes you to sin, pluck it out* [*and throw it away* (Matt.)]; *it is better for you to enter the kingdom of God* [*to enter life* (Matt.)] *with one eye than with two eyes to be thrown into Gehenna, where their worm does not die and the fire is not quenched.*

The last two verses (Mark 9:47–48), including their allusion to worm and fire in Isaiah 66:24, have been considered in chapter 5, no. 8.

The message here, as in the previous unit, concerns the absolute priority to be given to the needs of the Kingdom, the latter being short for life in the Kingdom. These sacrifices are depicted in all their shocking and gory details. It is better to get rid of a hand, a foot or an eye which hinders one's entry into the Kingdom of God than to end up in hell with a whole body. The metaphor of plucking out one's eye is associated with the Semitic idiom 'to follow your eyes (or lustful eyes)', indicating acts inspired by illicit sexual desire. The expression is commonly used in the Dead Sea Scrolls and in rabbinic literature (see Matt. 5:28 in chapter 5, no. 32, and in no. 18 below). The imagery reaches its climax with the hyperbolical counsel of self-castration in Matthew 19:12 (see no. 25 below).

7. Prohibition or restriction of divorce (Mark 10:11–12; Matt. 19:9; cf. Matt. 5:32; Luke 16:18)

Whoever divorces his wife [except for unchastity (Matt.)] *and marries another, commits adultery against her; and if she divorces her husband and marries another, she commits adultery.*

... and he who marries a woman divorced from her husband commits adultery (Luke).

The question of the legitimacy of divorce has been discussed in chapter 2, no. 9, and chapter 5, no. 6.

The absolute prohibition for a man to dismiss his wife, as distinct from the exception clause of fornication inserted by Matthew, corresponds to the idea of restoring in the final, messianic age the primeval ideal of the garden of Eden where one man and one woman were to form an indissoluble union of one flesh. This explains Jesus' insistence on the maintenance of the marital bond in the period leading to a new Paradise with the arrival of the Kingdom. A similar ban on divorce in Paul's church in Corinth in the days preceding the return of Christ at the Parousia is stated in 1 Corinthians 7:10–11. For the details of Jesus' teaching on divorce, including Mark's surprising assertion that a woman could initiate the proceedings, see chapter 2, no. 9, and chapter 5, no. 6. The rigorous doctrine taught by Jesus, even with the exception clause legitimizing divorce from a fornicating wife, provoked complete puzzlement on the part of his disciples, who thought that without the possibility of divorce it was 'not expedient to marry' (Matt. 19:10; see no. 25 below).

8. Giving up property (Mark 10:18–19; cf. vv. 21, 23, 25; Matt. 19:17, 21; cf. vv. 23–24; Luke 18:20, 22; cf. vv. 24–25)

See chapter 8, no. 14.

9. Giving up family (Mark 10:29–30; Matt. 19:28–29; Luke 18:29)

See chapter 8, no. 3.

II. THE Q TRADITION

10. Reconciliation before a court hearing (Matt. 5:25–26; Luke 12:58–59)

Make friends quickly with your accuser, while you are going with him to court, lest your accuser hand you over to the judge, and the judge to the guard, and you be put in prison; truly, I say to you, you will never get out till you have paid the last penny [*copper* (Luke)].

For earlier treatments of the saying see chapter 3, no. 13, and chapter 4, no. 7. For a similar injunction to seek instant reconciliation, see Matthew 18:15; Luke 17:3 in no. 15 below.

The details of judge, guard and prison seem to point to an ordinary social context. As noted earlier (see chapter 3, no. 13, and the parable of the cruel servant in chapter 4, no. 22), imprisonment for debt is not a known penalty in ancient Jewish law. So while the advice to make an instant settlement conforms to Jesus' ideas, the details of the punishment are likely to stem from the non-Jewish legal setting of the Gentile church.

11. Against retaliation (Matt. 5:38–42; Luke 6:29–30)

You have heard that it was said, 'An eye for an eye and a tooth for a tooth.' But I say to you, Do not resist one who is evil. But if anyone strikes you on the right cheek, turn to him the other also; and if any one would sue you and take your coat, let him have your cloak as well; and if anyone forces you to go one mile, go with him two miles. Give to him who begs from you, and do not refuse him who would borrow from you (Matt.).

To him who strikes you on the cheek, offer the other also; and from him who takes away your coat do not withhold even your shirt. Give to everyone who begs from you; and of him who takes away your goods do not ask them again (Luke).

The principle of non-retaliation has been treated in chapter 3, no. 14, and chapter 5, no. 21.

Employing his usual hyperbolical style, Jesus recommends in the perspective of the approaching Kingdom a Gandhi type of passive resistance, and an endeavour to shame a violent opponent into an attitude of repentance and generosity by granting him much more than he has demanded. Jesus' extreme teaching goes beyond the degree of magnanimity preached by the early rabbis, whose doctrine is preserved in the Talmud (bShab 88b). They simply recommended that the insulted person should abstain from insult in return. The difference between the two formulations may be due to the fact that the rabbis lived in the real world while the atmosphere surrounding Jesus was filled with abnormal eschatological fever.

12. The commandment to love one's enemies (Matt. 5:43–48; Luke 6:27–28, 32–36)

You have heard that it was said, 'You shall love your neighbour and hate your enemy.' But I say to you, Love your enemies and pray for those who persecute you, so that you may be sons of your Father who is in heaven; for he makes his sun rise on the evil and on the good, and sends rain on the just and on the unjust. For if you love those who love you, what reward have you? Do not even the tax-collectors do the same? And if you salute only your brethren, what more are you doing than others? Do not even the Gentiles do the same? You, therefore, must be perfect, as your heavenly Father is perfect (Matt.).

But I say to you that hear, Love your enemies, do good to those who hate you, bless those who curse you, pray for those who abuse you . . . If you love those who love you, what credit is that to you? For even sinners love those who love them. And if you do good to those who do good to you, what credit is that to you? For even sinners do the same. And if you lend to those from whom you hope to receive, what credit is that to you? Even sinners lend to sinners, to receive as much again. But love your enemies, and do good, and lend, expecting nothing in return; and your reward will be great, and you will be sons of the Most High; for he is kind to the ungrateful and the selfish. Be merciful, even as your Father is merciful (Luke).

The problem of the love of one's enemy has already been dealt with in chapter 3, no. 15, and chapter 5, no. 22.

This is the most overstated of all the hyperboles of Jesus. The interpretative details having been discussed in the earlier sections, it now remains to evaluate the teaching within the general context of the morality of the eschatological-messianic age. Both in Matthew and in Luke, the fundamental aim of the message is to give an extreme definition to the love which can turn a person into a child of God: 'so that you may be sons of your Father who is in heaven' (Matt. 5:45), 'and you will be sons of the Most High' (Luke 6:35). However, although their purpose is the same, the way in which to achieve it is differently described by the two evangelists. In Matthew's 'be perfect, as your heavenly Father is perfect', the main stress is laid on modelling one's conduct on that of God, who shows equal kindness and generosity to the wicked and the good, to the unrighteous and the virtuous. Hence the disciple is enjoined to extend his love beyond his friends and family so as to comprehend those who are the least dear to him, his enemies. The same argument is advanced in Luke too: 'Be merciful, even as your Father is merciful', but the emphasis is on the principle of disinterested love, the only love which earns merit and qualifies someone to be called a son of God. The doctrine of the imitation of God is fully illustrated in Matthew's parable of the last judgement (Matt. 25:35–36), mentioning the feeding of the hungry, giving drink to the thirsty, sheltering the stranger, etc. (see chapter 4, no. 26). Its ultimate source is Leviticus 19:2, 'You shall be holy; for I the Lord your God am holy', and the rule laid down in Deuteronomy 11:22 explaining that the love of God is to be implemented by 'walking in all his ways'. This concept of the imitation of God expressed in the New Testament finds a splendid later echo in the Talmud (bSotah 14a). There the heavenly Father is described as clothing the naked (Adam and Eve), visiting the sick (Abraham), comforting the mourner (Isaac) and burying the dead (Moses).

The precept of loving one's enemy is the climax of the hyperbolical teaching of Jesus regarding the right ethical behaviour on the eve of the advent of the Kingdom.

13. Severing family ties (Matt. 10:37; Luke 14:26)

See chapter 8, no. 3.

14. Saving of life overrides the Sabbath (Matt. 12:11–12; Luke 14:5)

See no. 1 above.

15. The duty to rebuke an erring brother (Matt. 18:15, 22; Luke 17:3–4)

If your brother sins against you, go and tell him his fault, between you and him alone. If he listens to you, you have gained your brother . . . Jesus said to him [Peter asking how often should one forgive], *I do not say to you seven times, but seventy times seven* [or rather *seventy-seven times*] (Matt.).

If your brother sins, rebuke him, and if he repents, forgive him; and if he sins against you seven times in the day, and turns to you seven times, and says, 'I repent', you must forgive him (Luke).

The original teaching attributed to Jesus, appropriate to the eschatological conditions of his age, recommends promptness and generosity in forgiving an offender. With the changed circumstances of the early church, the mode of rebuke is formalized (see Matt. 18:16–19 in no. 24 below). The figure of seventy-seven times (Matt. 18:22) is a customary exaggeration modelled on Genesis 4:24, 'If Cain is avenged sevenfold, truly Lamech seventy-sevenfold.' However, by applying a twist it indicates how often one has to forgive rather than the maximum number of permitted acts of vengeance.

III. THE *M* TRADITION

16. The permanence of the Torah (Matt. 5:17–20; cf. Luke 16:17)

Think not that I have come to abolish the law and the prophets; I have come not to abolish them but to fulfil them. For truly, I say to you, till heaven and earth pass away, not an iota, not a dot, will pass away from the law until all is accomplished. Whoever then relaxes one of the least of these commandments and teaches men so, shall be called least in the kingdom of heaven; but he who does them and teaches them shall be called great in the kingdom of heaven. For I tell you, unless your righteousness exceeds that of the scribes and Pharisees, you will never enter the kingdom of heaven.

But it is easier for heaven and earth to pass away, than for one dot of the law to become void (Luke).

The main purpose of this famous dictum is to define the status of the traditional Jewish religion during the ministry of Jesus in the run-up period to the Kingdom of God. Judaism is identified as 'the law and the prophets', but with the Law playing the dominant part. The eschatological perspective is made manifest by the threefold repetition of the 'kingdom of heaven' in Matthew 5:19–20. At first sight, the implied message is that there will be no change in the Law, no new Torah, during the final run-up period to the Kingdom. To this we need to add strict fidelity to the 'least . . . commandments'. These are to be observed, not in the manner taught by the scribes, but no doubt in the 'ethicized' understanding of the precepts. In other words, the duty to observe the individual laws is derived from the general notion of obedience to God.

This view, however, clashes with accepted scholarly ideas on two counts. In the first instance, already on the New Testament level, Matthew sees in Jesus a new Moses, and in the Sermon on the Mount an eternally valid new Torah. This understanding is confirmed by the saying of the Eschatological Discourse, 'Heaven and earth will pass away, but *my words* will not pass away' (Matt. 24:35; Mark 13:31; Luke 21:33), which is construed on the pattern of 'till heaven and earth pass away, not an iota, not a dot, will pass from *the law*' (Matt. 5:18). Secondly, it is an opinion held by many New Testament interpreters that Matthew 5:17–20 represents, not the stance of Jesus, but the viewpoint of his Palestinian Jewish followers in their polemic with Paul and the Gentile Christian church. A close scrutiny of the relevant passages regarding the lasting validity of the Torah reveals, however, that the basic saying comes from Jesus. This is shown by the attempts of the later editors of the Gospels to undermine Jesus' assertion of the permanence of the Law in its minute details, i.e. to its last iota or tittle.[1] Supplementary words introduced into Matthew and Luke try to set a limit to the age in which the Torah remains obligatory. In contradiction to Matthew 5:18 and Luke 16:17, both asserting that nothing in the Law will become void, the editorial glosses claim that the Torah has ended with John the Baptist: 'The law and the prophets

1. The iota or *yod* is the smallest letter of the Hebrew alphabet and the dot or tittle (*qots*, hook, or *keter*, crown) designates an artistic embellishment used in scribal calligraphy.

were until John; since then the good news of the kingdom of God is preached' (Luke 16:16). Again, 'For all the prophets and the law prophesied until John' (Matt. 11:13). Such later alterations were necessitated by the requirements of the non-Jewish church whose members no longer considered themselves subject to the burdensome rules of the Jewish religion. On the other hand, the fact that the non-Jewish Luke, addressing a Gentile Christian audience, still felt compelled to maintain that 'it is easier for heaven and earth to pass away, than for one dot of the law to become void' (Luke 16:17) speaks powerfully in favour of Jesus as the source of the logion.

17. Overcoming anger and the duty of swift reconciliation (Matt. 5:21–24)

You have heard that it was said to the men of old, 'You shall not kill; and whoever kills shall be liable to judgement.' But I say to you that every one who is angry with his brother shall be liable to judgement; whoever insults his brother shall be liable to the council, and whoever says, 'You fool!' shall be liable to the Gehenna of fire. So if you are offering your gift at the altar, and there remember that your brother has something against you, leave your gift there before the altar and go; first be reconciled to your brother, and then come and offer your gift.

The antithesis section (Matt. 5:21–23) and the Bible interpretation it contains have been investigated in chapter 5, no. 31.

Envisaged from the point of view of moral conduct, the main peculiarity of the passage consists in declaring that anger is the mainspring from which all hostile behaviour towards one's fellow derives, ranging from mere insult to the climax which is murder. The saying typifies Jesus' tendency to go straight to the heart of the matter, the inward motivation of moral action.

The command to interrupt the performance of an offering in the Temple as soon as one recalls an offence which has not yet been put right further illustrates the emphasis of Jesus on inner morality over ritual, including Temple worship. In this he is the heir and true embodiment of both the prophetic tradition and charismatic spirituality. Reference to an offering in the Jerusalem sanctuary also points to the age of Jesus rather than to the period of the Gospels. The Synoptics were all completed after the destruction of the Temple and the city of Jerusalem in AD 70, and consequently after the termination of all acts of worship in the Temple.

There is no reason to restrict the concept of the 'brother' with whom one is angry or whom one has insulted to a member of the church. In the Gospel context and on the lips of Jesus, the word would naturally designate a fellow Jew. The passage is entirely meaningful in the normal eschatological perspective of Jesus. The interpretation which transfers it to a church setting is more likely to be secondary.

18. Prevention of adultery by controlling sinful desire (Matt. 5:27–30)

You have heard that it was said, 'You shall not commit adultery.' But I say to you that every one who looks at a woman lustfully has already committed adultery with her in his heart. If your right eye causes you to sin, pluck it out and throw it away; it is better that you lose one of your members than that your whole body be thrown into Gehenna. And if your right hand causes you to sin, cut it off and throw it away; it is better that you lose one of your members than that your whole body go into Gehenna.

For the antithesis in Matthew 5:27–28, see chapter 5, no. 32. The counsel of self-mutilation has been treated in no. 6 above.

To prevent sin actually happening, the eschatological ethics of Jesus enjoin resistance to adultery's inward motive, the thought of lust. Hence the insistence on the concept of self-sacrifice in order to overcome all sinful tendencies. Jesus was not the first proponent of the idea of equivalence between lustful looks and adultery committed in the heart. It can already be found two centuries before the Gospel of Matthew in the Book of Jubilees: 'See that no woman commits fornication with her eyes or her heart' (Jub. 20:4).

19. Avoidance of oaths (Matt. 5:33–37)

Again you have heard that it was said to the men of old, 'You shall not swear falsely, but shall perform to the Lord what you have sworn.' But I say to you, Do not swear at all, either by heaven, for it is the throne of God, or by the earth, for it is his footstool, or by Jerusalem, for it is the city of the great King. And do not swear by your head, for you cannot make one hair white or black. Let what you say be simply 'Yes' or 'No'; anything more than this comes from evil.

For the interpretation of the biblical text and the Jewish anti-oath context see chapter 5, no. 33.

The teaching contained in this passage is not original, but as has been shown echoes Essene and rabbinic ideas. Nevertheless it is all of one piece with Jesus' main eschatological outlook, which seeks to go beyond the mainstream understanding and practice of the Torah. Early Jewish Christianity fully echoes the message, as can be seen in the Letter of James 5:12, 'Do not swear, either by heaven or by earth or with any other oath, but let your yes be yes and your no be no.' As for the phrase 'to swear by the head' of someone, it reflects a Jewish-Aramaic idiom. According to Targum Neofiti on Gen. 44:18, oaths are made 'on the life of the head' of Pharaoh and of Jacob.

20. No ostentation in piety: 1. Almsgiving (Matt. 6:1–4; cf. Gospel of Thos. 62)

Beware of practising your piety before men in order to be seen by them; for then you will have no reward from your Father who is in heaven. Thus when you give alms, sound no trumpet before you, as the hypocrites do in the synagogues and in the streets, that they may be praised by men. Truly I say to you, they have received their reward. But when you give alms, do not let your left hand know what your right hand is doing, so that your alms may be in secret; and your Father who sees in secret will reward you.

That which your right hand will do, let not your left hand know what it does (Gospel of Thos.).

The series of sayings assembled in Matthew 6 offer a positive counterpart to the hypocritical religious behaviour illustrated elsewhere (see chapter 2, no. 15, chapter 4, no. 40, and chapter 5, no. 34).

The main quality of true piety lies in its being directed towards God alone and kept hidden from the gaze of men. The key phrase here and in the next two sections is 'in secret'.[2] In other words, in the eyes of Jesus genuine devotion, performed exclusively for the sake of God, is by definition individual, personal and private. If it is enacted in public with a view to impressing other people, it becomes as valueless as love which seeks human reward (see no. 12 above). Consequently almsgiving must not be trumpeted but should be done discreetly with only God witnessing it. With typical exaggeration Jesus suggests that not even the donor should be conscious of his good deed: the left hand should not be aware of the action performed by the right hand. Depositing gifts in secret is also mentioned in rabbinic literature, but the purpose of secrecy is different. The Mishnah advises tactful benefactors to leave their gifts in the special 'chamber of secrets' in the Temple where the shy poor could help themselves without having to face the donors (mSheq 5:6). These benefactors were not intent on fighting hypocrisy by anti-hypocrisy, but were motivated by consideration for the sensitivities of the needy.

21. No ostentation in piety: 2. Prayer (Matt. 6:5–8)

And when you pray, you must not be like the hypocrites; for they love to stand and pray in the synagogues and at the street corners, that they may be seen by men. Truly, I say to you, they have received their reward. But when you pray, go into your room and shut the door and pray to your Father who is in secret; and your Father who sees in secret will reward you. And in

2. Some Matthew manuscripts mistakenly contrast God's seeing in secret with his rewarding openly. In the context the emphasis is laid exclusively on the secrecy element in the pious act.

praying do not heap up empty phrases as the Gentiles do; for they think that they will be heard for their many words. Do not be like them, for your Father knows what you need before you ask him.

For Jesus' advice on prayer with its ramifications in Jewish literature, see chapter 6, no. 7.

Just as with almsgiving, genuine prayer too should be strictly between the individual and God. Nothing is said in the Gospels about the view of Jesus on Temple or synagogue worship, on public prayer, or on individual prayer in public places. His eyes were focused on unwitnessed personal piety.

22. No ostentation in piety: 3. Fasting (Matt. 6:16–18)

And when you fast, do not look dismal, like the hypocrites, for they disfigure their faces that their fasting may be seen by men. Truly, I say to you, they have received their reward. But when you fast, anoint your head and wash your face, that your fasting may not be seen by men, but by your Father who is in secret; and your Father who sees in secret will reward you.

Instead of making themselves look miserable and thus publicizing their fasting, the truly pious followers of Jesus were encouraged to disguise asceticism and self-denial. Instead of following the custom of covering themselves with ashes (Dan. 9:3; 1 Macc. 3:47; Josephus, *Antiquities* 20:89), and abstaining from washing and from anointing themselves (mTaan 1:5), they were advised to cleanse their faces, pour oil on their heads, and thus appear normal. Jesus dispensed with the external signs of fasting, convinced as he was that God could read the secrets of the heart and recognize genuine spirituality.

Nowhere is the Gospel of Thomas more obviously contrary to the authentic message of Jesus than in its distortion of his teaching about genuine religiousness. Compare Jesus' praise for true Jewish forms of piety in Matthew 6:1–8, 16–18, with the Gospel of Thomas 14: 'Jesus said to them, "If you fast, you will bring sin upon yourselves, and if you pray, you will be condemned, and if you give alms, you will harm your spirits.' '[3]

23. The church built on Peter, the Rock (Matt. 16:17–19)

Blessed are you, Simon Bar-Jona! For flesh and blood has not revealed this to you, but my Father who is in heaven. And I tell you, you are Peter, and on this rock I will build my church, and the gates of Hades shall not prevail against it. I will give you the keys of the kingdom of heaven, and whatever you bind on earth shall be bound in heaven, and whatever you loose on earth shall be loosed in heaven.

The promise made to Simon, known as Peter, is the only passage in the Gospels where Jesus speaks of establishing a church. Also, whereas Peter is regularly depicted as the senior member or leader of the inner circle of Jesus, it is here alone that he is presented as the foundation stone of the community which was created by Jesus. The Greek term *ekklesia* (church) first appears in the Gospels at Matthew 16:18 and recurs only on one more occasion, in Matthew 18:17. The question of the authenticity of this momentous notion will be examined in no. 24 below.

In Matthew 16:17 Simon Bar-Jona is recognized as a man inspired by God to reveal that Jesus is the Messiah. He is rewarded in return by being declared the foundation stone of a new institution capable of resisting the attacks of the forces of hell. The Greek 'gates of Hades' is the equivalent of the Hebrew 'gates of Sheol', i.e. the underworld. From his first appearance in the Gospel story, Simon had been known by his Aramaic nickname, Cephas (*kepha*, rock), translated into Greek as *petros* (rock = Peter). St Paul designates him Cephas eight times and calls him Peter only once. It is to be assumed therefore that an already familiar sobriquet is used in the pun of Jesus in which Simon is called

3. It is amusing to note that some members of the Californian Jesus Seminar voted in favour of the authenticity of the Gospel of Thomas 14:1–3, but even in that peculiar company the majority thought otherwise. Cf. R. W. Funk, R. W. Hoover and the Jesus Seminar, *The Five Gospels* (San Francisco, 1997), 481.

the rock on which the stronghold of the church would stand. For the metaphor of rock as a symbol of solid construction in the Bible and at Qumran, see chapter 4, no. 8.

Peter is also entrusted with a twofold power. He receives the keys which open and lock the gates of the Kingdom of God, and the power of 'binding and loosing'. The image of the key is biblical and symbolizes authority. Eliakim, the newly-appointed chief minister of King Hezekiah (715–687 BC), had the key of the House of David placed on his shoulder (Isa. 22:22). One may infer therefore that Matthew's Peter, as leader of the disciples of Jesus, was empowered to admit or exclude people from the Kingdom of heaven.

The metaphor of 'binding and loosing' has a similar significance: entry into the Kingdom depends on being 'loosed', not 'bound'. We have encountered the phrase in connection with Satan binding a sick woman and making her his captive (see chapter 2, no. 5). But the use of the words here and in Matthew 18:18 (see no. 24 below), as well as in rabbinic literature, indicates the power to pronounce a decree or annul it. A similar Aramaic idiom, 'to loose and retain', is attested in rabbinic literature specifically in connection with forgiving and retaining sins. It is echoed in John 20:23, 'If you forgive the sins of any, they are forgiven; if you retain the sins of any, they are retained.' But in neither of the two passages in Matthew (Matt. 16:19 and 18:18) is forgiveness of sins explicitly mentioned or even alluded to; therefore the expression is related to decision-making or the cancellation of a decree.

The context in which this saying, exclusive to Matthew, appears is Peter's confession at Caesarea Philippi concerning Jesus' messianic status. The episode of Peter's confession that Jesus is the Christ is contained in all three Synoptic Gospels, but his appointment to be the rock does not figure in either Mark or Luke. Their silence on something as important as Peter's nomination as head of the *ekklesia* strongly intimates that Matthew 16:17–19 must be a secondary accretion. The lack of any mention of the church in the other Gospels, including John, also points in the same direction (see no. 24 below). In short, the words about Peter's promotion should be credited not to Jesus, but to Matthew or his editor in AD 80 or later.

24. Church rules (Matt. 18:15–20)

If your brother sins against you, go and tell him his fault, between you and him alone. If he listens to you, you have gained your brother. But if he does not listen, take one or two others with you, that every word may be confirmed by the evidence of two or three witnesses. If he refuses to listen to them, tell it to the church; and if he refuses to listen even to the church, let him be to you as a Gentile or a tax-collector. Truly, I say to you, whatever you bind on earth shall be bound in heaven, and whatever you loose on earth shall be loosed in heaven. Again I say to you, if two of you agree on earth about anything they ask, it will be done for them by my Father in heaven. For where two or three are gathered in my name, there am I in the midst of them.

For rebuke administered without witnesses, see no. 15 above. The first half of this unit (Matt. 18:15–17) sets out formal rules on how to bring back to the straight and narrow path an erring member of an organized community. The duty to reprimand a brother is based on biblical law: 'You shall reason with your neighbour' (cf. Lev. 19:17). At this initial stage, the issue is moral rather than legal. The next step in the procedure is a further remonstration with the impenitent offender in front of two or three witnesses. The rule comes from Deuteronomy 19:15, which postulates that for a valid indictment the testimony of two or three trustworthy persons is required. Here we are no longer in the domain of morality, but enter the juridical field where the requirement is the evidence of more than one witness.

A similar legislation is attested in the Dead Sea Scrolls, with the notable difference that in some specific cases the word of one witness is accepted as valid (CD 9:16–23).[4] In Qumran as well as in rabbinic law, reprimand is the necessary precondition for a matter to be brought before a court. In contrast, the purpose of the regulation introduced by Matthew is to persuade a sinner to repent by urging him first

4. See B. S. Jackson, *Essays in Jewish and Comparative Legal History* (Leiden, 1975), 172–201; L. H. Schiffman, *Sectarian Law in the Dead Sea Scrolls* (Scholars Press, Chico, 1983), 99–109.

privately, then in the presence of a small group, and finally in front of the whole congregation (i.e. the church), to mend his ways. It is only when moral pressure has failed that public expulsion from the community, i.e. excommunication, can be decreed.[5]

The mention of the power to bind and to loose conferred on church leaders, and not just on Peter as in Matthew 16:19, is no doubt directly linked with the authority to expel from the community, the emphasis resting on 'binding'. Taken separately, the notion of 'loosing' implies readmission after a temporary expulsion, as shown by Josephus' use of the same terms in connection with the jurisdiction of the Pharisees over the exclusion and readmission of members of their congregation (*War* 1:111). For the correspondence between binding and loosing made on earth and decisions enacted in heaven, thus reflecting the idea of strict symmetry between terrestrial and celestial realities, see chapter 2, no. 1.

The third communal saying in this unit, that regarding the impact made on God in heaven by the prayer agreed between two brethren on earth (Matt. 18:19), is mechanically associated by the evangelist with the preceding verse referring to binding and loosing on high and here on earth. Finally the phrase 'two or three' from Matthew 18:16 supplies the basis for the next statement: the meeting of two or three brethren in the name of Jesus ensures spiritual communion with the Master. The saying recalls a rabbinic teaching according to which when two Jews meditate together on the Torah, mystically they bring down on themselves the divine Presence (Shekhinah) (mAbot 3:2).

This whole complex of sayings has a peculiar ring when set against the bulk of Jesus' teaching in the Gospels. To begin with, to compare a sinning brother to a tax-collector is totally alien to the mentality of Jesus, who had a soft spot for publicans. In fact, Jesus was the object of disparagement by his opponents who called him a 'friend of tax-collectors and sinners' (Matt. 11:19; Luke 7:34; see chapter 7, no. 9). But above all, the reference to the church, twice in Matthew 18:17 and once previously in Matthew 16:18, clearly indicates that we are faced here with early Christianity and not with Jesus.

5. In 1 Corinthians 5:1–5 Paul seems to dispense with the two preliminary stages and proceeds at once with the order to 'deliver to Satan', i.e. to repudiate a member of the Corinthian church who has been sleeping with his stepmother.

The word *ekklesia* (church) is absent from Mark, Luke and even from John. By contrast, it appears twenty-two times in the Acts of the Apostles and, if the two occurrences in the Letter to the Hebrews are included, sixty-one times in the Pauline corpus. The great importance of the notion, both in Palestinian and in Hellenistic Christianity, is mirrored in the frequency of the term's use. If an external parallel is needed, it is provided by the variety of designations and their numerous instances at Qumran where the concept of the community, diversely called *yahad*, *'edah*, *'etsah*, *qahal*, plays a significant part. On the basis of the verbal statistics – no mention of *ekklesia* in three out of the four Gospels and a mention in only two passages in Matthew – we may safely conclude that Jesus himself left no teaching about a church. Neither did he employ any other term to denote a corresponding institution. Luke's 'little flock' (*poimnion*) figures only once (Luke 12:32); the 'flock' (*poimnê*) in Matthew 26:31 comes from a direct quotation of Zechariah 13:7, and the phrase 'little ones' (Matt. 10:42; 18:6; Luke 17:2) is too vague to serve as the designation of an institution. In brief, there is no evidence to support the idea that the foundation of the church was among the major concerns of Jesus.

25. The counsel of self-castration (Matt. 19:12)

For there are eunuchs who have been so from birth, and there are eunuchs who have been made eunuchs by men, and there are eunuchs who have made themselves eunuchs for the sake of the kingdom of heaven.

Self-mutilation resulting in the loss of an eye or a limb has already been referred to in no. 6 above.

Castration for the sake of the Kingdom stands at the summit of the ladder of sacrifices which Jesus hyperbolically recommended to his would-be followers. Bearing in mind the style of Jesus, often prone to exaggeration, the saying advocates complete abstinence from sex to allow the followers of Jesus to concentrate exclusively on entry into God's Kingdom. Though expressed in metaphorical language which is stronger than usual, the teaching is in harmony with the general message of the New Testament concerning marital life at the end-time. For example, the Eschatological Discourse proclaims woe on expectant women during the days of utmost misery before the Parousia, and implies that it is preferable not to be married and thus avoid the danger of pregnancy (cf. Mark 13:17; Matt. 24:19; Luke 21:23; see chapter 8, no. 22). The context shows that the passage on eunuchs shocked even Jesus' own disciples. For them, Matthew tells us, even the prohibition of divorce sounded intolerably harsh. So later editors of the Gospel tried to soften the stark message of Jesus. His doctrine on castration was not meant for everybody: 'Not all men can receive this saying, but only those to whom it is given' (Matt. 19:11). A similar limitation is appended in the concluding phrase: 'He who is able to receive this, let him receive it' (Matt. 19:12). In practice not even Paul, who basically shared Jesus' eschatological outlook, proposed full-scale rejection of matrimony and sex life. Those who were married should, so to speak, put up with it, but those who were without matrimonial ties had better remain free and devote themselves without restraint to work for the Kingdom of God (see 1 Cor. 7:26–35).

It is scarcely necessary to ask whether Jesus might have meant his advice on castration to be taken in the literal sense. Both his love of hyperbole and the fundamental Jewish teaching that sexually mutilated men were to be excluded from the assembly of God (Deut. 23:1) militate against voluntary self-inflicted emasculation. However, such reasoning did not stop certain Christian ascetics, including Origen (185–254), the greatest biblical scholar of the Greek church in antiquity, from adopting Jesus' counsel in Matthew 19:12 and implementing it in its crudest sense.

26. Modesty in using titles (Matt. 23:8–11)

But you are not to be called rabbi, for you have one teacher, and you are all brethren. And call no man your father on earth, for you have one Father, who is in heaven. Neither be called masters, for you have one master, the Christ. He who is greatest among you shall be your servant.

Part of this maxim has already been touched upon in chapter 2, no. 15C.

The saying has been inserted into the diatribe against scribes and Pharisees, but judging from the style, the original setting is didactic and not polemical. The general message, summarized in the concluding verse, is one of humility, which characterizes the preaching of Jesus. The same theme may also be found in Mark 9:35: 'If any one would be first, he must be last of all and servant of all' (see also Mark 10:43–44; Matt. 20:26–27; Luke 22:26).[6]

The workers for the Kingdom of God must shun honorific titles such as Rabbi. This was the polite way of addressing a teacher or a leading figure. In the age of Jesus it did not yet possess the later specific connotation, i.e. a person trained in the Jewish law and qualified to make binding legal decisions. While he was alive, Jesus alone was called Rabbi or Teacher (*didaskalos* in Greek) within the circle of his disciples. The other members of his group were referred to as pupils (*mathêtai*). The same point is made in Matthew 23:10, showing that in the terminology of the church there was only one *kathegêtês*, the Master *par excellence*, the Christ. Finally, the absolute prohibition on calling any human being 'father' because only God is truly Father is an exaggeration verging on the intolerable. The style belongs to the same class as the hyperbolic prohibition on addressing Jesus as 'good' because only God deserves this description (see Mark 10:17–18; cf. chapter 8, no. 14). But Jesus could hardly have objected to a child calling his or her father, 'father'. Is it conceivable that the criticism was aimed at pious individuals surnamed 'Abba' (Father), such as the miracle-worker Abba Hilkiah and others (see chapter 1, no. 9)? But Hasidim surely would not have agreed to be called 'Abba' if that entailed the usurpation of a title of God. An anecdote about Abba Hilkiah preserved in the Talmud makes this plain: 'When the world was in need of rain, the rabbis used to send schoolchildren to him [Hilkiah], who seized the hem of his cloak and said to him, "Abba, Abba, give us rain!" He said to God, "Lord of the Universe, help those who cannot distinguish between the Abba who gives rain and the

6. With the exception of Mark 10:44 and Matthew 20:27 where the term *doulos* (slave) is used, we always encounter *diakonos* (servant, helper, assistant).

Abba who does not"' (bTaan 23b). Consequently the most likely explanation of the prohibition issued by Jesus against calling anyone 'father' on earth lies in his fondness for exaggeration.

REFLECTIONS

Of the twenty-six rules of conduct listed in this chapter, of which four have already been discussed in chapter 8 (see nos. 3, 8, 9, 13), it is characteristic that twenty-two concern the behaviour of individuals and only four deal with aspects of communal life.

The regulations belonging to the individual category start with the assertion of the permanent validity of the Torah and its compulsory character for everyone (no. 16), and are distinguished mostly by their hyperbolical style. They aim at the innermost reality of religious and moral laws. Some of these, like the superiority of life over the Sabbath, (nos. 1, 2, 14), also belong to mainstream Jewish *halakhah*, or customary law, but are propounded more emphatically by Jesus. Other rules strive to reach the heart of the matter by pushing far beyond the line of normal duty. The antitheses pertain to this class, prohibiting divorce, oaths and retaliation, prescribing resistance to anger and to lustful desire, and imposing the duty of universal love which includes even the love of the enemy (nos. 7, 11, 12, 17, 18, 19). Furthermore, the internal causes of uncleanness and cleanness are stressed (no. 4) and so is the obligation to perform acts of piety such as prayer, fasting and almsgiving discreetly, without showiness (nos. 20–22).

Commandments enjoining, literally or figuratively, various kinds of extraordinary self-sacrifice form a special section; they are to facilitate an immediate and positive answer to the appeal issued by Jesus. The road towards the ultimate goal is depicted as exceedingly arduous. Not only does it impose a duty to give up family, titles and worldly possessions, but entails – symbolically speaking – self-mutilation and the carrying of the cross 'for the sake of the kingdom of heaven' (nos. 5, 6, 8, 9, 13, 25, 26). Patently the compulsory acceptance of such a burden could not be proposed for people who lived in normal circumstances: they would have been unable to tolerate it day in, day out, year after year. But if we assume that Jesus was contemplating an intensive struggle of brief duration before the onset of the *eschaton*, the demand would appear more bearable. Albert Schweitzer, who at the beginning of the twentieth century was the first to emphasize that Jesus' world view entailed the imminent coming of the Kingdom, described the demands addressed by Jesus to his entourage as a system of 'interim ethic'.[7] It was meant to be valid until the approaching day of the Lord. However, if these regulations are placed in the context of an extended future, they make no sense without a substantial reinterpretation.

It is the context of a changed outlook on a prolonged future that furnishes the remaining four precepts (nos. 10, 15, 23, 24) with a lasting home. The sayings which refer to reconciliation, the rebuke of the sinner, the keys of the Kingdom and the power to bind and to loose presuppose an organized society under a monarchic group leader. They mirror the needs, not of the small circle of the eschatologically animated companions of Jesus, but of a structured church prepared for a very long wait in an unchanged world for the Second Coming of the Lord.

7. *The Quest of the Historical Jesus* (London, 2000), 485.

10

Towards the Authentic Gospel

We have nearly reached the end of the road. In the preceding nine chapters every saying attributed to Jesus in the Synoptic Gospels has been classified, surveyed and furnished with brief essential comments. In the process, we have become familiar with the picture of the doctrinal legacy of Jesus handed down by the evangelists as representatives of nascent Christianity. Now the moment has come to separate the sheep from the goats, the genuine message of the Galilean Master from the developments, accretions and elaborations introduced by the writers, editors and glossators of the Gospels. For if there is one certain conclusion which no serious reader endowed with insight and logic the size of a mustard seed can escape, it is that these hundreds of sayings have not been produced by one and the same teacher. They patently represent irreconcilable variations; indeed again and again they display flat contradictions. Jesus could not declare the proclamation of the good news to be restricted to Jews alone, yet simultaneously wish it to be addressed to all the nations of the earth. He could not have expected the Kingdom of God to burst into the world in his own lifetime, yet maintain that it would be postponed until the infinitely distant consummation of the ages, thus making room for a long-lasting church, etc., etc. If one of these alternatives is true, the other must inescapably be false.

But is my antithetical picture too rashly drawn? Is it conceivable, for instance, that the contradictions were the result of Jesus' change of mind? Or put more tactfully, could he have allowed his views to evolve? While such a compromise solution is theoretically possible, two good reasons militate against it.

To start with, the public career of Jesus was too short to accommodate a progressive development of ideas. Even the two- to three-year-long chronology of the Gospel of John would not provide enough time for the gradual achievement of a U-turn. But with the exception of his account of the last days of Jesus, John's narrative is more fiction than history when it is compared with the Synoptics. It is enough to look at his invented lengthy speeches, which are totally incompatible with the style and content of the preaching of Jesus preserved in the first three Gospels. Mark wrote shortly after AD 70 and thus antedates John by some forty years. Yet he proposed a much shorter chronology, and Matthew and Luke in the last quarter of the first century AD adopted Mark's line of time reckoning and story-telling. There is no reasonable explanation why all three earlier evangelists should have reduced so considerably the length of the ministry of Jesus.[1] With a single Passover recorded in the Synoptics, the public career of Jesus had to be of a maximum of one year's duration. Indeed, it is not out of the question that it may have lasted less than twelve months. As a law-abiding Jew, resident in the Holy Land, Jesus was obliged to observe not one, but all three pilgrimage festivals: Passover (March/April), the Feast of Weeks or Pentecost (May) and the Feast of Tabernacles (September/October). On each of these holy days he had to attend the religious ceremonies in the Temple of Jerusalem. We find him there, indeed, during the days leading up to Passover. He was crucified in the Judaean capital just before that feast. But the Synoptics make no reference to his pilgrimage visit either for the Feast of Weeks or for that of Tabernacles which preceded the fateful Passover. As it is unlikely that he neglected his duty to visit Jerusalem on these occasions, his non-attendance suggests that the public life of Jesus did not cover the period of these festivals. The most sensible conclusion is therefore that he began his itinerant ministry in Galilee in the autumn, after the feast of Tabernacles, of one year (probably AD 29), and died in Jerusalem a mere six months later, in the following spring (AD 30).

The second reason for rejecting the idea of a complete volte-face on the part of Jesus is that he is nowhere portrayed as a hesitant, intellectually unstable person. The Gospels contain nothing to suggest that during his short career Jesus had reason substantially to alter his

1. For the dating of the Gospels, see *The Changing Faces of Jesus*, 8–10, 148–51.

conviction on the essential points of his teaching. Hence the only likely alternative is that the conflicting, sometimes diametrically opposite, statements do not all stem from Jesus himself. In other words, the Synoptic Gospels in their present form consist of an adjusted, supplemented and corrected version, a thoroughly revised edition, of the original message of Jesus. The words, idioms and images which a first-century AD Galilean master addressed to his compatriots and co-religionists were rephrased in the Gospels to suit a totally different public, imbued with Hellenistic thought, in the Greek-speaking part of the Roman empire. To cater for the requirements of this new audience and readership, ideas foreign to Jesus were introduced into the Gospels. Consequently it is up to us now to differentiate between the genuine and the accrued message.

Twentieth-century New Testament scholars undertook such quests for authenticity and pursued them along various paths. Some specialists, among them Gustaf Dalman and Matthew Black,[2] aimed high and attempted to retrieve the genuine words of Jesus by comparing the Greek of the Gospels with the Aramaic language spoken in ancient Palestine. This method pursues a laudable aim, but suffers, alas, from serious handicaps. Only a limited amount of suitable textual parallels are available and research is further undermined by scholarly disagreement concerning the type of surviving Aramaic which best represents the dialect spoken in Galilee in the first century AD. Nevertheless this kind of comparative philology occasionally works and I have employed it in chapter 7 in connection with the study of the phrase 'the son of man'.

The best-known and most commonly employed method in Gospel criticism is form history (*Formgeschichte*), the study of literary forms championed by Rudolf Bultmann and his school of twentieth-century German New Testament scholarship. In it the Gospel material is classified as wisdom sayings, prophetic and eschatological proclamations, polemics, church rules, etc., and their original setting or *Sitz im Leben* is sought either in the life of Jesus or in that of the early church. Whereas form criticism does not explicitly look for criteria of

2. G. Dalman, *Die Worte Jesu* (Leipzig, 1898, 2nd edn. 1930); English translation, *The Words of Jesus* (Edinburgh, 1902). M. Black, *An Aramaic Approach to the Gospels and Acts* (Oxford, 1946; 3rd edn. 1967).

authenticity, by assigning a major creative role to the church in the shaping of most literary units in the Gospels, it *ipso facto* leads to the rejection of the genuineness of a substantial amount of material attributed to Jesus by the evangelists.

Some adherents of the form critical school have tried, however, to devise principles whereby the authenticity of Gospel sayings can be ascertained. In an influential book entitled *Rediscovering the Teaching of Jesus*, Norman Perrin proposed three criteria to establish the pedigree of a limited number of Gospel passages.[3] The first criterion, *dissimilarity*, helps to identify as authentic the unparalleled sayings of Jesus, that is, those not attested elsewhere either in Jewish or in early Christian writings. The second criterion, *coherence*, is used to establish the genuineness of sayings which are compatible and consistent with those whose authenticity has already been established by means of the rule of dissimilarity. The third criterion, *multiple attestation*, serves to prove as genuine the sayings which have been preserved in more than one source (say, Mark and Q), or in a variety of literary forms (parables, stories, proclamations) in and outside the Synoptic Gospels.

The main difficulty arising from these criteria concerns the manner in which they have been formulated. Those who couched them wished to be so theoretically stringent that their rules are not fair; they are in fact definitely weighted *against* authenticity. Take for instance the criterion of dissimilarity, generally held to be the most effective, and consider its definition supplied by Bultmann apropos the parables of Jesus: 'We can only count on possessing a genuine similitude of Jesus where, on the one hand, expression is given to the contrast between Jewish morality and piety and the distinctive eschatological temper which characterized the preaching of Jesus; and when, on the other hand, we find no specifically Christian features.'[4] But in reality this rule asks for something absurd, because it disregards the fact that in the field of religion, as in philosophy, the same basic truths are investigated all the time. Novelty and originality usually consist in looking at familiar issues from an unfamiliar angle, in giving a new slant to classic ideas, in shedding fresh light on problems discussed

3. *Rediscovering the Teaching of Jesus* (London, 1967), 39–47.
4. R. Bultmann, *The History of the Synoptic Tradition* (New York, 1963), 205.

since time immemorial. How, then, can anyone imagine that a saying of Jesus, in order to be authentic, had to distance itself from every known expression of 'Jewish morality and piety'? Such an angle of approach is quite close to the old-fashioned antisemitic attitude according to which the aim of Jesus was to condemn and reject the whole Jewish religion and substitute for it something totally different and unprecedented. Again, Bultmann's exclusion of anything 'specifically Christian' from the genuine message of Jesus seems to imply the absurdity that Jesus and Christianity are self-contradictory. As for the additional principle often quoted by New Testament scholars, 'If in doubt, discard', it is also fundamentally inappropriate and definitely unhelpful. In Gospel research, certainty is a very scarce commodity floating adrift in an ocean of probabilities. In short, for a relatively successful quest for the authentic sayings of Jesus, we must discover new principles and devise a fresh procedure.

Let me put my cards on the table and disclose my presuppositions. I am convinced that the writers of the Synoptic Gospels intended to hand down what they believed was, according to Mark's opening sentence, 'the gospel of Jesus'. If, to some extent unavoidably, the evangelists conveyed or sought to formulate church doctrine, this was not their primary or avowed intention. In other words, in the perspective and belief of their authors, the Gospels intended to transmit the teaching which Jesus originally proclaimed to his own disciples and listeners. These teachings were to undergo numerous mutations after his death in the course of their transmission first to Jews in the Holy Land, later to diaspora Jews, and finally to Gentiles, both inside and outside Palestine. These mutations constitute a kind of continuously widening spiral in time and through changing cultures.

These various stages in the formulation and revision of the 'gospel' or message of Jesus are all merged in the traditions which finally resulted in the written Synoptic Gospels. If we can link these evolutionary stages to the successive phases of the early history of the Christian movement, we will be in a position to distinguish, on some solid basis, between the treasures left by Jesus and the later growth which affected them. We must also bear in mind that one and the same literary unit can reflect successive layers of significance throughout all the Gospels. The earliest level may represent Jesus, the next Jewish-Christianity, and the last the interpretation attached to the message of Jesus by the early non-Jewish church during the later decades of the first century.

Let us recall some basic facts. Jesus taught in Aramaic to Palestinian – and according to the Synoptics mainly Galilean – Jews. We must assume that he wanted to be understood by them, and to achieve this he used the words, phrases, images and teaching method with which his compatriots were familiar. Therefore no saying of Jesus can be reckoned authentic unless it was intelligible to first-century Jews in a Palestinian/Galilean setting.

Since Jesus did not record his message in writing, it had to be handed down by his disciples orally, first in Aramaic and later in Greek when the evangelization moved outside Palestine among Jews and Gentiles who spoke Greek. The written word soon became the medium of transmission in the various geographically distinct regions of the Graeco-Roman world and as a result the gospel was bound to acquire a considerable degree of variation. In such circumstances the possible rediscovery of a literally authentic saying is most of the time beyond reasonable expectation. Therefore it is wiser to lower one's aim and try to reconstruct, not the *ipsissima verba*, the original word-for-word version of a saying of Jesus, but the general gist of his message.

Our search for authenticity will begin with an analysis of contradictions and then proceed by way of eliminating the less likely alternatives. The survival of conflicting statements in the three Synoptics, and even in the same individual Gospel, demonstrates that the creation of coherence was not the paramount aim of the editors and redactors. Yet despite this, there exist many coherent features in Matthew, Mark and Luke. Since they are not the fruit of a process of revision but have come about as it were unintentionally, their accidental consistence is particularly significant. Therefore establishing genuine doctrines with the help of the criterion of coherence will form the second stage of the forthcoming quest.

The traditionally-minded may find some of my conclusions upsetting, but I would like to reassure them in advance that this investigation is not negatively motivated. Those who persevere may find that the tree of knowledge depicted in the forthcoming pages, despite its unusual shape and appearance, promises to bear good fruit. And as it is written, 'You will know them by their fruits'.

I. Search for authenticity by way of elimination

The most effective method to distinguish the authentic from the inauthentic is through the analysis and evaluation of contradictory statements. The most obvious clashes of opinion in the Gospels concern the identity of the addressees of the message of Jesus; the time of the advent of the Kingdom of God; and the question of whether the disciples of Jesus had any foreknowledge of his arrest and crucifixion. We shall therefore examine the following three questions:

(1) Did Jesus intend to address only Jews, or did he expect the gospel to benefit the entire non-Jewish world?

(2) Did Jesus believe and proclaim that the arrival of the Kingdom of God would take place in his lifetime, or after the Parousia, following closely his lifetime, or in the far distant future?

(3) Did Jesus clearly announce his suffering and death to his disciples? Or did his arrest, crucifixion and reported resurrection take them completely by surprise?

1. Did Jesus intend to address only Jews, or did he expect the gospel to benefit the entire non-Jewish world?

The definition of the fundamental purpose of the ministry of Jesus and of his first envoys is a *conditio sine qua non* for distinguishing what is authentic and what is not in his message. Did his thought proceed along a nationalistic line, or was his vision cosmopolitan and universal? There are sayings in the Gospels which point in either direction, and both stances are expressed in absolute terms so that no room is left for any compromise.

The most striking and incontrovertible statements are contained in Matthew's special section (*M*). There Jesus bluntly asserted that his mission was exclusively intended for Jews: 'I was sent only to the lost sheep of the house of Israel' (Matt. 15:24; see chapter 8, no. 49). He gave the same pro-Jewish directive to his apostles, too. Not only were they positively ordered to teach, heal and exorcize only 'the lost sheep of the house of Israel', but they were also expressly forbidden to minister among non-Jews: 'Go nowhere among the Gentiles, and enter no town of the Samaritans' (Matt. 10:5–6). In general terms, the

Kingdom of God was for Jews alone. Only they were given the honorific title 'sons of the kingdom' (Matt. 8:12). The substance of this assertion is backed by the story of all three Synoptic Gospels. Jesus preached his message only to Jews. When he acted as healer or exorcist in the neighbouring areas, in southern Lebanon (the Syrophoenician girl) or north-western Transjordan (the Gergesene/Gerasene demoniac), it was clearly the exception, and never included teaching.

These declarations, patent in themselves, are further supported by sayings in which Jesus declared non-Jews to be unworthy to receive his teaching. Here Mark joins Matthew and both speak with a single voice. In the story of the Syrophoenician woman Jesus states: 'It is not right to take the children's bread and throw it to the dogs' (Mark 7:27; Matt. 15:26; see chapter 8, no. 6). The meaning is clear: the 'dogs', a sarcastic nickname for Gentiles, should not usurp 'the [Jewish] children's bread'. Equally sharp is the proverbial wisdom maxim through which Jesus broadcasts the same message: 'Do not give dogs what is holy; and do not throw your pearls before swine' (Matt. 7:6; see chapter 3, no. 32). In these unequivocal utterances Jesus is presented as the champion of absolute Jewish exclusivism.

Yet against these programmatic pronouncements can be set another series of equally clear affirmations which plainly broadcast the opposite view. The most obvious of these is the final instruction which the apostles are said to have received. In it, as reported in Matthew and in the longer ending of Mark, the risen Christ charged them to evangelize the whole world: 'Go therefore and make disciples of all nations, baptizing them in the name of the Father and of the Son and of the Holy Spirit' (Matt. 28:19; Mark 16:15–16; see chapter 8, nos. 33 and 53). Similarly, at the end of Luke's last chapter, the same risen Jesus speaks of a mission of his disciples to all the peoples: 'Thus it is written, that the Christ should suffer and on the third day rise from the dead, and that repentance and forgiveness of sins should be preached in his name to all the nations, beginning from Jerusalem' (Luke 24:46–47; see chapter 7, no. 15). Matthew's version of the Eschatological Discourse also anticipates a universal promulgation of the message of Jesus: 'this gospel of the kingdom will be preached throughout the whole world, as a testimony to all nations' (Matt. 24:14; see chapter 8, no. 20).

To these direct affirmations should be added a number of incidental or indirect allusions. We read in the story of the woman who anointed Jesus in Bethany that her deed will be remembered 'wherever the gospel is preached in the whole world' (Mark 14:9; Matt. 26:13; see chapter 8, no. 29). In other passages, without being explicitly named, it is hinted that the Gentiles are the outsiders invited to the wedding feast: 'Go out to the highways and hedges, and compel people to *come in*, that my house may be filled' (Luke 14:23; see chapter 4, no. 13). People from the outside world will also be beneficiaries of the lamp lit inside the house: 'that *those who enter* may see light' (Luke 8:16; see chapter 3, no. 4).

Having considered the whole evidence, we are faced with the following dilemma. *Either* Jesus adopted a strictly pro-Jewish stance and the later introduction into the Gospels of pro-Gentile leanings must reflect the point of view of the early church, which was by then almost exclusively non-Jewish. *Or* it was Jesus who adopted the universalist stand, and this was replaced at a later stage by Jewish exclusivism. The pro-Jewish attitude was substituted for the cosmopolitan outlook by the Judaeo-Christian church of Peter and of James, the brother of the Lord, in its quarrels with Paul, who sought to free Gentile Christianity from the bonds of traditional Judaism. Bearing all these facts in mind, which alternative is the more likely?

As far as Jewish exclusivism is concerned, if it had nothing to do with Jesus, but was a later polemical insertion into the Gospels by Palestinian Judaeo-Christians fighting against the Hellenistic churches, it is highly unlikely that it would have remained unaltered after the victory of the Gentile church over the Jewish branch of the Jesus movement or indeed would have survived at all. For ultimately it was the Gentile church that provided a permanent home for the Synoptic Gospels. In the light of the criterion of dissimilarity, we must recognize that the view that the message of Jesus was meant only for Jews went strongly against the grain in the later, mostly Gentile, primitive church. It was the complete opposite of what the non-Jewish majority of the users of the Gospels wanted to hear. To the previously cited evidence we can further add Jesus' statements on the permanent validity of the Law of Moses: 'Think not that I have come to abolish the law and the prophets; I have come not to abolish them but to fulfil them. For truly,

I say to you, till heaven and earth pass away, not an iota, not a dot, will pass from the law until all is accomplished' (Matt. 5:17–18); and 'it is easier for heaven and earth to pass away, than for one dot of the law to become void' (Luke 16:17; see chapter 9, no. 16). Both these sayings are deeply confusing for Gentile Christians. Put differently, unless the claim concerning the validity of the Law had been known to have originated from, and enjoyed the authority of Jesus, it is quite unlikely that the evangelists would have freely invented it, and have produced a teaching which was plainly embarrassing and disturbing for their communities. On the other hand, the interpolation of a teaching which advocates an open approach to the Gentiles would have pleased, strengthened and encouraged those non-Jewish inhabitants of Syria, Asia Minor and Greece who accepted the gospel announced by Paul, while the mission of the rest of the apostles among Palestinian Jews was progressively failing.

The criterion of multiple attestation confirms this interpretation. Not only do we find Jewish exclusivism in Jesus' pronouncements in the Gospels already referred to, but it is also mirrored in the history of primitive Christianity as pictured in the Acts of the Apostles. In the early days of the Palestinian church, no Gentile was considered admissible into the Christian community without first joining the Jewish fold through becoming a fully-fledged proselyte (see Acts, chapters 10–11). It is true that Peter and his companions agreed to baptize the Roman centurion Cornelius and his household, but it was only after they had witnessed charismatic wonders that they had changed their minds (Acts 10:46; 15:8–9). None of them seems to have been aware of Jesus' command that the gospel was to be preached to non-Jews. It must also be recalled how hard Paul had to struggle to overcome the hostility of the Judaean churches whose leaders, previously of Pharisee persuasion, insisted on the compulsory circumcision of Gentiles before their admittance into the Jesus movement, and on their obligatory observance of the whole Law of Moses (Acts 15:5). After the initial clashes, the mission to the Gentiles was approved by James on condition that they would observe the Noachic laws (Acts 15:20, 29). Once more the concession was granted not on the ground that this was the wish of Jesus, but because of the charismatic events observed by Peter, and also because the conversion of the Gentiles was seen by the primitive church as the fulfilment of Old Testament prophecies (Acts 15:13–29). In consequence, Paul was allowed to pursue his evangelization of non-Jews, without obliging them to become proselytes, side-by-side with the other apostles' continuing ministry among the Jews (Gal. 2:7–9). In any case, both the Acts and Paul depict the preaching of the gospel to Gentiles as a definite novelty.

In short, the view that Jesus ministered only to the lost sheep of Israel and instructed his disciples to do the same is the historically correct alternative. Disturbing though this may sound to the uninformed, the order to proclaim the good news of salvation to all the nations must be struck out from the list of the authentic sayings of Jesus. How a religious teacher of his stature could have been – apparently – so narrow-minded will demand further reflection, which is reserved for the Epilogue (see p. 415).

2. *Did Jesus believe and proclaim that the arrival of the Kingdom of God would take place in his lifetime, or after the Parousia, following closely his lifetime, or in the far distant future?*

According to the evidence of the New Testament as it now stands, Jesus was as equivocal regarding the date of the arrival of the reign of God as about the identity of those (Jews or Gentiles) who were to become citizens of the Kingdom of God. In one set of sayings the Kingdom is definitely to be established during the lifetime of his generation. In a second set, the inauguration of the Kingdom follows the Parousia, the glorious return of the crucified and risen Christ from his heavenly habitat, after the earthly career of Jesus. In some texts this Parousia was to occur while Jesus' contemporaries were still alive, i.e. in the second half of the first century AD, whereas other forecasts appear to place it in the far distant future.

Fired by an absolute faith in his being chosen by God and commissioned to usher in the new age, Jesus spoke of the coming of the Kingdom as an imminent reality. Borrowing words from John the Baptist (Matt. 3:2), he proclaimed: 'The kingdom of God is at hand' (Mark 1:15; Matt. 4:17; see chapter 8, no. 1), and directed his disciples to present the same message about the impending fullness of time

(Matt. 10:7; Luke 10:9, 11; see chapter 8, nos. 5 and 49). In the course of his ministry, Jesus went further and stressed that the new age had already begun: 'behold, the kingdom of God is in the midst of you' (Luke 17:20–21; see chapter 8, no. 7). Even more clearly, 'if it is by the Spirit of God that I cast out demons, then the kingdom of God has come upon you' (Matt. 12:28; Luke 11:20; see chapter 8, no. 43). The same message pointing to an inceptive presence of the Kingdom is implicitly conveyed in Jesus' purported reply to John the Baptist's question whether he (Jesus) was God's specially chosen instrument: 'Go and tell John what you hear and see: the blind receive their sight and the lame walk, lepers are cleansed and the deaf hear, and the dead are raised up, and the poor have good news preached to them' (Matt. 11:4–5; Luke 7:22; see chapter 8, no. 7).

Finally there is the powerful statement of Jesus formally affirming the actual establishment of the Kingdom of God in his own generation: 'Truly, I say to you, there are some standing here who will not taste death before they see that the kingdom of God has come with power' (Mark 9:1; cf. Luke 9:27; see chapter 8, no. 8). This was also no doubt the original wording of Matthew. However, it was subsequently changed to 'there are some standing here who will not taste death before they see the son of Man coming in his kingdom' (Matt. 16:28). According to this reading the advent of the Kingdom follows the Parousia of the 'son of man', that is to say, not the historical ministry of Jesus, but his Second Coming. The formulation attested by Mark (9:1) represents without any doubt the authentic saying of Jesus. For no one would invent, and no community would preserve, an announcement of the imminent arrival of the Kingdom of God which was patently not fulfilled. Indeed, by the end of the first century, it created a serious embarrassment for the primitive church. Matthew's allusion to the Parousia was aimed at remedying the situation.

The evidence so far marshalled can be further strengthened by indirect means. Firstly, the coming of the Kingdom was dated to the era following the days of the Baptist, that is to say, to Jesus' own time. 'From the days of John the Baptist until now,' Matthew tells us, 'the kingdom of heaven has suffered violence, and men of violence take it by force' (Matt. 11:12), or as Luke puts it, 'The law and the prophets were until John; since then the good news of the kingdom of God is preached, and everyone enters it violently' (Luke 16:16; see chapter 8, no. 40). Moreover, the many examples indicating that Jesus was inviting not future believers in a later generation but his own listeners to enter at once the Kingdom of God suggest that for him the Kingdom was an incipient, present reality which was soon to reach its completion (see chapter 8, nos. 10, 13, 14, 15, 34; chapter 9, nos. 5, 6, 8, 9, 13, 16, 25). Add to these the parables of the Kingdom, which were meant to apply to the contemporaries of Jesus, and the Lord's Prayer, which asks not for the Parousia but for the coming of the Kingdom. Paul's Christians awaiting the return of Christ did not say, 'Thy kingdom come!', but 'Our Lord, come!' (*Marana tha*, 1 Cor. 16:22; cf. Rev. 22:20). They did not ask for the advent of the Kingdom, but for the reappearance of their Master.

Finally, we find more than one New Testament passage indicating that the followers of Jesus understood his words as implying an instantaneous manifestation of the Kingdom. When the apostles James and John (or their mother) asked for seats of honour in Jesus' realm, they seem to have envisaged the present time or a very near future (Matt. 20:21; cf. Mark 10:37; see chapter 8, no. 15). On one occasion Luke reports that the disciples of Jesus expected the Kingdom of God 'to appear immediately' (Luke 19:11). In a similar vein, according to the same Luke (and assuming that he was the author of the Acts of the Apostles), even on the way to the site of the Ascension the apostles are described as asking their risen Christ, 'Lord, will you at this time restore the kingdom to Israel?' (Acts 1:6). Needless to say, by the 'kingdom' God's reign was meant.

Against this substantial body of evidence indicating that the era of the Kingdom had already been started by Jesus, or was on the point of being launched in Galilee or in Jerusalem, we can exhibit those Parousia sayings which announce first the return of the exalted Christ from his heavenly glory, followed by the universal judgement and the beginning of God's triumphant rule over the whole universe. The texts are numerous and a selection of significant examples will suffice.

Most of the relevant passages figure among the 'Son of man' sayings, or in the parables of Jesus. Two 'Son of man' passages in Matthew actually include the uncommon Greek term *parousia* ('coming'): 'For as the lightening comes from the east and shines as far as the west, so will be the *parousia* of the Son of man' (Matt. 24:27; see chapter 8, no. 18); and 'As were the days of Noah [i.e. the sudden arrival of the flood], so will be the *parousia* of the Son of man'' (Matt. 24:37, 39; see chapter 7, no. 23). In the corresponding text of Luke the synonymous 'days of the Son of man' is substituted for 'the *parousia* of the Son of man' (Luke 17:26, 30, 31; see chapter 7, no. 23).

The central image, inspired by chapter 7 of the Book of Daniel, is that of the final judgement presided over by the 'Son of man' in the company of his heavenly attendants: 'The Son of man . . . comes in the glory of his Father with the holy angels', 'and then he will repay every man for what he has done' (Mark 8:38; Matt. 16:27; Luke 9:26; see chapter 7, no. 18). The theme is even more clearly put in the Eschatological Discourse: 'They will see the Son of man coming in clouds with great power and glory. And then he will send out the angels and gather his elect from the four winds' (Mark 13:26–27; Matt. 24:30–31; Luke 21:27–28; see chapter 7, no. 19; cf. also Matt. 13:41–43; 13:49; 25:31; see chapter 4, nos. 17, 20 and 26). The judgement executed by the 'Son of man', which introduces God's absolute dominion, is clearly envisaged as a future event when taken in comparison with the public life of Jesus. As judge, the 'Son of man' acts as a king and speaks of his kingdom, which is ultimately also the Kingdom of the Father (Matt. 13:37, 41–43; see chapter 4, no. 17). The same Kingdom figures also in the account of the enthronement of the 'Son of man' (Matt. 19:28; Luke 22:28–30; see chapter 7, no. 21).

This 'future' establishment of the Kingdom of God, as opposed to the one which was expected to crown immediately the career of Jesus, is contemplated on two different time scales. The Parousia was first believed to be imminent (see Matt. 10:23, 'you will not have gone through all the towns of Israel, before the Son of man comes'; see chapter 7, no. 24). The expectation of the return of Christ at an unpredictable moment of the night produced intense eschatological excitement. A number of parables testify to it, for example the parable of the doorkeeper (Mark 13:33–37; Matt. 24:42; 25:14–15; Luke 12:38; 19:12–13) and the parable of the burglar (Matt. 24:43–44; Luke 12:39–40; see chapter 4, nos. 6 and 14). Relying on the criterion of multiple attestation, we can also consider evidence from outside the Gospels. Paul, for instance, writing to the Thessalonians, declares: 'We

. . . who are left until the coming (*parousia*) of the Lord, shall not precede those who have fallen asleep [i.e. died]. For the Lord himself will descend from heaven with a cry of command, with the archangel's call, and with the sound of the trumpet of God. And the dead in Christ will rise first; then we who are alive . . . shall be caught up together with them in the clouds to meet the Lord in the air' (1 Thess. 4:15–17). This image can be complemented by another excerpt from Paul, explicitly alluding to the Kingdom: 'Then comes the end, when he [Christ] delivers the kingdom to God the Father' (1 Cor. 15:24). Such was the perspective in the early fifties of the first century AD.

As time passed with no Parousia of Christ on the horizon, the next stage of the expectation necessitated constant exhortation to patience on the part of church leaders. New or revised parables and 'Son of man' sayings began to encourage the need for quiet optimism and hopefulness. The bridegroom of the parable of the ten virgins is 'delayed' (Matt. 25:5; see chapter 4, no. 25). The return of the master who has entrusted the talents to his servants takes place 'after a long time' (Matt. 25:19; cf. Luke 19:15; see chapter 4, no. 16). Those waiting for the arrival of the 'Son of man' must maintain their faith and must not allow this-worldly concerns ('dissipation and drunkenness') to weaken their eschatological alertness (Luke 21:34–36; cf. also Luke 18:6–8; see chapter 7, no. 29). The author of one of the latest writings of the New Testament, the Second Letter of Peter (dating to AD 125 or later), had to combat boredom and scepticism among disillusioned Christians: 'Where is the promise of his [Christ's] *parousia*? For ever since the fathers fell asleep, all things have continued as they were from the beginning of the creation' (2 Peter 3:4). About a century had passed since the days of Jesus, and the church, which had no role to play during his life, had by then become institutionalized (see chapter 9, nos. 23, 24) and served to perpetuate the teaching of Jesus and of his envoys until an indefinitely postponed Parousia: 'Go therefore and make disciples of all nations . . . ; and lo, I am with you always, to the close of the age' (Matt. 28:19–20).

To recapitulate, the New Testament concept of the establishment of the Kingdom of God can neatly be divided into three phases. In the first, the Kingdom was expected to be realized during the Palestinian ministry of Jesus. In the second phase, the arrival of the Kingdom was to succeed the Parousia, which was expected to follow soon after the cross. In the third, the feverish waiting progressively quietened down, the date of the Second Coming was adjourned *sine die*, and the notion of the Kingdom metamorphosed into that of the church. In brief, both the Parousia doctrine and the identification of the Kingdom of God with the church are later correctives added to the authentic teaching of Jesus.

3. Did Jesus clearly announce his suffering and death to his disciples? Or did his arrest, crucifixion and reported resurrection take them completely by surprise?

The data providing the answer to these questions have been assembled and analysed in the 'Son of man' predictions of the death and resurrection of Jesus (see chapter 7, section II). It has been shown there that the Gospels supply contradictory evidence regarding the apostles' awareness of the events towards the end of Jesus' life.

The prediction of these events is presented in two different forms. On the one hand Jesus repeatedly foretells his death and resurrection to his closest followers. Most of the announcements are made in general terms: Jesus would be arrested, suffer, be killed, but rise after three days or on the third day (see chapter 7, nos. 12–17). One group of sayings, however, is furnished with extra details: he would be handed over to the Gentiles, mocked, spat upon, scourged, and crucified (Mark 10:32–34; Matt. 20:17–19; Luke 18:31–34; see chapter 7, no. 15; see also Matt. 26:2). The predictions are not mysterious; on the contrary, they are expressed in plain words. One of the evangelists explicitly stresses that Jesus intended to be understood, and his words remembered: 'Let these words sink into your ears' (Luke 9:44). In sum, we are left in no doubt that the apostles had been put in the picture by Jesus about the forthcoming happenings, not once or twice but several times.

On the other hand, how did these same apostles and disciples react when the predicted events began to materialize? They certainly showed no foreknowledge of the scenario. When Jesus was arrested, all his companions fled (Mark 14:50; Matt. 26:56). When confronted, Peter even denied that he had anything to do with Jesus or even that he knew him (Mark 14:66–71; Matt. 26:69–74; Luke 22:54–60). None of the apostles, or for that matter any member of the family of Jesus, accompanied him to Golgotha, according to the Synoptics. Only some courageous Galilean women watched him die on the cross (Mark 15:40–41; Matt. 27:55–56). Luke tries to improve on Mark's depressing report by adding that all the 'acquaintances' of Jesus 'stood at a distance' (Luke 23:49). But 'acquaintance' would hardly be the word to designate members of his inner circle or his family.

After the death of Jesus on the cross the apostles do not seek comfort in the thought that in three days' time all will be well. On the contrary, when the women who had gone to the tomb to complete the burial rites reported that the body of Jesus had disappeared, they encountered only total disbelief voiced with the customary male superiority of the age. In fact, for the apostles the words of the women were *lêros*, i.e. silly nonsense (Luke 24:11). According to Luke, neither the two disciples travelling to Emmaus nor the apostles in Jerusalem recognize Jesus when he appears to them after his resurrection. In Matthew's totally different account of the manifestation of the risen Jesus to his eleven disciples on a Galilean mountain, even some of these are said to have doubted (Matt. 28:17).[5] Would people who had been assured in advance by their charismatic and prophetic teacher that the tragic events would be followed promptly by a happy ending have displayed such profound incredulity? Even allowing for the momentary shock and natural fear caused by the arrest of Jesus in the depth of the night, the apostles should surely have recalled the sequence of events so often and so recently rehearsed before them by Jesus?

Hence the irreconcilable descriptions present us with the following dilemma. *Either* Jesus did not predict his fate, and the cowardly behaviour of the disoriented disciples resulted from natural distress, weakness and disarray; *or* he actually forewarned them, in which case the inglorious conduct of each single one of the apostles is inexplicable, and the distorted canvas must be entirely of the making of the writers of the Gospels. Weighing up the pros and cons, it is easier to account for the later insertion of inauthentic predictions than to provide a

5. The episode of doubting Thomas, unwilling to accept the reality of the resurrection, is well known from the account in the Fourth Gospel, too (John 20:24–25).

believable explanation for the undignified conduct of the closest associates of Jesus possessing full foreknowledge of the events to come.

The greatest difficulty which in the subsequent decades faced the apostles and early Christian missionaries was how to explain to Jews and to Gentiles the death and the resurrection of Jesus. It should be recalled that neither the death nor the resurrection of the Messiah formed part of the beliefs and expectations of the Jews in the first century AD. So the apostles and the evangelists endeavoured to account for this death and resurrection and make them acceptable by asserting that Jesus had full advance knowledge of them, that he conveyed this knowledge to his disciples, and that the subsequent events simply fulfilled his own predictions.

As is well known, the chief method adopted by the spokesmen of the early church in order to prove their message about the Messiahship of Jesus was to show that his story was prefigured in the Bible and consequently was foreordained by God. The teachers of the Dead Sea sect used the same technique, known as *pesher* interpretation. In the persons and events of the Qumran community the ancient predictions were realized. In retrospect, a similar fulfilment exegesis was inserted by the evangelists into the Gospel narrative regarding Jesus' suffering, death and resurrection.

In addition to Jesus' own announcements regarding his end, Mark and Matthew make him allude to prophecies foretelling his arrest: 'For the Son of man goes *as it is written of him*, but woe to that man by whom the Son of man is betrayed' (Mark 14:21; Matt. 26:24). They put words into Jesus' mouth: '*But let the scriptures be fulfilled*' (Mark 14:49); or 'But how then should *the scriptures be fulfilled*, that it must be so?' (Matt. 26:54). Elsewhere, in an ambiguous way Mark's Jesus asks, '*How is it written* of the Son of man, that he should suffer many things and be treated with contempt?' (Mark 9:12). In turn the Jesus of Luke remarks, '*Everything that is written* of the Son of man *by the prophets will be accomplished*' (Luke 18:31), and his risen Jesus also declares, '*Thus it is written*, that the Christ should suffer and on the third day rise from the dead' (Luke 24:46). It is highly remarkable, however, that none of these allusions actually cites the biblical passages in which the death and resurrection of Jesus are supposed to have found their realization. Neither does Paul reproduce any quotation from the Holy Books to support the claim that 'Christ died for our sins *in accordance with the scriptures*' (1 Cor. 15:3). This shows that the acceptability of the teaching concerning the death and resurrection of Jesus increases if it is assumed that these events had been foretold not just by him, but also by the prophets long before him.

In consequence, Jesus' appropriate predictions were incorporated into the Gospel narrative. The interpolation was then accompanied by further adjustments to make the behaviour of the apostles look less perplexing. The evangelists tried to excuse them by remarking that they could not understand Jesus, and that the meaning of his words was concealed from them (Luke 18:34). The apostles are made to pretend that they had no idea of what rising from the dead signified (Mark 9:10), although by the first century AD the concept of resurrection was common currency among Jews. The disciples' failure to ask Jesus for an explanation was due to their being too distressed (Matt. 17:23) or too frightened (Mark 9:32; Luke 9:45). Amazingly, it is even implied that some of them had simply forgotten the predictions! We learn that the angelic informants encountering the women in the empty tomb had to remind them of Jesus' prophecies and all of a sudden 'they remembered his words' (Luke 24:6–8). To give a semblance of coherence to their version of the story, the evangelists demand the apostles pay a high price: they are portrayed as obtuse and spineless.

In the light of the evidence cited and examined, the most likely verdict is that the apostles knew nothing in advance about the final stages of Jesus' career. In fact, '*Eloi, Eloi, lama sabachthani*' ('My God, my God, why hast thou forsaken me?') understood in its obvious sense (see chapter 5, no. 19, and chapter 6, no. 4) suggests that until the moment of the crucifixion Jesus himself did not expect any interruption of his mission, and looked forward to participating himself in the ceremony of inauguration of the Kingdom of God.

Further indirect evidence reinforces the view that Jesus looked forward to completing his predestined task. It is noteworthy that in the parables of the secretly growing seed (Mark 4:26–29; see chapter 4, no. 2) and of the weeds (Matt. 13:24–30; see chapter 4, no. 17), the sower is also the harvester, and no hiatus is foreseen between the two events. And more significantly, with one exception, none of the parables, the most typical literary form used by Jesus, has anything to say about the cross. The exception is the allegory of the wicked tenants of the vineyard who murder the owner's beloved son (Mark 12:1–9; Matt. 21:33–41; Luke 20:9–16; see chapter 4, no. 4). None of them alludes to the resurrection.

So far we have analysed three major problems in the Gospels: Jewish exclusivism against universalism; the inauguration of the Kingdom during the life of Jesus against its establishment after the Parousia; and the unexpectedness of the cross (and resurrection) against repeated forecasts. With the proposed resolution of these dilemmas, the door opens for the next stage of our journey towards the authentic gospel. Here the criterion of coherence will be called upon to enable us to identify the sayings of Jesus which are consistent with those which have already been accepted as authentic.

The further essential themes which appear to belong to the genuine message of Jesus are: (i) the role of faith or trust in religious life; (ii) the efficacy of prayer; (iii) belief in the fatherhood of God; (iv) the need to become like children; (v) a new eschatological concept of the family; (vi) healing and exorcism in the final age; and (vii) the need for hyperbolical speech and verbal twists in talking about the Kingdom.

II. Search for authenticity using the criterion of coherence

If in the light of the foregoing demonstration it is accepted that Jesus preached the imminent coming of the Kingdom of God, some ideas and attitudes seem to form an integral part of his religious outlook. Therefore if it can be shown that they regularly occur in the various segments of the general Gospel picture, they will have a primary claim to be recognized as genuine and essential constituents of this picture. In advancing this thesis, I do not presume that every saying that is not part of this sketch is necessarily inauthentic, or that those listed under the seven headings below actually emanated from the lips of Jesus in the form recorded in the Gospels. What I am prepared to argue is that these 'words of Jesus' reflect his true ideas, preoccupations and mentality.

1. *The role of faith or trust in religious life*

Throughout his whole preaching ministry Jesus laid heavy emphasis on the virtue of faith/trust, and considered it to be an absolute precondition for any valid action leading to the Kingdom of God. Negatively, he asserted the impossibility of achieving any efficacious act in the field of religion without such faith/trust. The evidence covers the whole spectrum of Gospel tradition, mostly Mark and Q, but also the special material of Matthew and Luke, and corresponds to the criterion of multiple attestation.

In the course of his whole life-work Jesus behaved as a man conscious of being endowed with God-given power to perform charismatic deeds. He also demanded from his prospective 'patients' total belief in his ability to cure them (see chapter 1, nos. 7, 9, 12, 14, 17, 19, 28, 29, 30, 36; chapter 8, no. 6). And as has been underlined again and again, he went so far as to credit the faith of the sick person with the achievement of the actual healing: 'Do you believe that I am able to do this?' Jesus asked two blind men (Matt. 9:28), but the accounts often conclude with 'your faith has made you well' (see chapter 1, nos. 9, 19, 29, 36).

Outside the sphere of healing, Jesus, in his capacity as teacher of wisdom, required from his followers the same unlimited trust in divine Providence in connection with the needs of the present moment. Such faith was necessary to overcome worry and persuade the believer that God would take care of the future: 'Therefore do not be anxious about tomorrow, for tomorrow will be anxious for itself' (Matt. 6:34). The disciples of Jesus had to believe that the heavenly protector of sparrows would *a fortiori* look after them, too. Such faith would not tolerate divided loyalty, the simultaneous service of God and mammon (see chapter 3, nos. 18, 19, 29).

The same theme of supreme faith also runs through the parables of Jesus. In the story of the secretly growing seed the sower has to wait and live on absolute trust until the soil produces the grain. In the parable of the demon returning to his former home the implicit message is that without repentance and constant confidence in God any liberation from satanic powers is likely to remain temporary. The anecdote of the unexpected guest conveys the teaching that childlike insistence and determined entreaties are efficient even when the addressee of the prayer is the heavenly Father. Similarly the parable of the widow and the wicked judge underlines the necessity of persistence and confident trust if one is to succeed: 'Because this widow bothers me, I will vindicate her, or she will wear me out by her continual coming' (Luke 18:5; see chapter 4, nos. 2, 29, 39).

Among the sayings directly related to the Kingdom of God, faith/trust once more plays the leading role. It supersedes blood ties and overrules neighbourliness and friendship. This explains the lack of success of Jesus as a charismatic prophet among his relations and all his acquaintances in Nazareth: 'A prophet is not without honour, except in his own country, and among his own kin, and in his own house' (Mark 6:4; see chapter 8, no. 4). Moreover, Jesus was convinced that only those who approached the Kingdom like children, that is to say, with complete trust in a caring father, could gain admittance to it (see (4) below). The power of faith could exceptionally inspire even Gentiles like the Syrophoenician woman and the Roman centurion: 'Not even in Israel have I found such faith . . . Be it done for you as you have believed' (Matt. 8:10, 13; Luke 7:9; see chapter 8, no. 37). According to the oft-repeated maxim, faith could even move mountains (see chapter 8, nos. 16, 35, 46).

2. *The efficacy of prayer*

The effective prayer may be considered as a sub-category of potent faith. In the view of Jesus prayer should be stimulated and activated by limitless trust if it is to produce the hoped-for result, even an outcome that in normal circumstances would seem impossible: 'Whatever you ask in prayer, believe that you have received it, and it will be yours' (Mark 11:24; Matt. 21:22; see chapter 6, no. 1). The man of prayer should address God in solitude to help concentration (Matt. 6:5–8; see chapter 9, no. 21). He must not be shy, and like a child he has to persist in asking. But even if the hyperbole of moving mountains is left aside, Jesus taught his disciples in the two final requests of the Lord's Prayer that confident supplication would defeat temptation and provide protection against the satanic Tempter. The prayer of petition must also be totally inspired by trust. Hence Jesus discouraged his disciples from presenting God with a shopping list because the heavenly Father knows in advance everyone's needs: 'In praying do not heap up empty phrases as the Gentiles do; for they think that they will be heard for their many words . . . your Father knows what you need before you ask him' (Matt. 6:7–8; see chapter 3, no. 19; chapter 6, nos. 1, 5, 7; chapter 8, nos. 16, 35, 46). The subject of the efficacy of prayer, like faith/trust, occurs in the diverse layers of Gospel tradition, in Mark, *Q* and *M*; that is, the criterion of coherence goes hand-in-hand with the criterion of multiple attestation.

3. *Belief in the fatherhood of God*

Jesus' habit of referring to and addressing God as 'Father' is well known and universally acknowledged.[6] 'Father' is the best metaphorical expression of a deity characterized by concern and care for the created world and is also the direct counterpart and consequence of Jesus' designation by others as 'Son of God'.

The concept is the legacy of the Bible and of early post-biblical Judaism (Apocrypha, Dead Sea Scrolls, etc.). It should be noted, however, that whereas in formal Jewish religious language and prayer the term 'Father' is less frequently employed than 'Lord', 'King', or 'Master of the Universe', in the terminology attributed to Jesus the use of 'Father', the Aramaic *Abba*, is dominant. It testifies to a genuine filial attitude: 'Abba, Father, all things are possible to thee; . . . yet not what I will, but what thou wilt' (Mark 14:36; see chapter 6, nos. 3 and 5).

The evidence is too extensive to be quoted item by item, but detailed documentation may be found in the sections on prayer (chapter 6, nos. 2, 3, 5–9) and on the Kingdom of God (chapter 8, nos. 3, 10, 14, 15, 20, 30, 35, 36, 39, 53). The examples are equally distributed among Mark, *Q*, *M* and *L*. The only case where the usual familiarity of the invocation *Abba* is absent and is replaced by the more formal 'My God' (*Eloi/Eli*) occurs in the last cry of Jesus on the cross according to Mark 15:34 and Matthew 27:46 (see chapter 6, no. 4). In Luke's edited version the cry 'My God, my God, why hast thou forsaken me?'

6. See *The Changing Faces of Jesus*, 198–201; *The Religion of Jesus the Jew*, 152–83.

is toned down and replaced by words of pious resignation, 'Father, into thy hands I commit my spirit' (Luke 23:46).

Since the use of 'Father' was part of the terminology of post-biblical Jewish prayer, it cannot be taken for granted that every Gospel passage in which 'Father' figures is a genuine saying of Jesus. But all other things being equal, the presence of the term, especially of the Aramaic *Abba*, lends powerful support to the case for authenticity.

4. *The need to become like children*

A powerful argument in favour of an authentic saying of Jesus can be built on the recurring feature emphasizing that those who seek admittance into the Kingdom must become and behave like children. It has been pointed out earlier (chapter 8, p. 284) that the central position assigned to children in defining the right spiritual attitude in the quest of the Kingdom is typical of the teaching of Jesus: 'Whoever does not receive the kingdom of God like a child shall not enter it' (Mark 10:15; Luke 18:17; see chapter 8, no. 10). This distinctive feature sets him apart both from the Bible and from later Jewish literature, as in neither of them did children play any significant part. The number of sayings is not particularly large (see chapter 8, nos. 10 and 34, and chapter 9, no. 12), but they mirror what seems to belong to the quintessence of Jesus' religious outlook. To become like a child in Jesus' parlance demands a conduct inspired by total openness and reliance on a caring heavenly Father. It is generally admitted that these sayings stem directly from the mouth of Jesus and truly reveal his personal filial piety and the piety which he sought to instil into all his disciples.

5. *A new eschatological concept of the family*

In the biblical and post-biblical age Jewish society had been characterized by particularly strong ties holding together members of the family and the clan. Jesus, in contrast, stood out as someone who proclaimed that in the eschatological age blood loyalty must come second to attachment to the community of those who wholeheartedly followed his teaching in their quest of the Kingdom of God: 'Whoever does the will of God is my brother, and sister, and mother' (Mark 3:35; Matt. 12:50).

The idea of a rift in families during the run-up period to the Kingdom derives from biblical prophecy. 'For I have come to set a man against his father,' etc. (Mic. 7:6) is quoted by Matthew and Luke (Matt. 10:34–36; Luke 12:51–53; see chapter 5, no. 24), and the same idea is expressed without citing Scripture in the saying 'And brother will deliver up brother to death, and the father his child,' etc. (Mark 13:12–13; Matt. 10:21–22; 24:9–13; Luke 21:16–17, 19; see chapter 8, no. 21). The anti-family angle is further accentuated in the case of Jesus because of the undisguised hostility of his relations, who frowned on, and tried to oppose, his prophetic-charismatic activity (Mark 6:4; Matt. 13:57; see chapter 3, no. 8). This attitude explains his sharp and provocative statements, 'Who are my mother and my brothers?' and 'My mother and my brothers are those who hear the word of God and do it' (Mark 3:33; Matt. 12:48; Luke 8:21). Add to these the exaggerated exclamation that loving one's father and mother more than Jesus excludes a candidate from the rank of his disciples, or even 'If any one comes to me and does not hate his own father and mother and wife and children and brothers and sisters, yes, and even his own life, he cannot be my disciple' (Matt. 10:37; Luke 14:26; see chapter 8, no. 3). In these circumstances the authenticity of the maxims which clash with the traditional Jewish attitude to kith and kin can hardly be questioned.

6. Healing and exorcism in the final age

The numerous references in the Synoptic Gospels demonstrate that healing and exorcism represent essential activities of Jesus. They find external support in the *Testimonium Flavianum*, Flavius Josephus' notice on Jesus, in which he is characterized not only as a 'wise man', but also as a 'performer of astonishing deeds' (*Antiquities* 18:63). To these *prima facie* authentic Gospel references belong not only the typical statements concerning the cure of the sick and the expulsion of demons (see chapter 2, nos. 1, 4, 5, 6, 7, 8), but sayings such as 'If it is by the Spirit [or 'finger'] of God that I cast out demons, then the kingdom of God has come upon you' (Matt. 12:28; Luke 11:20). As I noted earlier, by authenticity I do not necessarily mean strict verbal reproduction of an utterance of Jesus. It is quite possible, for example, that when Jesus described his charismatic deeds as signs heralding the messianic age he may have done so in general terms, and the subsequent introduction of the phraseology of Isaiah on the recovery of the blind and the lame, etc. may be the work of the later Gospel tradition (Matt. 11:4–5; Luke 7:22; see chapter 5, no. 25, and chapter 8, no. 7).

In this regard it is worth pointing out that contrary to the conventional understanding of the criterion of dissimilarity – sayings attributed to Jesus need to differ from Jewish tradition to count as authentic – certain utterances have a claim to genuineness just because they echo Jewish custom. I am thinking of the exorcistic-therapeutic vocabulary such as 'Come out!', 'Be silent!', '*Ephphatha!*' which Jesus, like other healers and exorcists, was bound to use.[7]

7. *The choice of hyperbolical speech and verbal twists*

The last two features selected as typical of Jesus are of a stylistic nature. They may be thought to be of lesser significance as they could easily proceed from the writers or editors of the Gospels. They are, however, of such uniformity and curiosity that their derivation from the teacher standing behind the teaching is a strong possibility verging on probability.

Hyperbolical speech or rhetorical exaggeration seems to be the hallmark of the poetic language of Jesus. An exhaustive list of examples would be tedious, but a selection of them will show that the theory is well founded. Here are some instances: 'straining out a gnat and swallowing a camel' (Matt. 23:24; see chapter 2, no. 15B); 'offering the other cheek' (Matt. 5:39; Luke 6:29; see chapter 3, no. 14); 'the camel going through the eye of a needle' (Mark 10:25; Matt. 19:24; Luke 18:25; see chapter 3, no. 12); 'loving one's enemy' as symbol of disinterested love (Matt. 5:44; Luke 6:27; see chapter 3, no. 15); 'sending sheep (or even lambs) among wolves' (Matt. 10:16; Luke 10:3; see chapter 3, no. 28); 'plucking out one's eye' or 'cutting off

7. For further examples of customary Jewish formulae, see chapter 1, nos. 2, 4, 6, 8, 10, 13, 17.

one's right hand' (Matt. 5:29–30; see chapter 5, no. 32) and even 'making oneself a eunuch' (Matt. 19:12; see chapter 9, no. 25); 'hating one's father and mother' (Luke 14:26; see chapter 8, no. 3); forbidding the application of the terms 'father' or 'good' to anyone except God (Mark 10:18; Luke 18:19; see chapter 8, no. 14, and Matt. 23:9; see chapter 9, no. 26), etc.

Another stylistic peculiarity notable in the sayings of Jesus consists in twists introduced into commonly used figurative speech. To provide a modern English illustration: the celebrated Oxford wit, Maurice Bowra, reversing the phrase 'to *cold*-shoulder someone', spoke of a person who gave him 'the *warm* shoulder'. The Gospels attest a number of examples where accepted idioms are given a similar unexpected turn. Thus when Jesus invites Peter and Andrew and others of his disciples to become 'fishers of men', he transforms a phrase usually implying destruction and killing into a metaphor of salvation (Mark 1:17; Matt. 4:19; cf. Luke 5:10; see chapter 1, nos. 1 and 34). In a somewhat different genre, king Solomon, who was seen as a symbol of luxurious living and as a generous host who gave lavish banquets, is made by Jesus into the proverbial model of sartorial elegance: 'Even Solomon in all his glory was not arrayed like one of these [lilies of the field]' (Matt. 6:29; Luke 12:27; see chapter 3, no. 19). For a final example, take the symbolical number 77. It is used in Genesis 4:24 as the upper limit of permissible revenge for wounding someone. On Jesus' lips the same figure, 'seventy-seven times' or 'seventy times seven', becomes the ideal ceiling for forgiveness, not for vengeance (Matt. 18:22; see chapter 9, no. 15).

Taken separately, these hyperbolical twists and slants may have little demonstrative value in themselves, but cumulatively they amount to a strong suggestion that a single original mind stands behind them, that is to say, that they are authentic words of Jesus.

Conclusion

In this quest for authenticity the parameters of the genuine sayings of Jesus have been defined. I first proceeded by way of elimination and set aside church-inspired alterations. This was followed by the selection of further topics which were compatible, indeed consonant, with the first group of genuine doctrinal statements by virtue of coherence and often of multiple attestation.

Two further tasks remain. For easy consultation, the reader will find in the Appendix on pages 419–36 a list of all the sayings attributed to Jesus in the Gospels, divided into two classes with the items judged certainly or probably genuine being distinguished from the rest by an asterisk (*).

More importantly, in the Epilogue I will endeavour to sketch, on the basis of the words considered most likely to be authentic, a portrait of Jesus, herald of the Kingdom of God, and an outline of the religion which he proclaimed to men, women and children blessed with eyes to see and ears to hear.

Epilogue: Jesus and his teaching in the light of his 'authentic' words

A final challenge still awaits us: the presentation in a nutshell and a summary assessment of the personality and message of Jesus, including a concise review of the purpose, motivation and form of his actions, and of the traits of his character. This survey will not amount to a systematic account of the teaching of Jesus. There was nothing systematic in his message. He was not a professional theologian who subjected the secret life of God to close scrutiny. He was an existentialist preacher who endeavoured to persuade his disciples to change their lives and to collaborate with him in the great enterprise of preparing the way towards the Kingdom of God. A glance at the relationship between the historical Jesus and modern Christianity from the perspective of a twenty-first-century observer will complete this historical sketch.

The personality of Jesus of Nazareth

The sayings of Jesus reveal practically nothing about his background and past life. In Mark, the oldest of the Gospels, he turns up suddenly like the hero of a novel or a film. We are told very little about his family, and nothing about his education or his early professional life. It was not his primary concern to reflect on his own person. The little 'biographical' information we have is due, not to Jesus, who never reminisces of his childhood or youth, but to the storytellers, the evangelists (Mark 6:3; Matt. 13:55; John 6:42). They tell us that Jesus hailed from the insignificant Galilean town of Nazareth, unknown to Josephus or to the Mishnah, where he was a *tekton*, the Greek word designating a builder or a carpenter.[1] The same Mark and Matthew also mention Mary (Maria, in Hebrew Miriam), the mother of Jesus. His father, Joseph, also a carpenter, appears by name only in Luke 4:22 and John 1:45 and 6:42, if we disregard the artificial genealogies and legendary infancy narratives of Matthew and Luke. Mark and Matthew name four brothers of Jesus (James, Judas, Joses or Joseph and Simon) and refer anonymously to his several sisters (Mark 6:3; Matt. 13:55–56). For Jesus, however, the real members of his family – mother, brothers and sisters – are not his flesh and blood, but those who listen to the word of God and are prepared to do his will (Mark 3:33–35; Matt. 12:48–50; Luke 8:21; see chapter 8, no. 3). One may deduce from these allusions that during his Galilean activity Jesus was not on good terms with his relations, who wanted to interfere with his calling (Mark 3:21). Further maxims of disillusioned wisdom intimate that Jesus met with a cool reception among his relatives and neighbours: 'A prophet is not without honour, except in his own country, and among his own kin, and in his own house,' he once remarked (Mark 6:4; Matt. 13:57).

According to his own words, the scene of his Galilean ministry was the northern shore of the Lake of Gennesaret. The places explicitly listed in a saying of Jesus are Chorazin, a townlet lying a few miles north of the lake, and the fishing villages of Bethsaida and Capernaum, where many of Jesus' healings and exorcisms are reported to have taken place (Matt. 11:21–23; Luke 10:13–15). None of the Synoptic evangelists, let alone Jesus himself, ever alluded to the larger towns of the area: Sepphoris, the regional capital, within a stone's throw from Nazareth, Gabara (or Araba), Tarichaeae, centre of the local fishing industry, and the new city of Tiberias, built in the lifetime of Jesus by Herod Antipas, ruler of Galilee, in honour of the reigning emperor Tiberius.[2] Jesus was not attracted to urban life; he was clearly a son of the Galilean countryside.

His first appearance in public is associated with John the Baptist, the eremitic prophet who called his Jewish compatriots to repentance in the wilderness lying alongside the river Jordan. Jesus, like many of

1. The Aramaic equivalent of 'carpenter' can also mean 'learned man', but it is unlikely that this signification is applicable to Jesus.

2. Tiberias figures in the Fourth Gospel (John 6:1, 23; 21:1), though not even John puts the name of the city into the mouth of Jesus.

his fellow citizens, responded to John's appeal. The Gospels have preserved no direct account of Jesus conveying to John his thought and appreciation of him. However, the fact that his original proclamation, 'Repent, for the kingdom of heaven is at hand' (Matt. 4:17; Mark 1:15), echoes John's theme (Matt. 3:2), and the incidental fulsome praises lavished by him on the Baptist – 'among those born of women there has risen no one greater than [he]' (Matt. 11:11; Luke 7:28) – prove the high esteem in which he held the man who, to all intents and purposes, can be recognized as his model and source of inspiration. Entering public life, he set out to continue in Galilee the mission of the Baptist, which came to an abrupt end when Herod Antipas imprisoned him in the Transjordanian hilltop fortress of Machaerus and ordered his execution by the sword (Mark 1:14–15; Matt. 4:12, 17; Josephus, *Antiquities* 18:116–19).

The three aspects of the public activity of Jesus, curing the sick, delivering people from demonic possession and preaching (already outlined in the narratives of chapter 1), are also disclosed in his sayings. His exhortation to adopt *teshuvah* or turning (repentance) and his proclamation of the way leading to the Kingdom of God (Mark 1:15; Matt. 4:17) were accompanied by charismatic acts of exorcism and healing: 'Behold, I cast out demons and perform cures' (Luke 13:32). Or even more powerfully, 'If it is by the Spirit/finger of God that I cast out demons, then the kingdom of God has come upon you' (Matt. 12:28; Luke 11:20). Jesus' unusual style of argument provoked amazement. He did not quote the Bible to prove his message, but displayed charismatic power instead. People commented that he introduced a new form of teaching, one 'with authority', in subjugating the forces of evil through the Spirit of God (Mark 1:21–22, 27–28; Matt. 7:28; Luke 4:32, 36; Matt. 12:28; Luke 11:20). His disciples were also entrusted with identical tasks: 'Preach as you go, saying, "The kingdom of heaven is at hand." Heal the sick, raise the dead, cleanse lepers, cast out demons' (Matt. 10:7–8; Luke 10:9, 17).

According to the evangelists, he occasionally showed compassion to Gentiles. The servant of the Roman centurion resident in Capernaum (Matt. 8:5–13; Luke 7:1–10), the Gergesene demoniac (Mark 5:1–19; Matt. 8:28–34; Luke 8:26–39) and the daughter of a Greek woman from the region of Tyre and Sidon (Mark 7:24–30; Matt. 15:21–28) became the beneficiaries of his charismatic power of healing and exorcism. Nevertheless these cases are given as exceptions. In fact, Jesus found it astonishing that Gentiles were able to display deep trust in God. While non-Jews were now and again healed by him, we do not encounter any example of his instructing them. What is more, he had no hesitation in declaring that his message was strictly for 'the lost sheep of the house of Israel' (Matt. 15:24). He spoke harshly to, and about, Gentiles, comparing them disparagingly to dogs and pigs (Mark 7:27; Matt. 7:6; 15:26). When Jesus dispatched his apostles on mission, not only did he specify that they were to address only Jews, but he also expressly forbade them to approach Gentiles, or even to enter Samaritan localities (Matt. 10:5–6). The only logical inference that can be drawn from these premisses is that Jesus was concerned only with Jews, because in his view citizenship of the Kingdom of God was reserved for them alone.

The religious and spiritual nature of the Kingdom will be the subject of our examination of the eschatological message of Jesus. Nevertheless it may be anticipated at this juncture that despite the patriotic fever that impregnated Jewish, and in particular Galilean, society in the age of Jesus, his ministry for the Kingdom was devoid of political, i.e. revolutionary inspiration. He had no anti-Roman bias. He embraced the doctrine of non-resistance to evil, and as a lover of hyperboles he even advocated love of one's enemies (Matt. 5:39; Luke 6:29; Matt. 5:44; Luke 6:27). In a more down-to-earth vein, in the memorable words, 'Render to Caesar the things that are Caesar's' (Mark 12:17; Matt. 22:21; Luke 20:25), Jesus approved of, or at least did not object to, paying tax to Rome, which was considered the ultimate betrayal by Jewish revolutionaries. The small company of his close disciples, mostly uneducated Galilean fishermen, whom he selected for spreading the good news of the Kingdom and dispensing the charisma of healing and exorcism, were not trained in warfare. He did not appoint them to be freedom fighters or guerrillas, but benevolent 'fishers of men' (Mark 1:17; Matt. 4:19; Luke 5:10).

As a representative of God, a latter-day prophet, a Hasid, Jesus devoted himself totally to the cause with which, he believed, God had entrusted him. His religious personality is reflected in his ideas about God, his Torah and his Kingdom. His character, personality and way of life are mostly revealed in *obiter dicta*, in incidental utterances. Convinced of the proximity of the day of the Lord, Jesus was happy to embrace the harsh existence of a wandering preacher. He forsook family life and declined the comforts of the home fire. 'Foxes have holes, and birds of the air have nests,' he told his followers, 'but the son of Man has nowhere to lay his head' (Matt. 8:20; Luke 9:58). His modesty is revealed not only in his choice of the humble and unshowy way of referring to himself as the 'son of Man', but also in his dislike for honorific titles: his disciples were not to be called 'rabbi' or 'master'. 'He who is greatest among you shall be your servant' (Matt. 23:8–11). He was an irenic spirit and sponsored non-violence: 'If anyone strikes you on the right cheek, turn to him the other also' (Matt. 5:39; Luke 6:29).

Jesus never chose to call himself 'Messiah' or 'Son of God' and even when others questioned him about his Messiahship, he usually declined to give a straight answer.[3] As for the epithet 'Son of God', disallowing the combined expression 'Messiah, the Son of God' in Matthew (Matt. 26:63; 16:16) where 'Son of God' and 'Messiah' are synonyms, it is never spoken by Jesus himself. One has to be foolish to believe the mockery of the chief priests and scribes, taunting Jesus to get down from the cross because he had claimed to be the 'Son of God' (Matt. 27:43). Only demons or people possessed by demons addressed Jesus by this title (Matt. 4:3; Luke 4:3, 9; Mark 3:11; Luke 4:41; Mark 5:7; Matt. 8:29; Luke 8:28). The only example in which the disciples call Jesus 'Son of God' and 'worship him' comes from a late legendary addition by Matthew to the story of Jesus walking on the water (Matt. 14:33). In the parallel passage of Mark the astonishment of the companions of Jesus is caused, not by his walking on the water, but by the earlier miraculous feeding of the five thousand with five loaves (Mark 6:51–52).

Though frequently and spontaneously acknowledged as leader and

3. For the exception in Mark 14:62 see chapter 1, no. 26. Jesus' only positive approval of being called 'Christ' follows the confession of Peter in Matthew 16:17–18. Against the authenticity of this saying speak the silence of Mark and Luke in the corresponding place, and the fact that the neighbouring reference to Peter, the rock on which a church is built, is also inauthentic, being unknown to Mark and Luke. Add to this that a few verses later Jesus disparagingly addresses Peter as 'Satan' (Mark 8:33; Matt. 16:23).

master, Jesus insisted that he was not there to rule but to serve (Luke 22:27). He saw himself as the champion of the weak and the despised; his appointed task was to 'seek and to save the lost' (Luke 19:10), to be the shepherd who spared no effort to find a missing lamb (Matt. 18:12–14; Luke 15:4–7). He cherished the proverbial pariahs of Jewish society, the repentant tax-collectors and harlots (Matt. 21:31–32), and scandalized the genteel pious by sharing the table of those ostracized by the conventionally devout bourgeoisie (Matt. 11:19; Luke 7:34). He loved children, and on account of their absolute faith in paternal goodwill he proclaimed them models of the genuine religious spirit: 'Let the children come to me, . . . for to such belongs the kingdom of God . . . Whoever does not receive the kingdom of God like a child shall not enter it' (Mark 10:14–15; Matt. 19:14; 18:3; Luke 18:16–17).

In Jesus the extremes met. He led the austere life of an itinerant prophet (Matt. 8:20; Luke 9:58), counselled his followers to carry their cross (Matt. 10:38; Luke 14:27), and hyperbolically speaking to undergo self-mutilation (Mark 9:43–48; Matt. 18:8–9; cf. Matt. 5:29–30; 19:12). He loved to employ exaggeration when teaching restraint and abnegation. Yet at the same time, in sharp contrast to his mentor John the Baptist who lived on a diet of locusts and wild honey, Jesus did not dislike a good meal. He sat at the table of wealthy publicans. In the famous parable of the prodigal son the father, symbolizing God, welcomes the return of his wayward child with a lavish party and orders his servants to roast the fatted calf (Luke 15:23). It is not surprising therefore that the convivial Jesus was vilified by his critics as 'a glutton and a drunkard, a friend [and table companion] of tax-collectors and sinners' (Matt. 11:18–19; Luke 7:33–34).

Next to these manifestations of kindness and compassion towards children and social outcasts, we find Gospel sayings which reveal in Jesus the fiery nature of his Galilean compatriots, bellicose from infancy according to Josephus (*War* 3:41). Jesus could utter impatient and sharp words, calling Peter 'Satan' (Mark 8:33; Matt. 16:23), the gravely ill daughter of the Syrophoenician woman a 'dog' (Mark 7:27; Matt. 15:26), and referring to the ruler of Galilee, Herod Antipas, as 'that fox' (Luke 13:32). He could be short-tempered with slow-witted disciples (Mark 10:14) and show his indignation towards the self-satisfied and the hypocrite (Mark 12:39–40; Luke 20:46–47; Matt. 23:5–7). Once when he was hungry, he is even depicted as unreasonable. Looking for figs on a fig tree but finding none, he pronounced a curse on it although the fruit harvest was still some time away (Mark 11:12–14; Matt. 21:18–19). Jesus was not exactly the gentle, sugary, meek and mild figure of pious Christian imagination.

He often spoke and acted with authority, but he was also ready to plead ignorance or confess incompetence. Although he proclaimed the imminent advent of the Kingdom of God, he also admitted that he was not privy to the exact time of its coming: 'of that day or that hour no one knows, not even the angels in heaven, nor the Son, but only the Father' (Mark 13:32; Matt. 24:36). Similarly he declared that he had no say in matters pertaining to the protocol of the eschatological banquet; God alone was in charge of the seating arrangements: 'To sit at my right hand and at my left is not mine to grant, but it is for those for whom it has been prepared by my Father' (Matt. 20:23).

The tragic end of Jesus came suddenly in the course of a fateful pilgrimage to Jerusalem, probably in AD 30. During his short charismatic ministry in Galilee, although he encountered some jealousy and hostility among small-minded local scribes and synagogue elders, he was on the whole a highly popular and much sought-after healer, exorcist and teacher. For the local people of the region of Lake Gennesaret, Jesus was a man of God, and even in Jerusalem he was hailed as 'the prophet from Nazareth in Galilee' (Matt. 21:11).

His downfall resulted from an act of prophetic zeal. He caused a fracas in the merchants' quarter in the Temple a few days before Passover. The nervous priestly authorities in charge of the maintenance of law and order sensed danger, and feared that the disorder might start a rebellion. They felt that it was their duty towards the Jewish nation to intervene. However, they preferred not to act directly, and handed over to the secular arm of Rome the man whom they considered a potentially dangerous revolutionary leader because of his influence on the crowds. Such a justification for the condemnation of Jesus is supported by Flavius Josephus' account of the execution of John the Baptist. Herod Antipas thought that John's eloquence might lead to sedition, so he took an appropriate preventive measure (*Antiquities* 18:117–18). Pilate, notorious for his cruelty, did not hesitate to put to death the 'king of the Jews', whom he believed to be an insurgent. Jesus expired on a Roman cross and was buried. But his disciples saw him in repeated visions and continued to perform charismatic deeds in his name, which persuaded them that he had been raised from the dead.

The diverse features of Jesus, which I have assembled from his genuine sayings, form a colourful, complex and rich human personality. It now remains for us to search for his spiritual characteristics so that we can reconstruct the religion preached and practised by him.[4]

The religion of Jesus

Contrary to the didactic style of John and Paul, who aimed to delve into the mystical relationship of Jesus to God and his 'mythical' function as redeemer of mankind, the genuine teaching of Jesus contains nothing abstract, theoretical and speculative. He was not intrigued by the nature of the Deity, even less was he concerned with his own part in the great drama of the *eschaton*. He rather tried to convey to his audience, especially to the inner circle of his apostles, how to draw near to God, and respond to his appeal through concrete religious behaviour and action. The basic and all-encompassing vision of Jesus was centred on the somewhat nebulous reality of the divine Kingdom. He was convinced that his God-given vocation was to persuade his Jewish contemporaries to strive whole-heartedly towards this Kingdom.

Five major themes constitute Jesus' message: (i) the Kingdom of God; (ii) the observance of the Torah in the final age; (iii) eschatological piety; (iv) the prayers of Jesus; and (v) his view of God.

(i) The Kingdom of God

Though it figures about eighty times in the Synoptic Gospels, the exact meaning of the expression 'Kingdom of God' or, according to Matthew, 'Kingdom of heaven', is never spelled out by Jesus. There is

4. For a fuller treatment of this subject see *The Changing Faces of Jesus*, 193–221, 249–58, and *The Religion of Jesus the Jew*, *passim*.

no doubt that in his mind it alluded to a new reality in which God's rule over Israel (and beyond) would become truly recognized and effective. As in the rest of Jewish literature of the period, the description of the Kingdom always proceeds by means of comparison. It is regularly likened by Jesus to various kinds of this-worldly reality, though significantly never to a political or military organization. In his thought, the Kingdom resembles a rich harvest (Mark 4:26–29), or a particularly tall mustard plant grown from the tiniest of seeds (Mark 4:30–32 and parallels). It may be compared to a small lump of leaven causing a large amount of dough to swell (Matt. 13:33; Luke 12:20–21), to an enormous treasure hidden in a field, or to a precious pearl (Matt. 13:44–46). True to his existential turn of mind, Jesus was only interested in the action leading to the goal, that is to say, the perfect observance of the Torah and correct behaviour in the new era of the last days. The Kingdom is always depicted by Jesus as the ultimate spiritual value. Its precise essence did not bother him; he was concerned with the ways and means which would secure admittance into it.

(ii) The observance of the Torah in the final age

The piety of Jesus, a Jew born and bred, was centred on the Torah, the fundamental charter and the principal distinguishing mark of the Jewish religion. But the Torah could be looked at from more than one angle, taught by many teachers of different schools and observed in various ways. Jesus, having adopted a feverish eschatological stance, perceived and practised the Law in his own characteristic fashion, which from time to time brought him into conflict with his more conventional and tranquil co-religionists.

He was deeply convinced of the centrality and permanent validity of the Mosaic heritage, which he approached from the point of view of a man of holiness living in the last age. From his perspective even the pedestrian rules and regulations of the Torah about agriculture, business, sex, food, etc., possessed a powerful inner spiritual significance. Therefore Jesus insisted on the necessity of obeying all the details of the Mosaic rules, including the ritual precepts, until the arrival of God's Kingdom (Mark 1:40–44 and parallels). His principle is clearly set out: 'Till heaven and earth pass away, not an iota, not a dot, will pass away from the law' (Matt. 5:18). Again, and even more significantly as it comes from the pen of the non-Jewish Luke, Jesus asserts: 'It is easier for heaven and earth to pass away, than for one dot of the law to become void' (Luke 16:17). The polemical edge to these sayings is due to frequent small-minded criticism voiced by narrow-minded country lawyers and leaders of village synagogues, incapable of grasping that the peculiar interpretation given by Jesus to certain commandments did not contradict, but deepened their meaning. For this reason he felt the need to reassure directly those attached to the observance of the Torah: 'Think not that I have come to abolish the law and the prophets; I have come not to abolish them but to fulfil them' (Matt. 5:17). Indeed, Jesus declared that faithfulness to 'the least of these commandments' would be highly regarded in the Kingdom of heaven (Matt. 5:19), and above all that the divine gift of life in the Kingdom would depend on the fulfilment of the precepts of the Decalogue (Mark 10:19; Matt. 19:17; Luke 18:20).

Complaints against Jesus' attitude to the Law mostly arose from his practice of healing and exorcism on the Sabbath, and from his prophetic internalization and ethical interpretation of ritual uncleanness. Healing on the Sabbath resulted from simple convenience: many sick people attended synagogue gatherings on the Sabbath, where they met Jesus and implored and obtained his help. For Jesus, as for many later rabbis, healing came under the heading of the saving of life, which by common consent was held to override Sabbath prohibitions: 'The sabbath was made for man, not man for the sabbath, so the son of Man is lord even of the sabbath' (Mark 2:27–28; Matt. 12:8; Luke 6:5). Leaving aside the legal issue of whether his method of healing by verbal command amounted to 'work' – I do not think that it did – Jesus simply adopted the common-sense attitude of ordinary people of his time and place. So he could rhetorically ask, 'Is it lawful on the sabbath to do good or do harm, to save life or to kill?' (Mark 3:4). Elsewhere he gave a more practical formulation to this question: 'What man of you, if he has one sheep and it falls into a pit on the sabbath, will not lay hold of it and lift it out? Of how much more value is a man than a sheep!' (Matt. 12:11–12). As for the matter of uncleanness, Jesus' emphasis on the primacy of morality over the ritual could only be misunderstood by a pedestrian mind: 'There is nothing outside a man which by going into him can defile him, but the things which come out of a man are what defile him . . . For from within, out of the heart of a man, come evil thoughts, fornication, theft, murder, adultery . . . and they defile a man' (Mark 7:15, 21–23; Matt. 15:11, 19–20).

This latter twist, the bringing to the foreground of the concealed, inward motivation, the root cause of the moral action, is manifest throughout Jesus' interpretation of the Torah. It underlies his understanding of all the biblical precepts, even of those commandments of the Decalogue which relate to ethics. For Jesus, the ultimate source of murder was anger, and adultery was the final outcome of an initial lustful desire. He held that neutralization of the cause would prevent the effect ever happening. Reliability stemming from constant veracity would render vows and oaths superfluous. And the best remedy against violence and retaliation – 'an eye for an eye' – would be a pacific and generous demeanour, hyperbolically the offering of the other cheek, that is, the disarming of an enemy with a gesture of love (Matt. 5:21–48; Luke 6:27–36). Seen through the prism of Jesus' piety, the purpose of the Law was not simply the regulation of everyday life and religious practice; it was above all intended to teach Jews the duty of obedience and total self-surrender to God. Jesus' various attempts at compressing the many precepts of the Torah to a few, to the Decalogue, to the biblical commandments of loving God and loving one's neighbour, or to the combined single precept of loving God *and* one's neighbour (Mark 12:30–31; Matt. 22:37–39; Luke 10:27), are simply meant to facilitate obedience. So also is the non-biblical Golden Rule: do as you would like to be done to, or negatively, don't do to others what you yourself would hate (Matt. 7:12; Luke 6:31).

(iii) The eschatological piety of Jesus

The conviction that the advent of the Kingdom was imminent instilled a sense of extreme urgency into the mind of Jesus, a sense which he attempted to transmit to his disciples. As the sayings assembled in chapters 8 and 9 indicate, all his followers were to become eschatological enthusiasts. They had to dedicate themselves unreservedly to the fulfilment of their divine vocation.

According to Jesus, the seekers of the Kingdom had to realize that the task was hard and pressing; the end was beckoning and time was in short supply. The narrow gate leading to the Kingdom stood at the end of an arduous path (Matt. 7:13–14), and progress towards it required continuous sacrifice. First, possessions had to go overboard. Even a camel could squeeze through the eye of a needle more easily than a wealthy man was able to enter God's Kingdom (Mark 10:25 and parallels). Consequently earthly goods were to be exchanged for an imperishable currency of treasure (Mark 10:21 and parallels; Matt. 6:19–21; Luke 12:33–34). No one could simultaneously 'serve God and mammon' (Matt. 6:24; Luke 16:13). The sacrifice of material wealth had to go hand-in-hand with a willingness to cut ties of kinship if they hindered the pursuit of a higher calling. In fact, following the example of Jesus, the worker for the Kingdom could be required to turn his back on his family, or according to his striking hyperbole 'hate his own father and mother and wife and children and brothers and sisters' (Luke 14:26; Mark 10:29–30; Matt. 19:28–29; Luke 18:29). The climax of this chain of rhetorical exaggerations is the total sacrifice of the self. It is pictured as willingness to 'take up [one's] cross' (Mark 8:34 and parallels), or – more gruesomely – as preparedness to sever a hand or a foot, pluck out an eye or castrate oneself 'for the sake of the kingdom of heaven' (Mark 9:43–48; Matt. 18:8–9; 19:12).

Because of the impending arrival of the day of the Lord, no delay would be tolerated. The straying sheep and the lost coin had to be retrieved at once (Matt. 18:12–14; Luke 15:4–10); the purchase of the field with the treasure trove in it, and the acquisition of the exceptionally precious pearl, were not to be deferred until the next day (Matt. 13:44–46). Departure on the great journey could suffer no postponement, not even for the fulfilment of such a sacred obligation as the burial of one's father (Matt. 8:22; Luke 9:60). The ploughman's duty was to look firmly ahead; he was not allowed to glance backward even for a single moment (Luke 9:62).

Jesus further combined the spirit of sacrifice and the element of extreme pressure with the positive virtues of generosity and trust. The munificent donor would receive extra recompense (Mark 4:24 and parallels) and the big-hearted penitent, like the reformed prostitute who anointed the feet of Jesus, could look forward to absolute forgiveness (Luke 7:41–47). Liberality would replace revenge (Matt.

5:38–42; Luke 6:29–30) and, paradox of all paradoxes, hate-filled enemies were to be disarmed with love (Matt. 5:44; Luke 6:27–28). This is the penultimate recipe given by Jesus to those who wished to become sons of the Most High in the Kingdom of God (Luke 6:35).

But the supreme virtue which his followers had to display in their pursuit of righteousness was faith-trust, the beginning and the end, the alpha and the omega, of the race towards the Kingdom. Faith defined his own piety and the piety which his disciples were to practise. Jesus believed in his own mission. He totally trusted his charismatic power which enabled him to perform extraordinary deeds (*paradoxa erga*), to use the terminology of the uncommitted Josephus (*Antiquities* 18:63). Both the parables and the sayings continually bring home to the audience of Jesus the paramount importance of faith. The trust of the widow in her just cause makes her triumph over the wicked judge (Luke 18:2–8). Firm belief procures for the man with an empty larder enough bread to feed an unexpected friend who turns up in the middle of the night (Luke 11:5–8). The parable of the foolish farmer reveals the superior value of reliance on God in comparison with careful forward planning (Luke 12:16–20). The missionaries of the Kingdom were urged by Jesus to rely on divine Providence alone, and were forbidden to carry gold, silver or provisions with them (Mark 6:8 and parallels). Jesus outlawed worry and anxiety on the ground that the God who feeds the birds cares also for those of his children who trust him (Matt. 6:25–34; Luke 12:22–32; Matt. 10:28–31; Luke 12:4–7). The same requirement of faith accounts for Jesus' refusal to provide premonitory signs announcing the arrival of the Kingdom (Mark 8:12; Luke 17:20).

The main religious and moral attributes required of the followers of Jesus are set out in the Beatitudes. In this manifesto, admittance into the Kingdom is promised to the poor, the hungry and the thirsty for justice, the generous and merciful, the irenic, those who are prepared to sacrifice everything (Matt. 5:3–12; Luke 6:20–26). But as I have noted, the one virtue encompassing all other virtues is faith-trust, the foundation stone of the biblical and post-biblical Jewish religion and of the eschatological piety of Jesus.

(iv) The prayers of Jesus

Since as a rule prayer provides the best insight into the religious mentality of an individual, a final glance at the relevant ideas of Jesus may serve as an 'experimental' check on the correctness of the total picture sketched so far. With the exception of the Lord's Prayer, which can be recited either by individuals or by groups, all the instances appearing in the Gospels are meant for personal devotion; in two cases they are for Jesus himself. Faith-trust is the kernel of the act of prayer, too. Boundless confidence in God lies at its heart. In the absence of such a complete dependence on Providence, words addressed to the heavenly Father remain empty phrases, and the prayer is futile. However, with faith everything that is good is obtainable: 'Ask, and it will be given you; seek, and you will find; knock, and it will be opened to you' (Matt. 7:7; Luke 11:9). Indeed in Jesus' habitual hyperbolical phraseology, faith as small as a mustard seed can move mountains (Mark 11:23–24; Matt. 21:21–22). He managed to express his totally God-centred piety in a brief and pithy exclamation, 'Abba, Father, . . . not what I will, but what thou wilt' (Mark 14:36), or even more briefly, 'Thy will be done', the memorable formula included in the Lord's Prayer.

There are two further essential features of prayer prescribed by Jesus. The first is readiness to forgive and the second seclusion. To receive divine absolution, the penitent must be prepared to pardon those who have offended him (Mark 11:25; Matt. 6:14). The requirement of seclusion is typical of the essentially private character of the religion taught by Jesus, who himself is often depicted as choosing solitude for prayer. Nowhere did he leave instructions about public worship in the synagogue or in the Temple. But he insisted that his disciples should speak to God, give alms and fast *in secret*, without ostentation (Matt. 6:2–6). In his eschatological perspective *personal* piety was paramount. The pomposity of the outwardly pious, who wanted their religiosity to be witnessed by all and sundry, provoked his anger: 'Beware of the scribes, who like to go about in long robes, and to have . . . the best seats in the synagogues . . . and for a pretence make long prayers' (Mark 12:38–40 and parallels). God is to be addressed behind closed doors and without a lengthy list of hoped-for goods in hand: 'When you pray, go into your room and shut the door and pray to your Father who is in secret; and your Father who sees in secret will reward you. And in praying do not heap up empty phrases . . . for your Father knows what you need before you ask him' (Matt. 6:6–8). So for Jesus the right spiritual disposition leading to efficacious prayer demands absolute trust in God, generosity and openness towards fellow humans, and a quiet, withdrawn approach to the heavenly Father with no exhibitionism of any kind. The familiar Lord's Prayer (fifty-six words in Matthew's Greek) embodies the most succinct epitome of the religion of Jesus.

(v) The God of Jesus

Our cursory glance at the true message of Jesus will appropriately end with his image of God. We already know that it would be pointless to expect from the Galilean prophet a theoretical definition or even a detailed description of the Deity. Such was not his genre. In Jesus' perception of religion practical reality supplants abstract elucidation. For him, God is what God does. In other words, God reveals himself in what Jesus and his followers acknowledge as divine interventions in their own lives during the final years of the present era, soon to become the transcendent age of the Kingdom.

Jesus' image of God is mirrored in sayings, parables and prayers. The picture is uncomplicated without being superficial or dull. Contrary to common Jewish tradition in which God is usually spoken of as 'King of the Universe', the royal title is never applied to him by Jesus. It figures only in parables which have been classified as inauthentic (for example, Matt. 22:1–14; 25:31–46).[5] Jesus always calls God 'Abba' or 'Father', save in his last cry of incomprehension on the cross, where he addresses him less intimately as 'My God' (Mark 15:34; Matt. 27:46).

Apart from this case, to which I will return, the God of Jesus is one who cares. He looks after the wild flowers and clothes them in beauty, and after the birds and foxes, providing them with shelter and food.

5. For instance in the Parousia scene of the last judgement the king is the glorified Christ, but he is clearly distinguished from God, alluded to as his heavenly Father (Matt. 25:34, 40).

Therefore, and *a fortiori*, humans also must pin their faith on him. In Jesus' eyes, worry, anxiety for the future, counts as a denial of God (Matt. 6:25–34; Luke 12:22–31). For the flock of his children God is like a loving shepherd, who spares no effort to find them if they stray, and rejoices when they are brought safely back into the sheepfold (Matt. 18:12–14; Luke 15:4–7). The God of Jesus is comparable to a warm-hearted and generous employer, like the owner of a vineyard who is ready to overpay some of his hired labourers (Matt. 20:1–16). He is also a solicitous paterfamilias, aware of the needs of all the members of the family (Matt. 6:32; Luke 12:30). He welcomes back with joy and forgiveness ungrateful and rebellious children (Luke 15:11–32), and pardons the sins of those who have forgiven those who have done them wrong (Matt. 6:12; Luke 11:4). However, this warm-hearted parent, anthropomorphically portrayed, is also declared by Jesus to be wholly superior to him. His God is the Master who alone knows and determines the precise moment of the advent of the Kingdom and there he alone is in charge of protocol (Mark 13:32 and parallels; Mark 10:40; Matt. 20:23).

When Jesus' many incidental references to God are gathered together, the portrait that emerges is of a loving Father. He makes the sun rise and the rain fall for the benefit of all; he gives his children their daily bread, knowing in advance, and providing for, all their necessities. Nothing remains secret before him, neither thoughts, nor deeds. He protects the little ones from temptation and delivers them from evil. Above all, he forgives them all, even the publicans and harlots, and welcomes them to his Kingdom. In short, there is not a shadow of harshness or severity in this portrait of the God of Jesus. This would suggest that he had an optimistic outlook on a successful outcome of his mission of gathering together the children of Israel and leading them safely to the gate of the Kingdom of God. He did not foresee the crisis and tragedy of the cross.

The religion of Jesus and Christianity

In the light of all that has been said, how can the religion of Jesus be summarized? His religion is a particular response to a specific situation by an extraordinary man. Christianity, on the other hand, is the general development of the religion of Jesus by practical people planning for the future in an ordinary time setting. The two are definitely connected, yet they are also radically different.

The specific situation arose from the political turmoil generated by the Roman rule in Palestine, first established in 63 BC. The unrest was clearly manifest in rebellious acts following the death of Herod the Great in 4 BC, which were violently suppressed by the Romans, and in the bitter resentment caused by the census or Roman tax registration imposed on Judaea by Quirinius, governor of Syria, in AD 6. The political unrest stirred up and nurtured a feverish longing for an impending divine intervention, especially in the wake of the widely influential ministry of John the Baptist in the late twenties. Jesus was to address and respond to this feverish expectation. The Kingdom of God was believed to be at hand. This Kingdom was a wholly Jewish issue, involving Jews alone, and requiring an exclusively Jewish solution. The non-Jewish world played no active part in it.

The extraordinary man was Jesus of Nazareth, provincial prophet, with no 'rabbinic' education, but filled with insight, compassion, magnetism and charismatic power, ready to throw himself headlong into the gathering movement launched by John the Baptist and take the lead in it.

His particular way of promoting the cause of the Kingdom stemmed from his total conviction of the necessity of the task for which he was commissioned. In consequence he demanded unfettered trust in God from his disciples. Owing to the eschatological nature of their task, its pursuit could not tolerate either slowness or procrastination and required absolute devotion irrespective of the cost. The goal in view was a seat at the eschatological banquet table prepared by God for those who responded to the invitation which Jesus conveyed to them with prophetic urgency. To follow his appeal and enter into the spirit of his eschatological Judaism, the disciples of Jesus were to leave behind uninspired religion, switch their sight to the highest ideals, and steam ahead at top speed.

What makes this religion particularly distinctive is the relentless effort imposed by Jesus on himself and on his followers. He never showed signs of hesitation, nor did he suffer delaying tactics or tergiversation on the part of a prospective disciple. The belief that the Kingdom is near, is coming, has come, carried with it a permanent air of urgency.

The religion revealed by the authentic message of Jesus is straightforward, without complex dogmas, 'mythical' images or self-centred mystical speculation. It resembles a race consisting only of the final straight, demanding from the runners their last ounce of energy and with a winners' medal prepared for all the *Jewish* participants who cross the finishing line. At this juncture, one may wonder today how a religious genius of the calibre of Jesus could have been such a narrow-minded chauvinist. But the Jewish eschatology of that age was exclusive and maybe Jesus was simply a child of his time. On the other hand, he may have embraced the prophetic idea manifest in the second half of the Book of Isaiah according to which the entry of the Jews into God's Kingdom would persuade the Gentiles to join them. If so, Jesus could easily have imagined that on the successful completion of his exclusively Jewish mission, God would step in and take care of the rest of mankind.

Compared with the dynamic religion of Jesus, fully evolved Christianity seems to belong to another world. With its mixture of high philosophical speculation on the triune God, its Johannine logos mysticism and Pauline Redeemer myth of a dying and risen Son of God, with its sacramental symbolism and ecclesiastical discipline substituted for the extinct eschatological passion, with its cosmopolitan openness combined with a built-in anti-Judaism, it is hard to imagine how the two could have sprung from the same source. Yet 2,000-year-old Christianity, responsible for the survival of the Gospel tradition, proudly considers Jesus as its founder and what I have reconstructed as the genuine religion of Jesus is espoused nowadays only by single individuals or is distorted and caricatured by cult groups and sects. Where does this leave us?

Let us first turn to Jesus. The historical Jesus believed in the coming of the Kingdom in his lifetime and this belief furnished the motivation of his eschatological action. However, this belief did not come true. Absolute trust in God prevented him from envisaging the possibility of the cross. Yet, one would imagine that detached observers familiar with the Roman world could easily have anticipated such a tragic outcome. It would seem that only when he let out the Aramaic cry, '*Eloi, Eloi, lama sabachthani*' ('My God, my God, why hast thou forsaken me'), did Jesus suddenly perceive that he would not be able to complete his task, a thought which previously had not even crossed his mind. What we know of his religious personality makes it unlikely that he died as a rebel against God. Indeed, it is easy to imagine that the further cry, mentioned by Mark and Matthew (Mark 15:37; Matt. 27:50) and creatively restored by Luke as 'Father, into thy hands I commit my spirit!' (Luke 23:46), was a sigh of final submission to God: 'Thy will be done'.

For a twenty-first-century person with genuine spiritual insight the absence of the literal fulfilment of Jesus' belief in the arrival of the Kingdom in his time does not count as a failure. Nor does it detract in any way from the fundamental truth that no religious attitude is real without an all-pervading sense of urgency which converts ideas into instant action. And death, which is never far distant from any human being, is a sufficient reason for anyone to feel constantly under pressure on account of the shortness of the allotted time.

The crucifixion raised two problems regarding the future of the Jesus movement. First, his disciples and friends had to ask themselves whether their understanding of the life, the charismatic cures and the message of Jesus was a monumental error? They obviously concluded that this was not the case and this is proved by their subsequent conduct. The success of their resumed charismatic activity of healing and exorcism, described in the Acts of the Apostles, which they continued in the name of Jesus persuaded them that their crucified Master was still alive and active through them, powerful and ready to return soon. For them he rose from the dead.

The second problem concerns eschatological motivation. Could the feeling of urgency which haunted Jesus still affect his followers after the crucifixion? Yes, it did. For Jesus' conviction that his mission and the arrival of the Kingdom of God formed a single and continuous act was replaced in the minds of his disciples by a drama in two acts. The life of Jesus in the recent past (Act 1) was to be followed by the inauguration of the Kingdom after the Parousia, his glorious Second Coming (Act 2). And by the time the feverish expectation of Christ's return began to cool down, spiritual encouragement and security were supplied by the church, a simultaneously maternal and authoritative this-worldly substitute for the Kingdom of God.

The same church, in the footsteps of St Paul, its true founder, succeeded in removing the major obstacle impeding the dissemination of Jesus' message. Jesus considered his mission to be restricted to Jews and explicitly ordered his envoys not to preach the gospel to Gentiles. The apostles, who were delivering a freshly tailored message to Jews about the Messiahship of Jesus, on witnessing the progressive fiasco of the evangelization at home gave in to Paul's insistent pressure, and opened the church to all the nations. The pagans entered in droves, first diluting and soon entirely transforming the Jewish heritage of Jesus. They justified the change by the belief, arising from the late Gospel of John, that the Holy Spirit was sent by Jesus to hand out new revelation and dispense afresh 'all the truth' (John 14:16–17; 16:13).

Hence understandably Christianity considers itself the transmitter to posterity of the legacy of Jesus, albeit one that has been converted by the church into a gospel for the whole human race. Yet on reading the original message, thinking and honest members of the various Christian faiths may (should?) feel the need for a thorough re-examination of the fundamentals of their belief, ethics and piety, a reconsideration which may demand a complete doctrinal restructuring, a new 'reformation'.

As for open-minded and unprejudiced Jews, the Jesus emerging from his authentic sayings must appear to them as a familiar, friendly, attractive and profoundly impressive figure who has something significant and unifying to offer, which Jews can share with mankind at large.

Some years ago I gave a lecture on the historical Jesus to the teaching staff and graduate students of an interdenominational theological faculty in Australia. At the end of a lengthy and lively discussion I was faced with a final question: 'How can we improve our understanding of Jesus?' I tried to be evasive and pleaded that it was not my task to 'preach', but the audience adamantly insisted. So I came up with the following counsel which, I believe, touches the heart of the matter: 'Look for what Jesus himself taught instead of being satisfied with what has been taught about him.'

The Authentic Gospel of Jesus is the tentative answer of a historian to inquiring minds, from all faiths or from none, who are fascinated by the figure of Jesus and seek to discover the real nature of his message.

Appendix:
A Classification of the Sayings of Jesus

Any attempt to try to reconstruct a word-for-word version of the sayings of Jesus is, I believe, a waste of time. The aim is unattainable because the original source, a written Aramaic collection of the sayings, if it ever existed, is no longer available. All we have is a secondary Greek reconstruction. In a domain such as this, at a distance of two thousand years, certainties are beyond the scholar's reach. The least unrealistic task is to weigh up and rank probabilities. On the less pessimistic side, it is worth observing that the fundamental principle of New Testament criticism, namely that the burden of proof rests on the claim of authenticity, is to a large extent misleading. The thesis that in the absence of definite proof of its genuineness a saying must be declared inauthentic is logically false. Inability to demonstrate that a maxim assigned by the evangelists to Jesus actually stems from him does not signify that he had nothing to do with it. It simply means that we are not in a position to prove that he had. Insufficiency of evidence does not automatically falsify a statement, but puts a question mark after it. Likewise lack of certainty is compatible with various degrees of probability.

Here follows the register of the sayings listed in chapters 1 to 9. An asterisk (*) marks those which are considered authentic or probably authentic. The rest will be called 'editorial'. These 'non-authentic' units range from the possibly genuine but heavily reworked to the almost certainly inauthentic, and are attributed to the writer or a later editor of a Gospel. They do not reflect the point of view of Jesus, but that of the early church for which the Synoptic Gospels in their present form were written between *circa* AD 70 and 100, forty to seventy years after the death of Jesus.

I

Narratives and Commands

1. *Call of the first disciples* (Mark 1:16–18; Matt. 4:18–20): 'Fishers of men' [unusual twist, probably stemming from Jesus] (*).

2. *The first exorcism of Jesus* (Mark 1:23–25; Luke 4:33–35): 'Be silent!', 'Come out!' [genuine exorcist's commands] (*).

3. *Jesus departs from Capernaum* (Mark 1:35–38; Luke 4:42–43): 'good news of the kingdom of God' [characteristic words of Jesus] (*).

4. *Healing a leper* (Mark 1:40–44; Matt. 8:2–4; Luke 5:12–14): 'Be clean' [genuine healer's command]; 'Show yourself to the priest' [obligatory ritual law contrary to the interest of the church] (*).

5. *The call of Levi* (Mark 3:1–3, 5; Matt. 12:9–10, 13; Luke 6:6–8, 10): [editorial].

6. *Healing a man with a withered hand* (Mark 3:1–3; Matt. 12:9–10; Luke 6:6–8): [editorial].

7. *Stilling the storm* (Mark 4:36–40; Matt. 8:23–26; Luke 8:22–25): [folkloric nature miracle, editorial].

8. *The Gerasene demoniac* (Mark 5:1–19; Matt. 8:28–34; Luke 8:26–39): 'Come out!' [authentic exorcist's command (*); the rest editorial].

9. *Healing a woman* (Mark 5:25–34; Matt. 9:20–22; Luke 8:43–48): 'Daughter, your faith has made you well' [characteristic charismatic words] (*).

10. *Raising the daughter of Jairus* (Mark 5:22–24, 35–43; Matt. 9:18–19, 23–26; Luke 8:41–42, 49–56): '*Talitha cum(i)*/Little girl, arise!' [genuine Galilean Aramaic (*); the rest editorial].

11. *Feeding five thousand* (Mark 6:31–43; Matt. 14:13–20; Luke 9:10–17): [editorial].

12. *Walking on the water* (Mark 6:45–51; Matt. 14:22–27, 32): [editorial – folk legend].

13. *Healing a deaf-mute* (Mark 7:32–36): '*Ephphatha*' [charismatic command in Aramaic] (*).

14. *Feeding four thousand* (Mark 8:1–9; Matt. 15:32–38; Mark 8:17–21; Matt. 16:8–10): [editorial – imitation of biblical example].

15. *Healing a blind man in Bethsaida* (Mark 8:22–26): 'Do you see anything?' [unusual question followed by words implying that the healing was not completely successful] (*); 'Do not even enter the village' [a usual command of secrecy] (*).

16. *Confession of Peter* (Mark 8:27–33; Matt. 16:13–16, 20–23; Luke 9:18–22): 'Who do men say that I am/the Son of man is?' ['Son of man' typical

terminology of Jesus] (*); 'Get behind me, Satan!' [addressed to Peter, unlikely to have been invented by the church (*); the rest editorial].

17. *Healing of an epileptic boy* (Mark 9:14–27; Matt. 17:14–18; Luke 9:38–43): 'All things are possible' [to the believer; standard formula used by Jesus] (*).

18. *Dispute about greatness* (Mark 9:33–34; Matt. 18:1; Luke 9:46): [editorial].

19. *Healing a blind man* (Mark 10:46–52; Matt. 20:29–34; Luke 18:35–43): ['Your faith has made you well', characteristic words of Jesus (*); the rest editorial].

20. *Entry into Jerusalem* (Mark 11:1–3; Matt. 21:1–3; Luke 19:29–31): [editorial].

21. *The cursing of the fig tree* (Mark 11:12–14; Matt. 21:18–19): 'May no one ever eat from you again' [unexpected illogicality which cannot be attributed to the evangelist] (*).

22. *Prediction of the destruction of the Temple* (Mark 13:1–2; Matt. 24:1–2; Luke 21:5–6): [the bulk of the Eschatological Discourse – editorial].

23. *Preparation for Passover* (Mark 14:12–15; Matt. 26:17–18; Luke 22:7–12): [editorial – Jesus died *before* the Passover].

24. *Jesus in Gethsemane* (Mark 14:32–42; Matt. 26:36–46; Luke 22:40–46): [editorial].

25. *The arrest of Jesus* (Mark 14:43–49; Matt. 26:47–56; Luke 22:47–53): [editorial – reference to fulfilment; see chapter 10, section I (2)].

26. *Jesus and the High Priest* (Mark 14:61–62; Matt. 26:63–64; Luke 22:67–70): [editorial – see chapter 10, section I (2)].

27. *Jesus before Pilate* (Mark 15:2; Matt. 27:11; Luke 23:3): [editorial, but standard answer of Jesus].

28. *The centurion's servant* (Matt. 8:5–13; Luke 7:1–10): 'Be it done for you as you have believed' [characteristic words of Jesus] (*).

29. *Healing two blind men* (Matt. 9:27–31): [editorial, but standard formulae to elicit faith and enjoining secrecy].

30. *Peter's failure to walk on the water* (Matt. 14:28–32): [editorial – folklore material].

31. *Instruction by the risen Jesus to his disciples* (Matt. 28:10): [editorial].

32. *The young Jesus in the Temple* (Luke 2:48–49): [editorial – childhood tale].

33. *Jesus in the synagogue of Nazareth* (Luke 4:16–19, 21): [editorial – claim of fulfilment].

34. *Miraculous catch of fish* (Luke 5:1, 3–6, 10): [editorial, but 'catching men' is a peculiar twist; cf. no. 1 above].

35. *Raising the widow's son at Nain* (Luke 7:11–15): [editorial, but 'Arise!' is a characteristic formula; cf. no. 10, above].
36. *The cleansing of ten lepers* (Luke 17:11–19): [editorial, but see no. 4 above].
37. *Zacchaeus* (Luke 19:1–6): [editorial].
38. *Preparation for Passover* (Luke 22:8): [editorial; see no. 23 above].
39. *Journey to Emmaus* (Luke 24:13–19): [editorial].
40. *Appearance of Jesus to his disciples in Jerusalem* (Luke 24:36–43, 48–49): [editorial].

2

Controversy Stories

Since the controversies regularly entail relatively long quotations, the hand of the evangelist is bound to have played a part in their formulation. Only some brief, sharp rejoinders or views typical of Jesus are placed in category (*). Polemics against the Pharisees are classified as editorial on historical grounds, but arguments with scribes are accepted as genuine.

1. *Healing or forgiveness of sins* (Mark 2:1–12; Matt. 9:1–8; Luke 5:17–26): 'My son, your sins are forgiven' and 'the son of Man has authority on earth to forgive sins' [formulae typical of Jesus] (*).
2. *Debate about fasting* (Mark 2:18–20; Matt. 9:14–15; Luke 5:33–35): [eschatological wedding feast (*); prediction of the removal of the bridegroom – editorial].
3. *Debate about plucking grain on the Sabbath* (Mark 2:23–28; Matt. 12:1–4; Luke 6:1–5): 'The Sabbath was made for man' [man is above ritual, typical of Jesus] (*).
4. *Debate about healing a man with a withered hand on the Sabbath* (Mark 3:1–2, 4; Matt. 12:9–10, 12; Luke 6:6–7, 9): 'Is it lawful on the sabbath to do good or to do harm', etc. [typical attitude of a charismatic healer] (*).
5. *Healing a sick woman whose illness was attributed to a demon* (Luke 13:10–16): 'Does not each of you untie his ox', etc. [principle characteristic of Jesus, combining healing and exorcism] (*).
6. *Healing a man with dropsy* (Luke 14:1–5; Matt. 12:11–12): 'Is it lawful to heal', etc. [man above ritual, typical of Jesus] (*); 'Which of you, having a son', etc. [characteristic principle of Jesus] (*).
7. *Dispute about demonic possession* (Mark 3:22–26; Matt. 12:24–26; Luke 11:15–18): [basic principle of Jesus as exorcist] (*).
8. *Dispute about defilement* (Mark 7:1–15; Matt. 15:1–11): 'Well did Isaiah

prophesy', etc. [editorial insertion of biblical proof]; 'There is nothing outside a man', etc. [moralization of the ritual law typical of Jesus] (*).

9. *Debate about divorce* (Mark 10:2–9; Matt. 19:3–8): [eschatology mirrors creation (*); the rest editorial].

10. *Debate about the authority of Jesus* (Mark 11:27–33; Matt. 21:23–27; Luke 20:1–8): [typical attitude of Jesus towards the Baptist] (*).

11. *Debate about tax to be paid to the emperor* (Mark 12:13–17; Matt. 22:15–22; Luke 20:20–26): 'Render to Caesar', etc. [characteristic attitude of the apolitical Jesus] (*).

12. *Debate concerning the resurrection of the dead* (Mark 12:18–27; Matt. 22:23–32; Luke 20:27–38): [editorial – Jewish-Christian church against Sadducees].

13. *Debate about the son of David* (Mark 12:35–37; Matt. 22:41–45; Luke 20:41–44): [editorial – Jewish-Christian biblical argument].

14. *Warning against the leaven of the Pharisees* (Mark 8:14–15; Matt. 16:5–6; Luke 12:1): [editorial on historical grounds].

15. *Polemics against Pharisees and lawyers* **A.** (Mark 12:38–40; Luke 20:46–47; Matt. 23:5–7): 'Beware of the scribes', etc. [consistent with Jesus' teaching on unostentatious prayer] (*). **B.** (Matt. 23:4, 13, 23–31; Luke 11:39–48, 52): 'Woes' against Pharisees [editorial on historical grounds, but characteristic phrases like 'straining out a gnat' and 'swallowing a camel' could be authentic]. **C.** (Matt. 23:2–3, 8–12, 15–22, 32–33): [editorial – Jewish-Christian hostility towards Pharisees, mixed with some sympathy, 'sit on Moses' seat'].

3

Words of Wisdom

Wisdom sayings by their nature are liable to have multi-level significance. Those marked (*) are taken in their earliest meaning attributable to Jesus.

1. *Who needs the physician?* (Mark 2:17; Matt. 9:12–13; Luke 5:31–32): [consistent with Jesus' way of life] (*).

2. *The new and the old* (Mark 2:21–22; Matt. 9:16–17; Luke 5:36–39): 'No one sews a piece', etc. and 'No one puts new wine', etc. [Kingdom sayings compatible with Jesus' outlook] (*); [Luke's modifications are editorial].

3. *Overpowering a strong man* (Mark 3:27; Matt. 12:29; Luke 11:21–22): [metaphor about the victory over Satan] (*).

4. *The purpose of a lamp* (Mark 4:21; Matt. 5:14–15; Luke 8:16; 11:33): [Mark: open teaching by Jesus (*); Matt., Luke, editorial].

5. *All hidden things will be disclosed* (Mark 4:22; cf. Luke 8:17; Matt. 10:26–27; Luke 12:2–3): [revelation of the secrets of the Kingdom characteristic of Jesus (*); Matt. 10:27; Luke 12:3 editorial].
6. *Measure for measure* (Mark 4:24; Luke 8:18; Matt. 7:1–2; Luke 6:37–38): [hyperbole about excessive generosity typical of Jesus] (*).
7. *Disproportionate remuneration* (Mark 4:25; Matt. 13:12; Luke 8:18): [hyperbole about excessive generosity typical of Jesus](*).
8. *No one is a prophet at home* (Mark 6:4; Matt. 13:57; Luke 4:23–27): [typical statement of a charismatic](*).
9. *Gaining the world but losing one's life* (Mark 8:36–37; Matt. 16:26; Luke 9:25; cf. Matt. 10:39; Luke 17:33): [giving up worldly values (*) possibly with editorial re-interpretation about persecutions].
10. *Millstone around one's neck* (Mark 9:42; Matt. 18:6; Luke 17:1–2): [threat to little ones: authentic teaching of Jesus (*); Luke 17:1 editorial].
11. *Salt without savour* (Mark 9:49–50; Matt. 5:13; Luke 14:34–35): [Mark eschatological formula (*); Matt., Luke: editorial].
12. *The camel and the eye of a needle* (Mark 10:24–25; Matt. 19:24–25; Luke 18:25): [Kingdom saying typical of Jesus both in substance and in style](*).
13. *Out of court settlement* (Matt. 5:25–26; cf. Luke 12:58–59): [editorial with possible underlying eschatological original].
14. *Generosity instead of retaliation* (Matt. 5:38–42; Luke 6:29–30): [typical hyperbole of Jesus](*).
15. *Love your enemies* (Matt. 5:43–48; Luke 6:27–28, 32–36): [typical hyperbole of Jesus (*); the pejorative allusion to tax-collectors – editorial].
16. *Treasures in heaven* (Matt. 6:19–21; Luke 12:33–34): [paramount importance of the values of the heavenly Kingdom](*).
17. *The healthy eye* (Matt. 6:22–23; Luke 11:34–36): [nothing specific].
18. *God and mammon* (Matt. 6:24; Luke 16:13): [Jesus' God-centredness excludes divided loyalties](*).
19. *Trust in the heavenly Father* (Matt. 6:25–34; Luke 12:22–32): [full trust in God against anxiety, characteristic ideas and style of Jesus](*).
20. *The chip and the beam* (Matt. 7:3–5; Luke 6:41–42): [simplicity against hypocrisy, characteristic style of Jesus](*).
21. *The Golden Rule* (Matt. 7:12; Luke 6:31): [traditional wisdom maxim given a peculiar twist](*).
22. *The narrow gate* (Matt. 7:13–14; Luke 13:24): [Matt.: narrow gate for few elect addressed by Jesus (*); Luke: editorial].
23. *Houses built on rock and sand* (Matt. 7:24–27; Luke 6:47–49): [see chapter 4, no. 8; popular simile possibly adopted by Jesus].

24. *The good tree and the bad tree* (Matt. 7:16–20; cf. Matt. 12:33–35; Luke 6:43–45): [common wisdom maxim given a new slant by Jesus](*).
25. *The homeless Jesus* (Matt. 8:20; Luke 9:58): [characteristic Jesus saying in substance and style](*).
26. *Burying the dead* (Matt. 8:22; Luke 9:60): [characteristic Jesus saying; no procrastination](*).
27. *The harvest and the labourers* (Matt. 9:37; Luke 10:2): [common simile with a possible twist].
28. *Sheep among wolves* (Matt. 10:16; Luke 10:3; cf. Matt. 7:15): [Matt. 10: typical paradoxical twist by Jesus (*); Matt. 7: prediction of the Parousia].
29. *Of sparrows and men* (Matt. 10:28–31; Luke 12:4–7; cf. Luke 21:18): [typical Jesus saying; total reliance on God](*).
30. *Blind leading blind* (Matt. 15:14; Luke 6:39): [editorial – anti-Pharisee].
31. *The corpse and the vultures* (Matt. 24:28; Luke 17:37) [Parousia].
32. *Dogs and swine* (Matt. 7:6): [Jewish exclusivism](*).
33. *Serpents and doves* (Matt. 10:16): [mixed images – editorial].
34. *A shrub not planted by God* (Matt. 15:13): [editorial – Pharisees].
35. *Exaltation – humiliation* (Matt. 23:12): [general wisdom saying coherent with Jesus' teaching].
36. *The ploughman and the Kingdom* (Luke 9:62): [eschatological urgency characteristic of Jesus](*).

4

Teaching in Parables

1a. *The parable of the sower* (Mark 4:3–9; Matt. 13:3–9; Luke 8:5–8): [the success of sowing, the mystery of the Kingdom in God's hand](*).
1b. *The explanation of the parable of the sower* (Mark 4:13–20; Matt. 13:18–23; Luke 8:11–15): [editorial – needs of the church; persecution].
2. *The parable of the secretly growing seed* (Mark 4:26–29): [success of the secretly growing Kingdom](*).
3. *The parable of the mustard seed* (Mark 4:30–32; Matt. 13:31–32; Luke 13:18–19): [unexpected growth](*).
4. *The parable of the wicked tenants of the vineyard* (Mark 12:1–9; Matt. 21:33–40; Luke 20:9–16): [editorial – murder of son; substitution of church for Jews].
5. *The parable of the fig tree* (Mark 13:28–29; Matt. 24:32–33; Luke 21:29–31): [editorial – premonitory signs, Parousia].

6. *The parable of the doorkeeper* (Mark 13:33–37; Matt. 25:14–15; 24:42; 25:13; Luke 19:12–13; 12:38): [editorial – delay of Parousia].
7. *The parable of reconciliation before appearing in court* (Matt. 5:25–26; Luke 12:58–59): [editorial – see chapter 3, no. 13].
8. *The parable of the two builders* (Matt. 7:24–27; Luke 6:47–49): [editorial metaphor of the Kingdom].
9. *The parable of children playing* (Matt. 11:16–19; Luke 7:31–35): [typical Jesus saying; friend of tax-collectors](*).
10. *The parable of the demon returning to his former home* (Matt. 12:43–45; Luke 11:24–26): [coherent with charismatic exorcism] (*).
11. *The parable of the leaven* (Matt. 13:33; Luke 13:20–21): [characteristic Jesus idea; the Kingdom's secret and peaceful coming] (*).
12. *The parable of the lost sheep* (Matt. 18:12–14; Luke 15:4–7): [typical Jesus idea; the lost sheep of Israel] (*).
13. *The parable of the wedding feast* (Matt. 22:2–14; Luke 14:16–24): [editorial – revenge on Jews, invitation of Gentiles built on a parable of Jesus].
14. *The parable of the burglar* (Matt. 24:43–44; Luke 12:39–40): [editorial – Parousia].
15. *The faithful and wise servant* (Matt. 24:45–51; Luke 12:42–46; cf. Luke 12:47–48): [editorial – delay of Parousia].
16. *The parable of the talents* (Matt. 25:14–30; Luke 19:11–27): [editorial – Parousia with a proverb of Jesus (chapter 3, no. 7) incorporated].
17. *The parable and interpretation of the weeds* (Matt. 13:24–30, 36–43): [editorial – a post-Parousia image probably built on a parable of Jesus].
18. *The parable of the hidden treasure* (Matt. 13:44): [urgency and total devotion to the cause] (*).
19. *The parable of the precious pearl* (Matt. 13:45–46): [urgency and total devotion to the cause] (*).
20. *The parable of the net* (Matt. 13:47–50): [encouragement to work for the Kingdom; the comment about the final judgement is probably editorial].
21. *The parable of the homeowner* (Matt. 13:52): [editorial – Jewish-Christian teachers].
22. *The parable of the cruel servant* (Matt. 18:23–35): [editorial – un-Jewish setting].
23. *The parable of the labourers in the vineyard* (Matt. 20:1–16): [generosity towards the unemployed] (*).
24. *The parable of the two sons* (Matt. 21:28–32): [typical attitude of Jesus towards social outcasts] (*).
25. *The parable of the ten virgins* (Matt. 25:1–13; cf. Luke 12:35–38; 13.25): [editorial – Parousia].

26. *The parable of the last judgement* (Matt. 25:31–46): [Parousia of the son of Man superimposed on the parable of the shepherd, and the idea of the imitation of God probably deriving from Jesus].
27. *The parable of the creditor and the two debtors* (Luke 7:40–47): [characteristic attitude of Jesus; sympathy towards a prostitute] (*).
28. *The parable of the good Samaritan* (Luke 10:30–36): [editorial; Jesus disliked Samaritans, loving-kindness though is typical].
29. *The parable of the unexpected guest* (Luke 11:5–8): [childlike persistence in prayer] (*).
30. *The parable of the rich farmer* (Luke 12:16–20): [eschatological urgency] (*).
31. *The parable of the fruitless fig tree* (Luke 13:6–9): [editorial – long-term perspective].
32. *The parable of choosing a seat at the wedding feast* (Luke 14:8–11): [common wisdom].
33. *The parable of the landowner and the king* (Luke 14:28–33): [editorial – Jesus against calculation].
34. *The parable of the lost drachm* (Luke 15:8–10): [similar to the parable of the lost sheep, see no. 12 above (*); final comment probably editorial].
35. *The parable of the prodigal son* (Luke 15:11–32): [repentance and fatherly love (*); conventional morality advocated by the faithful son – editorial].
36. *The parable of the crooked steward* (Luke 16:1–9): [editorial – calculation alien to Jesus].
37. *The parable of the rich man and the poor Lazarus* (Luke 16:19–31): [editorial – Pharisee teaching of Jewish-Christianity].
38. *The parable of the servant's reward* (Luke 17:7–10; cf. Luke 12:37): [church teaching reversing that of Jesus].
39. *The parable of the judge and the persistent widow* (Luke 18:1–8): [trust and insistence (*); editorial final section on Parousia].
40. *The parable of the Pharisee and the publican* (Luke 18:9–14): [sincerity of the publican authentic (*); Pharisee questionable].

5

Quoting or Interpreting Scripture

The exegesis of a biblical text qualified as *pesher* designates a fulfilment interpretation. The term is borrowed from the terminology of the Dead Sea Scrolls where sectarian commentators apply a prophetic text to the history of their own community. The style of argument is peculiar to the early church as is apparent from the Acts of the Apostles, etc., and should be treated as editorial.

1. *Plucking heads of grain* (Mark 2:23–28; Matt. 12:1–6; Luke 6:1–5) [1 Sam. 21:1–7; Num. 28:9–10]: [popular interpretative example (1 Sam.); editorial legal exegesis (Num.)].
2. *Concealment of meaning through parables* (Mark 4:11–12; Matt. 13:11–15; Luke 8:10) [Isa. 6:9–10]: [editorial distortion of the purpose of the parables].
3. *The parable of the secretly growing seed and the harvest* (Mark 4:26–29) [Joel 3:13]: [editorial colouring].
4. *The parable of the mustard seed* (Mark 4:30–32; Matt. 13:31–32; Luke 13:18–19) [Ezek. 17:23; 31:6; Dan. 4:10–12, 20–21]: [editorial elaboration].
5. *Corban and filial respect* (Mark 7:9–13; Matt. 15:3–6) [Exod. 20:12; Deut. 5:16; Exod. 21:17; Lev. 20:9] [editorial technical exegesis against Pharisees].
6. *Prohibition of divorce* (Mark 10:11–12; Matt. 5:31–32; 19:9; Luke 16:18) [Deut. 24:1]: [Mark: divorce followed by remarriage = adultery, typical teaching of Jesus (*); the rest editorial].
7. *The sign of Jonah and the queen of the South* (Mark 8:12; Matt. 12:39–42; (16:4); Luke 11:29–32) [Jonah 1:17; 3:5; 1 Kings 10:1–10]: [editorial elaboration].
8. *Punishment for making someone sin* (Mark 9:47–48; Matt. 18:9) [Isa. 66:24]: [editorial elaboration].
9. *How to gain eternal life* (Mark 10:19; Matt. 19:17–19; Luke 18:20) [Exod. 20:12–16; Deut. 5:16–20; Lev. 19:18]: [general trend followed by Jesus].
10. *The cleansing of the Temple* (Mark 11:17; Matt. 21:13; Luke 19:46) [Isa. 56:7; Jer. 7:11]: [editorial *pesher*].
11. *The parable of the wicked tenants of the vineyard* (Mark 12:1–11; Matt. 21:33–42; Luke 20:9–18) [Isa. 5:1–2; Ps. 118:22–23]: [editorial *pesher*].
12. *Proof of the resurrection of the dead* (Mark 12:18–27; Matt. 22:23–32; Luke 20:27–40) [Exod. 3:6]: [editorial elaboration; Pharisee technique].
13. *The first and the second commandments* (Mark 12:29–31; Matt. 22:37–40; cf. Luke 10:27–28) [Deut. 6:4–5; Lev. 19:18]: [common ideas, but also basic teaching of Jesus] (*).
14. *Debate about the son of David* (Mark 12:35–37; Matt. 22:41–45; Luke 20:41–44) [Ps. 110:1]: [editorial elaboration].
15. *The return of the son of Man* (Mark 13:24–27; Matt. 24:29–31; Luke 21:25–28) [Isa. 13:10; 34:4; Dan. 7:13–14; Ps. 65:7]: [editorial – Parousia].
16. *The flight of the disciples* (Mark 14:27; Matt. 26:31) [Zech. 13:7]: [editorial *pesher*].
17. *Words of sorrow in Gethsemane* (Mark 14:34: Matt. 26:38) [Ps. 42:6]: [editorial elaboration].

18. *Jesus' answer to the High Priest* (Mark 14:61–62; Matt. 26:63–64; Luke 22:67–69) [Ps. 110:1; Dan. 7:13]: [editorial – Parousia].
19. *The last cry of Jesus* (Mark 15:34; Matt. 27:46) [Ps. 22:2]: [disturbing cry in Aramaic] (*).
20. *Jesus' altercation with the devil* (Matt. 4:3–10; Luke 4:3–11) [Deut. 8:3; Ps. 91:11–12; Deut. 6:16; 6:13]: [editorial *midrash*].
21. *An eye for an eye and a tooth for a tooth* (Matt. 5:38–42; Luke 6:29–30) [Exod. 21:24]: [typical hyperbolical interpretation of a well-known text] (*).
22. *Love your neighbour and your enemy* (Matt. 5:43–48; Luke 6:27–28, 32–36) [Lev. 19:18; Deut. 18:13]: [typical hyperbolical interpretation of a well-known text] (*).
23. *The Golden Rule* (Matt. 7:12; Luke 6:31) [Tobit 4:15; Ecclus. 31:15]: [summary of the Law with a peculiar slant] (*).
24. *Bringing a sword* (Matt. 10:34–36; Luke 12:51–53) [Mic. 7:6]: [characteristic idea with questionable quotation].
25. *Jesus' answer to John the Baptist* (Matt. 11:4–6; Luke 7:22–23) [Isa. 35:5–6; 61:1]: [traditional type of quotation typical of Jesus] (*).
26. *The prophetic character of John the Baptist* (Matt. 11:7–10; Luke 7:24–27) [Mal. 3:1]: [editorial].
27. *The fate of Capernaum* (Matt. 11:23–24; Luke 10:15) [Isa. 14:13–15; Gen. 18–19]: [editorial interpretation by example and exaggeration].
28. *The sign of Jonah* (Matt. 12:39–42; Luke 11:29–32) [Jonah 1:17; 3:5; 1 Kings 10:1–10] [editorial; see no. 7 above].
29. *Persecution of messengers* (Matt. 23:34–36; Luke 11:49–51) [Gen. 4:8; 2 Chron. 24:20–21]: [editorial elaboration on persecution of Jewish-Christian preachers].
30. *The coming of the Son of man prefigured by the age of Noah and Lot* (Matt. 24:37–41; Luke 17:26–30, 32, 34–36) [Gen. 7:7; 19:1–26]: [editorial – Parousia].
31. *You shall not kill* (Matt. 5:21–23) [Exod. 20:13; Deut. 5:17]: [hyperbolical interpretation typical of Jesus] (*).
32. *You shall not commit adultery* (Matt. 5:27–30) [Exod. 20:14; Deut. 5:18]: [typical hyperbolical interpretation] (*).
33. *You shall not swear falsely* (Matt. 5:33–37) [Lev. 19:12]: [typical hyperbolical interpretation] (*).
34. *Praying unobserved* (Matt. 6:6) [Isa. 26:20]: [editorial stylistic elaboration].
35. *The annihilation of the wicked and the glorification of the just* (Matt. 13:41–43) [Dan. 3:6; 12:3]: [editorial – Parousia].

36. *Rebuke to be administered before witnesses* (Matt. 18:15–16) [Deut. 19:15]: [editorial – church teaching].
37. *Jesus hailed in the Temple* (Matt. 21:15–16) [Ps. 8:2]: [editorial – the evangelist's story].
38. *Jesus interpreting Isaiah* (Luke 4:16–21) [Isa. 61:1–2; 58:6] [editorial elaboration].
39. *Jesus alludes to his arrest* (Luke 22:37) [Isa. 53:12]: [editorial *pesher*].
40. *Jesus comforting the women of Jerusalem* (Luke 23:28–31) [Hosea 10:8]: [editorial *pesher*].
41. *The last cry of Jesus* (Luke 23:46) [Ps. 31:5]: [editorial corrective].

6

Prayers and Related Instructions

Most of the ideas expressed in prayers are in full conformity with the thought of Jesus.

1. *Effective prayer* (Mark 11:23–24; Matt. 21:21–22; cf. Matt. 17:20; Luke 17:6): [all-powerful faith characteristic of Jesus] (*).
2. *Forgiveness and prayer* (Mark 11:25; Matt. 6:14–15; cf. 11:25–26): [generosity towards offenders characteristic of Jesus] (*).
3. *The prayer of Jesus in Gethsemane* (Mark 14:36; Matt. 26:39; Luke 22:42): [absolute trust characteristic of Jesus; Aramaic invocation] (*).
4. *The last exclamation of Jesus* (Mark 15:34; Matt. 27:46): [Aramaic cry, counter-productive for the early church, unlikely to be invented] (*).
5. *The Lord's Prayer* (Matt. 6:9–13; Luke 11:2–4): [ideas typical of Jesus] (*).
6. *Jesus' thanksgiving prayer* (Matt. 11:25–27; Luke 10:21–22): [editorial theological elaboration on genuine ideas of Jesus].
7. *How to pray and how not to pray according to Jesus* (Matt. 6:5–8): [trust and privacy, characteristic ideas of Jesus] (*).
8. *Jesus' prayer for forgiveness* (Luke 23:33–34): [probably editorial].
9. *The last prayer of Jesus* (Luke 23:46): [editorial corrective].

7

'Son of man' Sayings

The meaning of the 'Son of man' sayings depends on their context, so that their claim to authenticity is to be judged according to special rules. In section I (reference to the speaker) the presence of an idiomatic Aramaism enhances the probability of genuineness. The examples assembled in section II (prediction of the death and resurrection of Jesus) and in section III (sayings connected with Daniel 7) are editorial; see chapter 10, section I (2) and (3).

1. *The right of the 'Son of man' to forgive sins* (Mark 2:9–11; Matt. 9:5–6; Luke 5:23–24): [see chapter 2, no. 1](*).
2. *The 'Son of man' is above the Sabbath* (Mark 2:27–28; Matt. 12:8; Luke 6:5): [see chapter 2, no. 3](*).
3. *Speaking against the 'Son of man'* (Mark 3:28–29; Matt. 12:31–32; Luke 12:10): [editorial].
4. *Question about the identity of Son of man/Jesus* (Mark 8:27; Matt. 16:13; Luke 9:18) [see chapter 1, no. 16] (*).
5. *The 'Son of man' as servant* (Mark 10:42–45; Matt. 20:25–28; Luke 22:25–27): [paradox typical of Jesus (*); the 'Son of man' phrase is editorial; see chapter 10, section I (3)].
6. *The betrayal of the 'Son of man'* (Mark 14:18, 20–21, 41; Matt. 26:21, 23–24, 45; Luke 22:21–22): [editorial – see chapter 1, no. 25].
7. *Persecution on account of the 'Son of man'* (Matt. 5:11; Luke 6:22): [editorial – see chapter 8, no. 34].
8. *The homelessness of the 'Son of man'* (Matt. 8:20; Luke 9:58): [see chapter 3, no. 25] (*).
9. *The 'Son of man' accused of gluttony* (Matt. 11:18–19; Luke 7:33–34): [see chapter 4, no. 9] (*).
10. *The 'Son of man' came to seek the lost* (Luke 19:9–10): [see chapter 1, no. 37] (*).
11. *The betrayal of the 'Son of man'* (Luke 22:48): [editorial – see chapter 1, no. 25].
12–17. *The 'Son of man' must suffer, die and rise on the third day* (Mark 8:30–31; Matt. 16:20–21; Luke 9:21–22 – Mark 9:9–10, 12; Matt. 17:9, 12 – Mark 9:30–32; Matt. 17:22–23; Luke 9:43–45 – Mark 10:32–34; Matt. 20:17–19; Luke 18:31–34; cf. Luke 24:44–47 – Matt. 12:40 – Matt. 26:1–2): [editorial – see chapter 10, section I (3)].
18–29. *The 'Son of man' and the Parousia* (Mark 8:38; Matt. 16:27; Luke 9:26; cf. Matt. 10:32–33; Luke 12:8–9 – Mark 13:26–27; Matt. 24:30–31; Luke 21:27–28 – Mark 14:62; Matt. 26:64; Luke 22:69 – Matt. 19:28; cf. Luke 22:28–30 – Matt. 24:26–27; Luke 17:22–24 – Matt. 24:37–44; Luke 17:26–27, 30, 34–35, 39–40 – Matt. 10:23 – Matt. 13:37, 41–43 – Matt. 25:31–32 – Luke 17:22, 29–30 – Luke 18:6–8 – Luke 21:34–36): [editorial; see chapter 10, section I (2)].

8

Sayings about the Kingdom of God

1. *The initial proclamation* (Mark 1:15; Matt. 4:17): [imminence of the Kingdom and repentance – essence of Jesus' preaching] (*).
2. *Healing and forgiveness of sins* (Mark 2:9–11; Matt. 9:5–6; Luke 5:23–24): [see chapter 2, no. 1] (*).
3. *New family ties* (Mark 3:33–35; Matt. 12:48–50; Luke 8:21; cf. Luke 11:27–28; Matt. 10:37; Luke 14:26; Mark 10:29–30; Matt. 19:28–29; Luke 18:29): [typical hyperboles of Jesus with editorial glosses] (*).
4. *No prophet is respected at home* (Mark 6:4; Matt. 13:57; Luke 4:24): [see chapter 3, no. 8] (*).
5. *Rules for the missionaries of the Kingdom* (Mark 6:8–11; Matt. 10:9–15; Luke 9:3–5; cf. Luke 10:4–11): [basic rules of eschatological ministry (*); with editorial retouches].
6. *Jesus' attitude to Gentiles* (Mark 7:27; Matt. 15:26): [Jewish exclusivism typical of Jesus; see chapter 10, section I (1)] (*).
7. *Request for a sign* (Mark 8:12; Matt. 16:4; 12:39; Luke 11:29; cf. Luke 17:20–21; Matt. 11:4–5; Luke 7:22): [refusal of signs on demand characteristic of Jesus (*); for Jonah, see chapter 5, no. 7].
8. *The coming of the Kingdom in Jesus' generation* (Mark 9:1; Matt. 16:28; Luke 9:27): [see chapter 10, section I (2)] (*).
9. *The coming of Elijah* (Mark 9:12–13; Matt. 17:11–12): [essential feature of eschatological teaching](*).
10. *The children and the Kingdom of God* (Mark 9:37; Matt. 18:5; Luke 9:48; cf. Mark 9:42; Matt. 18:6–7; Luke 17:1–2; Mark 10:15; Luke 18:17; Matt. 18:34; cf. Matt. 11:25; Luke 10:21): [prominent role of children typical of Jesus' teaching; see chapter 6, no. 6] (*).
11. *An uncommissioned exorcist* (Mark 9:39–41; Luke 9:50; cf. Matt. 12:30; Luke 11:23; Matt. 10:42): [whoever fights Satan is an ally of Jesus the exorcist] (*).
12. *Leading children astray* (Mark 9:42; Matt. 18:6–7; Luke 17:1–2): [see no. 10 above] (*).
13. *The children and the Kingdom of God* (Mark 10:15; Matt. 18:3; Luke 18:17): [see no. 10 above](*).
14. *How to gain eternal life* (Mark 10:18–19; cf. Mark 10:21; Matt. 19:17, 21; Luke 18:19–20, 22): [obedience to the Torah and renunciation of possessions – basic teachings of Jesus](*).
15. *Seating in the Kingdom of God* (Mark 10:35–45; Matt. 20:20–28;

cf. Luke 22:27): [allocation of a seat in the Kingdom does not belong to Jesus and service is a principal aim (*) with editorial changes (see chapter 7, no. 5)].

16. *The miraculously efficient prayer* (Mark 11:22–24; Matt. 21:21–22): [see chapter 6, no. 1](*).

17. *Prophecy of the destruction of the Temple* (Mark 13:1–2; Matt. 24:1–2; Luke 21:5–6): [Eschatological Discourse – editorial].

18. *Warning about false messiahs* (Mark 13:5–6; Matt. 24:4–5; Luke 21:8; cf. Mark 13:21–23; Matt. 24:23–25; cf. Matt. 24:26–27; Luke 17:22–24): [see chapter 7, no. 22].

19. *Preliminaries of the approaching end* (Mark 13:7–8; Matt. 24:6–8; Luke 21:9–11): [Eschatological Discourse – editorial].

20. *The persecution of the disciples as part of the preliminaries of the eschaton* (Mark 13:9–11; Matt. 24:14; Matt. 24:9; Matt. 10:17–20; cf. Matt. 10:24–25; Luke 6:40; Luke 21:12–15): [Eschatological Discourse; see also chapter 10, section I (1) – editorial].

21. *Conflict within the family* (Mark 13:12–13; Matt. 10:21–22; 24:9–13; Luke 21:16–17, 19): [see chapter 5, no. 24 – editorial].

22. *The apogee of the tribulation* (Mark 13:14–20; Matt. 24:15–22; Luke 21:20–24; cf. Luke 17:31): [Eschatological Discourse – editorial].

23. *Warning about false messiahs* (Mark 13:21–23; Matt. 24:23–27; Luke 17:23–24): [see no. 18 above].

24. *The return of the son of Man* (Mark 13:24–27; Matt. 24:29–31; Luke 21:25–28): [see chapter 5, no. 15 and chapter 7, no. 19 – editorial].

25. *The parable of the fig tree* (Mark 13:28–29; Matt. 24:32–33; Luke 21:29–31): [see chapter 4, no. 5 – editorial].

26. *The time of the Parousia* (Mark 13:30–32; Matt. 24:34–36; Luke 21:32–33): [the time of the arrival of the Kingdom unknown to Jesus (see also no. 8 above)] (*).

27. *Exhortation to watchfulness* (Mark 13:33–37; Matt. 25:14–15; 24:42; 25:13; Luke 19:12–13; 12:38): [editorial – see chapter 4, no. 6].

28. *Appearing before the 'Son of man'* (Luke 21:34–36): [editorial – see chapter 7, no. 29].

29. *The anointing in Bethany* (Mark 14:6–9; Matt. 26:10–13; cf. Luke 7:41–50): [editorial account using the characteristic themes of forgiveness and love of social outcasts].

30. *The words of Jesus during the Last Supper* (Mark 14:22–25; Matt. 26:26–29; Luke 22:15–20; 1 Cor. 11:23–26): [editorial, built round a saying of Jesus associating the drinking of wine with the imminent coming of the Kingdom].

31. *The forsaking of Jesus by his disciples and his denial by Peter* (Mark 14:27–28, 30; Matt. 26:31–32, 34; Luke 22:31–32, 34): [editorial *pesher*].
32. *Hearsay prophecy about the destruction and rebuilding of the Temple* (Mark 14:58; Matt. 26:61; cf. Mark 15:29; Matt. 27:40): [Hellenistic Jewish hostility to the Temple attributed to Jesus].
33. *The commission of the apostles in the longer ending of Mark* (Mark 16:15–18): [editorial – see no. 53 below].
34. *The beatitudes and woes: manifesto for the seekers of the Kingdom* (Matt. 5:3–12; Luke 6:20–26): [summary of the eschatological morality of Jesus (*) with editorial supplements].
35. *The power of prayer addressed to the heavenly Father* (Matt. 7:7–11; Luke 11:9–13, Matt. 26:53–54): [unconditional trust; see chapter 6, no. 1; Matt. 26:53–54 editorial](*).
36. *The condition of entry into the Kingdom* (Matt. 7:21–23; Luke 6:46; 13:26–27): [editorial account focusing in Matt. 7:21 (*) on basic teachings of Jesus].
37. *Jews replaced by Gentiles in the Kingdom* (Matt. 8:10–12; Luke 7:9; 13:28–29; cf. Matt. 21:43): [editorial – see chapter 10, section I (1)].
38. *Hostile audiences* (Matt. 10:16; Luke 10:3) [editorial – see chapter 3, no. 28].
39. *Acknowledgement or denial of Jesus* (Matt. 10:32–33; Luke 12:8–9): [editorial – lapsed disciples].
40. *Jesus on John the Baptist* (Matt. 11:11–15; Luke 7:28; 16:16): [see chapter 5, no. 26] (*).
41. *The ascetic John and the convivial Jesus* (Matt. 11:18–19; Luke 7:31–35): [see chapter 4, no. 9, and no. 40 above] (*).
42. *Failure of charisma in Galilean villages* (Matt. 11:21–23; Luke 10:13–15): [editorial – later perspective].
43. *The charismatic nature of exorcism* (Matt. 12:27–28; Luke 11:18–20): [see no. 8 above] (*).
44. *The blessedness of the disciples* (Matt. 13:16–17; Luke 10:23–24): [charismatic atmosphere] (*).
45. *Interpreting signs* (Matt. 16:2–3; Luke 12:54–56): [idea characteristic of Jesus if signs show the presence of the messianic age (*); if they are premonitory, editorial].
46. *The power of faith* (Matt. 17:20; Luke 17:6): [see chapter 6, no. 1, and no. 16 above] (*).
47. *Persecution of messengers* (Matt. 23:34–36; Luke 11:49–51): [see chapter 5, no. 29 – editorial].

48. *Lament over Jerusalem* (Matt. 23:37–39; Luke 13:34–35): [editorial – Jesus did not frequently try to save the children of Jerusalem].
49. *Mission to Jews alone* (Matt. 10:5–8; 15:24) [see chapter 10, section I (1)] (*).
50. *The messengers represent Jesus* (Matt. 10:40–41; cf. Luke 10:16): [see no. 5 above] (*).
51. *The yoke of Jesus* (Matt. 11:28–30): [editorial – the moral teaching of Jesus is not easy].
52. *Jesus on the use of force* (Matt. 26:52; cf. Luke 22:35–38): [Matthew agrees with Jesus' teaching on non-violence (*); Luke editorial].
53. *The universal mission of the apostles* (Matt. 28:18–20; cf. Mark 16:15–16): [editorial; see chapter 10, section I (1)].
54. *Power over the forces of evil* (Luke 10:18–20): [see no. 5 above] (*).
55. *Making the good choice* (Luke 10:41–42): [editorial account built on a basic idea of Jesus].
56. *Fire and baptism* (Luke 12:49–50): [editorial based on the idea of eschatological purification].
57. *Lesson to be drawn from bloodshed and disaster* (Luke 13:2–5): [unlikely to be invented] (*).
58. *The self-definition of Jesus* (Luke 13:31–33): [reference to exorcism and calling Herod a fox congruent with the teaching and personality of Jesus (*); the mention of three days: editorial apologetics].
59. *The Kingdom comes without premonitory signs* (Luke 17:20–21): [see no. 7 above] (*).
60. *Prophetic lament over the fall of Jerusalem* (Luke 19:41–44): [editorial – early Christian perception of the capture of Jerusalem].

9

Eschatological Rules of Behaviour

1. *Man is superior to the Sabbath* (Mark 2:27–28; Matt. 12:8; Luke 6:5; cf. Matt. 12:11–12; Luke 14:5; 13:15): [see chapter 2, nos. 3, 5, 6] (*).
2. *Performing acts of healing on the Sabbath* (Mark 3:4; Matt. 12:12; Luke 6:9): [see chapter 2, nos. 4, 5, 6] (*).
3. *Rules for missionaries* (Mark 6:8–11; Matt. 10:9–15; Luke 9:3–5; cf. Luke 10:4–11): [see chapter 8, no. 5] (*).
4. *The source of uncleanness* (Mark 7:15, 18–23; Matt. 15:11, 17–20): [see chapter 2, no. 8] (*).
5. *The doctrine of self-sacrifice* (Mark 8:34–37; Matt. 16:24–26; Luke

9:23–25; cf. Matt. 10:38; Luke 14:27): [everything to be sacrificed for the Kingdom] (*).
6. *The doctrine of self-mutilation* (Mark 9:43–48; Matt. 18:8–9; cf. Matt. 5:29–30): [everything to be sacrificed for the Kingdom] (*).
7. *Prohibition or restriction of divorce* (Mark 10:11–12; Matt. 19:9; cf. Matt. 5:32; Luke 16:18): [see chapter 2, no. 9, and chapter 5, no. 6] (*).
8. *Giving up property* (Mark 10:18–19; cf. vv. 21, 23, 25; Matt. 19:17, 21; cf. vv. 23–24; Luke 18:20, 22; cf. vv. 24–25): [see chapter 8, no. 14] (*).
9. *Giving up family* (Mark 10:29–30; Matt. 19:28–29; Luke 18:29): [see chapter 8, no. 3] (*).
10. *Reconciliation before a court hearing* (Matt. 5:25–26; Luke 12:58–59): [editorial – see chapter 3, no. 13, and chapter 4, no. 7].
11. *Against retaliation* (Matt. 5:38–42; Luke 6:29–30): [see chapter 3, no. 14, and chapter 5, no. 21] (*).
12. *The commandment to love one's enemies* (Matt. 5:43–48; Luke 6:27–28, 32–36): [see chapter 3, no. 15, and chapter 5, no. 22] (*).
13. *Severing family ties* (Matt. 10:37; Luke 14:26): [see chapter 8, no. 3] (*).
14. *Saving of life overrides the Sabbath* (Matt. 12:11–12; Luke 14:5): [see no. 1 above] (*).
15. *The duty to rebuke an erring brother* (Matt. 18:15, 22; Luke 17:3–4): [formalized church rebuke; see no. 24 below].
16. *The permanence of the Torah* (Matt. 5:17–20; cf. Luke 16:17): [unhelpful to the church] (*).
17. *Overcoming anger and the duty of swift reconciliation* (Matt. 5:21–24): [see chapter 5, no. 31] (*).
18. *Prevention of adultery by controlling sinful desire* (Matt. 5:27–30): [see chapter 5, no. 32, and no. 6 above] (*).
19. *Avoidance of oaths* (Matt. 5:33–37): [see chapter 5, no. 33] (*).
20. *No ostentation in piety: 1. Almsgiving* (Matt. 6:1–4): [God-centred devotion typical of Jesus] (*).
21. *No ostentation in piety: 2. Prayer* (Matt. 6:5–8): [see chapter 6, no. 7] (*).
22. *No ostentation in piety: 3. Fasting* (Matt. 6:16–18): [disguised self-denial] (*).
23. *The church built on Peter, the Rock* (Matt. 16:17–19): [church saying – editorial].
24. *Church rules* (Matt. 18:15–20): [editorial, see no. 15 above].
25. *The counsel of self-castration* (Matt. 19:12): [see no. 6 above] (*).
26. *Modesty in using titles* (Matt. 23:8–11): [anti-Pharisee polemic though the verbal exaggeration may derive from Jesus].

Chronological Table

Entries in italics relate to New Testament subjects

BC

197	Seleucid rule in Judaea
175–164	Antiochus IV Epiphanes
167	Abolition of Judaism
166	Maccabaean uprising
152–143	Jonathan Maccabaeus, high priest
143–135	Simon Maccabaeus, high priest and ethnarch
135–37	Hasmonaean rule
130(?)	Start of the Essene settlement at Qumran
65	Honi (Onias) stoned
63	Pompey in Jerusalem; Roman province of Judaea
37–4	Herod the Great
27–AD 14	Augustus, emperor
20–AD 50(?)	Philo of Alexandria
6/5(?)	*Birth of Jesus*
4–AD 6	Archelaus, ethnarch of Judaea and Samaria
4–AD 39	Antipas, tetrarch of Galilee

AD

6–41	Judaea governed by Roman prefects
14–37	Tiberius, emperor
18–36(?)	Joseph Caiaphas, high priest
26–36	Pontius Pilate
29(?)	*Ministry and execution of John the Baptist*

29–30(?)	*Ministry and crucifixion of Jesus*
37	Birth of Flavius Josephus
37–41	Gaius Caligula, emperor
41–44	Agrippa I, king
41–54	Claudius, emperor
44–66	Roman procurators
50–60(?)	*Letters of Paul*
54–68	Nero, emperor
62	*Death of James, the brother of Jesus*; Jesus son of Ananias
66–70	First war against Rome. Destruction of Jerusalem
68(?)	End of the Essene occupation of Qumran
68–69	Galba, Otho and Vitellius, emperors
69–79	Vespasian, emperor
70–75(?)	*Gospel of Mark*
73/74	Fall of Masada
75/79(?)	Josephus' *Jewish War*
79–81	Titus, emperor
80–100(?)	*Gospels of Matthew and Luke, Acts of the Apostles*
81–96	Domitian, emperor
93/94(?)	Josephus' *Jewish Antiquities* and *Life*
96–98	Nerva, emperor
96–100(?)	Josephus' *Against Apion*
98–117	Trajan, emperor
100(?)	*Letters of James, 1 Peter, 1–3 John, Jude; Revelation*
100–110(?)	*Fourth Gospel*; death of Josephus
117–138	Hadrian, emperor
125–150(?)	2 *Peter*
132–135	Second war against Rome

Index of Gospel Citations

Bold italics indicate passages with commentary.

INDEX OF GOSPEL CITATIONS